access to history

From Kaiser to Führer:
Germany 1900–45 for Edexcel

Geoff Layton

HODDER
EDUCATION
AN HACHETTE UK COMPANY

This material has been endorsed by Edexcel and offers high quality support for the delivery of Edexcel qualifications. Edexcel endorsement does not mean that this material is essential to achieve any Edexcel qualification, nor does it mean that this is the only suitable material available to support any Edexcel qualification. No endorsed material will be used verbatim in setting any Edexcel examination and any resource lists produced by Edexcel shall include this and any other appropriate texts. While this material has been through an Edexcel quality assurance process, all responsibility for the content remains with the publisher. Copies of the official specifications for all Edexcel qualifications may be found on the Edexcel website – www.edexcel.org.uk

Study Guide author: Angela Leonard (Edexcel)

The Publishers would like to thank the following for permission to reproduce copyright material:

Photo credits: akg-images, pages 37, 303; Otto Dix: © DACS 2009/akg-images/Erich Lessing, page 170; Heinrich Knirr – © DACS 2009/akg-images, page 242; © Austrian Archives/CORBIS, page 280; Bauhaus-Archiv, page 171; BPK, page 54; BPK/Kunstbibliothek, SMB/Knud Petersen, page 294; Henry Guttmann/Getty Images, page 20; Hulton Archive/Getty Images, page 9; © Hulton-Deutsch Collection/CORBIS, pages 247, 356; Imperial War Museum, page 84 (left); Keystone/Getty Images, page 179; Mary Evans Picture Library/WEIMA, page 319; Popperfoto/Getty Images, page 259; Punch Ltd, page 62; Süddeutsche Zeitung Photo/Scherl, pages 192, 220; Three Lions/Getty Images, page 145.

Acknowledgements: Cambridge University Press for an extract from *Nazism, Fascism and the Working Class* by Tim Mason, 1995; Grolier Publishing for an extract from *The Nazi Seizure of Power* by W.S. Allen, 1968; Hodder Arnold for an extract from *Imperial and Weimar Germany 1890–1933* by J. Laver, 1992; Hodder Murray for an extract from *Hitler's Germany* by Edgar Feuchtwanger, 2000; Oxford Paperbacks for an extract from *The Hitler Myth: Image and Reality* by Ian Kershaw, 1984; Palgrave Macmillan for an extract from *A History of Germany 1815–1945* by W. Carr, 1979; Penguin for an extract from Hitler 1936–45 by Ian Kershaw, 2000; I.B. Tauris for an extract from *German Society and the Resistance Against Hitler* by Hans Mommsen, 1999.

Every effort has been made to trace all copyright holders, but if any have been inadvertently overlooked the Publishers will be pleased to make the necessary arrangements at the first opportunity.

Hachette UK's policy is to use papers that are natural, renewable and recyclable products and made from wood grown in sustainable forests. The logging and manufacturing processes are expected to conform to the environmental regulations of the country of origin.

Orders: please contact Bookpoint Ltd, 130 Milton Park, Abingdon, Oxon OX14 4SB. Telephone: (44) 01235 827720. Fax: (44) 01235 400454. Lines are open 9.00–5.00, Monday to Saturday, with a 24-hour message answering service. Visit our website at www.hoddereducation.co.uk

© Geoff Layton, 2009
First published in 2009 by
Hodder Education,
an Hachette UK Company
Carmelite House, 50 Victoria Embankment,
London EC4Y 0DZ

Impression number   13
Year   2016

Cover image: A view of the Brandenburg Gate, © Photodisc/Photolibrary Group Ltd. Typeset in 10/12pt Baskerville and produced by Gray Publishing, Tunbridge Wells Printed and bound by CPI Group (UK) Ltd, Croydon, CR0 4YY

A catalogue record for this title is available from the British Library.

ISBN: 978 0340 990 155

Contents

Dedication

Keith Randell (1943–2002)

The *Access to History* series was conceived and developed by Keith, who created a series to 'cater for students as they are, not as we might wish them to be'. He leaves a living legacy of a series that for over 20 years has provided a trusted, stimulating and well-loved accompaniment to post-16 study. Our aim with these new editions is to continue to offer students the best possible support for their studies.

Acknowledgement

I have been very fortunate with the help of various friends who have given advice and encouragement in the preparation of this text; in particular Chris Moreton and Barbara Klass. I would like to thank them both.

G.L.

1 Germany in 1900

POINTS TO CONSIDER

Germany had only become a unified state in 1871. The Prussian statesman Otto von Bismarck undoubtedly played a crucial role in this, yet at the time few regretted his fall from power in 1890. The country was changing rapidly and many Germans mirrored the growing confidence of the new young emperor, Wilhelm II. This chapter aims to give a broad overview of Germany in 1900 and will examine the following themes:

- Bismarck's legacy
- The German economy
- The changing spirit of the age: New ideas
- German society
- The Wilhelmine political system
- Key debate: Who actually ran Germany?

Key dates

1815	Creation of German Confederation
1864–71	Unification wars
1864	Defeat of Denmark
1866	Defeat of Austria
1870–1	Defeat of France in the Franco-Prussian War
1871	Creation of the German Empire (*Kaiserreich*)
1888	Death of Emperor Wilhelm I, followed by the death of his son Friedrich III just 99 days later
	Wilhelm II succeeded as Emperor
1890	Forced resignation of Bismarck

1 | Bismarck's Legacy

German unification

By the early twentieth century Germany was a new country which had emerged from the **nationalism** of nineteenth-century Europe. Yet, in 1800 there had been some 400 states in what was known then as the **Holy Roman Empire** – each with its own ruler and proud of its independence. In the wake of the Napoleonic Wars, the Holy Roman Empire came to an end and the number of German states was reduced to 39. This loose grouping of states became the German Confederation in 1815.

During the years that followed, the two most powerful states, Prussia and Austria, competed for the leadership of the Confederation. In 1834, Prussia gained an advantage by setting up a free trade area or **Zollverein** and achieved the upper hand. Afterwards, Prussia, under the leadership of Chancellor Otto von Bismarck from 1862, worked to exclude Austria from German affairs, and set out to achieve a unification of the other German states under Prussian leadership. Bismarck famously warned that this would not be brought about 'by speeches and the resolutions of majorities but by blood and iron'. Following the unification wars of 1864, 1866 and 1870–1 Bismarck finally achieved his aim and in January 1871, King Wilhelm I of Prussia was proclaimed the **Kaiser** of Germany.

Key question
When and how did Germany become a nation state?

Key dates

Creation of German Confederation: 1815

Unification wars: 1864–71

Defeat of Denmark: 1864

Defeat of Austria: 1866

Defeat of France in the Franco-Prussian War: 1870–1

Creation of the German Empire (*Kaiserreich*): 1871

Key terms

Nationalism
The belief in – and support for – a national identity.

Holy Roman Empire
Formed in the ninth century, but by 1800 had become a loose empire of separate states.

Zollverein
The customs union of German states. It created a free trade area by removing internal customs, but upholding customs on imports from foreign trade partners.

Kaiser
Emperor. The regime of 1871–1918 is known as the *Kaiserreich*, translated as Imperial Germany or the Second Empire.

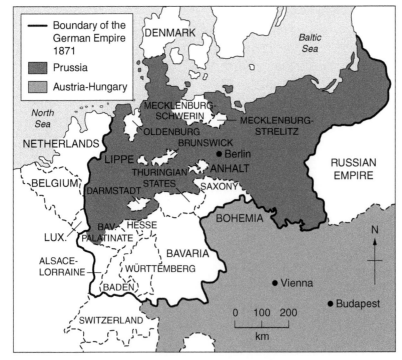

Figure 1.1: Germany in 1871.

Key question
What were the main features of the German Empire's constitution?

Key terms

Constitution
The principles and rules that govern a state.

Federalism
A government in which several states divide responsibilities between central and regional authority.

Authoritarianism
A broad term meaning government by strong non-democratic leadership.

Annexation
Taking over of another country against its will.

Reichstag
The Imperial Parliament elected by all male voters aged over 25.

Bundesrat
The Federal Council 1871–1918. It comprised 58 members nominated by the assemblies of the 25 states.

Kanzler
The Chancellor.

The constitution

Bismarck stamped his mark on the creation of the new nation state, but the **constitution** was an uneasy compromise between three political forces and principles:

- liberal nationalism: the unification of the Germans into one state
- **federalism**: the traditional authority of the German states in the regions
- **authoritarian** monarchy: the military power of Prussia.

Indeed, it has been said that the constitution drawn up by Bismarck 'did not fit easily into any category known to the political scientists'.

The *Reich* consisted, in fact, of 25 sovereign states: four kingdoms, six grand duchies, four duchies, eight principalities and three free cities – plus the imperial territory of Alsace-Lorraine **annexed** in 1871 after the Franco-Prussian War. The new constitution drawn up by Bismarck was a complex balance of power between the Emperor, the Chancellor, the Federal Council and the Imperial Parliament. See Figure 1.1 on page 2.

Emperor (Kaiser)

The King of Prussia was also automatically the Emperor of Germany. In this capacity he enjoyed great authority as of right and he was able to:

- appoint and dismiss the Chancellor
- dissolve the *Reichstag* (but in consent with the *Bundesrat*)
- direct Germany's foreign policy
- command all armed forces as commander-in-chief within the Empire both in peace and in war.

Such were the powers available to Wilhelm II, if he had the will to use them.

Chancellor and imperial government

The Chancellor (*Kanzler*) was in effect the chief minister of the *Reich* and normally combined it with the post of Minister-President of Prussia. He was:

- responsible to the Emperor alone
- responsible for shaping the framework of *Reich* policies
- not accountable to the *Reichstag*, i.e. a vote or resolution of no confidence could be ignored
- responsible for appointing all the state secretaries, who had no power of their own.

In addition, he had to sign all decrees of the Emperor.

Federal Council (*Bundesrat*)

It is all too easy to underestimate the individual powers of the 25 regional states. Although the imperial government had complete control over foreign policy and defence, currency, banking and matters relating to trade, responsibility for education, justice, health and cultural matters remained in the hands of the states.

Bismarck's concession to federalism was enshrined in the creation of the Federal Council (*Bundesrat*). This meant it had:

- 58 representatives nominated from all of the states (with 17 seats for Prussia)
- the right to make changes to the constitution
- the responsibility to ratify all legislation
- the ability to reject any military or constitutional issue with just 14 votes.

Imperial Parliament (*Reichstag*)

The *Reichstag* (the Imperial Parliament) was elected directly by universal male suffrage and secret ballot. However, this apparent concession to liberal democracy was in reality limited in scope. For, although Bismarck always desired the co-operation of the *Reichstag* in the passage of legislation, he went to considerable lengths to make sure that the parliament with majorities did not have the same privileges and status as those enjoyed in Britain by the House of Commons at the end of the nineteenth century.

The *Reichstag* was run according to the following terms:

- It was elected by all males over 25 years of age by secret ballot and served for five years unless dissolved by the Emperor.
- It could discuss and agree those proposals put forward by the *Bundesrat* and the imperial government, including the budget.
- It was not permitted to introduce its own legislation.
- It did not allow the Chancellor and the state secretaries to be members.
- The imperial government was not accountable to it.

Implications of the constitution

Aspects of the *Reich* constitution caused concern long after Bismarck's day. It had aimed to ensure the position and power of Bismarck himself and to preserve the privileges of Prussia and its

Key question
What were the main concerns about the constitution?

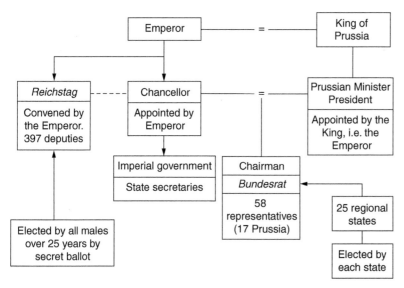

Figure 1.2: The constitution of Imperial Germany.

ruling class. Yet, even with Bismarck at the helm, the system of checks and balances led to political tensions between monarchical and parliamentary claims to power and between federal and state authority:

- The universal suffrage of the *Reichstag* was not as dramatic as it first looked. It was a representative assembly without real power, which, of course, was as Bismarck had intended when it was created. Yet, as more democratic parties came to dominate the *Reichstag*, it became more difficult for the imperial government to manage the assembly.
- The position of Chancellor was independent of the *Reichstag*. Yet, it had a fundamental weakness, as he and his ministers were solely responsible to the Kaiser. As Bismarck and Kaiser Wilhelm I worked together effectively, this weakness was disguised, but the very system made government difficult, unless the Chancellor and Emperor showed a mutual respect and shared a common political outlook.
- In theory, the states came together voluntarily, enjoying equal status and maintaining some of their rights. However, Prussia made up two-thirds of the territory of the German *Reich* and so, in reality, Prussia enjoyed a privileged status in the federal system. It was entitled to 17 seats in the *Bundesrat*, which was crucial, as any fundamental changes could be vetoed with a vote of just 14. Moreover, Prussia's own regional assembly (**Landtag**) had retained an archaic voting system, which disproportionately divided the electors into three classes based on the amount of tax they paid. This allowed the landed aristocracy and big business to have much more political influence.
- There was also a fundamental problem over taxation and expenditure. Only the states could raise **direct taxes**; the imperial government was prohibited from levying a national income tax. As a result, the *Reich* was dependent on **indirect taxes**, such as customs duties and taxes on goods and services, but, as a modernising and expanding state, its spending was increasing. This lack of funds put more dependence on the Prussian civil service and increased its influence.

It was already obvious that the power structure was confused and unclear. From 1888, the weaknesses of the constitution were exacerbated by the accession of an Emperor who was no longer prepared to sit on the sidelines.

The Bismarckian era

Wilhelm I, King of Prussia (1861–88) and Emperor of Germany (1871–88), once said about his relationship with Bismarck: 'It isn't easy to be an Emperor under a Chancellor like this one.' However, in spite of the heartache and frustration implied by this comment, Bismarck and his sovereign worked together most effectively for just over a quarter of a century.

Key terms

Landtag
Within the federal structure each state had its own assembly.

Indirect/direct taxes
Direct taxes are on income. Indirect ones are customs duties and taxes on goods and services.

Key question
What was Bismarck's legacy?

Bismarck controlled affairs from 1871 to 1890 and Germany developed into a powerful industrial nation protected by a well-equipped and modern army. He introduced an advanced system of welfare to help the workers and to put off the appeal of socialism. This included:

- Sickness Insurance Law (1883)
- Accident Insurance Law (1884)
- Old Age Pensions Law (1889).

However, Bismarck did not have things all his own way. The traditional structure of society was changing and there were significant groups who were dissatisfied with his powerful nationalist German state. As a result:

- he declared a 'war for civilisation' or *Kulturkampf* against the Roman Catholic Church in 1873
- he took measures from 1878 to reduce the influence of socialism and its political party, the **Social Democratic Party** (see pages 13 and 25–6).

Such problems would not have been impossible to overcome if only the political system had shown a degree of flexibility. However, the firmly fixed framework of Bismarck's constitution proved to be a major weakness. There was only very limited scope for adjusting to changing circumstances at a time when important major changes were taking place.

In 1888, the old Kaiser died and the Chancellor's relationship with his son and successor, Frederick III, was less friendly. Within 99 days the new Kaiser had also died to be succeeded by his son, the 29-year-old Wilhelm II, on 15 June 1888. Differences of opinion between the new Kaiser and his Chancellor on both a personal and a political level caused Bismarck to offer his resignation on 18 March 1890. Wilhelm II gladly accepted it.

Few contemporaries in Germany regretted Bismarck's fall from favour. The 'Iron Chancellor', as he was known, had successfully forged the unification of Germany out of a collection of independent and self-governing states and had then managed the new nation's affairs for nearly 20 years, by which time Germany had developed into the most powerful state on mainland Europe. Even so, there were many who believed that Bismarck had outlived his usefulness and that the young Kaiser should assume the personal rule of the German Empire.

Key terms

Kulturkampf
A struggle for culture or civilisation. Bismarck's anti-Catholic policy of the 1870s.

Social Democratic Party
The SPD was the main working-class party in Germany.

Key dates

Death of Emperor Wilhelm I, followed by the death of his son Friedrich III just 99 days later. Wilhelm II succeeded as emperor: 1888

Forced resignation of Bismarck: 1890

Summary diagram: Bismarck's legacy

German unification:
- Decline of Holy Roman Empire
- German Confederation
- *Zollverein* (customs union)
- Unification wars 1864–71

↓

The Empire's constitution:
- Emperor (*Kaiser*)
- Chancellor (*Kanzler*)
- Federal Council (*Bundesrat*)
- Imperial Parliament (*Reichstag*)

↓

Bismarckian era 1871–90:
- *Kulturkampf*
- Anti-socialist laws
- State welfare
- Accession of Wilhelm II
- Forced resignation

Table 1.1: Output of heavy industry (in millions of tonnes)

a) Coal

Year	Germany	UK
1871	37.7	119.2
1880	59.1	149.3
1890	89.2	184.5
1900	149.5	228.8
1910	222.2	268.7

b) Steel

Year	Germany	UK
1871	0.14	0.41
1880	0.69	1.32
1890	2.13	3.64
1900	6.46	4.98
1910	13.10	6.48

2 | The German Economy

In 1871 unified Germany had already completed what economic historians describe as the 'take-off' into sustained economic growth. Industries associated with the first stages of industrialisation – coal, iron, heavy engineering and textiles – were well established and production continued to increase. Germany was already a respectable economic power, though clearly second to Great Britain.

By 1914, Germany had become Europe's industrial superpower. It had already exceeded Britain's level of iron production and had nearly caught up with its coal production (see Table 1.1a). Also steel production increased nearly nine-fold in this period, so that by 1914 German output was double that of Britain (see Table 1.1b).

Germany's 'second industrial revolution'

German economic expansion was not just built on the 'old industries'; the very nature of the expansion was more advanced, which suggested that it had gone through 'a second industrial revolution'.

Key question
What were the main features of Germany's 'second industrial revolution'?

New technology

What really marked out the German economy in the 25 years before the First World War was the development and exploitation of its range of new industries:

- Electrics. The first transmission of electricity in the 1880s made an immediate dramatic impact, as it provided a source of light, heat and power. Two German firms, AEG and Siemens, came to dominate the world market in the production of electrical goods to such an extent that by 1913 it is estimated that nearly 50 per cent of the world's electrical products originated from Germany.
- Chemicals. The production of potash and potassium salts massively increased the availability of fertilisers which significantly improved the yield of fruit, vegetables and grains. In the meantime, research and development in the manufacture of chemicals gave Germany a world lead in the preparation of dyes, pharmaceutical products and artificial fibres dominated by the two companies, Bayer and Hoescht. By 1900, Germany produced 90 per cent of the world's synthetic dyes.
- Cars. It was two Germans, Daimler and Benz, who developed the first automobile. By 1900 cars were already being manufactured, although mass production in Germany did not develop until the 1920s.
- Precision equipment. There was an extraordinary growth in research and development into new technologies, such as Zeiss in optics and cameras, and Bosch in mechanical engineering.

Table 1.2: The expansion of the German economy measured by the index of industrial production (1913 = 100)

Year	Index
1871	21.0
1880	25.0
1890	40.0
1900	74.0
1910	84.0
1913	100.0

Table 1.3: Major cities with over half a million inhabitants in 1910. Note the growth of urbanisation (in thousands)

City	1875	1910
Berlin	976	2071
Breslau	239	512
Cologne	135	516
Dresden	197	548
Hamburg	265	931
Leipzig	127	590
Munich	193	596

The labour force

The population had been steadily growing through the nineteenth century, yet in the last quarter it increased markedly and the curve of urbanisation started to rise (see Tables 1.3 and 1.4). Moreover, in the **Wilhelmine** era the expansion of industry and commerce changed the balance of the workforce. The number of Germans employed in the primary sector (e.g. agriculture, forestry and fishing) may have increased slightly, but the number employed in the secondary sector (e.g. industry, mining, handicrafts) and the tertiary sector (e.g. commerce, banking and transport), increased far more dramatically. This meant that in a relatively short time the very nature of the German economy was being transformed. In the 20 years before the First World War the proportion of Germans dependent on agriculture for their livelihood fell from 42 per cent to 34 per cent, still a much higher proportion than Britain, whereas those dependent on the secondary and tertiary sectors for employment

Key term

Wilhelmine
A term for the period of German history, 1890–1918. It refers to the rule of Wilhelm II, in contrast to the Bismarckian era, 1871–90.

The gun-finishing workshop in the Krupp factory in Essen.

Table 1.4: Population (in millions)

Year	Total	Percentage of population in towns of over 2000 people
1871	41.1	36.1
1880	42.2	41.4
1890	49.4	42.5
1900	56.4	54.4
1910	64.9	60.0

Key term

GNP
Gross national product: the total value of all goods and services in a nation's economy (including income derived from assets abroad).

grew from 34 per cent to 38 per cent and from 24 per cent to 28 per cent, respectively (see Table 1.5).

During this time, the percentage of contribution to Germany's **GNP** made by the different sectors changed substantially. In 1888 the three sectors were fairly equally balanced; by 1913 agriculture had fallen to less than 25 per cent, whereas industry had risen to 45 per cent. Therefore, clearly, industry was the real driving force in the economic change and Germany had been transformed from being a country of agriculture to one of industry centred round the urbanised towns and cities (Table 1.5).

Nevertheless, it would be false to suggest that agriculture was in marked decline, and if it was, then it was only 'relative'. In terms of production, in fact, agricultural output rose dramatically by over 42 per cent between 1888 and 1913, and this success was

Table 1.5: Structure of labour force (in millions of workers and as a percentage)

Sectors	1875	1895	1913
Primary (agriculture, fishing, forestry)	9.23 (49%)	9.79 (42%)	10.70 (34%)
Secondary (industry, mining)	5.49 (29%)	7.95 (34%)	11.72 (38%)
Tertiary (banking, transport, commerce)	3.97 (22%)	5.66 (24%)	8.55 (28%)
Total	18.64	23.40	30.97

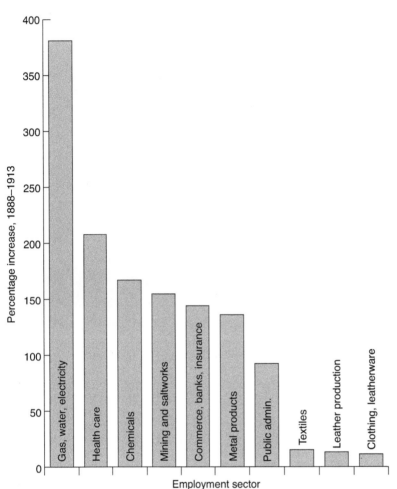

Figure 1.3: The percentage increase in employment sectors for 1888–1913.

despite fierce competition from other countries, especially the USA and Canada. German agriculture was very productive and the country remained more self-sufficient in terms of food supplies than Britain.

Reasons for German success

For once, the economic figures present a clear-cut picture. Germany had built on its earlier economic foundations and from 1890 to 1914, despite occasional **recessions** such as in 1891 and 1901, witnessed a period of real economic expansion. In those years its annual average growth was 4.5 per cent. It had grown into the most powerful industrial economy on the European continent, with a share of world trade which rivalled that of Britain and its Empire. How and why did this come about?

Long-term causes of German success

The success of the German economy was built on a number of long-term factors over the nineteenth century.

Recession
Period of economic slowdown, usually accompanied by rising unemployment.

Key term

Key question
What were the long-term causes of German success?

Key terms

Imports
Goods purchased from foreign countries.

Balance of trade
The difference in value between exports and imports. If the value of the imports is above that of the exports, the balance of the payments has a deficit that is often referred to as being in the red.

Exports
Goods sold to foreign countries.

Population

Germany's population continued to grow rapidly. There were one-third more Germans in 1910 than in 1890. This provided both the market and the labour force for an expanding economy. Moreover, a younger population was more willing to move from job to job and adapt to new skills. Both were essential in the change-over to a more advanced level of economic production.

Raw materials

Germany had an abundance of natural resources. There was coal from the Ruhr, Saar and Silesia; iron-ore from Alsace-Lorraine and the Ruhr; and potash from Alsace-Lorraine. Thus, the huge demand for energy, iron–steel products and chemicals could largely be met from domestic supplies instead of depending on **imports**. This was a huge benefit for the **balance of trade** (see Table 1.6).

Table.1.6: Balance of payments (in millions of marks)

Year	Imports	Exports	Visible balance	Invisible balance	Overall balance
1880	2814	2923	+109	+168	277
1890	4162	3335	−827	+1249	422
1900	5769	4611	−1158	+1566	408
1910	8927	7475	−1452	+2211	759

Visible balance refers to the payment and receipts for the import and **export** of goods; invisible balance refers to the payment and receipts for the import and export for services such as banking, insurance and shipping.

Geography

Other geographical advantages included major navigable rivers, such as the Rhine and the Elbe, and easy access to the Danube. The broad flat northern plain was well suited to the construction of its excellent railway system.

Short-term causes of German success

Key question
What were the short-term causes of the 'second industrial revolution' in the late nineteenth century?

Education

Alongside the natural advantages, must be added the skills and efficiency of the German people. Germany had probably the best elementary education system in the world, and between 1890 and 1914, enrolment to university doubled. More importantly, its institutes of higher education not only provided for the traditional scholar, but also made increasing provision for those with technical skills; in that way highly qualified scientists and technicians worked closely with the major firms.

Banks

German banking proved to be a real stimulus to economic expansion with its policy of credit for investment in industry. Free from any kind of state control, German banks pursued an adventurous policy of providing generous long-term loans. This in turn led the big banks to become directly involved in industry. This helped to create a close partnership between the banking and commercial sectors of the economy. Indeed, the relationship between banks and industrial firms became so close that they often had representatives on each other's boards of directors.

Protection

From 1879 Bismarck decided to abandon free trade and to follow a policy of **tariffs** to protect both agriculture and industry. This was based on the following economic reasons:

- to protect infant industries and provide a secure domestic market, especially after the beginning of the economic downturn from 1873
- to counter the falling prices of wheat from Russia and the USA; this also led to a shortage of wheat and a marked rise in food prices
- to raise revenue for the *Reich* government.

The Tariff Law of 1879 undoubtedly caused political divisions, but generally it helped to stimulate the growth of a large internal market and to consolidate the regions of the *Reich*.

Cartels and syndicates

In the final decade of the century the banking system expanded enormously which contributed to the development of a distinctly German feature of industrialisation, the growth of **cartels**. Whereas in Britain and the USA the idea of a group of businessmen combining together to control prices, production levels and marketing was frowned on for being against the spirit of free enterprise, and was indeed illegal in the USA after 1890, in Germany cartels were accepted and legally protected. Indeed, the state even encouraged their development. Since they restricted competition and encouraged development and investment, such measures were considered sensible as a means of achieving advantages of large-scale production and economies of scale. This was especially important in times of recession. By keeping domestic prices high, cartels could subsidise low export prices to undercut opposition and gain markets abroad.

As a result, according to a government investigation, by 1905, 366 cartels existed compared to only 90 in 1885. In effect, whole areas of German industry had been 'cartelised', most famously by the creation of the Rhineland–Westphalia coal syndicate of Thyssen and Krupp in 1893 and the deal between AEG and Siemens from 1908. Similar arrangements were established in every area: banking, shipping, textiles, paper and even perambulators (prams). To many at that time, the cartels were typical of the efficient large-scale and productive nature of the German economy. Yet, economic historians today have questioned the extent to which cartels really benefited the German economy since, by restricting the entry of new manufacturers, they reduced competition and maintained artificially high prices.

Key terms

Tariffs
Taxes levied by an importing nation on foreign goods coming in, and paid by the importers.

Cartel
An arrangement between businesses to control the level of production and prices. This in effect creates a joint monopoly.

Government ownership

Unlike in nineteenth-century Britain, the German government pursued a more rigorous policy of state intervention and ownership. Stretches of railways were nationalised from the very earliest stages (although the creation of a unified single system was not established until the Weimar years). The approach of government ownership, either state or federal, had a crucial role in developing various enterprises. It allowed mixed ownership of services like gas and water, and complete state ownership of the post service, telephones and the telegraph.

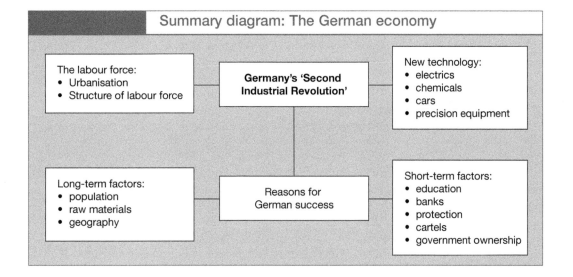

Summary diagram: The German economy

The labour force:
- Urbanisation
- Structure of labour force

Germany's 'Second Industrial Revolution'

New technology:
- electrics
- chemicals
- cars
- precision equipment

Long-term factors:
- population
- raw materials
- geography

Reasons for German success

Short-term factors:
- education
- banks
- protection
- cartels
- government ownership

3 | The Changing Spirit of the Age: New Ideas

In the latter half of the nineteenth century different beliefs and ideas had an influence on the politics of the early twentieth century. These were socialism, nationalism, imperialism, **anti-Semitism** and Social Darwinism.

Socialism

As Germany became more industrialised, **Marxism** gained ground among various workers' parties in the latter half of the nineteenth century. This led to the creation of the Social Democratic Party (SPD) in 1875 with its declared aim to overthrow the existing political and economic system, albeit by legal means. Indeed, Bismarck saw socialism as such a real threat to the established order that Anti-Socialist Laws were passed in 1878 and remained in force until 1890.

However, far from killing socialism, the movement was strengthened by this kind of persecution. By the time it was liberated in 1890 with the end of the Anti-Socialist Laws, the SPD had organised itself into a nationwide mass party. At the Erfurt Congress of 1891, the party adopted a fully Marxist programme aimed at overthrowing the Wilhelmine class system. It proved to be a popular policy manifesto and in the election of 1893 the

Key question
How did the socialist movement become so well established in Germany?

Key terms

Anti-Semitism
The hatred of Jews.

Marxism
The ideology of Karl Marx, who believed that the working classes will overthrow the ruling classes by revolution.

SPD had won nearly a quarter of the vote with 23.4 per cent (see also page 35).

Nationalism

In the first half of the nineteenth century nationalism was seen as a liberal progressive force leading the way to the creation of a parliamentary democracy. Yet, following the failure of the revolutionary events of 1848 and the creation of the *Kaiserreich* in 1871, the nature of nationalism was to change by 1900.

This was partly because of the dominating political influence of Bismarck, who was able to stay in power longer than expected, and partly because of the effects of the economic recession after 1873. More significantly, German nationalists changed their priorities; they had become more conservative, backing the semi-authoritarian regime and preserving their interests. After all, liberal nationalism failed in 1848, whereas conservative nationalism succeeded in 1871.

The nationalism emerging from the 1880s took a different form. It was a harsher nationalism directed against the internal minorities: Jews (see below), French, Danes and especially against Poles who formed five per cent of the German population. The existence of these minorities with their own different religions, languages and cultures was in conflict with German nationalists who aspired to a united nation state. As a result, when the minorities tried to maintain their own identities and to establish rights, the imperial government became increasingly determined to 'Germanise' the areas. In Polish-speaking regions the German language was strictly enforced in schools and it caused much discontent, leading to 40,000 pupils holding a strike against the authorities in 1906–7.

This radical nationalism, with its appeal of **imperialism**, sought also to extend German power and influence beyond the *Reich*. In its most chauvinistic and racist form was the idea of Germany as a nation destined for world power through a *Lebensraum* policy of creating German settlements both overseas and to the east. This ideology was exemplified by the **Pan-German League** and many other organisations, which were to gain much support at the turn of the century (see page 27). These groups were anti-socialist, racist, anti-Semitic, expansionist and inevitably strong supporters of any policy that advanced German power and influence.

Anti-Semitism

There is a long tradition of anti-Semitism in European history. It certainly had never been just a purely German phenomenon. It was rooted in the religious hostility of some Christians towards the Jews (as being seen as responsible for the death of Christ) that could be traced back to medieval Europe. However, by the mid-nineteenth century it had become politically non-influential and in 1869 the Jews enjoyed equal legal and civil rights.

Key question
How did German nationalism change in the latter half of the nineteenth century?

Key terms

Imperialism
Rule by an Emperor. It has come to mean one country taking political and economic control of another territory.

Lebensraum
Living space.

Pan-German League
Alldeutscher Verband. A right-wing nationalist movement formed in 1893. It supported expansionism and many of its supporters were anti-democratic, anti-socialist and anti-Semitic.

Key question
How did the nature of anti-Semitism change?

During the nineteenth century a more clearly defined anti-Semitism based on racism and national resentment as well as religion emerged in Germany. By 1900, a number of specifically anti-Semitic *völkisch* political parties were winning seats in the *Reichstag* and, although comparatively few in number, their success shows that anti-Semitic ideas were becoming more prevalent and generally more acceptable. As a consequence, extreme right-wing racist parties made significant gains compared to the election of 1893. One of the leaders of these right-wing anti-Semitic parties was the imperial court chaplain, Adolf Stöcker.

Although anti-Semitism may be seen partly as a by-product of the nationalist passions, it was more a response to intellectual developments arising from those nationalist passions and to changing social conditions. The Jews became an easy scapegoat for the discontent and disorientation felt by many people as rapid industrialisation and urbanisation took place. Since many of the Jews were actually immigrants from eastern Europe, they were easily identifiable because of their different traditions. Moreover, although many members of the Jewish community were impoverished, wealthier ones became the focus of envy because they were viewed as privileged. Although Jews comprised less than one per cent of the German population, they composed a much higher percentage of bankers, lawyers, doctors, editors and writers.

Social Darwinism

In the late nineteenth century anti-Semitism began to be presented in a more intellectual vein by the application of the racial theories of **Social Darwinism**. According to such thinking, nations were like animals and only by struggling and fighting could they hope to survive. In this way, an image of intellectual and cultural respectability was given to those anti-Semites who portrayed the Jews as an 'inferior', or 'parasitic', race and the **Aryans** as superior. Most notable of those anti-Semites were:

- Heinrich von Treitschke, the leading historian, who publicly declared 'the Jews are our misfortune'.
- Richard Wagner, the musician and composer whose operas glorified German mythology and often portrayed Jewish characters as evil.
- Houston Stewart Chamberlain, an Englishman, who in his bestselling book, *The Foundations of the Nineteenth Century*, celebrated the superiority of the German *Volk*.

The modern historian Noakes has suggested that by 1900 anti-Semitism 'had succeeded in permeating broad sections of German society from the Kaiser down to the lower middle class. Ominously, it was particularly strongly entrenched within the academic community, thereby influencing the next generation.'

Key terms

Völkisch
Nationalist views associated with racism (especially anti-Semitism).

Social Darwinism
A philosophy that portrayed the world as a 'struggle' between people, races and nations. It was deeply influenced by the theory of evolution based on natural selection.

Key question
How influential was Social Darwinism?

Key terms

Aryan
Technically it refers to the family of Indo-European languages. Yet, racists in the nineteenth century defined it as the non-Jewish people of northern Europe.

Volk
Often translated as 'people', although it tends to suggest a nation with the same ethnic and cultural identities and with a collective sense of belonging.

Summary diagram: The changing spirit of the age – new ideas

```
                        ┌──────────────┐
                        │  Socialism   │
                        └──────┬───────┘
                               │
┌──────────────────┐   ┌───────┴────────┐   ┌──────────────┐
│ Social Darwinism │───│ The changing   │───│ Nationalism  │
│                  │   │ spirit         │   │              │
│                  │   │ of the age     │   │              │
└──────────────────┘   └───────┬────────┘   └──────────────┘
                               │
                        ┌──────┴───────┐
                        │ Anti-Semitism│
                        └──────────────┘
```

4 | German Society

The impact of the rapid economic change meant that millions of ordinary Germans were forced to come to terms with changes in their way of life. In some of the more rural areas, such as much of Bavaria and almost all of Pomerania, time stood still, but few could fully escape the consequences of change. The difficulty for the historian is trying to draw some meaningful conclusions about the social effects of these changes without being too generalised. Such difficulties are even more noticeable in German social history. Here, any attempt to consider the make-up of the German people on the basis of class is complicated by the existence of other lines of division such as those of religion and regional identity. However, the nation could still be divided into broad social groups.

Class divisions
Junkers

The landed nobility or *Junkers* continued to be an extremely powerful force in society. In economic terms many in this class were beginning to experience less prosperous times. Agriculture was in relative decline, as measured against industry, and those landowners who failed to modernise their production methods or who did not adapt to changing market conditions were likely to find their financial position under threat, despite widespread tax evasion. Yet the nobility still regarded their privileged and highly state-subsidised social status not only as essential to maintaining the traditions and values of German society, but also as a right and proper reflection of their social superiority built up over many generations. Nowhere was this determination more apparent than in the army officer corps, which the *Junkers* were determined to keep under their control, even to the extent of opposing the expansion of the army in case it diluted the aristocratic nature of the officer class (see pages 27–8).

Key question
What were the main social groups in the Second Empire?

Junkers
The conservative landowning aristocracy, especially those from eastern Germany.

Key term

Key terms

Bourgeoisie
The upper and middle classes who owned the capital and the means of production (factories and mines).

Mittelstand
Can be translated as 'the middle class', but in German society it tends to represent the lower middle classes, e.g. shopkeepers, craft workers and clerks. Traditionally independent and self-reliant, but it increasingly felt squeezed out between the power and influence of big business and industrial labour.

Industrial *bourgeoisie*

The greatest potential threat to the nobility's supremacy came from the wealthy new industrial **bourgeoisie**. However, most research suggests that successful German businessmen were willing to purchase privileges and to flaunt their wealth in an attempt to copy the *Junkers* rather than to replace them. Indeed, the policies and the actions of the National Liberal Party (see page 24), who were in the main representatives of business and industry, became increasingly conservative in their outlook and supportive of the existing system.

Middle classes

The middle ranks of the middle class were also becoming more numerous. Professional and clerical workers in industry, education and the bureaucracy were in great demand for their scientific, technical or administrative skills. Even so, the tendency was to maintain the status quo rather than to seek change. Teachers, civil servants and others employed in the public services, for example, were classified as *Beamte*, or state officials, and in return for accepting the state's strict regulations of employment, they were guaranteed rights of employment and certain privileges, such as pensions. This status was highly cherished and widely respected.

Mittelstand

However, this period was not so good for the **Mittelstand**, the lower-middle class of skilled workers and small traders. The problems they faced went a lot deeper than merely coping with difficult times. The *Mittelstand* found itself squeezed between the more powerful workers who had formed trade unions and the larger, more productive enterprises of big business. As a result, resentment led many in this class to regard the old times, before the age of industrialisation, as a golden bygone era. This also led to a simple and unrealistic belief that their fears might be overcome by supporting the views and solutions offered by the extreme right in politics. The changing attitudes of the peasantry and the *Mittelstand* led to growing support in the 1890s for populist right-wing movements (see page 27).

Working classes

At the bottom of the social pyramid was the mass of the population who made up the labouring classes in both the towns and countryside. For the smallholders and landless labourers life was particularly difficult. The economic problems of agriculture at this time, combined with the growth in population, meant that it was difficult for farming to be profitable because of competition from the USA and Canada (see pages 9–10). In the south and west of Germany, where the land was mainly farmed as smallholdings, families were often forced to divide the land between their children who then combined farming with other part-time occupations. In the east, the labourers (and many were

Poles) on the estates of the aristocratic and landed *Junkers* had little option but to accept wage cuts. Not surprisingly, to many on the land, the appeal of industrial employment with the prospect of regular work and wages seemed an attractive option. This meant that the drift of rural workers to the cities continued.

Life in the industrial areas, however, had its own problems. Although employment rates were very good and unemployment only went above three per cent in one year between 1900 and 1914, and the average wage increased by 25 per cent between 1895 and 1913, living and working conditions remained dismally poor. It was this discontent that led to a rise in trade union membership during these years (see Table 1.7). For most working people, life was divided between long hours in often unhealthy workplaces and the cold, cramped accommodation of their unsanitary homes. As a leading historian has put it: 'Some 30 per cent of all family households in this prosperous Second Empire lived in destitution and abject misery.'

Table 1.7: Trade union membership, in thousands, 1890–1913

Year	No. of people (thousands)
1890	357
1895	327
1900	849
1905	1653
1910	2455
1913	3024

A national identity

Bismarck may have unified Germany and the economy may have been rapidly modernised, but religious and national (and regional) feelings were still very powerful influences that cut across all classes of society.

Key question
Was unified Germany socially united?

The policy of *Kulturkampf* (see page 6) had alienated Catholics in Germany, especially in Bavaria and the Rhineland. Their support for the Catholic Centre Party and the success of Catholic trade unions in providing an alternative to the socialist trade unions, underlined the importance of religious affiliation. Germany still had strong regional loyalties despite the political dominance of Prussia. The federal system conceded responsibilities to each state for such things as education and police. Also, economically, the regions had maintained strong regional specialisation. Moreover, it is telling that over 10 per cent of the *Reichstag*'s seats continued to be won by deputies supporting one of the minority nationalist groupings (see pages 25 and 35).

Most significantly, in spite of the economic changes, German society seems to have remained divided along traditional class lines. Although as a nation Germany was becoming wealthier, the inequalities between the upper and upper-middle classes and the lower-middle classes and working classes seem to have increased, not reduced. What movement there was tended to be within a class rather than movement between the different classes. Divisions were maintained and it was difficult to achieve higher social status simply on the grounds of wealth or expertise. As summed up by the historian Kaelble, 'the large majority of working class sons did not leave their class; the majority of the lower-middle class continued to come from the lower-middle class'.

There is little doubt therefore that the rapid pace of economic change in Imperial Germany had an important effect on the stability of an already mixed society. However, the prejudices of class, religion and race acted as very effective barriers to the breaking down of class differences. This was seen in the education system, the professions, the business world, and most prominently at the top levels of society, where the higher ranks of the civil service and the army remained predominantly the preserve of the nobility. While the traditional social ties and values were still very strong, economic progress inevitably led to rivalry, tensions and disorder. It was the problem of balancing the old with the new, of accommodating the various groups in German society, which the political system somehow had to manage.

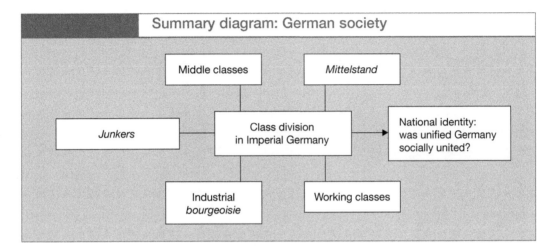

Summary diagram: German society

5 | The Wilhelmine Political System

Whether one should start studying the political system of Imperial Germany with a consideration of the role of the Kaiser is an issue of historical debate in itself (see the key debate on pages 29 and 45). Some historians would strongly argue that a biographical approach with an individual would be at the expense of other important issues. Nevertheless, it is still difficult to ignore the personality and role of Wilhelm II, who has remained the focus of much discussion and controversy.

Key question
How did the Kaiser
exert influence?

The Emperor and his court

Wilhelm II was born in 1859, the eldest child of Crown Prince Friedrich (Kaiser Friedrich III for just 99 days in 1888) and Victoria, the eldest daughter of Queen Victoria. Even his birth has become the focus of historical study: the breech delivery resulted in the partial paralysis of his left arm and damage to the balance mechanism in his ear. These 'physical' problems have prompted great speculation about their possible psychological consequences on the young prince. For instance, his tutor taught him to ride a horse simply by putting him back on after he fell off time after time after time until he found his balance, despite the child's pain and humiliation. Close attention has also been paid to the strained relationship with his parents, especially his mother. Certainly, he grew apart from them during his adolescent years.

An official painting of Wilhelm II in the uniform of the Garde de Corps (1901).

He opposed their liberal sympathies and he despised his father's deference to his strong-willed mother. Instead, he preferred the company of his grandfather and the Bismarcks and found solace in the regimental life of the military garrison at Potsdam.

Wilhelm's personality

The nature of the personality of the young Wilhelm II has been the focus of great analysis. He was intelligent and at times an extremely charming man. He had a broad range of interests and took great pride in his country and ancestry. However, his understanding of the crucial issues was usually slight and distorted by his own personal prejudices. Above all, he was very sensitive to criticism and so taken up by his own self-importance that his moods and behaviour were liable to wild fluctuations.

Later profiles have suggested that the Kaiser's behaviour can be seen as symptoms of insanity, megalomania (delusions about his own greatness) and sadism (pleasure in inflicting pain on others). More recently, it has been suggested that he was narcissistic (showed signs of excessive self-love), a repressed homosexual and suffered from a mental condition which revealed itself in his irrational behaviour. It is difficult to be sure about any of these claims, but the general opinion now is that Wilhelm II, if not insane, was at least deeply disturbed. However, besides attempting to draw conclusions about Wilhelm the man, the historian must also try to decide the extent to which Wilhelm's personality actually shaped the history of Imperial Germany.

Wilhelm's 'personal rule'

Wilhelm II once boasted that he had never read the German constitution. Bearing in mind the complications of Bismarck's constitutional plans, his failure to do so was perhaps understandable. However, the story gives an interesting insight into the outlook of Germany's sovereign. He had no doubts about his position. He considered himself to be all-powerful, with his authority based on the **divine right of kings**. He was accountable to God alone. He was also of the Hohenzollern dynasty of kings and, as such, was a warrior king who led and commanded his people militarily. In 1891 he spoke to some new recruits as follows:

> Recruits! You have sworn Me allegiance. That, children of My Guard, means that you are now My soldiers. You have given yourselves over to Me body and soul. There is only one enemy for you and that is My enemy. With the present Socialist agitation, it may be that I shall order you to shoot down your own families, your brothers, yes, your parents – which may God forbid – but then too you must follow my orders without murmur.

Of course, it is true that the constitution did indeed grant the Emperor extensive powers, but his ignorance of its other aspects was a dangerous misunderstanding and self-deception. His desire to establish 'personal rule' was made possible by his total control over appointments to the imperial government. He also enjoyed the same right over the government of Prussia. Bismarck had at least given the system a degree of unity and direction, but the Kaiser possessed neither the character nor the ability of his former Chancellor and his leadership amounted to little more than flights of fancy and blundering interventions. This situation was allowed to continue because he made all the important appointments. By this means the Kaiser was able to surround himself at court and in government with men who were prepared to bolster his own high opinion of himself by sympathising with his views. In this sense it is perhaps possible to speak of the Kaiser's 'personal rule'.

Key term

Divine right of kings
The belief that kings are God's representatives and have the authority to rule their subjects.

Profile: Wilhelm II 1859–1941

1859 – Born in Berlin, the eldest son of Crown Prince, Friedrich, and Victoria, the eldest daughter of British Queen Victoria

1869 – Commissioned as a second lieutenant in the Pomeranian Regiment

1878 – Embarked on his studies at the University of Bonn

1881 – Married Princess Augusta-Victoria of Schleswig-Holstein

1888 – Became Kaiser on the death of his father which followed just 99 days after the death of his grandfather

1890 – Dismissed Bismarck as Chancellor

1897 – Supported the policy of *Weltpolitik* (see pages 36–8)

1908 – Homosexual scandal at royal court, involving his close friend Count Philip von Eulenburg
– *Daily Telegraph* affair (see pages 41–2)

1914 – Start of First World War: his position in the 'July Crisis' did not help to prevent the war (see pages 70–5)

1916 – Overshadowed by the leadership of the Supreme Army Command (see page 92)

1918 – Abdicated on 9 November, fled to the Netherlands and spent the rest of his life living there in exile

1940 – Declined Hitler's offer to return to Germany as a private citizen

1941 – Died and buried at Doorn in the Netherlands

Key term

Weltpolitik 'World policy'; the imperial government's strategy from 1897 to expand Germany's military and political influence.

The background and personality of Wilhelm II have long been the focus of much gossip and discussion:

- his difficult birth and subsequent deformity
- his difficult relationship with his parents
- his increasing isolation leading him to find solace in the daily routine of the military garrison at Potsdam
- the closeness of his friendship with some colleagues at the court leading to suggestions of repressed homosexuality.

Despite these problems Wilhelm II was not unintelligent, he had a very good memory and the political power to direct things. Yet, his moods were so violent and changed so rapidly that they disturbed the balance of effective government policy. Clashes with Bismarck led him to choose four more pliable Chancellors with very different weaknesses. Most significantly, he lacked the real skills and charisma to co-ordinate the leadership and government of a major power. He failed to appreciate the changes that were happening so that, at home, he opposed the development of parliamentary rule and, abroad, he supported increasingly dangerous foreign policies. He might have wanted to see himself as the German autocrat, but in the few years up to 1914 it became difficult to say who really controlled Germany.

During the course of the war, Wilhelm's influence rapidly declined and he was forced to play a subordinate role to Germany's military leaders Hindenburg and Ludendorff.

Key question
How much influence
was exerted by the
Chancellors?

The Kaiser and his Chancellors

If Wilhelm II's ability to govern the country was limited, the responsibility fell first on his appointed Chancellor. However, none of Bismarck's successors was able to or was allowed to take up the mantle of leadership with any kind of real authority or conviction.

Caprivi

The short-lived Chancellorship of Count Leo von Caprivi (1890–4) is proof enough that good intentions, integrity and a friendly approach were not sufficient in the political environment of Wilhelmine Germany. Ironically, he was appointed in 1890 by Wilhelm II in order to legalise socialism in Germany, which had been outlawed earlier under Bismarck (see page 13). Yet, in 1894 Caprivi felt obliged to resign when his master demanded the drafting of measures directed against that very same party!

Hohenlohe

Prince Hohenlohe-Schillingfurst (1894–1900) was an 80-year-old Bavarian aristocrat. His reputation for indecision and long windedness offered exactly the kind of weak leadership that allowed others to exercise influence. Hohenlohe was soon reduced to little more than a figurehead.

Bülow

Even before Bernhard Bülow became Chancellor (1900–9), he had come to exert powerful political influence as Foreign Minister (1897–1900). He astutely kept the affection and trust of the Kaiser and he effectively managed the *Reichstag* so, for a decade he successfully combined the roles of courtier and Chancellor. However, Bülow's domination from 1897 to 1909 should not be mistaken for genuine authority and purpose. Bülow was a manipulator, whose main concern was to further himself. Eventually, when he failed to show sufficient loyalty to the Kaiser during the '*Daily Telegraph* affair' (see pages 41–2), he lost that all-important support and his removal soon followed.

Bethmann

Germany's final Chancellor before the First World War was Theobald von Bethmann-Hollweg (1909–17). He was a hard-working and well-meaning bureaucrat, whose virtues were not really suited to the demands of the situation. At a time of growing international tension between the great powers in Europe his lack of experience in foreign affairs and his ignorance of military issues were highly significant.

Conclusion

These men were very different in character and background. Yet, none of them was ever really willing or able to dominate the German political scene decisively. It is tempting to say that their weaknesses and limited political experience were the reasons for the problems of government. This would be an over-simplification. Imperial Germany got the Chancellors it deserved. They were the products of a constitution that made them accountable first and foremost to the Kaiser. Under Wilhelm I this had not mattered, since he had relied on Bismarck, but his grandson was determined to be more involved in the affairs of state. Political survival for Germany's four post-Bismarck Chancellors was therefore dependent on showing loyalty to the Kaiser. This was far from easy when Wilhelm II's personal involvement was often erratic and blundering.

The *Reichstag*

The problems of government were made more difficult in the years after 1890 by the constitutional position of the *Reichstag*. Bismarck had always been obliged to secure the support of the *Reichstag* for government legislation and by one means or another he had usually managed to achieve that. After 1890 the balance of power in the *Reichstag* shifted significantly. What were these changes in political representation and what were their implications?

Key question
What were the main political parties in Imperial Germany?

Conservatives

On most issues – and there were some important exceptions covered in the next chapter – the Kaiser and his governments could always depend on the backing of the three right-wing parties: the German Conservative Party, the Free Conservative Party and the National Liberal Party. However, the voting strength of these parties was on the decline. In 1887, they gained 48 per cent of the vote and 220 of the seats in the *Reichstag*. By the time of the election of 1912 their share of the vote had further fallen to 26 per cent, which gave them only 102 seats. During this period, the traditional support for the imperial government was slowly being eroded; this increased the problem of finding majority support from other parties to ratify legislation.

Liberals

The Left Liberals though supportive of the government at times, were generally more critical. However, from 1893 they were divided into at least three factions and were incapable of having a decisive say in the *Reichstag*. These divisions help to explain the failure of German liberalism to make the sort of impact that their counterparts were making in other industrialised countries.

Centre Party

The same could not be said of the Centre Party. Its importance increased during Bismarck's *Kulturkampf* and afterwards it consistently won between 90 and 110 seats which made it the largest party in the *Reichstag* until the election of 1912. Although it had a religious base, its members embraced a wide range of political views, ranging from right-wing conservatism to progressive social reform. Its parliamentary numbers were sufficiently large to ensure that the Centre Party enjoyed a pivotal role in German politics. Earlier, even Bismarck had been forced to recognise this. It exploited this position by a sensible, down-to-earth approach to the parliamentary process. At times this led to co-operation and at others to downright opposition. Therefore the Centre Party deputies could not be taken for granted and the imperial government dared not ignore its views.

Social Democrats

As referred to on page 13, the spread of socialism in Germany went hand in hand with the creation and rise of the SPD. Of course, the introduction of the Anti-Socialist Laws significantly reduced left-wing representation to a handful of seats in 1878–90,

Table 1.8: The major political parties represented in the *Reichstag* 1890–1918

Party	Description
German Conservative Party (*Deutschkonservative Partei*, DKP)	The party of the landowning farming community. Its outlook was ultra-conservative and distinctly hostile to socialism and liberalism. It was especially strong in Prussia.
Free Conservative Party (*Reichspartei*, RP)	Conservative in outlook, it was backed by both industrialists and landowners. Its geographical base of support was not so narrow as DKP.
National Liberal Party (*Nationalliberale Partei*, NLP)	Traditionally the party of economic and political liberalism. It represented bankers and industrialists and was becoming increasingly conservative in its policy.
Centre Party (*Zentrumspartei*, ZP)	Formed in 1871 to uphold the interests of the Catholic Church against the dominance of Protestant Prussia. Its appeal was therefore denominational rather than class based. Despite the *Kulturkampf* (Bismarck's anti-Catholic policy of the 1870s) it had become an influential political voice in the *Reichstag*.
German Free Thought Party (Left Liberals) (*Deutsche Freisinnige Partei*, DFP)	Formed in 1884 following the secession of the more radical elements from the NLP. It attracted support from intellectuals and certain elements of the commercial and professional middle class. In 1893 it split into three and was only reunited in 1910 under the new name of the *Fortschrittliche Volkspartei* (FVP), Progressive People's Party.
Social Democratic Party (*Sozialistische Partei Deutschlands*, SPD)	A Marxist party that was closely connected with the trade unions and supported by the working classes. Restricted by anti-socialist legislation from 1878 to 1890. Afterwards it grew rapidly.
National minorities	Such parties represented the interests of ethnic minorities living in Germany such as Poles, Danes and the French in Alsace-Lorraine.
Right-wing extremists	There were a number of small extreme right-wing conservative parties. They were nationalistic, anti-socialist and often anti-Semitic.

although once it lapsed, the Social Democrats rose rapidly as a parliamentary force. In 1887 the Social Democrats had polled only 10.1 per cent of the vote and gained 11 seats; in 1912 the figures were 34.8 per cent with 110 seats and it had merged as the largest party.

Yet, although the party had gathered the majority of the working classes behind its banner and it was committed to a Marxist programme, there were clear divisions within the ranks. On the one hand, there were many members who were trade unionists who came to believe that a policy of '**gradualism**' or '**reformism**' was the best way to create a socialist society. According to this view, they supported democratic socialism with reforms that improved the living and working conditions of working people. On the other hand, traditional Marxists, such as Rosa Luxemburg (see profile on page 105) and August Bebel, remained thoroughly against this approach, since it involved co-operation with the *bourgeoisie*; they were still committed to **revolutionary socialism**.

The differences between reformist and revolutionary socialists were to be significant, but up to 1914, they did not greatly weaken the increasing electoral appeal of the Social Democrats. In theory the party remained committed to bringing about revolutionary changes in society, but in practice many of the deputies in the *Reichstag* were content to talk of revolution while working for social and political change through the parliamentary system. Such moderation was not generally recognised by the opponents of the Social Democrats. The party was seen as a force for evil, which had to be isolated and controlled. There was no question of its taking part in the imperial government.

Conclusion

At the start of the twentieth century, the balance of political forces in the *Reichstag* was important to Germany's political and constitutional problems. The *Reichstag* itself was divided between those who wished to see no change in the existing order and those who wanted the creation of a truly parliamentary democracy. This may not have presented any problems had the conservative forces been able to maintain a majority. However, the gradual decline in their electoral fortunes, combined with the strength of the Centre Party and the increase in the popularity of the Social Democrats, only served to worsen the problem of finding majority support for the passing of legislation. By 1914 this situation showed no sign of being solved since the constitution did not permit measures to be taken to allow for changing circumstances.

Pressure groups

Political life in the Wilhelmine era also saw a real growth in the number of pressure groups which campaigned to advance their interests in the *Reichstag*. They took various forms.

Key terms

Gradualism or reformism
The ideas of evolutionary socialism grew out of the writings in the late 1890s of Eduard Bernstein, who argued that capitalism was not in economic demise and he refuted Marx's predictions. He therefore believed that socialism would be achieved through capitalism – as workers gradually won rights, their cause for grievance would be diminished.

Revolutionary socialism
The belief of socialists in the need for revolution to bring about fundamental social change.

Key question
How and why were pressure groups so influential?

Key terms

Agrarian League
A *Junkers*-led
organisation formed
in 1893 with a third
of a million
members of farmers
and landowners.

Hakatisten
The German
Society for the
Eastern Marches
was known as the
Hakatisten, named
after its founders
Hansemann,
Kennemann and
Tidemann. It
campaigned for a
repressive anti-
Polish policy.

Kaiserreich
Translated as
Imperial Germany
or the Second
Empire.

Economic lobby groups
- The **Agrarian League**, a *Junkers*-led organisation with a third of a million members, mainly peasants, committed to tariffs to protect their agricultural interests.
- The Centre of Association of German Industrialists, geared to promoting the interests of heavy industry.
- The Imperial German *Mittelstand* Confederation, committed to preserving traditional values.

Nationalist organisations
- The Pan-German League, which was committed to an aggressive expansionist foreign policy to achieve Germany's world role.
- The Navy League, to advance the Kaiser's policy of expanding the German navy (see page 38).
- The German Society for the Eastern Marches, also known as the *Hakatisten*, which campaigned for a repressive anti-Polish policy.

Politically affiliated groups
- The working-class trade unions, which were represented by the SPD, campaigning for improving living and working conditions.
- Catholic education and youth organisations and Catholic trade unions which were closely linked with the Centre Party.

Single-issue campaigns
As diverse as the National Soil Association and the Zionists campaigning for Jewish interests and the creation of a Jewish state.

Conclusion
On one level pressure groups could be seen as a sign of development of a greater political participation. Yet, it is questionable whether this increase in parliamentary debate brought about a more sophisticated democratic process. Some simply came to see the process as merely political bargaining between the different interest groups, which Germans derogatively called 'cow-dealing'.

Key question
How influential was
the army in Germany?

The German army
In Germany the military tradition went back a long way into the nation's past. The French statesman Mirabeau had observed in the late eighteenth century: 'Prussia is not a country with an army: it is an army with a country.' It was the power of the Prussian military machine which had enabled Bismarck to forge German unification out of the three wars, 1864–1871. Although the forces of Bavaria, Saxony and Württemberg were theoretically independent, the German army from 1871 was essentially a Prussian one. The all-important role the army had played in the unification process helped to raise out of all proportion the status of its members in the *Kaiserreich* society.

Therefore, the German army was to be found at the centre of the political and social life of Imperial Germany:

- The oath of loyalty signed by German officers was to the military leader, the Emperor, not the state and so the military élite enjoyed great social status.
- The system of **conscription** for two to three years helped to instil its military values throughout the country. The educational drill system and the national pride and patriotism of the military helped to imbue society with values such as: strict discipline and order, blind obedience and deference to uniformed authority.
- The army was virtually independent of the *Reichstag* and was not constrained by annual approval, since the military budget had a five-year grant.
- Within society the prestige of the army was high. Civilians got out of the way of officers on the pavement, and being a reserve army officer enhanced social status.

Conscription
The length of time of compulsory service for men in the army.

Key term

Not surprisingly, the majority of army officers were conservative and unsympathetic to democracy – while liberalism and socialism were seen as dangerous ideas, which were not to be tolerated.

In a way the fall of Bismarck exacerbated the situation further, as the new Chancellors lacked the authority to stand up against the military chiefs, as they had the sympathy of the Emperor. The lack of effective civil control over the military had important consequences for domestic and international policies: most significantly (and unfortunately) was the drawing up of the Schlieffen Plan in 1905 (see pages 73–4).

In one sense the aristocratic dominance in the army was beginning to wane slightly by 1914, as most of the lower officers came from the middle classes, rather than the landed aristocracy. However, they tended to model themselves on their upper-class colleagues so the mentality of the army stayed very much the same and the majority of the highest ranks were still 'chosen' by birth and class, not by merit. As a result, the army remained a conservative right-wing force glorifying its traditional values and resisting political modernisation.

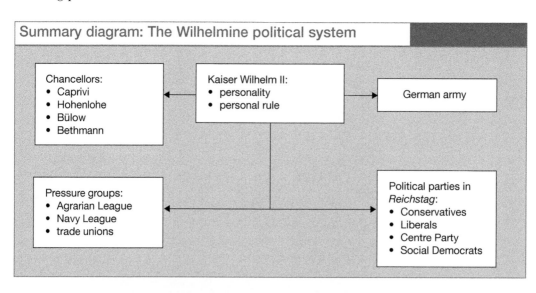

Summary diagram: The Wilhelmine political system

Chancellors:
- Caprivi
- Hohenlohe
- Bülow
- Bethmann

Kaiser Wilhelm II:
- personality
- personal rule

German army

Pressure groups:
- Agrarian League
- Navy League
- trade unions

Political parties in *Reichstag*:
- Conservatives
- Liberals
- Centre Party
- Social Democrats

6 | The Key Debate

This section can be seen as a preparation for Chapters 2 and 3 in that this key debate raises more questions than answers:

Who actually ran Germany?

The 'personal rule' of the Kaiser

The view that the Kaiser's 'personal rule' was a system of government centred on the imperial court has been most strongly argued by the historian John Röhl. Following extensive research of the private letters of leading contemporary figures, he has built up a portrait of the Kaiser to support this view. He concludes that aspects of the Kaiser's personality do suggest that he was a mentally unbalanced character. His behaviour was often manic and on occasions turned into uncontrollable rage. Röhl goes on to argue that this erratic character, flattered and charmed by an inner circle of friends, advisers and military officers, created a situation in which he gained control over all other sources of power.

At the centre of this 'system' were the two friends Eulenburg and Bülow. Eulenburg and the Kaiser were undoubtedly very close; the Kaiser spoke of him as his only 'bosom friend', and Eulenburg 'loved [the Kaiser] above everything else'. Bülow's relationship with the Kaiser was also close. He was an insincere flatterer who tailored his letters and conversations to satisfy Wilhelm, a successful strategy that in the end helped him to achieve his aim in becoming Chancellor. In 1898 he wrote to Eulenburg in apparently unambiguous terms:

> I grow fonder and fonder of the Kaiser … In a way I have never before seen he combines genius – the most authentic and original genius – with the clearest *bon sens* [good sense]. His vivid imagination lifts me like an eagle high above petty detail, yet he can judge soberly what is or is not possible and attainable. And what vitality! What a memory! How quick and sure his understanding! In the Crown Council this morning I was completely overwhelmed!

Röhl therefore has placed Wilhelm's personality at the very centre of his interpretation of Imperial Germany. Moreover, the German constitution granted the Kaiser extensive powers if he exerted them. He alone had the right to appoint and dismiss the Chancellor and his state secretaries completely independent of the wishes of the *Reichstag*.

However, it is worth bearing in mind several points:

- The Kaiser's grasp of politics was limited.
- He was essentially a lazy and pleasure-seeking man.
- He was never able to settle down to the regular routine required of government and administration.
- He much preferred to spend his time playing the social and ceremonial roles of a monarch.

- He liked to travel and to take part in military manoeuvres and was absent from Berlin for long periods.

The Kaiser may have appeared and behaved as an all-powerful autocrat, but was his claim that 'there is only one Ruler in the *Reich* and I am he' perhaps just another example of his own delusion of power?

The élites

The problems caused by the political system have led some German historians to move the emphasis of their views about the *Kaiserreich* away from the political centre. The so-called '**structuralist**' school appeared in the mid-1970s, which sought to explain history through a detailed examination of the various social, political and economic forces that influence events. Foremost amongst the supporters of this approach is Hans-Ulrich Wehler.

Wehler and his fellow structuralists have rejected the idea that Kaiser Wilhelm II was the main influence behind German policy and political affairs. They have argued that, whereas Bismarck had earlier provided strong leadership, the Kaiser had neither the ability nor the strength of character to do so. In addition they have claimed that, as the powers of both the Chancellor and the *Reichstag* were limited by the constitution, after 1890 a power vacuum developed. This led to a situation in which the arrogant and overbearing leadership of the Kaiser hid the fact that there was an ongoing crisis in German politics. In Wehler's words, the *Kaiserreich* was suffering from 'a permanent crisis of the state behind its façade of high-handed leadership'.

Wehler has suggested that other forces were able to take advantage of this situation and that these emerged and exerted a major influence over the nation's affairs. By 'other forces' he meant five groups:

- Prussia's landowning and aristocratic *Junkers*
- the officer class of the army
- those who held high-ranking professional positions in the civil service
- the judiciary
- senior members of the diplomatic service.

Collectively, these five groups are referred to as 'the élites'. He argued that these non-elected élites were able to exercise power because they were Prussians and the constitution had deliberately allowed Prussia to dominate the other German states. Such a situation might have prevailed if Germany had remained socially and economically frozen in 1871, but this was not the case. Germany was undergoing rapid change and new forces were emerging; most notably powerful industrialists, bankers and others engaged in trade and commerce.

It was the desire of the traditional élites to maintain their power against what they regarded as a threat to democracy that prompted them to seek an alliance with the newly emerging élites

Key term

Structuralists Interpret history by analysing the role of social and economic forces and structures. Therefore, they tend to place less emphasis on the role of the individual.

of industry and commerce. They hoped to bring this about by offering them a stake in the system and the promise of armaments contracts and colonial markets overseas. This plan of bringing together the two dominant social élites in order to protect their own status and power has been called *Sammlungspolitik*, a 'policy of concentration'. This strategy was further developed by deliberately disregarding the forces of democracy and socialism and portraying them as unpatriotic enemies of the Reich.

The structuralist interpretation has had enormous influence on our understanding of the *Kaiserreich*, nevertheless it has also attracted much criticism for concentrating on the élites and ignoring other elements. The main points of criticism are:

- it exaggerated the unity of purpose within the élites
- it failed to recognise the declining influence of the *Junkers*
- it did not emphasise the fears of the German middle classes – who did *not* take their lead from the traditional élites – about revolution and full democracy.

Mass politics movements

The structuralist theories and the concept of *Sammlungspolitik*, which have held such sway, have come to be questioned by a new generation of British and American historians, such as Geoff Eley and David Blackbourn. In essence, they have tried to put the emphasis of political developments in the late nineteenth century on 'history from below', rather than 'from above', by recognising the importance of popular movements. In their view the élites lacked any real unity of purpose and, therefore, they struggled to come to terms with the social upheavals that accompanied the tremendous economic changes in Germany at this time.

Their research has focused not only on the trade unions, *Mittelstand* and agrarian pressure groups, but also on the non-Prussian regions and the influence of Catholicism. They have tried to shift the historical emphasis away from Prussia and its élites and instead show that the *Kaiserreich* was a state of many regions with very different political and cultural traditions. Many of these interest groups were demanding a genuine voice for the first time, particularly in the wake of the relatively depressed years before 1895. In this way, such historians have successfully highlighted the tremendous growth of political activity in the *Kaiserreich* and also its diversity. This, in turn, has led them to suggest that Germany's political leaders were not so much using, but actually responding to public opinion. If this was indeed the case then the policies of Wilhelmine Germany were the result of rather more complicated developments than has previously been thought.

The above interpretations in this key debate have highlighted the different ways of seeing the make-up of the *Kaiserreich*. Now, it is necessary to examine the developments in domestic politics and foreign policy in the years before 1914.

Key term

Sammlungspolitik
A 'policy of concentration' to integrate the range of conservative forces.

Some key books in the debate

D. Blackbourn and G. Eley, *The Peculiarities of German History* (Oxford, 1984).

J. Retallack, *Germany in the Age of Kaiser Wilhelm II* (Palgrave Macmillan, 1996).

J.C.G. Röhl, *The Kaiser and his Court* (Cambridge, 1994).

H.-U. Wehler, *The German Empire* (Berg, 1985).

Summary diagram: Who actually ran Germany?

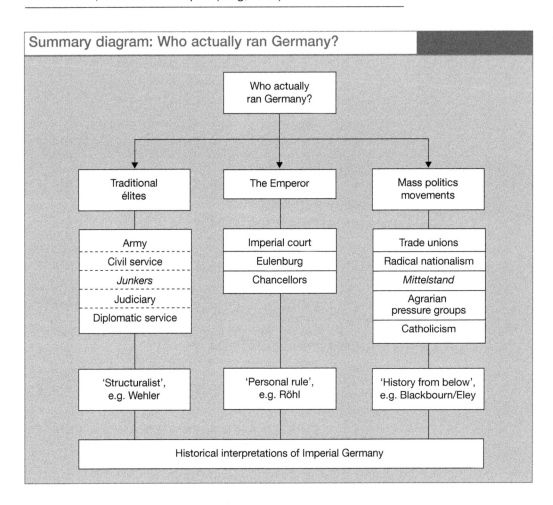

2

Domestic Politics in Wilhelmine Germany 1890–1914

POINTS TO CONSIDER
Chapter 1 highlighted many of the key features of Germany in 1900, yet it raised one key question, which remains the focus of this chapter: who really ran Germany? This will be considered in the following themes:

- The 'new course' of Wilhelm II and Caprivi
- The advent of *Weltpolitik*
- Bülow and the problems of *Weltpolitik*
- Political stalemate
- Key debate: Was Wilhelmine Germany an entrenched authoritarian state?

Key dates

1890	Resignation of Bismarck; Caprivi appointed Chancellor
	Anti-Socialist Laws lapsed
1893	Agrarian League formed
1894	Hohenlohe appointed Chancellor
1897	Government reorganised; *Weltpolitik* initiated
1898	Navy League formed
	First Naval Law passed, followed by the laws of 1900, 1906, 1912
1900	Bülow appointed Chancellor
1908	The *Daily Telegraph* affair
1909	Bethmann appointed Chancellor
1912	Major socialist gains in *Reichstag* elections
1913	Zabern affair
1914	Outbreak of the First World War

1 | The 'New Course' of Wilhelm II and Caprivi 1890–4

Key question
In what ways did Caprivi embark on a 'new course'?

If the new young Kaiser had assumed that Bismarck's departure in 1890 would give him a free hand, Wilhelm II was to be disappointed. The new chancellor, Caprivi, soon proved himself to be more astute and independent-minded than the Kaiser had bargained for. He spoke of embarking on a 'new course', with a more consultative approach to government and a conciliatory attitude to previously hostile forces, such as the Centre Party and the Social Democrats. The Anti-Socialist Laws lapsed. In contrast to the stalemate between Bismarck and the *Reichstag* in the late 1880s, Caprivi was able to depend on a fair degree of backing from the *Reichstag*. This allowed him to push through a number of social measures in 1891:

- Sunday work was prohibited.
- Employment of children under 13 years of age was forbidden.
- Women were not allowed to work for more than 11 hours a day.
- Industrial courts were set up to arbitrate disputes.

Resignation of Bismarck; Caprivi appointed Chancellor: 1890

Anti-Socialist Laws lapsed: 1890

Agrarian League formed: 1893

Key dates

Caprivi's success paved the way for an even more important change – the reform of Germany's tariff policy (see page 12). Ever since 1879 Germany had followed a policy of protection for both agriculture and industry. In order to encourage the export of German manufactured goods, Caprivi negotiated a series of commercial treaties with Austria-Hungary, Italy, Russia and a number of smaller states. These treaties were bilateral, which meant that each country agreed changes likely to benefit the other. These agreements led to the reduction in German tariffs on agricultural goods in return for favourable reductions in the tariffs imposed on exported German manufactured goods. Therefore, they not only acted as a vital spur to the growth of the German economy, but also represented a political triumph for Caprivi. His policy of tariff reform gained broad support as most parties, except the Conservatives, recognised the benefits of lower food prices. It seemed as if the new Chancellor could perhaps make Bismarck's system work in a flexible and progressive fashion. It was not to last.

Growing opposition

The Kaiser had been so taken by the success of tariff reform that Caprivi had been given the noble title of count. However, powerful voices quickly and effectively raised doubts:

Key question
Who opposed the 'new course' and why?

- Court conservatives. To start with, Wilhelm II himself backed Caprivi's social policy in the belief that the improvements would discourage people from supporting the socialists. Yet, Wilhelm II's sympathy began to wane and many of Wilhelm's advisers at court disagreed with Caprivi's 'socialist' policies. Some encouraged the Kaiser to ditch him and to assume a more authoritarian 'personal rule'.
- Landowners. They were deeply upset by the commercial treaties since they threatened to reduce their profits. In 1893 the Agrarian League was formed to put pressure on parliament and to win support and privileges for landowners. It quickly grew into an effective and well-organised lobby of a third of a million members that acted as a powerful pressure group on behalf of the conservative parties.
- Military. In 1893 there had also been resentment in military circles when Caprivi made concessions over the Army Bill in the *Reichstag* by reducing the length of conscription for national service from three years to two (see also page 28).

The Army Bill was actually rejected, resulting in the *Reichstag* being dissolved and the following election brought things to a head. There were conservative concerns about anarchist outrages across Europe and the increase in the total number of Social Democrat seats to 44 (see Table 2.1). Opponents of Caprivi now reinforced Wilhelm II's own doubts about his Chancellor's suitability for office and Wilhelm II pressed Caprivi to draw up an anti-socialist Subversion Bill. The Chancellor refused and this led to an extraordinary plan by Wilhelm II and his supporter, Eulenburg. Their plan was to set aside the powers of the *Reichstag*, crush socialism and establish a more authoritarian system centred on the Kaiser himself. This was the final straw for Caprivi. He successfully talked the Kaiser out of such a course of action, but he had lost the will to carry on. In October 1894 Caprivi resigned and gladly retired from the political scene.

Table 2.1: *Reichstag election results (total number of deputies = 397)*

Party	1887	1890	1893	1898	1903	1907	1912
Conservatives							
Seats	121	93	100	79	75	84	57
Per cent of vote	25	19	19	16	13	14	12
National Liberals							
Seats	99	42	53	46	51	54	45
Per cent of vote	22	16	13	12	14	14	14
Left Liberals							
Seats	32	76	48	49	36	49	42
Per cent of vote	14	18	15	11	9	11	12
Centre Party							
Seats	98	106	96	102	100	105	91
Per cent of vote	20	19	19	19	20	19	16
Social Democrats							
Seats	11	35	44	56	81	43	110
Per cent of the vote	10	20	23	27	31	29	35
Minorities							
Seats	33	38	35	34	32	29	33
Per cent of vote	8	9	8	11	10	9	8
Right-wing extremists							
Seats	3	7	21	31	22	33	19
Per cent of vote	0.2	1	4	3	3	4	3
Turn-out (%)	77	71	72	68	75	84	84

Key question
How successful was Caprivi's 'new course'?

Conclusion

Caprivi's four years as Chancellor neatly illustrate the difficulties of trying to cope with the pressures of the various political forces in Imperial Germany. In his attempt to create a genuine base of parliamentary support for the government, Caprivi showed his understanding of the need, in a modern industrial society, for a political approach that recognised the concerns and aspirations of the mass of the population. However, Caprivi's 'new course' foundered because it was opposed by the established forces of power and influence. He was subjected to considerable abuse from the conservative press and he was the focus of opposition intrigue at court. In the end, he could not rely on the consistent support of the Kaiser whose delusions of greatness were now taken up with thoughts of 'personal rule' and *Weltpolitik*.

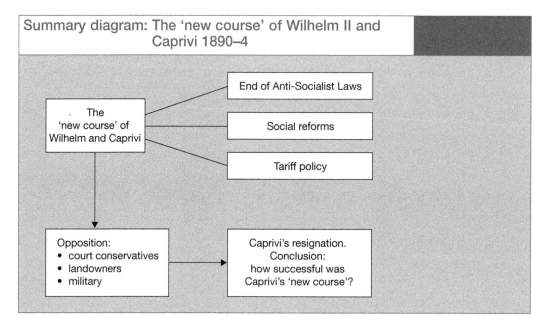

Summary diagram: The 'new course' of Wilhelm II and Caprivi 1890–4

2 | The Advent of *Weltpolitik*

Although Hohenlohe was appointed Chancellor in 1894 and held the office for six years, the government was increasingly dominated by men who supported the policies of the Kaiser. Indeed, there was even talk of a military *coup* and overthrowing the constitution. Nothing came of it. Yet, the ageing Hohenlohe could not counter the intrigue at court and in government circles. By 1897, a group of key political figures had emerged who sympathised with the Kaiser's wish to embark on what he saw as 'personal rule'. In that year there were three new important appointments in the government:

Key question
How was the imperial government reorganised?

Key dates

Hohenlohe appointed Chancellor: 1894

Government reorganised; *Weltpolitik* initiated: 1897

- most importantly Bülow, as Foreign Secretary
- Admiral von Tirpitz, as Navy Secretary
- Count Posadowsky-Wehner, as Interior Secretary.

In addition, two long-serving figures began to assume even greater prominence:

- Friedrich von Holstein, a senior official in the Foreign Office
- Johannes von Miquel, Prussian Finance Minister (and the leader of the National Liberals).

The creation of the new government team has led many historians to view 1897 as a turning point in history since it coincided with the drive to achieve world power status for Germany, or *Weltpolitik*. This not only marked a decisive shift in the emphasis of Germany's foreign policy (see Chapter 3), but also raised implications for the future of German domestic politics.

The motives of *Weltpolitik*

Key question
How and why did
Weltpolitik become
government policy?

Bismarck had thought of Germany as essentially a European power. While he had no objections to overseas colonies, his priority was to maintain Germany's powerful position on the continent without alienating Britain. However, the Kaiser himself believed that *Weltpolitik* would satisfy Germany's destiny which he aimed to do in the following ways: colonial acquisitions, the establishment of economic **spheres of influence** and the expansion of naval power to complement the strength of the army. In the government team assembled in 1897 he was supported by a number of like-minded ministers.

Key term

Sphere of influence
An area or region
over which a state
has significant
cultural, economic,
military or political
influence.

However, there were also other powerful intellectual and economic forces at work in Germany that favoured the new policy:

- Nationalism (see page 14).
- Imperialism (see page 14). Industrial changes had created economic demands for the acquisition of raw materials and markets beyond Europe.
- Social Darwinism (see page 15).

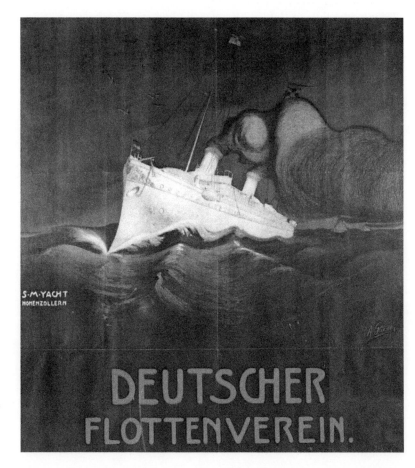

A German poster of 1902 glorifying the Navy League. Such images were popular as a kind of mass propaganda for the league and the fleet.

- Radical nationalism (see pages 14–15). These nationalists formed a series of pressure groups which performed a two-fold purpose. On the one hand, they popularised the idea of *Weltpolitik* and encouraged mass support for the policy. On the other, they exerted political pressure on the imperial government to pursue the policy to the full.

The German navy

Of greater importance to *Weltpolitik* was the decision to expand the German navy. The appointment of Tirpitz meant that there was a man prepared to do this, for he not only enjoyed the full confidence of Wilhelm II, but also recognised the importance of gaining parliamentary support and popular backing for such plans. In 1898, he established the Navy League in order to further these aims. The Navy League argued that naval expansion was a patriotic national symbol of Germany's new status in the world. With the backing of leading industrialists, it was able to gain a membership of over a million and this large-scale public support strengthened Tirpitz's position in his handling of the *Reichstag*. When he presented the Naval Bills of 1898 and 1900 they were both passed with substantial majorities, largely because they were supported by the Centre Party.

Key dates

Navy League formed: 1898

First Naval Law passed: 1898, followed by the laws of 1900, 1906, 1912

The political impact of *Weltpolitik*

The introduction of *Weltpolitik* succeeded where Caprivi's 'new course' had run into difficulties because it achieved a greater acceptance from the various political parties. It successfully rallied both the middle and upper classes and their political representatives in the *Reichstag* behind the Kaiser and the government. The support of the Centre Party represented an important step forward, since it helped to secure an effective majority for the government in the *Reichstag*. *Weltpolitik* even won the support of many of the ordinary people by playing on their feelings of patriotism and loyalty to the crown. Finally, the policy closely coincided with the aspirations of the Kaiser, who convinced himself that *Weltpolitik* must be under his personal rule. However, in the coming years it was shown that *Weltpolitik* did not prove to be the complete cure for the problems of government.

Key question
Was *Weltpolitik* politically successful?

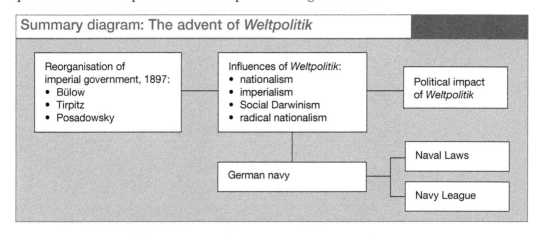

Summary diagram: The advent of *Weltpolitik*

Reorganisation of imperial government, 1897:
- Bülow
- Tirpitz
- Posadowsky

Influences of *Weltpolitik*:
- nationalism
- imperialism
- Social Darwinism
- radical nationalism

Political impact of *Weltpolitik*

German navy

Naval Laws

Navy League

Key question
How successful was Bülow in managing the imperial government?

Key date

Bülow appointed Chancellor: 1900

3 | Bülow and the Problems of *Weltpolitik*

In 1900, Hohenlohe, tired of being ignored and not consulted on policy matters, resigned and Bülow replaced him. He was a very competent administrator and handled the *Reichstag* effectively. Significantly, his main interest was foreign policy and he enjoyed the trust of the Kaiser. He therefore hoped to reduce the conflicting interests on the domestic front by rallying support for the *Weltpolitik*. As he himself said in a private letter to Eulenburg:

> I am putting the main emphasis on foreign policy ... Only a successful foreign policy can help to reconcile, pacify, rally, unite. Its preconditions are of course, caution, patience, tact, reflection.

Yet, despite Bülow's aspirations and skills, it was not always so easy to maintain support for the government in the *Reichstag*.

Social reform

Bülow did try to revive the 'new course' initiated by Caprivi by the inclusion of the socially minded Posadowsky as Interior Secretary. The aim was to expand the social welfare provision in order to pacify the working classes to the imperial state. As a result, new measures were introduced such as:

- an extension of accident insurance in 1900 (see page 6)
- a law making industrial courts compulsory in towns with a population above 20,000 people
- an extension of the prohibition of child labour.

Tariffs

Tariff policy had been an ongoing issue in Germany and in 1902 it revived again with renewed controversy. The landowning interest working with the Conservatives and the Agrarian League had long bitterly opposed Caprivi's commercial treaties (see page 34). They now demanded the imposition of higher tariffs to protect agriculture. In contrast, the Social Democrats and Left Liberals called for lower tariffs to reduce the price of bread for the benefit of the working classes. In the end the compromise Tariff Law of 1902 was comfortably passed which restored tariffs to pre-1892 levels with the combined support of the Centre, the National Liberals and the Free Conservatives. On one level, Bülow's compromise was endorsed by the *Reichstag* election result of 1903 where the Centre maintained its dominant position (see Table 2.1). Nevertheless, on another level, the election revealed that:

- The Social Democrats, who had opposed the tariffs, saw their popular vote go up significantly and their number of seats increased from 56 to 81.
- The Conservatives, who had demanded even higher tariffs, saw their vote narrowly decline.

Budget

Weltpolitik generated its own problems too. The budget had run into debt as the mounting costs of maintaining the army, expanding the navy and running the empire took effect. If the 'glories' of *Weltpolitik* were to be continued then substantial tax increases had to be introduced. Bülow was astute enough to realise that this was likely to cause a political storm – and so it did. In 1905 he suggested a two-pronged attack on the deficit by proposing an increase in indirect taxes and an **inheritance tax**. The proposals came to nothing because first, the Centre and the Social Democrats voted down the indirect taxes that would have hit the working classes most severely; and secondly, the Conservatives and their allies weakened the inheritance tax proposals, so as to make them financially insignificant. The Reich treasury deficit continued to grow.

The 'Hottentot' election

Bülow's government was also being attacked for its policy in the colony of German South West Africa (modern Namibia). The local population was crushed in 1904–5 and subsequent revelations of awful brutality, corruption and incompetence in the administration of the colony were made public. The government's proposals of compensating the white settlers and of finding extra money for suppressing the rebels and for the new administration were not well received in the *Reichstag*. To Bülow's shock, not only the SPD, but also his normal ally, the Centre Party, voted against the government, leading to its defeat.

Bülow was determined to bring the unruly Centre Party to heel, so the *Reichstag* was dissolved. The government's election campaign was known as the **'Hottentot election'** as it played on the campaign in Africa, but was also anti-socialist, anti-Catholic and nationalistic.

The result was an encouraging one for Bülow, as the number of Social Democrat seats was halved and the parties of the right made some good gains (see Table 2.1, page 35). This enabled Bülow to bring together the Conservatives, Free Conservatives, National Liberals and Left Liberals in a **coalition** dubbed the 'Bülow bloc'. Posadowsky was replaced by the conservative bureaucrat, Bethmann, as Interior Secretary. Yet, Bülow's coalition was extremely fragile and his triumph was not to last long.

Conclusion

In the early years of the twentieth century, the German political system became increasingly sophisticated. New political forces were emerging in the country and yet imperial government showed only a limited ability to come to terms with these forces. Powerful interest groups, such as the trade unions and the Catholic Church wanted their wishes to be taken into account by their political representatives in parliament. Moreover, economic forces also exerted new pressures; the dilemma of government finance and tariff reform reveals clearly the limitations of implementing government policy. By 1908 it seemed as if Bülow's

Key terms

Inheritance tax
The tax on the estate, or total value of the money and property, of a person who has died. Also known as estate tax and death duty.

'Hottentot election'
The name given to the *Reichstag* election of 1907, when the government's nationalist patriotic campaign played on the colonial war against the rebels in German South West Africa.

Coalition
A government made up of members from several parties.

Profile: Bernhard von Bülow 1849–1929

1849	– Born near Hamburg, the son of Bismarck's Foreign Minister
1870–1	– Served as a volunteer in the Prussian army during Franco-Prussian War
1873	– Studied law and entered the diplomatic service
1873–97	– Served as a diplomat in various embassies across Europe
1897–1900	– Appointed as Foreign Minister and initiated *Weltpolitik*
1900–9	– Chancellor of Germany
1906	– Made Prince of Bülow
1908	– *Daily Telegraph* affair
1909	– Forced to resign by the Kaiser
1914	– Appointed as special envoy in Rome in an unsuccessful attempt to prevent Italy joining the war against Germany
1915–29	– Retired from public life and died in Rome in 1929

Bülow was a scheming politician by nature who found that he was able to further his own position by pandering to the Emperor. He was also a skilled and effective administrator and dominated the German political scene for a decade. Nevertheless, in domestic policy, he had few new ideas and his control of the *Reichstag* became increasingly difficult, despite the creation of the Bülow bloc in 1907. His main interest was foreign policy and he enjoyed the trust of the Kaiser for developing the *Weltpolitik*. However, his muddled **diplomacy** was responsible for strengthening the ties between Britain, France and Russia which led to the Triple Entente (see page 59).

In 1909, he was forced to resign when he failed to give the Kaiser adequate support following Wilhelm's indiscreet interview with the *Daily Telegraph*. Later, as ambassador to Italy, he failed to prevent that country entering the First World War on the side of the Allies. After his retirement, he sought to redeem himself by writing an autobiography that revealed the political corruption and personal jealousies that existed within the German government.

Key term

Diplomacy
The art and practice of negotiating between states with regard to issues of peace-making, trade, war and economics.

government, far from controlling events, was increasingly at the mercy of them.

The *Daily Telegraph* affair

Key question
What is the significance of the *Daily Telegraph* affair?

In the winter of 1908–9 the political crisis came to a head, although in a somewhat bizarre fashion. The German public had already been treated to a moral scandal by the revelation that the Kaiser's close friend, Eulenburg, was at the centre of an extensive ring of homosexuals at court, when the *Daily Telegraph* affair broke.

Key date

The *Daily Telegraph* affair: 1908

In an interview with a journalist, the Kaiser expressed his wishes for closer relations with Britain. Yet, his comments attracted much criticism for making such an important statement on foreign policy to the foreign press and there were demands in the *Reichstag* for constitutional limitations to be placed on the Kaiser. Bülow himself was in a difficult position, as he had actually cleared the article before publication, which made the situation all the more constitutionally delicate.

Its impact

In the end, caught between loyalty to his friend, the Kaiser, and the demands of the *Reichstag*, Bülow sided with the latter. He secured a promise from the Kaiser that, in future, the terms of the constitution would be respected. Thereafter, the crisis petered out and no constitutional changes followed. It seemed as if Bülow, nicknamed 'the eel', had once again slithered his way out of a tight corner. Yet, the Kaiser's trust in his Chancellor had been fatally weakened by these events and when Bülow's new budget proposals were rejected by the *Reichstag* in 1909, the Kaiser took the opportunity to secure the Chancellor's resignation.

The *Daily Telegraph* affair is an illuminating insight into the power politics of the Wilhelmine age. Bülow had survived for over a decade at the very centre of German politics by playing the part of the old-fashioned courtier with a sound grasp of how to satisfy all the vested interests. He retained the backing of the Kaiser through flattery and by turning situations to his advantage. He also gained a degree of broader political support through the nationalistic policy of *Weltpolitik*. However, his failure to stand by the Kaiser in the *Daily Telegraph* affair underlined how vulnerable the office of Chancellor was to the personal whims of the Kaiser. The Chancellor remained accountable to the Kaiser alone, not to the *Reichstag*. This was in spite of the fact that there was a growing belief that the Kaiser could no longer behave as an authoritarian monarch and had to conform to some constitutional changes. Yet now when the opportunity presented itself for constitutional reform, the *Reichstag* showed a marked reluctance to assert itself and its authority.

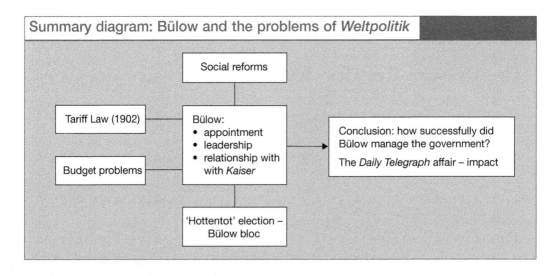

Summary diagram: Bülow and the problems of *Weltpolitik*

4 | Political Stalemate

German government was nominally in the hands of Chancellor Bethmann in the last few years of peace. However, powerful forces between 1909 and 1914 limited his capacity to direct affairs and he generally backed away from introducing major initiatives. It seemed as if the German government had reached political stalemate.

The *Reichstag*

Key question
What was the significance of the 1912 *Reichstag* election result?

With the collapse of the Bülow bloc, Bethmann's parliamentary base of support was narrow, as his conservative views meant that his natural allies came from the right-wing parties. Any attempt to broaden his support by appealing to the centre or left would have offended his conservative and right-wing supporters. In this situation Bethmann tried to avoid depending on any particular party, although this allowed other forces to exert their influence outside parliament.

The *Reichstag* elections of 1912 further added to the Chancellor's parliamentary difficulties, since there was a distinct shift to the left. Indeed, it was historically significant and the Social Democrats became the largest party in the country with 35 per cent of the vote (see Table 2.1, page 35). The Social Democrats and the Left Liberals won 110 and 42 seats, respectively, and the Conservative–Centre alliance could no longer dominate the *Reichstag*. However, this created a situation of virtual deadlock for Bethmann's government.

Key dates
Bethmann appointed Chancellor: 1909

Major socialist gains in *Reichstag* elections: 1912

Outbreak of the First World War: 1914

All these figures served to increase the fears of conservatives of a possible democratic and socialist revolution. The SPD would have been even stronger in the *Reichstag* if constituency boundaries had been revised to reflect growing urbanisation. Yet, although the SPD had become the largest party in the *Reichstag*, there were emerging two clear factions within it: the orthodox Marxists and the moderates (see page 26). It is important to note

A cartoon from 1912 which tries to challenge the fears of the middle classes who saw the stereotype of the socialist as a bloodthirsty assassin and revolutionary. 'A Sozi depicted by the enemies. What a "Sozi" (really) looks like.' (Sozi was a nick-name for a socialist.)

that the majority of SPD supporters were to be found in the latter group – and they were proud patriots concerned about Germany's diplomatic isolation from Russia, France and Britain.

Military spending

The problem of imperial finance remained the key stumbling-block and in 1912–13 it came to a head over defence expenditure. In the wake of the second Moroccan crisis (see page 63) the army and the navy both submitted plans involving major increases in expenditure. The idea of an inheritance tax was again proposed as the only possible means of raising the required money, but Bethmann feared a hostile political reaction and resorted to the stop-gap measure of taxing spirits. In early 1913 Moltke, the Chief of Staff, went even further and demanded a second Army Bill to increase the peacetime strength of the army by 20 per cent to 800,000 men in 1914 (see page 68).

Fortunately for Bethmann, the inheritance tax was accepted on this occasion. This was partly because the worsening international situation acted as a significant stimulus; but also, there were increasing vocal demands by the nationalist associations for a more vigorous defence of German interests. The confused state of German politics was further revealed by the Conservatives, who, while supporting the increased military expenditure, opposed the inheritance tax. By contrast, the Social Democrats, who were traditionally against military spending, supported it as the tax established a precedent of a property-based tax.

The Zabern affair

Just before the outbreak of war Germany was rocked by the Zabern affair, named after the town in Alsace which had been annexed from France by Germany in 1871 (see page 2). Friction between the French inhabitants and German soldiers led to a series of disturbances and, in November 1913, officers ordered the locals to clear the streets. Twenty-eight citizens were arrested and detained in the military barracks; in one incident an officer used his sabre to cut down a disabled cobbler. This led to widespread protests, well beyond Alsace, that the army officers had acted above the law and overridden the civilian authorities and the courts. In effect, it was felt that the army had infringed the liberties of citizens.

The army defended itself by claiming to be accountable to the Kaiser alone and Wilhelm condoned the action. In the *Reichstag*, Bethmann, unlike Bülow in 1908, stood by the army and the Kaiser, but the political opposition was intense and the Chancellor received a massive **vote of no confidence**. Yet, nothing really happened.

The Zabern affair crystallised the divisions in German politics and society. For Röhl (see page 29), the incident shows how, right up to 1914, the *Kaiserreich* was still dominated by the actions, decisions and personality of the Kaiser and his supporters. The very fact that Bethmann was able to continue as Chancellor, despite a major defeat in the *Reichstag*, is seen as proof enough of

Key question
What were the implications of the imperial government's financial problems?

Key term

Vote of no confidence
A motion put before a parliament by the opposition in the hope of defeating or weakening the government. In Britain, the passing of a vote of no confidence would lead to a general election.

Key question
What was the significance of the Zabern affair?

Key date

Zabern affair: 1913

how the Kaiser still ultimately controlled policy and political decision-making. However, for the structuralists, Wilhelm II was never more than a 'shadow Kaiser'. He was considered a front for the élites who were determined to manipulate him, the system and government policy in order to preserve their own privileged positions. By this interpretation, the Zabern affair is seen as a classic example of how the army was able to preserve its own authority and status. Nevertheless, the huge public outcry against the army's action with the Kaiser's support also gave strong evidence that popular movements were on the increase. Pressures were 'bubbling up' to bring about genuine democratic and social change.

Summary diagram: Political stalemate

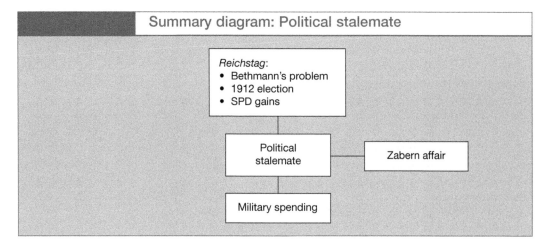

Reichstag:
- Bethmann's problem
- 1912 election
- SPD gains

Political stalemate

Zabern affair

Military spending

5 | The Key Debate

The *Kaiserreich* was, therefore, both socially and politically very complicated. It was just as complex as the Kaiser's own eccentric personality. As the historian P. Kennedy has written: 'the Kaiser both reflected and inter-meshed [was involved in] the country's broader problems'. So this leaves the question:

Was Wilhelmine Germany an entrenched authoritarian state?

It is a demanding task for almost all students seeking a conclusion and it is likely to be frustrating for those who crave certainty.

It is impossible to cast aside Kaiser Wilhelm II entirely. It has been suggested that Wilhelm II came to symbolise the inconsistencies of the *Kaiserreich*. On the one hand, he was a defender of traditional privileges of the Prussian monarchy. On the other, he was an enthusiast for technology, new industries and a world role for Germany. From 1890 to 1914, his personal influence enabled him to set the tenor of government policy. Between 1897 and 1908 his influence was most marked. This represented the high point of the Kaiser's personal rule and it coincided exactly with the years of supremacy of Bülow, who recognised that his own position depended on flattery and the promotion of the Kaiser's personal views.

However, the *Kaiserreich* was not an absolute monarchy, like Russian Tsarism, nor a dictatorship like the **Third Reich**. The Kaiser and the imperial government had to work within the constitutional framework created in 1871. German citizens enjoyed certain civil liberties as a *Rechtsstaat*: the freedom of expression, of press, and of assembly. All men over 25 had the right of universal suffrage, which gave Germany a broader franchise than Britain until 1918. The *Reichstag* could not be ignored as it had the power to endorse or reject legislation initiated by the imperial government, including finance bills. Indeed, as Germany developed more into a modern industrial society, the amount of legislation discussed in the *Reichstag* increased significantly. It must not be forgotten that the turn-out of the *Reichstag* elections increased substantially from 50 per cent in 1871 to nearly 85 per cent in 1912. Clearly the German people no longer saw it as a meaningless institution, but one of increasing relevance. The tremendous growth of the SPD was so politically telling that the reintroduction of repressive laws was no longer really a feasible option. In many senses, pre-1914, the country of Germany was a developed, sophisticated and highly educated society. It would be easier to explain the rise of Nazism if this was not so.

Nevertheless, although there is evidence of Germany potentially developing into a parliamentary democracy, the monarchical system was strongly upheld and supported by powerful forces, especially the Prussian élites. This was recognised by Bülow, who generally developed policies to protect their interests, unlike Caprivi, who had paid the price of alienating them in the early 1890s.

First, the constitution was fundamentally weakened in several key ways:

- The Kaiser retained the power to appoint the Chancellor and the government ministers; the Chancellor therefore was not obliged to be accountable to the *Reichstag* (even after Bethmann's massive vote of no confidence in 1913).
- The **federal structure** was obviously unfair and undemocratic; Prussia covered two-thirds of Germany and it still had the three-class electoral system (see page 5).
- Prussia continued to block any change in the *Bundesrat* (see pages 4–5).

Secondly, there was a lack of will on the part of the political parties to take responsibility for bringing about changes. This was for three reasons:

- All the parties distanced themselves from the Social Democrats. The Conservatives saw them as anathema, but even the more moderate middle-class parties were scared of their growing influence and they refused to co-operate actively as they feared constitutional reform might lead to radical reforms.

Key terms

Third Reich
Third Empire: the Nazi dictatorship 1933–45. It was seen as the successor to the Holy Roman Empire and Imperial Germany 1871–1918.

Rechtsstaat
A state under a rule of laws.

Federal structure
Where power and responsibilities are shared between central and regional governments, for example, the USA.

- There were a lot of parties and each one tended to act more like an interest group rather than acting for the common good of government.
- The prestige and status of the Kaiser were still deeply ingrained in the minds of many *Reichstag* deputies. They actively supported the patriotic and expansionist policy of *Weltpolitik*.

Therefore, the balance of power still rested with the forces of conservatism, although their right to govern was under threat from forces of change. The conflict between these two groups was the source of great political tension and frustration. So, although in 1914 Imperial Germany was not ungovernable, partly because of its economic well-being and partly because there was still general respect for the monarchy, it had reached a situation of political stalemate. This made for weak and confused government in the hands of an entrenched authoritarian regime in 1914, and fundamental change did not seem imminent. It was only to collapse after four years of war and defeat.

Some key books in the debate
V. Berghahn *Imperial Germany, 1871–1914* (New York, 2005).
D. Blackbourn and G. Eley, *The Peculiarities of German History* (Oxford, 1984).
David Blackbourn, *The Long Nineteenth Century* (Fontana, 1997).
P. Kennedy, *The Rise of Anglo-German Antagonism* (Allen & Unwin, 1982).
Annika Mombauer, *New Research on Wilhelm II's Role in Imperial Germany* (Cambridge, 2003).
J. Retallack, *Germany in the Age of Kaiser Wilhelm II* (Palgrave Macmillan, 1996).
J.C.G. Röhl, *The Kaiser and his Court* (Cambridge, 1994).
H.-U. Wehler, *The German Empire* (Berg, 1985).

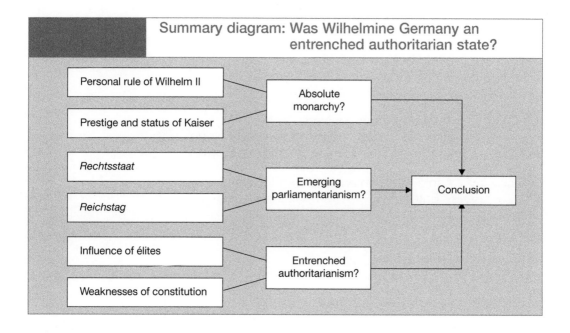

Summary diagram: Was Wilhelmine Germany an entrenched authoritarian state?

3 German Foreign Policy 1890–1914

POINTS TO CONSIDER

Inevitably, any analysis of European foreign affairs in the years 1890–1914 must involve the causes of the First World War. This is particularly true of Wilhelmine foreign policy, since much attention has been given by politicians and historians over the years to the question of German 'responsibility' in the debate about the origins of the war. Indeed, the so-called war guilt controversy has been described as one of the most famous historical debates.

This chapter will examine the following themes:

- German foreign policy and the origins of the First World War
- The European alliance system and how its balance changed after the fall of Bismarck
- The coming of *Weltpolitik* 1897–1904
- International crises and tensions 1904–11
- 1911–14: The final years of peace
- Sarajevo and the July 1914 crisis
- Key debate: Was Germany really responsible for pursuing a war of aggression and conquest?

Key dates

1894	Franco-Russian Alliance ratified
1897	Bülow's 'place in the sun' speech; advent of *Weltpolitik*
1898	First German Naval Law (second in 1900)
1904	Anglo-French Agreement (which later became the Anglo-French *Entente Cordiale*)
1905	Schlieffen Plan devised
	First Moroccan crisis: the Tangier incident
1906	Launch of the first Dreadnought by Britain
	Third German Naval Law
1907	Anglo-Russian *entente* forming the Triple Entente
1908–9	Bosnian crisis
1911	Second Moroccan crisis: the Agadir incident
1912	Fourth Naval Law
	Anglo-French naval agreement
	First Balkan War
	War Council meeting

1913		Second Balkan War
1914	June 28	Assassination of Franz Ferdinand
	July 5	'Blank cheque' given by Germany to Austria
	August	Start of First World War

1 | German Foreign Policy and the Origins of the First World War

Key question
Why is the foreign policy of Imperial Germany so significant in historical debate?

A student of Wilhelmine foreign policy is confronted by a major problem: it is only part of a much broader historical debate. This has important implications. By concentrating on Germany there is a danger of exaggerating its role in the origins of the First World War and, by extension, minimising the responsibility of other countries. Also, the complementary themes of nationalism, imperialism and the **arms race**, which some historians have identified as central to the outbreak of war in 1914, could be seen as less important. Wilhelmine foreign policy must be seen in a broader perspective, although the focus of this book is to explain and analyse the German role in particular.

Why has the foreign policy of the *Kaiserreich* been such an important area of historical debate? The Allies insisted that Germany accept responsibility for the war by signing a **war guilt** clause in the Treaty of Versailles (see pages 122 and 126). Extensive debate in the inter-war years resulted in a general agreement that the European Great Powers had 'stumbled' into war because of the system of alliances and the state of international relations, with no one country to blame. This was a view that proved acceptable to many German historians.

The interpretation of Fritz Fischer

The above viewpoint remained the standard German interpretation of the origins of the First World War until 1961 when Fritz Fischer's *Grasp for World Power: Germany's Aims in the First World War* suggested that the German government did bear the decisive share of responsibility for starting the war in 1914. Fischer argued this on the basis of what he saw as its unquestionable desire to achieve German predominance throughout Europe. Fischer's interpretation caused enormous controversy among German historians. This led to protracted squabbling and even to offensive name-calling. However, Fischer himself was not moved from his point of view and in 1969 he published another book, *War of Illusions*. In this he suggested that from the time of the second Moroccan crisis in 1911 (see page 63) the German leadership consistently pursued a policy aimed at fighting a European war as a means of achieving world-power status for Germany.

Fischer's views led to a historical controversy, the reverberations of which continue to this day. Although the bad feeling is now less, there remain basic differences of opinion about the motives and direction of German foreign policy during the pre-war years.

Key terms

Arms race
A competition between two or more powers for military supremacy. Each power competes to produce larger numbers of weapons, greater armies or superior technology.

War guilt
The term originated from the Treaty of Versailles 1919, which forced Germany to accept blame for causing the war. Later, it became the focus of great historical discussion.

There are five key questions that need to be addressed in this chapter:

1. Did the break-up of the Bismarck system of alliances after 1890 set in motion a chain of disasters that led towards the outbreak of the First World War?
2. Did the coming of *Weltpolitik* pose a real threat to the existing European situation at the start of the century?
3. What were the causes of the crises of 1904–11 and why did attempts to bring about some improvement in Anglo-German relations fail?
4. How convincing is the evidence that Germany was planning a war in the years before 1914?
5. How far was Germany responsible for the turn of events in the summer of 1914?

Great Power
A nation or state that has the ability to exert its influence on a global scale through its economic, military and diplomatic strengths. In 1900 the five major continental Great Powers were Britain, France, Germany, Russia and Austria-Hungary.

Key term

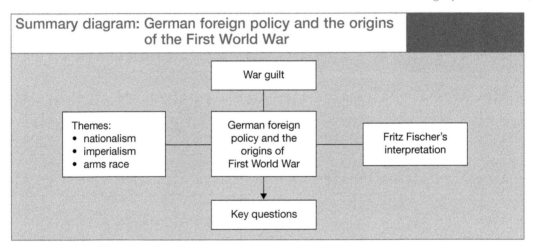

Summary diagram: German foreign policy and the origins of the First World War

2 | The European Alliance System

In the 20 years after German unification Bismarck successfully enabled Germany to dominate the **Great Powers** on the continent. He cleverly used diplomacy to ensure the isolation of Germany's major continental enemy, France, in the following ways:

Key question
What were the main features of Bismarck's alliance system?

- By creating the **Triple Alliance** between Germany, Austria-Hungary and Italy in 1882, it was agreed that:
  - if any of the signatories were attacked by two or more powers, the others promised to lend assistance
  - if France attacked Germany, Italy would support its partner
  - if Italy was attacked by France, both Germany and Austria agreed to back Italy. Italy made it clear that it would not be drawn into a war with Britain, but there seemed to be no possibility of that at the time.

Triple Alliance
The military alliance of Germany, Austria and Italy was formed in 1882 out of the Austro-German Dual Alliance of 1879.

Key term

Key terms

Three Emperors' Alliance
An informal alliance between Austria-Hungary, Germany and Russia, announced officially in 1872 and renewed in 1881.

Reinsurance Treaty
An agreement signed in 1887 between Russia and Germany accepting that that if either were at war, the other would remain neutral, unless France or Austria were the object of attack.

- By maintaining a close relationship with Russia. Although the **Three Emperors' Alliance** (1881) had lapsed, Bismarck was delighted in 1887 to secure the signing of the three-year **Reinsurance Treaty** and it was agreed that:
  - if either Russia or Germany were at war, the other would remain neutral, unless France or Austria were the object of attack.
- By making a conscious effort *not* to antagonise Britain and to persuade it to play a more important role in European affairs in the Near East. The success of this was shown in 1887 when Britain signed the **Mediterranean Agreements** with Germany's allies, and even contemplated joining the Triple Alliance in 1889.

So, in 1890 Germany was in a secure position: on good terms with Britain, holding a treaty with Russia and allied with Austria and Italy. Yet, by 1914 at the onset of the First World War three of these would fight against Germany.

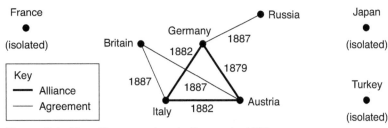

Figure 3.1: The alliance system in Europe in 1890.

Key question
How much did Germany's position deteriorate in international affairs?

Key term

Mediterranean Agreements
A series of agreements signed by Britain, Austria and Italy to maintain the status quo in the eastern Mediterranean, which was clearly directed against Russia.

German diplomacy after Bismarck 1890–7

Although Bismarck's diplomatic juggling was certainly under severe pressure in his final few years, his fall from power had important consequences for Germany's international position. The Kaiser himself wanted to be his own man and to embark on a 'new course' in German foreign policy. Yet, Caprivi, who was sympathetic to this new change of direction, was not really an expert in foreign affairs, while Bismarck's protégé in the foreign office, Holstein, lacked his skills.

Caprivi and Holstein believed that the Reinsurance Treaty conflicted with Germany's other commitments, especially with Austria, while the Kaiser's attitude was framed by his own anti-Russian prejudices and his pro-British position. In March 1890, it was decided to allow the Reinsurance Treaty to lapse, which Bismarck himself saw as an act of criminal stupidity. The result was to push Russia into the arms of France.

The Franco-Russian Alliance

France and Russia were to become strange friends: one, a democratic republic, the other, a tsarist autocracy. Yet a common concern of Germany was the obvious basis of their *rapprochement*. Russia had really no serious conflict with Germany, but it was increasingly unsettled by the growing relationship of Austria and

Germany and Wilhelm II's pro-British sympathies. France which, to all purposes, had been diplomatically isolated since 1871, for a long time had wanted to improve national security to protect herself from a German attack. It was the French who really took the initiative, which led to two agreements: a political *entente* in 1891 and a military convention in 1892, which was ratified by the creation of the **Franco-Russian Alliance** of 1894. This alliance made a reality of what Bismarck called a 'nightmare of coalitions' since it meant that at some time in the future Germany might have to fight a war on two fronts: France in the west and Russia in the east.

Anglo-German relations

This new threat to Germany could have been reduced by an understanding with Britain. Unfortunately, diplomatic moves in 1894 failed to achieve this and attempts to provide a firm basis for a mutual understanding came to nothing. Indeed, only two years later Anglo-German relations went sharply into reverse over the 'Kruger Telegram'.

In 1896, tension between the British and former Dutch (Boer) settlers in South Africa reached crisis point following an attempted invasion by the **Jameson Raid** on the Transvaal, a Boer republic. Many Germans objected to the military raid as the Boers were related to their Dutch neighbours, but the British were offended when the Kaiser sent a congratulatory telegram to the President of the Transvaal, Paul Kruger, in effect supporting the independence of Transvaal from Britain. Not surprisingly, the British felt that the Kruger telegram was a tactless interference in British imperial affairs. Wilhelm II's intention was to show to the British that they were diplomatically isolated and should become friendly with Germany. However, this sadly backfired and the incident aroused the first real wave of popular hostility against Germany in Britain. This set a pattern for the future – the Germans never grasped that Britain would not succumb to such pressure, and each attempt increased British distrust.

Conclusion

It is clear that by 1896 the Bismarckian system had collapsed and that Berlin was no longer the centre of the European balance of power. The 'new course' of German diplomacy had not been successful. Anglo-German relations had cooled. More significantly, Russia had allied with France, which raised serious points about German security. It is tempting to conclude that Germany's international standing was in decline, and in the hands of lesser politicians. It was to an extent, but this should not be exaggerated. Bismarck's system of alliances was not itself without fault and cracks had already begun to appear. Relations between Germany and Russia had already deteriorated before Bismarck's dismissal and the Reinsurance Treaty merely papered over the cracks. Moreover, since 1890, Germany had deliberately pursued what has been referred to as a 'free hand' policy. It was hoped that disagreements might occur among the other

Key terms

Franco-Russian Alliance
A military alliance signed between Russia and France in 1894.

Jameson Raid
In 1895–6 Leander Jameson, a British colonial administrator, led a force of 500 into the Transvaal in the hope of overthrowing the Boer government. It was a complete failure.

Key date

Franco-Russian Alliance ratified: 1894

Key question
Was the end of the Bismarckian system a mistake?

European powers and that this, combined with more friendly German approaches, would lead to Germany having a major voice in European affairs. By 1896, Germany had allies in Austria and Italy as well as an improved relationship with France. Relations with Russia were also slowly recovering. Although the Kruger Telegram had upset Britain, it was a fact that Britain was on far worse terms with Russia and France than it was with Germany. German foreign policy had moved on from the days of Bismarck and, although the Franco-Russian Alliance was still regarded as a threat, the situation was not seen as immediately dangerous by the German government at the time.

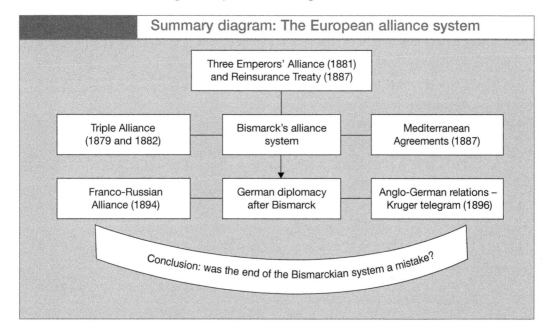

Summary diagram: The European alliance system

Three Emperors' Alliance (1881) and Reinsurance Treaty (1887)

Triple Alliance (1879 and 1882) — Bismarck's alliance system — Mediterranean Agreements (1887)

Franco-Russian Alliance (1894) — German diplomacy after Bismarck — Anglo-German relations – Kruger telegram (1896)

Conclusion: was the end of the Bismarckian system a mistake?

Key question
What was the purpose of *Weltpolitik*?

Key dates

Bülow's 'place in the sun' speech; advent of *Weltpolitik*: 1897

First German Naval Law (second in 1900): 1898

3 | The Coming of *Weltpolitik* 1897–1904

The decision to pursue *Weltpolitik* in 1897 was a turning point in German history. We saw in Chapter 2 how this coincided with important changes on the political scene at home; and it marked an even more important change in the development of German foreign policy.

Aims

The decision to build the German navy by the two naval laws of 1898 and 1900 (see page 38) was obviously a significant one, yet *Weltpolitik* did not have a very clear purpose even among the politicians. Bülow declared in the *Reichstag*: 'We have to put no one in the shade, but we too demand our place in the sun.' This echoed the idea of the British Empire 'on which the sun never set'. And the Kaiser enthusiastically said: 'Germany has great tasks to accomplish outside the narrow boundaries of Europe.' Such political claims led a German army commander to state more cynically: 'We are supposed to pursue *Weltpolitik*. If only we knew what it is supposed to mean.'

Weltpolitik meant different things to different people. For some, it meant the chance to create a larger overseas empire by the acquisition of colonies and to stimulate the expansion of the German economy. For others, it was simply a policy to assist German business to establish areas of economic influence in as many parts of the world as possible. Another view, epitomised by the Pan-German League, amounted to nothing less than racist *Lebensraum* which encouraged colonial expansion and the conquest of neighbouring countries, particularly those bordering Germany's eastern frontiers.

Of course, historians have tried to give a shape to the history of the advent of *Weltpolitik*. For the structuralists Wehler and Berghahn, *Weltpolitik* was a manoeuvre in domestic politics (see pages 30–1). They have seen it as essentially a diversionary tactic to distract the masses of the people from social and political reform. They simply believed that the prestige of the navy and *Weltpolitik* was no more than '**social imperialism**' aimed at rallying public opinion to stabilise the *Kaiserreich*. In contrast, Fischer maintained that in 1897 Germany 'embarked on a course aiming at nothing less than parity with the British world empire, if not more'.

Social imperialism
A phrase suggesting that a government played on imperialism to preserve the domestic social peace.

Key term

The Kaiser's hand-drawn diagram of the navy schedule.

Objectives

This push for world hegemony was to be achieved by a range of objectives, each of which carried dangers:

- the expansion of the navy, which was bound to be perceived as a threat by Britain
- the creation of a large colonial empire in central Africa (*Mittelafrika*), including the Congo, and the Portuguese colonies of Angola and Mozambique, lands already owned by someone else, increasing the perception of German imperialism as aggressive
- the economic domination of central Europe to Germany's interests (*Mitteleuropa*), including Austria-Hungary, the Balkan states and the Ottoman empire.

In Fischer's view, *Weltpolitik* was a grand plan involving both continental and overseas expansion in order to attain world-power status.

Achievements

Attractive as Fischer's interpretation may seem, it gives the impression that the direction of German foreign policy from 1897 had a clear shape and order. If Fischer's understanding of *Weltpolitik* is accurate, why was German policy so unclear and lacking direction?

Between 1897 and 1904 the real achievements of *Weltpolitik* were very limited. Certainly, naval construction was started and German economic influence was extended into South America, China, the Near East and the Balkans. Yet, Germany's small and costly empire made only a few gains:

- the Chinese port of Kiaochow (1897) as a naval base
- some islands in the Pacific: the Mariana Islands (1899), the Caroline Islands (1899) and German Samoa (1900)
- an attempt to gain access to Angola and Mozambique by exploiting Portugal's indebtedness was thwarted by British diplomacy in 1898.

Moreover, *Weltpolitik* had important diplomatic consequences.

The end of British splendid isolation

Bülow and Holstein believed that the policy of maintaining a 'free hand' from commitments with other powers, such as Britain and France, was consistent with *Weltpolitik*. Essentially this was because they assumed that Britain would remain at loggerheads with France (over African colonies) and with Russia (over central Asia). Indeed, some British political leaders, particularly Joseph Chamberlain, the Colonial Secretary, were concerned with Britain's foreign policy keystone of '**splendid isolation**'. It was he who led the British overtures in 1898–1901 for an Anglo-German agreement. Yet, the negotiations came to nothing, because Bülow was convinced that Britain's rivalry with Russia and France was likely to lead to war anyway. Therefore, it would be naïve for

Key term

Splendid isolation
In the nineteenth century Britain had been the strongest power because of its navy and empire, therefore it had no need to sign alliances with others. (However, although Britain was still isolated in 1900, it faced increasing pressures from France, Germany and Russia and the isolation appeared less attractive.)

Key question
Did *Weltpolitik* alienate Britain?

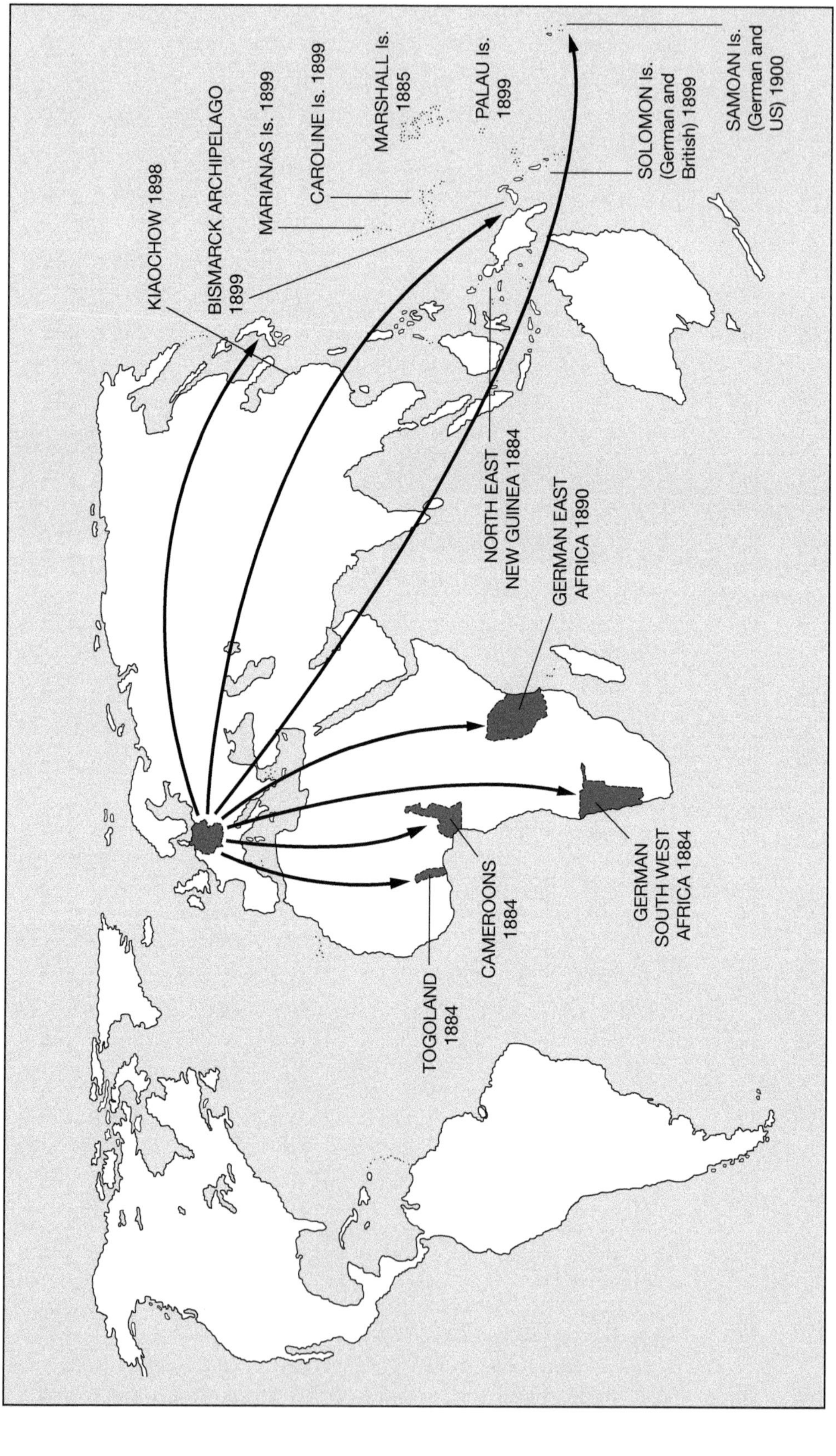

Figure 3.2: German overseas expansion 1884–1900.

Germany to befriend Britain, as it would alienate Russia. An alliance with Britain was not really a good deal – and Bülow let the negotiations lapse in 1901 with significant consequences. Also, the British Prime Minister, Lord Salisbury, did not see how Germany could give practical help to Britain over its worldwide commitments.

Public opinion fuelled by the press, in both Germany and Britain, complicated matters. Anglophobia was exacerbated by the Boer War, 1899–1902, as most Germans sympathised with the Boers. At the same time, growing commercial rivalry and the British determination to maintain naval supremacy increased anti-German feelings in Britain.

Germany had never considered that Britain would reduce her fears of isolation by signing an alliance with Japan (1902) and the Anglo-French Agreement (1904). The 1902 Anglo-**Japanese Alliance** grew out of mutual fears about expansionist Russia, although the terms were clearly limited to the Pacific area. In a way, it confirmed Britain's traditional 'isolation' from the European powers, but it enabled Britain to withdraw naval forces from the Pacific to reinforce the North Sea fleet against the growing German naval presence there. More significant was the **Anglo-French Agreement**, which later became known as the *Entente Cordiale*. This was not an alliance, but merely an understanding to settle colonial differences and to encourage future diplomatic co-operation between the two countries; Lord Lansdowne, the British Foreign Secretary, was keen to underline that it was in no way directed against Germany. Nevertheless, it was difficult to disguise the serious implications of British diplomacy in 1898–1904. Britain and Germany were no longer so close, while Germany itself could no longer rely on Anglo-French hostility to strengthen its own hand.

Key date
Anglo-French Agreement (which later became the Anglo-French *Entente Cordiale*): 1904

Key terms

Japanese Alliance
An alliance signed by Japan and Britain in 1902 but limited to the Pacific region.

Anglo-French Agreement
A colonial agreement signed by France and Britain in 1904, which evolved into the *Entente Cordiale*.

Key question
How successful was *Weltpolitik* 1897–1904?

Conclusion

At first the decision to embark on *Weltpolitik* in 1897 was probably no more than a desire felt in Germany that it was time for the country to catch up with the other major European powers. It was rather a mixture of hopes and fears, and there was no real consensus among the leading figures about planning. Consequently, by 1904 Germany found itself in a state of diplomatic confusion. The real benefits of *Weltpolitik* remained limited to the commercial advantages from overseas economic expansion and the prestige arising from possessing a powerful army and navy. However, Germany's colonial possessions remained few. In this sense, at very considerable financial cost, *Weltpolitik* had made very little progress towards promoting Germany to world-power status. Therefore, it could be argued, as many Germans did at the time, that *Weltpolitik* did not pose a real threat to anyone else. However, it was not seen this way outside Germany. Britain had been alienated and was soon to take steps to maintain its naval lead (see pages 61–3). At the same time, it had aligned itself with France. As a result, Germany's diplomatic and strategic position was weaker in 1904 than it had been for a generation or so before. In this sense the early years of *Weltpolitik* contributed to an important change in the European balance of power.

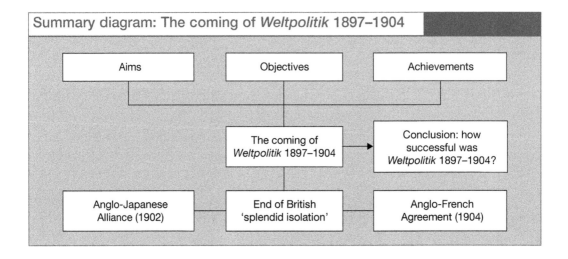

Summary diagram: The coming of *Weltpolitik* 1897–1904

4 | International Crises and Tensions 1904–11

German politicians and newspapers expressed concerns about the Anglo-French Agreement, but these were brushed aside by Bülow saying in the *Reichstag* that it was a purely colonial agreement and was not directed against Germany. The onset of the **Russo-Japanese War** in 1904 then seemed to work to Germany's advantage. Admittedly, German hopes of Britain being drawn into the conflict never materialised, but the war fundamentally weakened Russia, which descended into the 1905 Revolution. Suddenly, France was diplomatically undermined by the political weakness of Russia, whereas Germany felt more secure and confident of exploiting the international situation in its favour.

Russo-Japanese War
The war fought between Russia and Japan in 1904–5 over the clash of ambitions in Asia.

Key term

The first Moroccan crisis 1905–6

Initially, the Kaiser had reacted to the diplomatic shift by hoping to resurrect an understanding between Germany and Russia through his close personal relationship with his cousin, Tsar Nicholas II. This came to nothing – partly because of Bülow's concerns, but also because of Russia's ministers' doubts that it was at odds with the Franco-Russian Alliance. More significantly, the Kaiser and Bülow also decided to provoke the Moroccan crisis of 1905–6 in the hope of breaking the Anglo-French Agreement.

Morocco had become an accepted French sphere of influence in the latter half of the nineteenth century. In March 1905 Wilhelm II melodramatically landed at the Moroccan port of Tangier and made a speech in which he upheld the independence of the Sultan and supported German interests.

The Tangier incident was a clear German challenge and it shocked many in European capitals. Bülow demanded an

Key question
How did German diplomacy poison international relations?

First Moroccan crisis: the Tangier incident: 1905

Key date

Key terms

Brinkmanship
The strategy of pushing one's opponent to the limit in a dangerous situation with the aim of forcing them to concede.

Triple Entente
The name given to the alignment of the powers Russia, France and Britain, which evolved between 1894 and 1907. Only France and Russia were actually in alliance.

Key question
Was Europe divided by 1907?

Key date

Anglo-Russian *entente* forming the Triple Entente: 1907

international conference to review the question of Morocco, confident that it would show that the Anglo-French Agreement was flimsy and that Britain was not a reliable partner. He therefore hoped to humiliate France and to score a major German diplomatic victory. This was not to be. At the international conference held at Algeçiras in 1906, Germany suffered a major humiliation. Apart from Austria, it found itself diplomatically isolated and France essentially got its way over Morocco. Algeçiras therefore proved to be a severe blow to German prestige. More significantly, the whole crisis had actually strengthened the Anglo-French relationship, which developed into the *Entente Cordiale*. The new British Liberal government had become very concerned about the **brinkmanship** of German foreign policy. The Foreign Secretary, Edward Grey, quickly came to believe that Germany was a threat to the balance of power in Europe and to the British Empire. Within months he initiated secret military conversations between Britain and France. The Moroccan crisis had ended in a diplomatic humiliation for Germany, with an outcome for Anglo-French relations which was the reverse of what Germany had intended.

The Triple Entente
Growing concerns and frustrations in Berlin worsened in August 1907 when Britain and Russia signed an *entente*. With France now close to Britain as well as allied to Russia, this agreement closed the circle and underlined Germany's isolation. The Anglo-Russian *entente* was fundamentally a colonial agreement to settle differences in Asia over Tibet, Persia and Afghanistan by regulating spheres of influence; again, like the Anglo-French *entente*, it was not overtly directed at Germany. Yet, Germany's growing military power and diplomatic pressure had shaped British foreign policy under Grey. The agreement clearly underlined Germany's isolation and it closed the circle of the **Triple Entente**: Britain, France and Russia.

By 1907 the major powers of Europe were already divided along lines that would parallel those of 1914. Germany was alone except for Austria and the doubtful support of Italy in any war with Britain, which left the country much less secure than in 1890. Perhaps understandably, German newspapers accused the Triple Entente of an 'encirclement' aiming to undermine Germany. On the other side, there were also certainly growing suspicions within the *entente* of German aggression.

It might be thought that there was now no turning back. However, such a view cannot be held with certainty. A series of crises in Bosnia (1908–9) and Morocco (1911), as well as the Balkan Wars (1912–13), passed off without the outbreak of major European war. It should also be remembered that genuine efforts were made during that time to improve the relationship between Britain and Germany. If an Anglo-German *entente* had been agreed, then the situation that arose in 1914 would have been very different indeed!

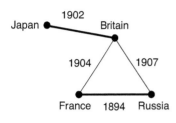

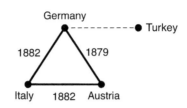

Figure 3.3: The European alliance system in 1907.

Key
— Alliance
— Understanding
--- Growing co-operation

The Bosnian crisis

The Balkans had long been a major problem in international relations:

- The **Ottoman Empire** had been in decline and had lost its power and influence in southern Europe.
- The Slavic people (Serbs, Croats and Slovenes) wanted to be independent and to create their own state (and were supported by Russia, as fellow Slavs).
- Austria hoped to keep control over the southern Slavs within its empire to prevent it being eaten away by external forces (especially Russia and its close fellow Slav state, Serbia).

Bismarck had tried to dissuade Austria from its ambitions in the Balkans. Yet, Bülow was increasingly prepared to back Austria with its aim of maintaining its empire against Balkan nationalism, mainly because Germany, in its deteriorating diplomatic position, could no longer ignore its one major ally.

In 1908, Austria annexed the neighbouring province of Bosnia, which it had administered since 1878, but was nominally part of the Ottoman Empire. As that empire declined in the face of Slavic nationalism, Austria feared that its own Slav peoples might break away to join their brothers to the south. The Triple Entente demanded an international conference, but Austria bluntly refused to co-operate and the possibility of war dragged on for five months. Although Germany did not want to alienate Turkey, as they enjoyed good relations, Bülow felt obliged to give full support to Austria. Indeed, in January 1909 Helmuth von Moltke, the German Chief of General Staff (and the nephew of the great general, Moltke the Elder), made it clear to his Austrian equivalent that Germany would be prepared to mobilise if Serbia and Russia took military action.

Tensions continued and came to a head when Germany asked Russia to recognise the annexation. This amounted to an ultimatum. Russia was in a weak and embarrassing position since the war with Japan (see page 58) and the 1905 Revolution, and France was unprepared to commit itself over Bosnia. Eventually, in March 1909, the annexation was recognised and war was avoided.

Key question
Was the Bosnian crisis really such a triumph for Germany?

Ottoman Empire
The Ottoman Empire, or Turkish Empire, lasted from 1299 to 1922. The sultanate was dissolved in 1922 and the state of Turkey became a republic.

Key term

Bosnian crisis: 1908–9

Key date

Figure 3.4: The Balkans in the early twentieth century.

The Bosnian crisis was a diplomatic triumph for Germany. In the short term, Germany with Austria could claim victory over the incident; it strengthened the alliance between Austria and Germany, while it highlighted the weaknesses of the Triple Entente. However, the implications were costly, causing increased resentment and distrust. Serbia was embittered and Russia publicly humiliated. Both were determined not to back down again. Most importantly, doubts within the Triple Entente about the true purpose of German foreign policy were markedly growing.

Navy rivalry

Key question
Why did Anglo-German *rapprochement* fail?

In 1909, Anglo-German relations reached a decidedly low point. This was partly because of the Bosnian crisis, but for Britain it coincided with a renewed concern over the worrying issue of increasing German naval strength.

British military and naval strategy had begun to be reviewed as early as 1902 in response to the early German naval laws and the Anglo-Japanese Alliance. By 1905, Britain had started to concentrate three-quarters of the fleet in European waters. It had also developed a new type of battleship and cruiser. The keel of the prototype battleship, HMS *Dreadnought*, was laid down in 1905 and completed in December 1906; it was faster and more heavily gunned and armoured than any other ship.

Despite the financial problems faced by the German imperial government (see page 40), the Kaiser, Bülow and Tirpitz were still keen to expand the German navy and to put it on equal terms with Britain. They succeeded in getting their proposal for two supplementary naval laws in 1906 passed by the *Reichstag* to build Germany its own Dreadnoughts.

British projections estimated that by 1911 Germany would have 11 Dreadnoughts and Britain would have 12. The Admiralty was so concerned about the threat to British supremacy over the German navy that in spring 1909 public anxiety came to a head (see Table 3.1, page 63). The increasingly populist anti-German campaign of the press was 'we want eight and we won't wait' and the British government decided to increase naval expenditure to maintain its lead by building four more ships with the possibility of more if necessary. However, this proved to be only a short-lived compromise, and not a long-term solution to the German threat. In the years 1910–13 the British government continued to expand its navy and the two main countries were drawn into an expensive arms race that worsened an already uneasy relationship. Britain was bound to see German naval expansion as a challenge whatever Germany's real motives were.

Key dates

Launch of the first Dreadnought by Britain: 1906

Third German Naval Law: 1906

'Poker and Tongs', *Punch*, 8 January 1908. The Kaiser playing poker with John Bull. Kaiser: 'I go three Dreadnoughts.' John Bull: 'Well, just to show there's no ill-feeling, I raise you three.'

Table. 3.1: The naval race. Battleships planned 1905–14

	1905	1906	1907	1908	1909	1910	1911	1912	1913	1914	Total
Britain	1	3	3	1	6	4	4	5	5	0	32
Germany	0	2	2	3	3	3	3	1	2	2*	21 (19)

Notes: date is by planned programme, not by delivery.
* The two German battleships of 1914 were not completed.

Anglo-German differences

The appointment of Bethmann as Chancellor was followed by an attempt to improve Anglo-German relations. He recognised that an agreement with Britain to limit naval construction would not only reduce his country's financial difficulties, but could also loosen Britain's ties to the Triple Entente. There were also influential people in Britain who saw the advantages of a settlement of Anglo-German differences. During negotiations carried out between 1909 and 1911, Britain pressed for a real reduction in German naval strength while Germany demanded a promise of British neutrality in the event of an attack by France or Russia. The demands placed by each country on the other were impossible for either to accept and the gap could not be bridged. The Kaiser and Tirpitz did not seriously consider making any concessions over the fleet and Bethmann was prepared only to offer a slowing down in construction. Britain, in turn, viewed the German request for British neutrality as too high a price to pay and the talks were to collapse with the onset of the second Moroccan crisis.

The second Moroccan crisis

Key question
How did Germany mishandle the second Moroccan crisis?

Key date
Second Moroccan crisis: the Agadir incident: 1911

Perhaps both Germany and Britain had expected too much. Or perhaps, with time, the negotiations could have laid the basis for a better understanding. Instead, the Germans responded to the failure of these talks with an action which would challenge Britain either to abandon its French ally, or publicly support it. The crisis blew up in April 1911 over Morocco, when French troops were sent to the town of Fez following the outbreak of a revolt.

In a way Germany did have a real grievance over this French action, which was in conflict with the Algeçiras agreement of 1906 (see page 59). Even France implied that some compensation from the French Empire was appropriate. Unfortunately, the German Foreign Minister, Kiderlen, with his combative approach mishandled the situation. In his hope of pulling off a 'great stroke' to impress public opinion, he sent the gunboat *Panther* to the port of Agadir in southern Morocco. Ostensibly, this was to protect German citizens in the area, although only one could be found. In reality it was intended as a lever to win the whole of the French Congo as compensation for the French action. Instead, Kiderlen's diplomacy went wrong. France broke off negotiations and Britain stood by its side, which developed into a major Anglo-German dispute. In the face of what was regarded as German intimidation, Lloyd George, the British Chancellor of

Profile: Alfred von Tirpitz 1849–1930

1849	– Born in Brandenburg, the son of a senior civil servant
1865	– Joined the Prussian navy and attended the Kiel Naval School
1877	– Rose steadily through the ranks and became an admiral in 1895 to command a fleet of cruisers representing Germany's military and colonial interests in the Far East
1897–1916	– Secretary of State of the Imperial Naval Office
1898	– Proposed the first of four navy laws of 1898, 1900, 1906 and 1912 to enlarge the German navy
1916	– Fell out with Bethmann over submarine policy and resigned
1917	– Became head of the short-lived German Fatherland Party and later a deputy of the right wing DNVP, 1924–8 (see pages 110 and 158)
1930	– Died

Tirpitz was undoubtedly talented and he advanced his naval career by his technical skills and his flair for managing men. He was recalled to Berlin in 1897 because of his success as an energetic supporter of an enlarged fleet which would lead to stronger world power status. An interesting and significant figure on several counts because:

- he proved in the years 1897–1914 to be masterful in handling public opinion and an effective administrator of the Tirpitz Plan to develop the German navy
- he developed the military strategy of '**risk fleet theory**'.

Tirpitz was a strong supporter of **unrestricted submarine warfare** (see page 83) from 1914 which he felt could break the British stranglehold on Germany's sea lines of communication.

Key terms

Risk fleet theory
As Germany was unable to challenge the Royal Navy directly in terms of size, the expansion of the German fleet was based on what Tirpitz described as the 'risk fleet theory'. The aim of this was to build a fleet based in the North Sea of sufficient size to pose a serious threat to British strategy.

Unrestricted submarine warfare
Germany's policy in the First World War to attack all military and civilian shipping in order to sink supplies going to Britain.

the Exchequer, bluntly warned Germany in a major speech that Britain's interests were at stake. In growing tensions the Royal Navy was put on alert; once again Britain had diplomatically stood firmly by France, its *entente* partner.

In the end, the German government was not prepared to force the issue and risk war. Instead, by the agreement in November 1911, it backed down and accepted a narrow strip of the French Congo as compensation and France secured its domination of Morocco. In fact, little was gained by the episode and much was lost. Kiderlen may have enjoyed broad support from conservatives for his patriotic bombast; yet, the political tension had sharply increased, particularly between Britain and Germany. The press in both countries stirred up hatred of each other and pressed for further increases in arms expenditure.

Anglo-French naval agreement: 1912

Once again German clumsiness had made things worse, and within a year Britain and France had concluded a naval agreement whereby the Royal Navy would concentrate in the North Sea and the French in the Mediterranean. This gave Britain an informal commitment to defend the French Channel ports, which proved to be significant in 1914.

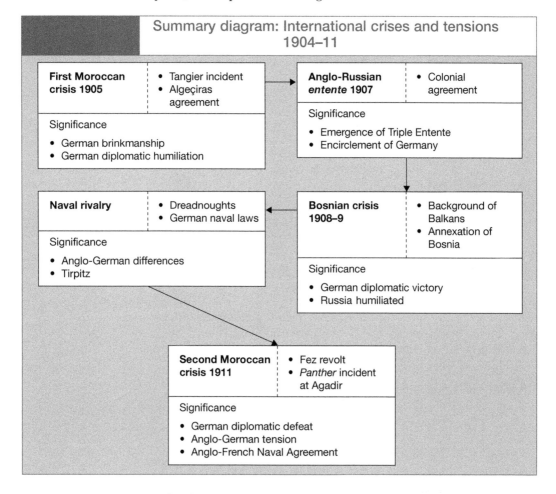

Summary diagram: International crises and tensions 1904–11

First Moroccan crisis 1905
- Tangier incident
- Algeçiras agreement

Significance
- German brinkmanship
- German diplomatic humiliation

Anglo-Russian *entente* 1907
- Colonial agreement

Significance
- Emergence of Triple Entente
- Encirclement of Germany

Naval rivalry
- Dreadnoughts
- German naval laws

Significance
- Anglo-German differences
- Tirpitz

Bosnian crisis 1908–9
- Background of Balkans
- Annexation of Bosnia

Significance
- German diplomatic victory
- Russia humiliated

Second Moroccan crisis 1911
- Fez revolt
- *Panther* incident at Agadir

Significance
- German diplomatic defeat
- Anglo-German tension
- Anglo-French Naval Agreement

5 | 1911–14: The Final Years of Peace

The final three years of peace have been the subject of much investigation by historians studying the causes of the First World War. Fischer maintains that the 'excitement and bitterness of nationalist opinion over what was seen to be the humiliating outcome of the [Moroccan] crisis were profound and enduring'. He argues that 1911 was an important year in German foreign policy because, from that point, there existed a clear continuity of German aims and policies that directly led to war in August 1914. Important to Fischer's view and our general understanding of the origins of the First World War are:

- the Balkan Wars 1912–13
- the War Council meeting
- the military plans of the Great Powers.

The Balkan Wars

In 1912 the focus of international affairs shifted back again to the Balkans. The small Balkan states of Serbia, Montenegro, Bulgaria and Greece formed the Balkan League and attacked Turkey, winning two major battles. Yet, there was a real danger of the conflict developing into a broader European war unless a peace was negotiated. Russia was determined to back the Balkan League to force concessions from Turkey; whereas Austria felt that the fall of the Turkish Empire would be fatal because of the possible growth of Serbia at the expense of its own empire. In particular, Austria feared that Serbia's gains could lead to access to the Adriatic coastline and to the Mediterranean Sea.

The Austrian military, led by Conrad von Hotzendorff, was keen to join the war straightaway to crush Serbia. However, Foreign Minister Berchtold, was more cautious – tying in with Germany's conciliatory approach urged by Bethmann, the Kaiser and Moltke. This laid the basis for an international conference of the Great Powers in London in 1913, which significantly revised the territorial map (see Figure 3.4 on page 61) including the creation of the new independent state of Albania, which Austria wanted in order to deny Serbia access to the sea. The interests of Russia and Austria had thus been protected. These optimistic signs gave way to discontent when the victors quickly fell out over the spoils. This led to the second Balkan War. Greece and Serbia made further gains at the expense of Bulgaria. The Turks regained some land, and Romania gained some Bulgarian land. The various client states of the Great Powers had all gained something from the two wars.

The Balkan Wars had changed the international atmosphere:

- Turkey had lost nearly all of its European territory.
- Serbia had doubled its size, yet it still felt resentful at the creation of Albania – blaming Austria for denying it access to the sea.
- Russia had won a diplomatic victory from Serbia's military victory.
- Austria feared that its state was fundamentally threatened by the expansionist Serbia, but was happy to have set up Albania.

Also, significantly, Germany's position stiffened during 1913 when Serbian troops, flushed by success, moved across the border into Albania. Austria was dismayed and presented an ultimatum for the troops to withdraw in one week, which was backed by Germany. In a flamboyant gesture Wilhelm II assured the Austrian Kaiser, 'I am prepared to draw the sword whenever your move makes it necessary.' On this occasion the Serbs withdrew, as Russia did not give its support, and the ultimatum had proved to be successful. Once again the international tension and the local wars had not escalated, but it was to be for the last time.

Key question
How did the Balkan Wars change the European balance of power?

Key dates

First Balkan War: 1912

Second Balkan War: 1913

Key question
How significant was the 'War Council' meeting?

Key date

War Council meeting: 1912

The 'War Council' meeting 1912

The increasing sense of isolation and encirclement of the Triple Alliance was underlined by a further attempt to reach an Anglo-German *rapprochement*, which failed. Indeed, the British War Minister, Lord Haldane, who was pro-German, having attended Göttingen University, passed on to the German ambassador in London that Britain would stand by France unconditionally in the event of a continental war; Britain could not allow the balance of power in Europe to change in Germany's favour. This was unofficial, as there was no treaty commitment to do so, but was realistically true. The Kaiser was livid and the upshot of this was the summoning of a meeting of Germany's army and navy chiefs on 8 December 1912.

This meeting, which became known as the War Council meeting, provides for the supporters of the Fischer view conclusive evidence of German intentions to fight a war at a time most suitable to German military interests. Moltke observed that if Germany should go to war, then 'the sooner the better' and Wilhelm II called for increased armaments to confront the 'racial struggle' with Russia. Other historians have not been so convinced. They have highlighted the informal nature of the meeting, which was simply another example of a hastily assembled gathering in response to an outburst by the Kaiser. Attention has been drawn to the fact that Bethmann did not even attend. Tirpitz warned against war and Müller commented that 'the result amounted to almost nothing'. More generally, it has been questioned whether the chaotic nature of Wilhelmine government was actually capable of such clear-sighted long-term planning. Therefore, it does not seem that Germany was set on war in that meeting. War was not deliberately planned for 1914; nevertheless, there was a feeling that it was just a question of time.

Key question
How and where did military expenditure grow?

The arms race

The alliance system and the imperial tensions at the turn of the century grew in conjunction with the arms build-up. From the 1890s the military budgets of the Great Powers rose both on sea and on land, but in the three years leading up to 1914 concerns about military strategy markedly increased expenditure (see Table 3.2).

Table 3.2: Growth in German military expenditure

Expenditure	1900	1906	1910	1913
Millions of marks	1080	1359	1659	2312
GNP (%)*	3.7	3.8	3.9	4.7

* Gross national product. The figures technically are GNP minus social benefits.

From the German perspective, the cost of the German navy had put financial pressures on the treasury) and by 1912 it was becoming clear that Germany could not afford and could not really win the naval race war. As a result, the Navy Law of 1912 was more limited than Tirpitz's hopes. In addition, there was a growing concern for Germany's capacity to fight a land war on the continent against France and Russia; not just because of the long-standing strategic dilemma since 1894, but also because Germany and Austria were being outspent by their rivals. This, therefore, led the powers to initiate a marked upgrading of their war machines:

Fourth Naval Law: 1912

Key date

- Germany. Moltke pushed for increases in the Army Law of 1912 and 1913, which increased the peacetime strength of the army by 20 per cent from 663,000 to 800,000 men in 1914 (see Table 3.3).
- France. In August 1913 it extended military conscription from two to three years.
- Russia. In December 1913 it added 500,000 men to its forces.

However, the Russian and French reforms would take up to three years to take effect, which gave Germany a short-term advantage.

Table 3.3: Military personnel 1900–14 (in thousands)

Country	1900	1910	1914
Germany	524	694	891
France	715	769	910
Russia	1162	1285	1352
Britain	624	571	532
Austria-Hungary	385	425	444

The mood of 1914

By 1914, in Germany there was definitely a growing mood of pessimism and uncertainty about the future. The country had been forging an even closer friendship with Austria that increased the possibility of Germany being drawn into a Balkan conflict. The early months of 1914 witnessed a worsening in Russo-German relations. Some influential people in the German establishment held the belief that war provided the only solution. However, in the final few months of peace, Bethmann still saw hopeful signs in Germany's position. He was encouraged by the extent of Anglo-German co-operation during the Balkan Wars and by the peaceful settlement of several colonial disputes.

To suggest that evidence proves that the German government was actually planning a war in the summer of 1914 is to go too far. War plans certainly existed. It would have been irresponsible if they had not. The Schlieffen Plan (see pages 73–4) had been evolving for over 20 years. The War Council meeting of December 1912 is clear evidence of how war was considered to be a possible option. From 1912 German leaders were aware in their own minds of the extent to which 1914–15 was the most advantageous time for war, as Russian and French military reforms would come on stream in 1916. These considerations must surely have been very influential when the Sarajevo crisis (see page 70) developed. But this is not the same as claiming that Germany had decided to go to war whatever happened.

Key question
Was Germany planning for war?

A cartoon from the satirical magazine *Simplicissimus* which implied that the Kaiser was having sleepless nights because of the dominating presence of Tirpitz (see the shadow).

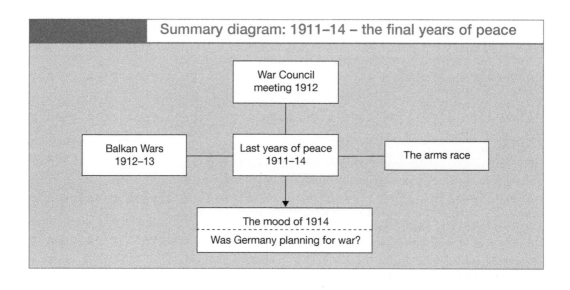

Summary diagram: 1911–14 – the final years of peace

War Council meeting 1912

Balkan Wars 1912–13 — Last years of peace 1911–14 — The arms race

The mood of 1914

Was Germany planning for war?

6 | Sarajevo and the July 1914 Crisis

On 28 June 1914 in Sarajevo, Archduke Franz Ferdinand, the heir to the Austrian throne, was assassinated by Gavrilo Princip, a member of the Bosnian Serb terrorist group, 'Death or Unity'. The deaths of the Archduke and his wife shocked the world and sparked the crisis that led to the outbreak of the First World War in August. Over the years the focus of study has been on the impact of those six weeks on the whole of Europe, but this section will concentrate mainly on what happened in Germany during this time and why.

Key dates

Assassination of Franz Ferdinand: 28 June 1914

'Blank cheque' given by Germany to Austria: 5 July 1914

Start of First World War: August 1914

The 'blank cheque'

Following the assassination, the Austrian leaders were agreed on the need to take strong action against Serbia. Yet, measures against Serbia might well have led Russia to defend its ally, so Vienna and Berlin consulted to discuss their options. On 5–6 July Wilhelm II and Bethmann gave their full unconditional support to Austria, a deal which has become known as the **'blank cheque'**. They urged Austria to send a harshly worded ultimatum and indeed went further, recommending immediate action against Serbia. In communication to the Austrian ambassador Bethmann wrote: 'Austria must judge what is to be done to clear up her relations with Serbia. But whatever Austria's decision, she could count with certainty upon it that Germany would stand behind her ally.'

In the context of 1908 and 1912–13 this German support is not surprising, especially as Hotzendorff renewed his demand for immediate action. The German pressure for swift and decisive action, combined with its knowledge of the severity of the ultimatum being prepared against Serbia, suggests that it was taking more than just defensive measures on behalf of its ally. Bethmann seemed to have recognised that the situation provided a fine opportunity for Austria to assert its power over Serbia in a localised war. An Austrian victory would also prove a significant diplomatic victory over Russia and over the *Entente* in general. Even so his assessment was a gamble, since there was a risk that Russia would stand by Serbia and thus broaden the conflict.

Bethmann reported to the Austrian ambassador: 'If war must break out, better now than in one or two years' time, when the *Entente* will be stronger.' The German leadership seemed to have been prepared to take that chance in the belief that Germany would win such a war, as is shown in this illuminating extract from the diary of K. Riezler, secretary to Bethmann:

Key question
How and why did Germany support Austria?

'Blank cheque'
The name given to the telegram sent by Wilhelm II and Bethmann telling Austria that Germany would support whatever action was necessary to deal with Serbia.

7.7.1914 … Our old dilemma in every Austrian move in the Balkans. If we encourage them, they will say we pushed them into it; if we try to dissuade them, then we're supposed to have left them in the lurch. Then they turn to the western powers whose arms are open, and we lose our last halfway reliable ally. This time it's worse than 1912; for this time Austria is on the defensive against the subversive activities of Serbia and Russia. A move against Serbia can lead to world war.

Profile: Theobald Bethmann-Hollweg 1856–1921

1856 – Born in Brandenburg
1905 – Appointed Prussian Minister for the Interior
1907 – Appointed State Secretary in the Imperial Interior
        Office
1909 – Replaced Bülow as Imperial Chancellor
1914 – Played a major role in events leading to the First
        World War
1917 – Opposed unrestricted submarine warfare and wanted to
        negotiate for peace. Forced to resign
1921 – Died

When appointed Chancellor in 1909, Bethmann was a skilled
bureaucrat but relatively inexperienced in political affairs. He
was an earnest and conscientious man, but lacked authority. He
faced ongoing political criticism from the reactionary forces and
the left and, as a result, he found it increasingly difficult to
manage legislation in the *Reichstag*.

Bethmann is best remembered for his part in the crises leading
up to the First World War. Although he never expected those
events to escalate into a major European conflict, it seems he
hoped that a limited war would divert opposition from domestic
problems. A critical comment claims that 'he was a weak
politician who stumbled into war through sheer incapacity'. As
the war progressed, he became deeply unpopular with both
conservatives and liberals in the *Reichstag* and the military
forced him to resign from office in 1917.

At this stage Germany did not necessarily want war, but it
certainly seemed to have been prepared to risk it. Twenty-five
years of diplomacy had left them so dependent on Austria as
their only ally that they had no choice but to take the risk.

The historical sources now available suggest that the 'blank
cheque' initiated the international crisis. Yet, for three weeks at
the time, there was no real indication of Europe drifting into war.
The Kaiser left for his yachting holiday. The diplomatic alarms
were not yet ringing in the foreign offices. And on 23 July, Lloyd
George said in Parliament that British and German relations were
better than they had been for years! On that very day Austria sent
its ultimatum to Serbia.

Key question
Why was the Sarajevo
crisis not resolved
diplomatically?

The looming crisis

The Austrian ultimatum to Serbia shocked many foreign
ministers. Its 10 demands were undoubtedly severe and insisted
on a reply within a 48-hour time limit. To the surprise of many,
the Serbs, after consulting with their Russian ally, accepted most
of the terms, except the one which gave Austrian police access to
its territory. This was enough for Austria to regard it as a rejection
and break off diplomatic relations.

For the first time since the assassination, the events of 23–25 July brought home to the major powers the danger of the situation. Britain, in particular, tried to mediate by calling for an international conference, but Germany ignored such proposals. Privately it urged Austria to take military action because 'any delay in commencing military operations is regarded as a great danger because of the interference of other powers'.

It would seem therefore that until 27 July there was a reasonable degree of agreement among the German leaders. However, afterwards doubts began to appear among some of the leading figures and there were disagreements over policy. The Kaiser returned from his holiday on 28 July having decided that the Serb reply represented a victory. He proposed that the Austrians should 'halt in Belgrade' and then negotiate on the basis of the Serbian reply to the Austrian ultimatum; meanwhile German generals were pressing the government to take the military initiative. Yet, the confusion was not completely clarified by Bethmann. Either he was hesitating and having doubts about the wisdom of taking such great risks, or he was playing a cunning diplomatic game to win over German public opinion to support a war by making Germany appear an innocent party in the face of Russian aggression. This uncertainty was implied by Riezler in his diary:

> 23.7.1914 … The Chancellor believes that if there is war it will be unleashed by Russian mobilisation … In this case there will be little to negotiate about because we shall have to wage war immediately in order to have a chance of winning. Yet, the entire nation will then sense the danger and rise in arms.

The contrasting German messages did not help Austria and Berchtold is famously reported as saying in frustration: 'What a laugh – who actually rules in Berlin?' Nevertheless, Austria seized the initiative and declared war on Serbia on 28 July, bombarding Belgrade on the next day. Therefore, war had started, albeit a local one at that stage.

Mobilisation and war

At this point the international crisis was propelled forward by the involvement of military and strategic planning. It was war by railway timetable, as historian A.J.P. Taylor described it (see Table 3.4, page 73). Russia decided to order a partial mobilisation straight after Austria's declaration of war on Serbia. Yet, that defensive action by Russia had serious implications for the German generals, who were to use the situation to exert increasing influence.

In addition to military pressure, there was increasing political pressure. For example, Erich von Falkenhayn, the War Minister, had already tried unsuccessfully to force Bethmann into ordering a mobilisation alert; Moltke also deliberately deceived his own government by urging his opposite number in Austria to mobilise

Key question
Why did Germany go to war?

Table 3.4: Timeline: war timetable 1914

Date	Event
28 June	Assassination of Franz Ferdinand and his wife at Sarajevo
5 July	The 'blank cheque' offered by Germany to Austria
23 July	Austria sent its ultimatum to Serbia
28 July	Austrian declaration of war on Serbia and Belgrade attacked
29 July	Partial mobilisation by Russia
31 July	Full mobilisation by Russia
1 August	German declaration war on Russia
3 August	German declaration of war on France and invasion of Belgium
4 August	British declaration of war on Germany

and prepare for an immediate war which would be a general mobilisation against Russia.

The important strategic point is that Moltke saw the summer of 1914 as the best opportunity for war; even before the assassination, he had declared in the May that Germany was ready for war, but, by 1917, its position would be much weaker because of Russia's rearmament. Also, Moltke and the generals recognised that once Russia had fully mobilised, Germany would be strategically committed to fight. By 30 July military matters were beginning to take precedence over diplomacy. As Bethmann himself had stated at a meeting: 'things are out of control and the stone has started to roll'. This would bring into play Germany's military plan drawn up by Moltke's predecessor, Alfred von Schlieffen.

The Schlieffen Plan

Germany's military leaders had long recognised the weakness of their position if faced by a combined attack from Russia in the east and France in the west. The **Schlieffen Plan**, named after the former German Chief of the General Staff, had been deliberately devised as a means of dealing with such a possibility. This would be achieved by an all-out assault in the west in order to defeat France before Russia could mobilise; once France had been defeated, the German armies could turn east to face the Russians.

In simple terms, the plan involved a surprise move in the west through Belgium and Luxembourg so as to encircle Paris and the French fortress towns close to the Franco-German frontier. It was hoped that this would bring about the defeat of France within six weeks. This would then enable the transfer of German troops to the east to face the Russian armies which, because of the state's backwardness, it was thought would take six weeks to mobilise.

Although attractive in theory, the final draft of the plan produced by Schlieffen in 1905 raised a number of points. In order to advance on a broad front the plan would need to violate the neutrality of Belgium, the Netherlands and Luxembourg without regard to the possible political consequences of such actions. This was yet another indication of the dominating influence of the military in the decision-making process of

Key term

Schlieffen Plan Germany's military strategy in 1914. Its purpose was to avoid a two-front war by winning victory on the Western Front before dealing with the threat from Russia on the Eastern Front. It aimed to defeat France within six weeks by a massive German offensive in northern France and Belgium in order to seize Paris quickly.

Key date

Schlieffen Plan devised: 1905

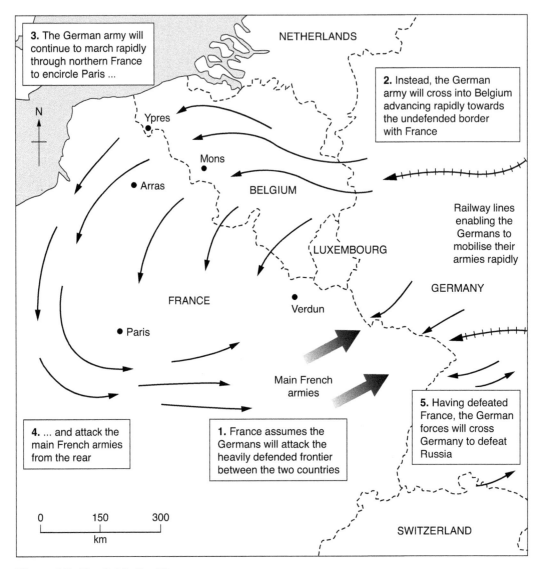

3. The German army will continue to march rapidly through northern France to encircle Paris ...

NETHERLANDS

2. Instead, the German army will cross into Belgium advancing rapidly towards the undefended border with France

N

Ypres

Mons

Arras

BELGIUM

Railway lines enabling the Germans to mobilise their armies rapidly

LUXEMBOURG

GERMANY

FRANCE

Verdun

Paris

Main French armies

5. Having defeated France, the German forces will cross Germany to defeat Russia

4. ... and attack the main French armies from the rear

1. France assumes the Germans will attack the heavily defended frontier between the two countries

0   150   300

km

SWITZERLAND

Figure 3.5: The Schlieffen Plan.

Imperial Germany. In addition, the plan was made at a time when Tsarist Russia had political and military difficulties and consequently it was assumed that Russian mobilisation would be slow. So, although amendments to the plan were made before 1914, this timescale was unchanged and assumed a six-week window of opportunity (see Figure 3.5).

The outbreak of world war

Russia's partial mobilisation on 29 July was a diplomatic tool to put pressure on Austria. However, Bethmann made it clear to Russia that unless it cancelled the partial mobilisation Germany would be compelled to mobilise their forces fully. This put Russia in an invidious position: either to face another climb-down (like Bosnia) or to order full mobilisation to defend itself against a possible German attack. When Russia then, understandably, decided on 31 July to go for the second option, the German political and military leadership took the lead and raised the stakes by:

- giving an ultimatum that Russia demobilise its forces within 12 hours
- asking France to state its position in the event of a Russo-German war.

In response, France replied that 'she would be guided by her own interests' and mobilised its troops; while Russia did not reply to the ultimatum. The diplomatic gamble had failed and Bethmann recognised what now had to be done. War was declared on Russia on 1 August and against France, two days later, on 3 August. Because of crucial strategic timing of the Schlieffen Plan, Germany had no time to lose.

By the end of July the chances of Britain remaining neutral were already waning. Grey and the British ambassador had both made it clear that it was *not* in Britain's interests to stand aside and allow Germany to dominate Europe, although opinion in the cabinet was somewhat divided over entry into the war. However, the prospect of Belgium being invaded as part of the Schlieffen Plan clarified the government and public opinion in favour of drawing Britain into war with Germany. Once Belgium refused to accept Germany's request for free passage to Belgian territory, German troops marched across the frontier. Britain protested at the violation of **Belgian neutrality** and demanded the withdrawal of German troops. When Germany ignored this ultimatum, Britain declared war at midnight on 4 August.

Key term

Belgian neutrality
Britain had guaranteed Belgian neutrality by the 1839 Treaty of London. Notoriously, Bethmann referred to it in 1914 as 'a scrap of paper', a comment which contributed to the harshness of the Treaty of Versailles, as it was taken to mean that Germany did not respect treaties.

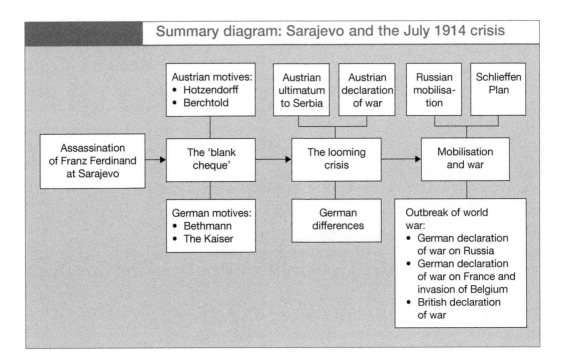

Summary diagram: Sarajevo and the July 1914 crisis

7 | The Key Debate

The majority of historians now do acknowledge the responsibility of Germany for the outbreak of the First World War. As Berghahn bluntly states: 'the historian does not any longer have to undertake a round-trip through the capitals of Europe to locate those primarily responsible. They were sitting in Berlin.' This, however, leaves the rather more debatable question:

> Was Germany really responsible for pursuing a war of aggression and conquest?

'A planned and executed war of aggression'

Fischer's interpretation has been massively influential. He maintained that German policy of *Weltpolitik* from 1897 was consciously working towards expansionism. More controversially, he believed that the German leadership from 1911 consistently pursued a policy aimed at fighting a European war as a means of achieving world-power status for Germany. However, Fischer's views and approach have not been without significant criticism. In particular, the evidence suggesting that Germany was actively planning an offensive war from as early as 1911, is limited.

'Escape forwards'

In the 1970s many of the structuralist historians, like Wehler (see pages 30–1), were strongly influenced by Fischer. However, in their attempt to explain the outbreak of war, they very much place their emphasis on domestic factors and highlight the crucial effects of the accumulating domestic pressures in 1912–14: the budget deficit, the growing political power of the Social Democrats and the Zabern affair (see page 44). They see these events as indicative of a fundamental internal crisis which encouraged the Prusso-German élites to pursue a war policy as a means of deflecting political opposition and thereby preserving their own threatened position. This is generally referred to as the 'escape forwards' theory. Some go even further and suggest that the *Kaiserreich* was virtually 'ungovernable'; that it had become 'a **polycracy** of forces' which counteracted each other and made coherent decision-making impossible. According to such an analysis, the structure of the *Kaiserreich* was so chaotic that the pursuit of an offensive war policy was effectively beyond the government's capability.

> **Key term**
>
> **Polycracy**
> A term used to describe a government system with an increasing range of competing power blocs.

'An offensively conducted defensive war'

Some conservative German historians have come to criticise Fischer severely for over-emphasising Germany's aggressive and expansionist tendencies. They have revived the view from the inter-war years that Europe had stumbled into war. Indeed, they have suggested that 1914 was an 'offensively conducted defensive war' by Germany resorting to a preventive strike as an attempt to break free from the pressures brought about by diplomatic isolation and the threatening power of Russia. This has most recently been taken further and placed on an even more abstract level by Stürmer, who argues that the exposed **geostrategic** position of Germany must be seen as one of the vital factors in the making of German foreign policy.

'Calculated risk'

Alternatively, it has been suggested by historians, like Pogge von Strandmann, that the German leadership undertook a 'calculated risk' to strengthen Germany's domestic and diplomatic situation. He does not believe that the Kaiser and Bethmann actually planned the war, though he maintains that German foreign policy was a consistently expansionist one before 1914. Significantly, he thinks that in July 1914 Germany assessed war as a viable option – one seen as a limited war, mainly because it could be won.

Conclusion

In a chapter on German foreign policy, it must be remembered that the outbreak of the First World War happened in the context of Europe at the turn of the century. Powerful forces – technological, economic, ideological and demographic – were at work and they helped to shape the international situation and make the war possible. However, to emphasise the primacy of such long-term factors is dangerously close to suggesting that the war was somehow inevitable. An interesting modern comparison might be that all the ingredients existed from the late 1940s to the late 1980s for another worldwide conflict, but the flashpoints of the Cold War never did actually develop into a Third World War. As J. Röhl has written:

> To argue that an event had deep causes and profound consequences is surely not to say that the deep causes were sufficient in themselves to bring about the event. It is my belief that the deeper causes ... were necessary, certainly, to produce the kind of war which broke out in 1914, but that those deeper factors (which had after all been present in the European situation for several decades prior to the outbreak of war) did not lead by themselves to a self-activation of war. The deeper causes were necessary but not sufficient. What is still missing is the decision-making dimension.

When one looks at the evidence from this level, it is difficult to escape from the conclusion that the German leadership must shoulder the major responsibility for both the worsening international climate in the years before 1914 and also for turning the July crisis of 1914 into a European war.

You will have learned from this chapter that German *Weltpolitik* and the ham-fisted diplomacy that accompanied it contributed to an increase in international tension and, by 1907, to a deterioration in Germany's position. Significantly, in the following years there was no real attempt by Germany to overcome this. There was no willingness to compromise as a way to encourage conciliation and trust or to improve the prospects for peace. Instead, German foreign policy was generally of a warmongering nature that was prepared to take risks. In part, this was made necessary by Germany's determination to stand by its one remaining reliable ally, Austria-Hungary.

This policy and approach came to a head in the German response to events in the crisis of July 1914. From early July, Bethmann chose a policy that involved taking calculated risks in the hope of winning a diplomatic victory that would decisively weaken the *Entente*. To this end, the crisis was deliberately worsened and there were no attempts at constructive mediation. All this was done because it was believed that the failure of diplomacy would lead to a war with the *Entente* powers, which, in the view of the generals, Germany could win. Thus, when Russia did mobilise in July 1914, Germany willingly accepted the challenge, declared war on Russia and France and began to implement the Schlieffen Plan.

Some key books in the debate

V. Berghahn, *Germany and the Approach of War in 1914* (London, 1973).

P. Kennedy, *The Rise of Anglo-German Antagonism* (Allen & Unwin, 1982).

H. Koch (ed.), *Origins of the First World War* (Macmillan, 1984).

G. Schöllgen (ed.), *Escape into War? The Foreign Policy of Imperial Germany* (Berg, 1991).

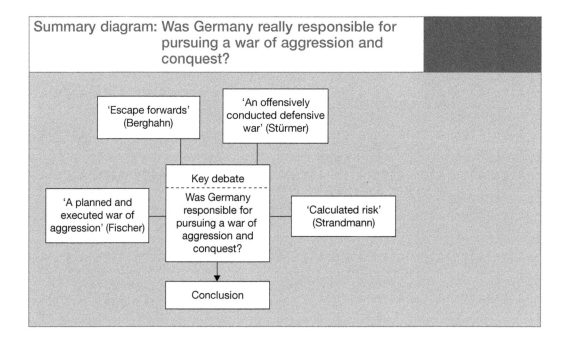

Summary diagram: Was Germany really responsible for pursuing a war of aggression and conquest?

Study Guide: A2 Question

How far do you agree with the view that Germany's miscalculations explain the outbreak of war in 1914? Explain your answer, using Sources 1–3 and your own knowledge of the issues related to this controversy.

Source 1

From: Geoff Layton, From Kaiser to Führer: Germany 1900–45 for Edexcel, *published in 2009.*

From early July [1914], Bethmann chose a policy that involved taking calculated risks in the hope of winning a diplomatic victory that would decisively weaken the *Entente*. To this end, the crisis was deliberately worsened and there were no attempts at constructive mediation. All this was done because it was believed that the failure of diplomacy would lead to a war with the *Entente* powers, which, in the view of the generals, Germany could win. Thus when Russia did mobilise in July 1914, Germany willingly accepted the challenge.

Source 2

From: W. Carr, A History of Germany 1815–1945, *published in 1979.*

Everything pointed to 1914 as the year of decision for Germany; she could either seize this last chance of breaking the ring of encirclement and asserting her 'right' to absolute hegemony in Europe, or, if a diplomatic victory was no longer possible, she would at least fight for hegemony in the most favourable circumstances. When a Great Power is prepared to run such appalling risks, it must bear a major share of responsibility for the outbreak of war should the gamble fail. This by no means exhausts the question of war guilt. Other powers contributed to the general deterioration in the international situation and committed tactical errors in July 1914.

Source 3

From: J. Laver, Imperial and Weimar Germany 1890–1933, *published in 1992.*

The extent to which Germany was culpable of bringing about war through support of Austria in the crisis of 1914; the country's bellicose behaviour generally; and the extent to which Germany, like other Powers, was simply caught up in the rush to the abyss, characteristic of 'war by timetable' – these are issues of debate. Other contentious issue include: the extent to which German Governments simply miscalculated, for example in their estimates of British intentions.

Exam tips

The cross-references are intended to take you straight to the material that will help you to answer the question.

This question provides you with sources that contain different views on the reasons why the First World War broke out and asks you to use them, together with your own knowledge, to discuss the statement. It is important to treat questions of this type differently from the way you would plan an essay answer. If you ignore the sources, you will lose more than half the marks available. The sources raise issues for you. You can use them as the core of your plan since they will always contain points which relate to the claim stated in the question. Make sure you have identified all the issues raised by the sources, and then add in your own knowledge – both to make more of the issues in the sources (add depth to the coverage) and to add new points (extend the range covered). In the advice given below, links are made to the relevant pages where information can be found.

The claim in the question, that war came about as a result of Germany's miscalculations, is contained in Source 3. In contrast, Source 1 emphasises 'calculated risk' and suggests that Germany was following a policy designed to strengthen Germany's diplomatic position and was prepared to pursue it into open conflict.

Source 2 also agrees that German diplomatic policy was prepared to run 'appalling risks' and, if need be, fight in 'favourable circumstances'. You should use your own knowledge to extend this discussion of the 'defensive aggression' (page 76) explanation.

The sources also introduce other issues on which you should expand:

- how far Germany's support of Austria was culpable (page 70)
- how far Germany was caught up in a war by timetable (page 73)
- how far other powers contributed to the deterioration in the international situation by 1914 (page 73)
- how far other powers committed tactical errors in July 1914 (pages 70–5).

Additionally, you should consider the 'escape forwards' (page 76) theory which also lends weight to the view that Germany was following a policy designed to produce conflict.

You should reach a clearly stated judgement on whether you favour 'miscalculation' or other explanations after consideration of the weight of evidence in the sources and in your reading.

4 Germany in War and Revolution 1914–19

POINTS TO CONSIDER

The First World War has fundamental significance for the history of Germany, as it served as the stimulus for key changes. Germany entered the First World War still largely an authoritarian monarchy; four years later in 1918 following humiliating defeat at the hands of the Allies, the *Kaiserreich* was to collapse. Its long-term consequences were to affect Germany for a generation. These points will be covered in Chapters 5–14.

This chapter will examine the following themes:

* The course of the war 1914–18
* The impact of the war on Germany: Social, economic and political effects
* The German Revolution 1918–19
* The National Constituent Assembly
* The key debate: Did Ebert and the SPD leadership betray the German Revolution?

Key dates

1914	September	Battle of Marne: failure of Schlieffen Plan
1915		Unrestricted submarine warfare began (but ended after the sinking of the *Lusitania*)
1916		Battles of Verdun and Somme
	August	Establishment of 'the silent dictatorship' under Hindenburg and Ludendorff
	December	Auxiliary Service Law introduced
1917	February	Unrestricted submarine warfare restarted
	April	Entry of USA into the war
	April	Split of SPD; creation of USPD
	July	Resignation of Bethmann and replacement by Michaelis
		Peace resolution
1918	March	Treaty of Brest-Litovsk
	August 8	'Black day' of German army
	October 3	Prince Max of Baden appointed Chancellor

	November 2	Grand Fleet mutiny at Kiel
	November 9	Kaiser fled to the Netherlands; Ebert appointed Chancellor; Germany proclaimed a republic
	November 11	Armistice signed at Compiègne
1919	January 5	Start of Spartacist uprising in Berlin
	February 6	National Constituent Assembly met at Weimar

1 | The Course of the War 1914–18

It is tempting to suggest that Germany's eventual military defeat in autumn 1918 is a good example of how one factor can prove decisive in the outcome of a major ongoing event, such as a war. In this case it seems that Germany's inability to achieve a quick victory in the autumn of 1914 resulted in a lengthy war for which the country was militarily and economically unprepared and strategically ill suited.

Battle of Marne: failure of Schlieffen Plan leading to stalemate: September 1914

Key date

The breakdown of the Schlieffen Plan

The Schlieffen Plan had been deliberately devised as a means of dealing with the possibility of combined attack on both Western and Eastern Fronts (see pages 73–4). The plan had dangers from the start, but Moltke, the Chief of the **Supreme Army Command**, made a number of significant changes. The proposed advance through the Netherlands was abandoned to prevent the risk of any Dutch involvement in the war and, because of concern about the strength of the likely French assault in Alsace-Lorraine, some forces were moved to the south. Whether the effects of these changes were decisive in the failure of the plan has long been disputed. What does seem clear is that, even before the first shots had been fired, the military odds were not in Germany's favour. The Schlieffen Plan did not provide any guarantee of success, and yet its failure was likely to draw Germany into a war with a doubtful outcome.

Although in late August the Allies were in retreat and the Schlieffen Plan was coming close to success, Germany's optimism ebbed away in September when they faced the realities of the military situation:

- Russia had mobilised faster than expected and in desperation Moltke transferred additional German army units to the Eastern Front.
- The main offensive came up against stiffer than expected Belgian resistance.
- The invasion of Belgium led to the arrival of the British Expeditionary Force (BEF) to bolster the left flank of the Allies.

The German lines of communication lengthened, so the speed of their advance slowed. Moltke then decided not to encircle Paris, but to move to the east of the French capital. This exposed his flank to a counter-attack and, in September 1914, at the Battle of

Key question
Why did the Schlieffen Plan fail?

Supreme Army Command
The highest level of command in the German army.

Key term

the Marne, the Germans were forced to retreat. The Schlieffen Plan had failed. Moltke suffered a nervous breakdown and resigned and was replaced by Falkenhayn as the chief of Army Command. Admittedly, on the Eastern Front the Germans had gained a couple of memorable victories against Russia, but that country was still very much in the war and a very real threat to Austria, Germany's major ally.

The implications of Germany's inability to gain the intended quick victory were far-reaching. It was **stalemate** and along the Western Front the two sides had dug in trenches for 400 miles. By November 1914 Germany was confronted with a war on two fronts for which it was not prepared militarily, or economically. The generals had long recognised the dangers of such a situation, but in the end their plan had been unable to prevent it. If Germany was to win the war, it had to develop a workable alternative strategy.

Key question
What were the limitations of German strategy in 1915–16?

Key terms

Stalemate
A deadlock in war where neither side makes progress.

Dardanelles campaign
Took place at the Gallipoli peninsula of Turkey in 1915. British (and Empire) and French troops aimed to capture Constantinople and secure a sea route to Russia. The attempt failed, with heavy casualties on both sides.

Key date

Unrestricted submarine warfare began (but ended after the sinking of the *Lusitania*): 1915

The failure of alternative strategies

Throughout 1915 Germany struggled to come up with an appropriate long-term strategy to overcome the military stalemate. Victories on the Eastern Front against Russia and the withdrawal of the Allies from the **Dardanelles campaign** could not alter the fact that time was against Germany. The Allies had already gained the maritime advantage by seizing German colonies and destroying its roving cruisers that had successfully preyed on unarmed British merchant vessels. More significantly, Britain had imposed a naval blockade, which severely limited Germany's ability to import essential foodstuffs and raw materials.

Unrestricted submarine warfare

The German response to this threat is telling evidence of the leadership's inability to develop a co-ordinated and purposeful strategy. Although Admiral Tirpitz wanted to engage the British Fleet in battle in order to break the blockade, other voices felt that this was far too dangerous since it risked the loss of the German High Seas Fleet. When the risk was taken, at the Battle of Jutland in 1916, the outcome was inconclusive, and the German fleet never ventured out from its base again. As an alternative, Tirpitz consequently pressed for the use of unrestricted submarine warfare and the sinking of all ships bound for Britain irrespective of their nationality. This too led to fierce controversy. There were doubts about the morality, as well as the effectiveness of the policy. Bethmann was also rightly aware of the possible diplomatic consequences for the neutral USA.

However, the Chancellor accepted military advice and in February 1915 unrestricted submarine warfare was introduced. It was short lived and, following the sinking of the liner *Lusitania* in September with the loss of 1098 lives, it was brought to an end. In February 1916 the policy was readopted only to be dropped again within a few weeks when the USA threatened to break off diplomatic relations. At this point Tirpitz resigned. Such inconsistency was a sign of the divisions and uncertainties within the German leadership about how the war could be brought to a successful conclusion.

Attrition

The limitations of German planning were further revealed in 1916. Falkenhayn believed that the war could only be won on the Western Front and, to this end, his plan to launch a massive assault against the key French fortress town of Verdun was accepted. His declared aim was to 'bleed the French army white on the anvil of Verdun'. The casualties on both sides were horrifying but the French held on. The failure at Verdun along with the losses suffered in the Battle of the Somme, fought later in the same year, undermined Falkenhayn's position completely and he was replaced in the summer of 1916 by the joint leadership of Paul von Hindenburg and Erich Ludendorff (see profiles on pages 161 and 93).

During the years 1915–16 Germany had been unable to break the deadlock created by the failure of the Schlieffen Plan. As one military historian has put it: 'What they [the Germans] could not do was escape from the remorseless logic of a two-front war.' And as victory failed to materialise the economic pressures of conflict grew more intense.

> Battles of Verdun and Somme: 1916 Key date

German propaganda of the First World War: (*left*) a 1917 poster uses the image of a submarine to encourage Germans to buy war bonds; (*right*) Germanica appears above the slogan 'God punish England'.

Submarine warfare and the entry of the USA into the war

Key question
How effective was unrestricted submarine warfare?

Key terms

Convoy system
Organised naval protection of the merchant navy. From 1917 the British Admiralty introduced a system for the Royal Navy to counter the threat of submarines to merchant ships.

Central Powers
The name for Germany and its allies: Austria-Hungary, Turkey and Bulgaria.

Although Hindenburg and Ludendorff were determined to pursue the war with the utmost vigour, they were unable to offer any new military strategy. There was no way out of the deadlock on the Western Front and the passage of time simply played further into the hands of the Allies. It was this dilemma which encouraged the military to press for the reintroduction of unrestricted submarine warfare in the belief that this would bring Britain to its knees. Bethmann remained unconvinced by this 'miracle cure' and its possible side-effects. Even so, by January 1917 he had become unpopular and was politically too isolated to offer effective opposition to the plan (see pages 96–7). The following month a new submarine campaign was launched.

Within a few months, the failure of the policy was only too apparent. Admittedly, Britain initially suffered catastrophic losses, but the introduction of the **convoy system** proved decisive in reducing the losses to tolerable levels. By 1918 it was clear that the Germans were losing the submarine war. More significantly, the US decision to enter the war in April 1917 proved a major contributory factor to the Allied military campaign. The military situation was now stacked against Germany. The resources of the world's greatest economic power were mobilised in the interests of the Allies while the economic strains on Germany and the **Central Powers** continued to increase.

The final German offensive

Key question
How and why did Germany fail to exploit the collapse of Russia?

Key terms

Bolsheviks
Followers of Bolshevism – Russian communism.

Armistice
An agreement to cease fire before drawing up a peace settlement.

Reparations
Payments of money (and gold) and the transfer of property and equipment from the defeated to the victor after war.

As 1917 drew to a close, Germany's defeat seemed only a matter of time. The fact that Germany did not actually surrender until November 1918 was mainly due to events in Russia. There, the revolution and the establishment of the **Bolsheviks**' regime in November 1917 resulted in Russia seeking an **armistice** with Germany followed by a negotiated peace in March 1918, the Treaty of Brest-Litovsk, with the following terms:

- the previously Russian territories of Poland, Lithuania and Latvia were annexed by Germany
- the territories of Estonia and Ukraine became in effect German spheres of economic or military influence
- Russia had to pay three billion roubles in **reparations**.

These events provided a window of opportunity for the German leadership. Not only did they boost civilian and military morale at a critical time, but they also freed Germany from the two-front war and opened up the chance to snatch victory by concentrating German military might on the Western Front.

Although Germany's intended victory offensive in the west at first made considerable progress, the Allied lines were never decisively broken and the offensive slowly ground to a halt. There were several reasons for this. Ironically, the German Supreme Command still kept one and a half million men on the Eastern Front to maintain control over the won territory. Such numbers

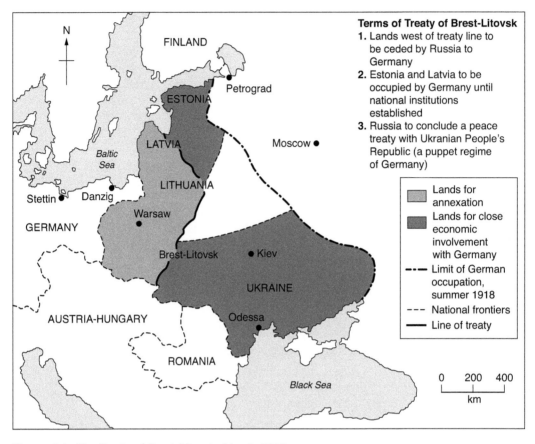

Terms of Treaty of Brest-Litovsk
1. Lands west of treaty line to be ceded by Russia to Germany
2. Estonia and Latvia to be occupied by Germany until national institutions established
3. Russia to conclude a peace treaty with Ukranian People's Republic (a puppet regime of Germany)

Figure 4.1: The Treaty of Brest-Litovsk, March 1918.

could have provided vital reserves to keep the momentum of advance during the offensive on the Western Front. Instead, German troops on the Western Front were faced by ever-increasing numbers of US troops. These men were fresh and had not been subjected to the demoralising effects of trench warfare over the previous three years. When the Allies counter-attacked on 8 August, the German army's 'black day', its troops proved incapable of withstanding the assault, although their retreat remained an orderly one. By mid-September the final German defensive positions had been broken and the western region of Germany faced the very real possibility of invasion. In south-eastern Europe, Germany's allies all faced imminent collapse. Even Hindenburg and Ludendorff at last recognised the extent of the crisis and on 29 September they advised the Kaiser that Germany must make enquiries to request an armistice. The war had been lost.

Unrestricted submarine warfare restarted: February 1917

Entry of USA into the war: April 1917

Treaty of Brest-Litovsk: March 1918

'Black day' of German army: 8 August 1918

Key dates

Conclusion

When the war broke out in 1914 it was assumed in Germany, as well as in all the Great Powers, that the conflict would not last very long. However, by late September 1918, after four years of bloody war, Germany faced military defeat. The reasons for its eventual collapse go right back to the early days of August 1914, but the pressures had developed over the years that followed. The main factors can be identified as follows:

- *Germany's failure to achieve rapid victory in the summer of 1914.* The German Supreme Command's strategy was built on the notion of a quick victory in order to avoid a long, drawn-out conflict with the Allies. By the autumn of 1914 the Schlieffen Plan had failed to gain a rapid victory.
- *Stalemate.* Germany was forced to fight the war on two fronts: the east and the west. The balance of military power resulted in a war of stalemate that put immense pressures on Imperial Germany. The situation was made particularly difficult for Germany by the Allies' naval blockade, which seriously limited the import of all supplies. And, although the German policy of unrestricted submarine warfare at first seriously threatened Britain, it did not decisively weaken the country.
- *Strengths of the Allies.* Britain and France were major colonial powers and could call on their overseas empires for personnel, resources and supplies. Furthermore, from April 1917, the Allies were strengthened by the USA's entry into the war, which resulted in the mobilisation of two million men. In contrast, Germany was supported by relatively weak allies (see Table 4.1).
- *Limitations of German war economy.* Imperial Germany was totally unprepared for the economic costs of a prolonged war. It made great efforts to mobilise the war effort and arms production was dramatically increased. However, the economy was seriously dislocated, which wrecked the government's finances and increased social tension.

Table 4.1: Military capacity of the two sides

	Central Powers	Allied Powers (excluding USA)
Population in 1913 (millions)	119.0	259.2
Percentage of world's manufacturing in 1913	19.2	27.9
Mobilised forces (millions)	24.7	36.9

A last German chance to escape from the military defeat came when Russia signed the Treaty of Brest-Litovsk in March 1918. This immediately enabled Germany to launch its last major offensive on to the Western Front. Unfortunately, it was unable to maintain the momentum and, by August, German troops were being forced to retreat. The hoped-for military victory had not materialised.

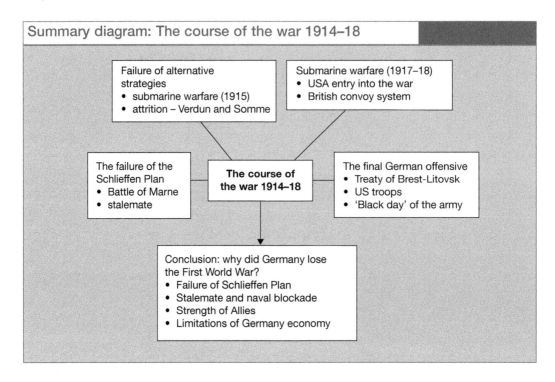

Summary diagram: The course of the war 1914–18

Failure of alternative strategies
• submarine warfare (1915)
• attrition – Verdun and Somme

Submarine warfare (1917–18)
• USA entry into the war
• British convoy system

The failure of the Schlieffen Plan
• Battle of Marne
• stalemate

The course of the war 1914–18

The final German offensive
• Treaty of Brest-Litovsk
• US troops
• 'Black day' of the army

Conclusion: why did Germany lose the First World War?
• Failure of Schlieffen Plan
• Stalemate and naval blockade
• Strength of Allies
• Limitations of Germany economy

2 | The Impact of the War on Germany: Social, Economic and Political Effects

Germany went to war in August 1914 united in a patriotic fervour against what was perceived as the threat posed by 'barbaric Russia'. Numerous writers, who saw the war as a mixture of adventure and liberation, caught the mood of the moment. Bruno Frank's contemporary poem was typical:

Proud Times, 1914
Rejoice, friends, that we are alive
And that we're young and nimble!
Never was there a year like this,
And never such a gift for youth!
It is given to us to take our stand or to strike out
Eastwards or westwards.
The greatest of all of earth's ages
Sets its brand upon our young hearts.

Burgfriede

This view was reflected at a political level as well. A political truce, *Burgfriede*, was agreed between all the political parties and the laws for necessary loans to finance the war were passed unanimously. In the words of the Kaiser to the *Reichstag*: 'I know no parties any more, only Germans.'

Even the Social Democrats, who for so long had been viewed as unpatriotic pacifist 'enemies of the state', promised their support for a defensive war. Their attitude came as a surprise to many in the military who had been seriously considering the need to make

Key question
How strong was the *Burgfriede* in Germany?

Burgfriede
A (political) truce.

Key term

mass arrests and to impose press censorship as a way of keeping them in check. However, such methods were not required for several reasons. First, the party was taken in by the way the government successfully managed to portray the war as a defensive war. Secondly, many Social Democrats were naturally very patriotic and were genuinely proud of their country's achievements. This led to a belief that, by showing loyalty in the nation's hour of crisis, the party could gain political recognition. In the long run, they thought that this would increase the possibility of Germany becoming a truly democratic nation.

The failure to secure a quick victory and the onset of military stalemate by Christmas 1914 certainly did much to undermine the enthusiastic spirit of August 1914. However, critical views remained few in number during the first half of the war. Lulled into a false sense of security by the power of the military censors and government propaganda, the public mood remained confident of eventual victory. It was only during 1916, with the losses at Verdun and on the Somme, that doubts began to be expressed about the way the war was going. The *Burgfriede* had lasted well over the first two years during which time the government had faced no real opposition from the public or the *Reichstag*. There, debates were limited to the leadership, where individuals and factions competed to exert the greatest influence.

Key question
What were the economic consequences of the war?

Germany's economic limitations

The imposition of the blockade and the demands of a long, drawn-out war created enormous economic strains:

- German banks and export industries were badly disrupted.
- Germany's capacity to produce enough food to feed the population was limited.
- The ability to import raw materials was severely curtailed; materials such as oil, rubber, nitrates, copper and mercury were vital for war production.

Of course, Germany was not alone in experiencing such problems, but surrounded by enemies, its circumstances meant that the situation was more difficult. Therefore, success in the war necessitated the total mobilisation of the nation's economy.

KRA

The urgency of the situation was soon recognised. Walther Rathenau, the owner of AEG (see page 8), worked to create the **KRA** (War Raw Materials Department), within the War Ministry. The KRA oversaw a range of companies whose job it was to acquire, store and distribute the most vital raw materials in the interests of the war effort. Such direct government intervention was most clearly shown over the shortage of nitrates. These were central to the manufacture of explosives. The KRA not only established a chemicals section, but also backed the construction of several plants to produce nitrates by an artificial process. Within six months, the KRA had successfully organised the

Key term

KRA
Kriegsrohstoffabteilung: War Raw Materials Department.

provision of most essential supplies and prevented the looming munitions crisis.

Labour

State intervention also became increasingly apparent in other fields. Labour was affected by the role of the War Ministry in deciding who should be conscripted and who exempted from military service. There was also the need to prevent industrial unrest. This led to the creation of local War Boards made up of representatives of management and labour. There were also attempts to control consumption by means of rationing and price controls and so ensure a fair distribution of scarce goods. Even so, there was still growing discontent amongst the civilian population (see pages 97–8).

In the short term, the measures to regulate the war economy were reasonably successful. However, when military victory was not forthcoming in 1915–16, two important economic weaknesses continued to erode Germany's capacity to maintain the fighting. These were the government budget and the provision of food.

Finance

Germany had already been running a massive government debt in peacetime, and it saw it increase rapidly once the war started. The sale of **war bonds** represented the only real attempt to narrow the gap between income and expenditure. The idea of raising taxes on income and industrial profits, the burden of which would have fallen mainly on the rich, was rejected on political grounds. The cost of the war was simply put to one side until the end of the war when compensation in the form of reparations could be demanded from the defeated countries. Altogether, only 16 per cent of the cost of the war was met from taxation; the rest of the cost was met from funding such as war bonds and the printing of more money. Such a massive expansion of the amount of money in circulation not only started inflation within Germany, but also reduced the value of the mark internationally.

Food

Perhaps even more disturbing was Germany's inability to feed itself. The effects of the blockade and the conscription of so many able-bodied males, who had formerly worked on the land, led to a decline in grain supply and production. However, attempts to establish government control over the powerful lobby of the agricultural landowners were unsuccessful. Eventually, a War Nutrition Office was set up to regulate food supplies, but it met massive resistance from the powerful agricultural lobby and its measures proved inadequate. Production continued to decline and, because insufficient food was made available at the regulated prices, a **black market** flourished.

Key terms

War bonds
In order to raise money for the war, Imperial Germany encouraged people to invest into government funds in the belief they were helping to finance the war and their savings were secure.

Black market
The underground economy where goods are sold at unregulated prices.

Key date

Auxiliary Service Law introduced: December 1916

Auxiliary Service Law

By the end of 1916 the economic situation was such that the Supreme Army Command was determined to intensify the war effort by a clearly defined set of targets. The Hindenburg programme aimed to increase arms production massively by placing contracts directly with heavy industry, while the introduction of the Auxiliary Service Law was supposed to achieve 'the mobilisation of the entire civilian population for war service'. The law demanded service for all able-bodied Germans during the war and curtailed the freedom of workers to change jobs. In fact, both ideas fell short of their objectives and problems of labour and production continued to hinder the German war effort.

'Total war'

Key term

Total war
A war that spared neither the military nor the civilian population, forcing Germany to use the power of the state as a means of mobilising its economic potential.

The onset of '**total war**' forced Germany to use state power as a means to mobilise its economic potential. However, there were limits to how far this policy could go because of the reaction of certain key interest groups. Ironically, authoritarian Germany failed to achieve the same degree of mobilisation as in democratic Britain where wartime agreement among the civilian population proved to be more productive in the long run. In Germany, the First World War did not result in a state-controlled economy:

- Government financial policy was unchanged.
- Industries were not nationalised.
- The property rights of landowners were left relatively untouched.

In this sense the German economy was never fully mobilised to meet the military demands of the situation. Yet, as we will see, the consequences of this economic policy were to be disastrous in the long term for the stability of the *Kaiserreich*, since the political blame for the nation's problems was increasingly laid on the state.

Political change

Key question
How and why did Germany become a military dictatorship?

It has already been seen how Germany's military leaders supported intervention in the nation's economy on the grounds that it was necessary in order to win the war. However, as the war progressed the military leadership became increasingly involved in political affairs.

First, there was the position of the Kaiser himself. Whatever controversies may exist about the Kaiser's political influence in the pre-war years, there is little doubt that he exerted no real control over political and military affairs during the war. His self-confidence and determination, already badly shaken by the *Daily Telegraph* affair, seemed to desert him with the onset of war and all its accompanying problems. Despite being supreme warlord, he was kept in the dark about military developments and his advice was rarely sought. As a political leader he was no more than a figurehead and an increasingly distant one at that. He did not even make a serious attempt to project a propaganda image of himself as the caring leader of his people, preferring instead to while away his time on his estates.

However, the impotence of the Kaiser also had important consequences for the power exerted by the Chancellor. Bethmann did not have popular backing and the *Burgfriede* in the *Reichstag* was pursued because of patriotic loyalty, not out of respect for the Chancellor. All along, Bethmann's power base was built on the support of the Kaiser and yet, as the war progressed, that support became increasingly unreliable. This left the Chancellor and his government more and more isolated and incapable of resisting the interference of the military.

The 'silent dictatorship'

In the summer of 1916 the developing political crisis came to a head. By this time, of course, the military situation was a cause of grave concern and many conservatives looked to blame Bethmann for abandoning the policy of unrestricted submarine warfare which had been introduced for the second time. This, in turn, made him conscious of the need to shore up his own political position by winning popular support. Therefore, he decided to ditch Falkenhayn and to replace him with the popular military hero Hindenburg, who had so successfully led the German forces on the Eastern Front. On 29 August 1916 Hindenburg and his deputy Ludendorff became joint leaders of the Supreme Command.

Establishment of 'the silent dictatorship' under Hindenburg and Ludendorff: August 1916

Key date

The emergence of Hindenburg and Ludendorff was indeed a turning point, but not in the way intended by Bethmann. Far from strengthening his position, the Chancellor soon found that the authority of both himself and the Kaiser had been seriously weakened. Neither of them enjoyed the popularity of Hindenburg and Ludendorff. By the simple means of their threatening resignation, the Supreme Command was able to exert a powerful influence over political, economic and military events. With the authority of the Emperor and the Chancellor so weakened, the two main props of Bismarck's constitution had been undermined.

To all intents and purposes effective power for the next two years lay with the so-called 'silent dictatorship' of the Supreme Army Command. As a result:

- Several opportunities for a negotiated peace were turned down.
- The Auxiliary Service Law was introduced to militarise society (see page 91).
- Hindenburg and Ludendorff forced the unfortunate Bethmann out of office (see pages 96–7) and on their instructions they replaced and promoted ministers.

In the final year of the war, the power of the Supreme Army Command reached new heights. The constitutional authority of the Emperor and the Chancellor was effectively sidelined. Even the *Reichstag*, having expressed its desire for peace, proved unable or unwilling to exert any further political pressure. Instead, the power of the army, which had been such a key feature of the *Kaiserreich* since its foundation, had, under the conditions of total war, eventually become obvious to everyone. The real masters of Germany were the 'silent dictators', Hindenburg and Ludendorff.

Profile: Erich Ludendorff 1865–1937

1865 – Born at Posen in Prussia

1914 – Appointed Chief-of-Staff to Hindenburg

1916 – Transferred to Western Front. Promoted to the post of Quartermaster General – virtual military dictator, 1916–18

1917 – Responsible for the dismissal of Chancellor Bethmann

1918 – Masterminded the German final offensive
– Fled to Sweden

1919 – Returned to Germany and took part in Kapp *putsch* of 1920 (see pages 131–3)

1923 – Collaborated with Hitler and was involved in Munich *putsch* (see pages 134–5)

1937 – Died

Ludendorff was a soldier of considerable ability, energy and enthusiasm. In the campaign in Belgium he showed considerable initiative and was soon sent to the Eastern Front with Hindenburg, he won major victories over the Russians. In 1916, the two men were posted to the Western Front and during the years that followed they were able to assume Supreme Command of the German war effort. By the end of the war, Ludendorff was, in effect, the wartime dictator of Germany and directed German military and political affairs. When it was clear that Germany had lost the war, he tried to direct the control of the constitutional reform in October 1918 and proposed the theory of the 'stab in the back' (see page 100). Afterwards, he became associated with the activities of Hitler's Nazi Party whose racial views he shared.

Key question
To what extent did the war affect the everyday lives of ordinary German people?

The human experience
Military morale

For those directly involved, the First World War was unlike any previous conflict. It is hard to convey in words the real horrors of that war. Its impact on millions of Germans was severe in the extreme. Germany's war dead totalled 1.8 million – 16 per cent of those conscripted. Millions more suffered permanent disabilities, both physical and mental (see Table 4.2). Of course, such statistics fail to convey the human and emotional consequences. Few families escaped the trauma of a death or a casualty. By 1918, a popular joke was circulating – 'What family is going to survive the

Table 4.2: Casualties of the First World War

Country	Dead	Wounded
Germany	1,773,700	4,216,058
Russia	1,700,000	4,950,000
France	1,357,800	4,266,000
Austria-Hungary	1,200,000	3,620,000
British Empire	908,371	2,090,212

war with all six sons alive?' The Kaiser had six sons and the joke was a bitter comment on Germany's human tragedy and the declining popularity of the royal family.

Any assessment of the results of such war experiences is fraught with difficulty. It is easy to generalise and it would be easy to be wrong. Perhaps the safe conclusion is the most accurate one: different people were affected in different ways. Some soldiers serving in the trenches were drawn into left-wing politics in the hope of creating a socialist society after the war. Others, like Adolf Hitler, found the discipline and camaraderie of the trenches fulfilling and so turned their experiences of patriotism and death into heroic ideals they wished to transfer to post-war German society. Many more simply grew resentful of the sacrifices made while rumours circulated about the luxury and indulgence to be found behind the lines among the higher ranking officers. Within the ranks of the navy things were very different, since the lack of military action led to boredom and frustration.

However, it should be noted that despite signs of resentment within the German military, there was no large-scale breakdown of discipline and order until the final few weeks of the war. Only when the war was lost and the political changes had begun did the discontent within the military machine lead to growing unrest (see page 102).

The home front

In 1914, the vast majority of Germans supported the war and for the first two years the effects were generally those of inconvenience rather than real hardship. Yet, by the winter of 1916–17 the declining living standards, as well as the bleak military situation, began to affect the everyday lives of ordinary Germans. Discontent on the home front grew because of:

- Food and fuel shortages. The exceptionally cold winter of 1916–17 contributed to severe food and fuel shortages in the cities. It was nicknamed the 'turnip winter' because the failure of the potato crop forced the German people to rely heavily on turnips, which were usually used for animal fodder.
- Civilian deaths. The number of civilian deaths from starvation and hypothermia increased from 121,000 in 1916 to 293,000 in 1918.
- Infant mortality. The number of infant deaths increased by over 50 per cent in the course of the war years.
- The flu epidemic. In 1918 Europe was hit by the 'Spanish flu', which killed between 20 and 40 million people – a figure higher than the casualties of the First World War. It has been cited as the most devastating epidemic in recorded world history probably because people's resistance to disease was lowered by the decline in living conditions.

The cartoon indicates that after two years of war the German people had not entirely lost their sense of humour. It reads: 'Look here woman, we've been at war with each other for some 20 years – and all this fuss about just two years!'

- Inflation. Workers were forced to work even longer hours, but wages fell below the inflation rate. Average prices doubled in Germany between 1914 and 1918, whereas wages rose by only 50–75 per cent (see Table 4.3).

Table 4.3: Indices of real wages 1913–19, where 1913 = 100

Year	Railway workers	Printers	Miners	Civil servants
1914	97.2	97.2	93.3	97.2
1916	69.2	60.6	74.4	58.9
1918	83.9	54.1	63.7	55.0

Social discontent, therefore, increased markedly in the final two years of the war. Considerable anger was expressed against the so-called 'sharks' of industry, who had made vast profits from the war. Resentment grew in the minds of many within the middle class because they felt that their social status had been lowered as their income declined. Above all, opposition began to grow against the political leaders, who had urged total war, but seemed incapable of ensuring equality of sacrifice. Such hostility was further evident in the heated political debate over Germany's war aims and came to a head in the events of 1918.

War aims

Key question
In what ways was Germany divided over the issue of war aims?

The issue of war aims was central to the political and economic changes taking place in wartime Germany and this went beyond a debate over mere territorial gains. It directly concerned the question of what kind of Germany was to exist after the war. Bethmann was keen to avoid a public debate on war aims. He saw the maintenance of the *Burgfriede* as essential and he feared that discussion of war aims would cause arguments at home and damage Germany's status, especially among neutral powers abroad.

Siegfriede

Bethmann's dilemma was that once the military stalemate had set in, two very different versions of the future peace began to emerge in Germany. On the one hand, there were those who believed that Germany was fighting a purely defensive war and not one aimed at conquest. This view was most clearly expressed within the ranks of the SPD, which believed that the peace should be based on compromise, reconciliation and no territorial gains. On the other hand, there were those who argued for a **Siegfriede**, a victory peace, by which Germany would use its position of strength to win control over Europe and finally achieve its long-cherished world-power status.

Siegfriede found expression in its most extreme form in the programme of the Pan-German League. The League stood for:

- the creation of a central African empire
- the annexation of key military and industrial regions in the Netherlands, Belgium and northern France
- the economic domination of western Europe for the benefit of Germany
- the annexation from Russia of extensive territories in the east.

Such ideas were not limited to a lunatic fringe of the extreme conservative right wing. The basic ideas of a *Siegfriede* were widely supported by many of the political parties (with the exception of the SPD) and among broad sections of the middle classes, as well as the upper classes.

However, this was not just a case of the nationalists wanting territorial gains. It was the result of a fear that, unless Germany achieved a decisive victory with territorial gains and compensation from the defeated countries, it would prove impossible to prevent Germany from undergoing great change. In this sense, the pursuit of the *Siegfriede* was seen as essential in order to maintain the status quo at home. A peace aimed at reconciliation would only encourage internal changes and reform.

> **Key term**
>
> *Siegfriede*
> A victory peace, which would establish Germany's supremacy in Europe.

The July 1917 crisis

The emergence of these two conflicting viewpoints created all sorts of problems from the start for Chancellor Bethmann, who wanted to maintain a united political front in the *Reichstag*. He worked hard to avoid creating divisions in the nation at large; he had even drafted a reform to the Prussian voting system to placate the public, although no date was fixed for this and it would not happen until after the war.

In the spring of 1917 the growing pressure from both left and right came to a head because of Germany's deteriorating situation – two factors were domestic and two were external:

- the worsening military position
- the increase of social discontent in Germany
- the entry of the USA into the war in April 1917
- the abdication of the Tsar in the Russian Revolution.

The dominating role of the Supreme Command totally undermined Bethmann's position and by April 1917 he felt obliged to endorse the *Kreuznach* programme of the military. This was a list of war aims that included extensive territorial gains in both east and west. Although the Chancellor claimed that this document would not stand in his way if a genuine chance of a negotiated peace came along, it was clear that his opportunity for manoeuvre was running out. Moreover, his apparent support for the *Kreuznach* programme inevitably reduced further his standing with the non-conservative forces on the left.

Key dates

Resignation of Bethmann and replacement by Michaelis: July 1917

Peace resolution: July 1917

In early July 1917, the leading Centre Party deputy Matthias Erzberger at last came out in a powerful speech and publicly declared that a negotiated peace was not only desirable, but necessary. He succeeded in forging a coalition of forces in the *Reichstag* suggesting a motion for peace without territorial gains:

> The *Reichstag* strives for a peace of understanding and permanent reconciliation of peoples. Forced territorial acquisitions and political, economic and financial oppressions are irreconcilable with such a peace.

The peace resolution was passed by 212 votes to 126 and it should have been a dramatic turning point. Wilhelm may have been unwilling to let his Chancellor go, and yet Bethmann was forced to resign. However, ironically, nothing was really achieved by the peace resolution. Ludendorff was not prepared to work with a Chancellor who sympathised with political change. Significantly, therefore, the newly appointed Chancellor was the colourless and unknown Georg Michaelis, who was described by one SPD deputy as 'the fairy angel tied to the Christmas tree at Christmas for the children's benefit'. By the end of the year Michaelis was removed and replaced by Georg Hertling, who was unable to satisfy the conflicting demands of the Supreme Command, the *Reichstag* and public opinion. It was clear where the real power still lay, and it was not with the *Reichstag*.

Polarisation

Key question
How did polarisation contribute to the collapse of Imperial Germany?

The *Reichstag* may have voted decisively in favour of the peace resolution, yet it did not seize the opportunity to press its own claims to political authority or to demand immediate peace negotiations with Allies. Instead, the political divisions polarised between the right and the left.

The right

Key term

Fatherland Party
Vaterlandspartei. A conservative right-wing party which supported the government's pursuit of the war and annexations.

The Supreme Army Command did not change its policy. Indeed, the position of the Chancellor merely served to strengthen further the political hold of Hindenburg and Ludendorff, who rejected out of hand anything less than the *Kreuznach* programme. To this end, a few months later Hindenburg and Ludendorff played an instrumental role in the creation of the **Fatherland Party**. This deliberately set out to mobilise mass support for the right wing in favour of maintaining the status quo and winning a *Siegfriede*. Led by Tirpitz and Kapp (see profiles on pages 64 and 132) and financially backed by some leading industrialists, it proved remarkably successful. By 1918 it boasted 1.2 million members.

The left

In contrast, the left was calling for a compromise peace without forced annexations and for constitutional reform. Its increasing influence was shaped not just by domestic developments, but also by the revolutionary events in Russia.

Split of SPD; creation of USPD: April 1917 — *Key date*

The SPD had already shown its differences before 1914 over the debate between evolutionary and revolutionary socialism (see page 26). In the spring of 1917, 42 deputies of the SPD broke away from the party and formed a new party, the USPD. It was wholly committed to bringing about a speedy end to the war and constitutional reform. On the far left there was the small **Spartacus League**, which was encouraged by the Bolsheviks (Communists) in Russia, and which aimed to overthrow capitalism in a socialist revolution.

This radicalisation was also evident in the masses. Dissatisfaction and unrest were expressed in a growing number of strikes and demonstrations (see Table 4.4), which were organised by the emerging **revolutionary stewards** in the factories and workshops. They were to play an increasingly significant role in the last year of the war and contributed to the creation of the workers' councils in the German Revolution, 1918–19 (see pages 100–8).

Table 4.4: Strikes and lock-outs 1915–19

Year	No. of strikes	No. of workers	Working days lost
1915	141	15,000	40,000
1917	562	668,000	1,860,000
1919	3719	2,132,000	33,080,000

Defeat in 1918

By early 1918 the *Kaiserreich* was under great pressure. The social discontent came to a head in January in widespread strikes in the major cities. In the capital Berlin half a million workers struck for five days in protest. The authorities effectively suppressed the strikes, but that did not quell the resentment of the war – especially the hostility to food rationing and the coal shortages (see pages 94–5).

Nevertheless, it seemed as if the forces of conservatism could emerge supreme, when the Bolshevik regime in Russia negotiated a peace in the Treaty of Brest-Litovsk in March 1918. It represented a decisive victory for the supporters of *Siegfriede* (see Figure 4.1 on page 86) which not only liberated Germany from the two-front war and made victory in the west now possible, but also greatly strengthened the political standing of the military leadership. The *Reichstag* backed the treaty by a large majority,

Key terms

Spartacus League
A small group which believed that Germany should follow the same path as communist Russia. The fundamental aim of the Spartacists was to create a soviet republic based on the rule of the proletariat through workers' and soldiers' councils.

Revolutionary stewards
Obleute. Left-wing activists who organised strikes and demonstrations against the war. They did much to create the workers' councils (soviets) in 1918–19.

A cartoon drawn in 1918 by the German artist Raemaeker. It underlines the serious situation faced by Kaiser Wilhelm II who is held by two ominous figures: war and starvation.

which was very much in contrast to the 1917 peace resolution. Only the USPD voted against the treaty.

When Ludendorff launched his 'last offensive', military gains were made but with no decisive breakthrough. A German military victory in 1918 would almost certainly have defused the crisis and in so doing slowed the process of political reform for a generation or more. Instead, four years of total war which ended in defeat brought the *Kaiserreich* to its knees. It had a dramatically adverse effect on the German economy by further damaging the government's already difficult financial position. This, in turn, was to lead to run-away inflation and the severe strains that this placed on the German economy and society. In pre-war Germany there had been instability and the occasional political crises. By the autumn of 1918 Ludendorff and Hindenburg recognised the seriousness of Germany's position – and decided to seek peace with the Allies.

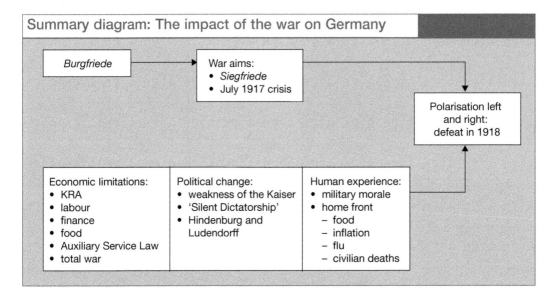

Summary diagram: The impact of the war on Germany

3 | The German Revolution 1918–19

Once Ludendorff came to appreciate that an Allied invasion of Germany would lead to destructive internal disturbances, he pushed for political change. Ever since Imperial Germany had been created in 1871, it had been an authoritarian monarchy. Now Ludendorff wanted to change Germany into a **constitutional monarchy** by the Kaiser's handing over political power to a civilian government. In other words, he aimed to establish a more democratic government, while maintaining the German monarchy.

October reform

Ludendorff's political turnaround had two aims. First, he wanted to secure for Germany the best possible peace terms from the Allies – it was believed that the Allied leaders would be more sympathetic to a democratic regime in Berlin. Secondly, he hoped the change would prevent the outbreak of political revolutionary disturbances.

However, Ludendorff had a third and a more cynical ulterior motive. He saw the need to shift the responsibility for Germany's defeat away from the military leadership and the conservative forces, which had dominated Imperial Germany, e.g. landowners and the army. Instead, he intended to put the responsibility and blame for the defeat on the new leadership. Here lay the origins of the **'stab in the back' myth**, which was later to play such a vital part in the history of the Weimar Republic. It was a theme soon taken up by sympathisers of the political right wing (see pages 127–35).

It was against this background that on 3 October 1918 Prince Max of Baden, a moderate conservative, was appointed Chancellor. He had democratic views and also a well-established international reputation because of his work with the Red Cross.

Key question
Why did Ludendorff support constitutional reform?

Key terms

Constitutional monarchy
Where the monarch has limited power within the lines of a constitution.

'Stab in the back' myth
The distorted view that the army had not really lost the First World War and that unpatriotic groups, such as socialists and Jews, had undermined the war effort. The myth severely weakened the Weimar democracy from the start.

Key date
Prince Max of Baden appointed Chancellor: 3 October 1918

In the following month a series of constitutional reforms came into effect, which turned Germany into a parliamentary democracy:

- Wilhelm II gave up his powers over the army and the navy to the *Reichstag*.
- The Chancellor and his government were made accountable to the *Reichstag*, instead of to the Kaiser.
- At the same time, armistice negotiations with the Allies were opened.

The effects

Key question
Did the constitutional changes of October 1918 represent a 'revolution from above'?

The changes of the October reform have traditionally been portrayed as a 'revolution from above'. This suggests that they were brought about by those in power and not forced as a result of a 'revolution from below'. Structuralists, like Wehler, regard the events of October 1918 as proving their theory that Germany had long been controlled and manipulated by the conservative traditional forces. He writes: 'The conservative bastions of the monarchy and the army were to be preserved as far as possible behind the façade of new arrangements intended to prevent the radical overthrow of the system and prove acceptable to the Allies.'

However, some historians, such as Eberhard Kolb, have suggested that the steps taken by the military leaders coincided with increasing pressure from the *Reichstag* to bring about political change. The most telling evidence supporting this interpretation is the resolution passed (on the same day as Ludendorff proposed an armistice) demanding 'the creation of a strong government supported by the confidence of a majority of the *Reichstag*'. Furthermore, Prince Max was appointed only after consultation with the majority parties in the *Reichstag*.

The idea that it was the *Reichstag* that brought about these changes certainly cannot be ignored but, on balance, it would be wrong to read too much into its actions. Over the years the German *Reichstag* had shown no real inclination to seize the initiative. This still applied in 1918. The *Reichstag* suspended proceedings on 5 October and went into recess until 22 October, when it adjourned again until 9 November. These were hardly the actions of an institution that wished to control events decisively. It seems that the October reforms were shaped from above and the *Reichstag* was happy to go along with these. However, it would be an exaggeration to see these as a constitutional revolution. The forces that had dominated Imperial Germany were still in position at the end of the month.

What pushed Germany, in such a short space of time, from political reform towards revolution was the widespread realisation that the war was lost. The shock of defeat, after years of hardship and optimistic propaganda, hardened popular opinion. By early November it was apparent that the creation of a constitutional monarchy would not defuse what had become a revolutionary situation.

The November revolution

On 29 October, a mutiny began to spread among some sailors who refused to obey orders at Wilhelmshaven, near Kiel. Prince Max's government quickly lost control of the political situation and by 2 November sailors gained control of other major ports, such as Kiel and Hamburg. These take-overs had been prompted by a real fear among the sailors that their officers were planning a suicide attack on the British Fleet, in order to restore the honour of the German navy. The news of the Kiel mutiny fanned the flames of discontent to other ports, Bremen and Lübeck, and soon throughout Germany. By 6 November, numerous workers' and soldiers' councils, similar to the **soviets** that had been set up by the Bolsheviks in Russia, were established in the major cities of Berlin, Cologne and Stuttgart. In Bavaria, the final member of the House of Wittelsbach, King Louis III, was deposed and the socialist Kurt Eisner proclaimed Bavaria an independent democratic socialist republic.

By the end of the first week of November it was clear that the October reforms had failed to impress the German people. The popular discontent was turning into a more fundamental revolutionary movement whose demands were for an immediate peace and the abdication of Kaiser Wilhelm II. The disturbances were prompted by:

- The realisation by troops and sailors that the war was lost and nothing was to be gained by carrying on.
- The sense of national shock when the news came of Germany's military defeat – propaganda and censorship had really delayed the reality for too long.
- The increasing anger and bitterness over the socio-economic conditions.

Prince Max would certainly have liked to preserve the monarchy, and possibly even Wilhelm II himself, but the Emperor's delusions that he could carry on without making any more political changes placed the Chancellor in a difficult position. In the end, Prince Max became so worried by the revolutionary situation in Berlin that on 9 November he announced that the Kaiser would renounce the throne and that a coalition left-wing government would be formed by Friedrich Ebert. It was in this chaotic situation that Philipp Scheidemann, one of the provisional government's leaders, appeared on the balcony of the *Reichstag* building and proclaimed Germany a republic. (Actually, an hour later Germany was also declared a 'soviet republic' – a statement crucial for the shaping of the next few months of the German Revolution.) It was only at this point in the evening of 9 November that the Kaiser, who was in Belgium, accepted the advice of leading generals. In that way, the Kaiser did not formally abdicate, he simply walked away and went into exile voluntarily in the Netherlands.

Key question
How and why did the October reform fail?

Key dates

Grand Fleet mutiny at Kiel: 2 November 1918

Kaiser fled to the Netherlands; Ebert appointed Chancellor; Germany proclaimed a republic: 9 November 1918

Key term

Soviet
A Russian word meaning an elected council. Soviets developed during the Russian Revolution in 1917. In Germany many councils were set up in 1918, which had the support of the more radical and revolutionary left-wing working class.

Key question
In what ways was the left-wing movement divided?

Key terms

Socialist republic
A system of government without a monarchy that aims to introduce social changes for collective benefit.

Soviet republic
A system of government without a monarchy that aims to introduce a communist state organised by the workers' councils and opposed to private ownership.

Proletariat
The industrial working class who, in Marxist theory, would ultimately take power in the state.

The left-wing movement

A genuinely revolutionary situation existed in Germany in early November 1918. However, the revolutionary wave that swept Germany was not a united force. In fact, the left-wing movement behind it consisted of three main strands (see Table 4.5).

The SPD (German Social Democratic Party)

The SPD represented moderate socialist aims and was led by Friedrich Ebert and Philipp Scheidemann. In the election of 1912 it had become the largest party in the *Reichstag* with a membership of over one million. Its fundamental aim was to create a socialist republic, but being wholly committed to parliamentary democracy, it totally rejected anything that might have been likened to Soviet-style communism.

The Spartacists

On the extreme left stood the Spartacus League (otherwise known as the Spartacists), led by Karl Liebknecht and the Polish-born Rosa Luxemburg, one of the few women to be prominent in German political history (see profile on page 105).

The Spartacists had been formed in 1905 as a minor faction of the SPD. By 1918 it had a national membership of about 5000. From 1914, they had opposed the war and they were deeply influenced by Lenin and Bolshevism. They had come to believe that Germany should follow the same path as communist Russia. The fundamental aim of the Spartacists was to create a soviet republic based on the rule of the **proletariat** through workers' and soldiers' councils.

The USPD (Independent German Social Democratic Party)

The USPD had been formed in 1917 as a breakaway group from the SPD (see page 98). It was led by Hugo Haase and Karl Kautsky. Although the USPD was a minority of the assembly in the *Reichstag* it had a substantial following of 300,000 members.

The USPD demanded radical social and economic change as well as political reforms. However, as a political movement, it was far from united and internal divisions and squabbles seriously

Table 4.5: The German left-wing movement

	Moderate socialists	Radical socialists	Revolutionary socialists
Party names	SPD: Social Democratic Party of Germany	USPD: Independent Social Democratic Party of Germany	Spartacists: Spartacus League
Aim	To establish a **socialist republic** by the creation of parliamentary democracy	To create a socialist republic governed by workers' and soldiers' councils in conjunction with a parliament	To create a **soviet republic** based on the rule of the workers' and soldiers' councils
Leaders	Friedrich Ebert and Philipp Scheidemann	Karl Kautsky and Hugo Haase	Rosa Luxemburg and Karl Liebknecht

Profile: Friedrich Ebert 1871–1925

1871		– Born in Heidelberg of humble background
1885–8		– Trained as a saddler
1889		– Became a trade union organiser and SPD member
1912		– Elected as a member of the *Reichstag*
1916		– Chosen as leader of the party
1918	9 November	– Became Chancellor of the provisional government when Imperial Germany collapsed
	10 November	– Ebert–Groener agreement (see page 106)
1919	11 February	– Chosen as the country's first President, a position he held until his death in 1925

Ebert rose from a humble background as a saddler to become leader of the SPD and first president of Germany. His character and achievements significantly shaped the development of Weimar democracy.

When Germany collapsed in autumn 1918, Ebert wanted a democratic parliamentary government with a constitutional monarch, but when events got out of hand the monarchy collapsed and he accepted the chancellorship. It was a major success to manage to hold the first truly democratic German elections; these were to lead to the National Constituent Assembly and the creation of the Weimar Constitution. However, Ebert has been criticised for endorsing the use of the army, the *Freikorps* (see page 108) and other conservative forces to brutally suppress the more radical elements of the left.

As the country's first President from 1919 until his death, he oversaw the years of crisis and applied the emergency decrees of Article 48 (see page 115) with success. However, he became the focus of scurrilous criticism from the extreme right – which almost certainly contributed to his early death. He was a man of great integrity and decency and, despite the critics, he was a patriot and served his office with distinction and correctness.

Key term

Freikorps
Means 'free corps' who acted as paramilitaries. They were right-wing, nationalist soldiers who were only too willing to use force to suppress communist activity.

curtailed its influence. The main disagreement was between those who sympathised with the creation of a parliamentary democracy and those who advocated a much more revolutionary democracy based on the workers' councils.

Ebert's coalition government

Because of the different aims and methods of the socialist movement, there was a lack of unity in Ebert's coalition government. Moreover, it should also be remembered that German society was in a chaotic state of near collapse, so the

Key question
What were the main problems faced by Ebert?

Profile: Rosa Luxemburg ('Red Rosa') 1871–1919

1871 – Born in Poland of Jewish origins. Badly disabled and walked with a limp, endured continual pain

1905 – Took part in the revolutionary troubles in Russia
    – Founded the Spartacist League

1914 – Imprisoned for the duration of the war. Only freed in 1918

1917 – Welcomed the Bolshevik revolution in Russia (but soon came to criticise Lenin's repressive methods)

1919 – Supported the creation of KPD (German Communist Party) from the Spartacist League
    – Opposed the Spartacist uprising in January 1919
    – Murdered while in police custody in Berlin

After her death, Luxemburg was described as 'arguably one of the finest political theorists of the twentieth century' who famously said, 'Freedom is always for the person who thinks differently.' She championed the cause of armed revolution that would sweep the capitalist system away. Ironically, she spoke against the uprising in January 1919 (see page 108) because she felt that Germany was not ready for communism. Although she died a committed revolutionary, she had a humane and optimistic view of communism which was at odds with the brutality of the Bolsheviks in Russia.

leading political figures at the time had little room to manoeuvre when they had to make hasty and difficult decisions.

On 9 November 1918 Ebert created a provisional coalition government:

- 'Provisional' in the sense that it was short term until a national election was held to vote for a National Constituent Assembly (parliament).
- 'Coalition' in the sense that it was a combination of parties, the SPD and the USPD.

Ebert himself was a moderate and was frightened that the political situation in Germany could easily run out of control. In Table 4.6 on page 106, the nature of Ebert's major problems can be seen.

Ebert's main worry was that the extreme left would gain the upper hand. He recognised the growing number of workers' councils and feared that they might threaten his policy of gradual change. He was determined to maintain law and order to prevent the country collapsing into civil war. He also feared that the return of millions of troops after the Armistice agreement, which was eventually signed on 11 November, would create enormous social and political problems. These were the main concerns in the minds of Ebert and the SPD leadership in the months that followed and were the main reasons why they made agreements with the army and industrialists.

Key date

Armistice signed at Compiègne: 11 November 1918

Table 4.6: Ebert's main problems

Socio-economic	Left-wing opposition	Right-wing opposition	Military
Inflation Wages were falling behind prices, which was increasing social discontent.	*Strikes* From the autumn of 1918 the number of strikes and lock-outs increased markedly.	*Freikorps* A growing number of right-wing, nationalist soldiers were forming paramilitary units.	*Demobilisation* About 1.5 million German soldiers had to be returned home to Germany.
Shortages From the winter of 1916–17 fuel and food shortages were causing real hardship in the cities.	*German communists* Inspired by the events of 1917–18, communists aimed to bring about a revolution in Germany.	*The army* The army was generally conservative, but also deeply embittered by the military defeat.	*Allied blockade* The Allies maintained the naval blockade even after the Armistice. Social distress was not relieved until June 1919.
Flu epidemic 'Spanish flu' killed thousands. The most serious flu epidemic of the twentieth century.	*Workers' and soldiers' councils* Hundreds of councils were created and many wanted changes to the army and industries.	*Nationalists* Nationalist–conservatives were deeply against the abdication of the Kaiser and did not support the creation of a democratic republic.	*Peace terms* The Armistice was when they agreed to stop fighting, but there was great public concern about the actual effects of the peace treaty.

Ebert–Groener agreement

On 10 November, the day after the declaration of the Republic, General Wilhelm Groener, Ludendorff's successor, telephoned Chancellor Ebert. Their conversation was very significant. The Supreme Army Command agreed to support the new government and to use troops to maintain the stability and security of the new republic. In return, Ebert promised to oppose the spread of revolutionary socialism and to preserve the authority of the army officers. The deal has become known simply as the Ebert–Groener agreement.

Stinnes–Legien agreement

A few days later, on 15 November, Karl Legien, leader of the trade unions, and Hugo Stinnes, leader of the industrial employers, held another significant discussion. The Stinnes–Legien agreement was, in effect, a deal where the trade unions made a commitment not to interfere with private ownership and the free market, in return for workers' committees, an eight-hour working day and full legal recognition. Ebert's provisional government endorsed this because the German trade unions were a powerful movement and traditionally closely tied with the SPD.

So, on one level, the agreement to bring about some key, long-desired reforms was a real success. However, these two agreements have been severely criticised over the years, particularly by the left wing. Critics have accused Ebert of having supported compromises with the forces of conservatism. The army was not reformed at all and it was not really committed to democracy.

Employers resented the concessions and were unsympathetic to the Weimar system. Nevertheless, there is a counter-argument that Ebert and the SPD leadership were motivated by the simple desire to guarantee stability and a peaceful transition.

Key question
Why did the left-wing movement split?

Left-wing splits

By the final days of 1918 it was clear that the SPD had become distanced from its political 'allies' on the left and their conflicting aims resulted in fundamental differences over strategy and policies.

SPD

The SPD government became increasingly isolated. It moved further to the political right and grew dependent on the civil service and the army to maintain effective government.

Aim
To establish a socialist republic by the creation of parliamentary democracy.

Strategy
To make arrangements for a democratic *Reichstag* election leading to a National Constituent Assembly.
To introduce moderate changes, but to prevent the spread of communist revolution.

Policies
To maintain law and order by running the country with the existing legal and police systems.
To retain the army.
To introduce welfare benefits.

USPD

In late December 1918, the USPD members of Ebert's government resigned over the shooting of some Spartacists by soldiers. However, the split had really emerged over the USPD's desire to introduce fundamental social and economic changes that the SPD did not want to adopt.

Aim
To create a socialist republic governed by workers' and soldiers' councils in conjunction with a parliament.

Strategy
To introduce radical social and economic changes.

Policies
To reform the army fundamentally.
To nationalise key industries.
To introduce welfare benefits.

Spartacists

On 1 January 1919 the Spartacists formally founded the *Kommunistische Partei Deutschlands*, the KPD – the German Communist Party. It refused to participate in the parliamentary elections, preferring instead to place its faith in the workers' councils, as expressed in the Spartacist manifesto:

> The question today is not democracy or dictatorship. The question that history has put on the agenda reads: bourgeois democracy or socialist democracy? For the dictatorship of the proletariat is democracy in the socialist sense of the word. Dictatorship of the proletariat does not mean bombs, *putsches*, riots and anarchy, as the agents of capitalist profits deliberately and falsely claim. Rather, it means using all instruments of political power to achieve socialism, to expropriate [dispossess of property] the capitalist class, through and in accordance with the will of the revolutionary majority of the proletariat.

Aim
To create a soviet republic based on the rule of the workers' and soldiers' councils.

Strategy
To oppose the creation of a National Constituent Assembly and to take power by strikes, demonstrations and revolts leading to fundamental social and economic changes.

Policies
To replace the army by local militias of workers.
To carry out extensive nationalisation of industries and land.
To introduce welfare benefits.

The Spartacist revolt

In January 1919 the Spartacists decided that the time was ripe to launch an armed rising in Berlin with the aim of overthrowing the provisional government and creating a soviet republic.

On 5 January they occupied public buildings, called for a general strike and formed a revolutionary committee. They denounced Ebert's provisional government and the coming elections. However, they had little chance of success. There were three days of savage street fighting and over 100 were killed. The Spartacist *coup* was easily defeated and afterwards, most notoriously, Liebknecht and Luxemburg were brutally murdered while in police custody.

The events of January 1919 showed that the Spartacists were strong on policies, but detached from political realities. They had no real strategy and their 'revolutionaries' were mainly just workers with rifles. By contrast, the government not only had the backing of the army's troops, but also 5000 'irregular' military-style groups, *Freikorps*.

This event created a very troubled atmosphere for the next few months. The elections for the National Constituent Assembly duly took place in February 1919 (see pages 109–11), although the continuation of strikes and street disorders in Berlin meant that, for reasons of security, the Assembly's first meeting was switched to the town of **Weimar**. More serious disturbances in Bavaria in April resulted in a short-lived soviet-type republic being established there. The *Freikorps* brought the disturbances under control, although, in each case, at the cost of several hundred lives. The infant republic had survived the traumas of its birth.

Key question
Why did the Spartacist revolt fail?

Start of Spartacist uprising in Berlin: 5 January 1919

Key date

Weimar Republic
Took its name from the first meeting of the National Constituent Assembly at Weimar. The Assembly had moved there because there were still many disturbances in Berlin. Weimar was chosen because it was a town with a great historical and cultural tradition.

Key term

Summary diagram: The German Revolution 1918–19

The birth of the Republic:
October reforms and failure

↓

Mutiny and revolt

↓

Abdication of the Kaiser

↓

Declaration of republic

The left-wing movement:
• SPD
• USPD
• Spartacists

Ebert's leadership:
• the coalition government
• Ebert–Groener and
  Stinnes–Legien agreements

Early problems:
• socio-economic factors
• left-wing opposition
• right-wing opposition
• military consequences

The Spartacist uprising
Why did it fail?

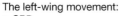

Key question
Was the election a success for democracy?

Key date
National Constituent Assembly met at Weimar: 6 February 1919

4 | The National Constituent Assembly

Despite the disturbances across Germany, in the months after the collapse of Imperial Germany, the new republic was still able to hold its first elections for a National Constituent Assembly on 19 January 1919. Most political parties took the opportunity to retitle themselves, but new names did not disguise the fact that there was considerable continuity in the structure of the party system (see Table 4.7).

The election results (see Figure 4.2 on page 111) quickly led to the creation of the National Constituent Assembly on 6 February. In many respects the results represented a major success for the forces of parliamentary democracy:

• The high turn-out of 83 per cent in the election suggested faith in the idea of democracy.
• 76.1 per cent of the electorate voted for pro-democratic parties.
• The solid vote for the three main democratic parties, the SPD, the DDP and the ZP, made it straightforward to form a coalition government, which became known as the 'Weimar Coalition'.

Table 4.7: The major political parties in the Weimar Republic

Bavarian People's Party (*Bayerische Volkspartei*, BVP)	Leader: Heinrich Held	The BVP was a regional party formed from elements of the ZP in 1919 in order to uphold Bavaria's local interests. It was conservative, but generally supported the Republic.
German Democratic Party (*Deutsche Demokratische Partei*, BVP)	Leaders: Walther Rathenau and Hugo Preuss	Formed from the National Liberals party in the old *Reichstag*, it attracted support from the professional middle classes, especially the intellectuals and some of the businessmen. The party supported the democratic republic and was committed to constitutional reform.
German National People's Party (*Deutschnationale Volkspartei*, DNVP)	Leaders: Karl Helfferich and Alfred Hugenberg (see page 159)	The DNVP was a right-wing party formed from the old conservative parties and some of the racist, anti-Semitic groups, such as the Pan-German League. It was monarchist and anti-republican. Generally, it was closely tied to the interests of heavy industry and agriculture, including landowners and small farmers.
German People's Party (*Deutsche Volkspartei*, DVP)	Leader: Gustav Stresemann (see page 166)	A new party founded by Gustav Stresemann, who was a conservative and monarchist and at first suspicious of the Weimar Republic and voted against the new constitution. From 1921, under Stresemann's influence, the DVP became a strong supporter of parliamentary democracy. It attracted support from the protestant middle and upper classes.
German Communist Party (*Kommunistische Partei Deutschlands*, KPD)	Leader: Ernst Thälmann	The KPD was formed in January 1919 by the extreme left wing, e.g. Spartacists. It was anti-republican in the sense that it opposed Weimar-style democracy and supported a revolutionary overthrow of society. Most of its supporters were from the working class and strengthened by the defection of many USPD members in 1920.
National Socialist German Workers' Party – Nazi Party (*Nationalsozialistische Partei Deutschlands*, NSDAP)	Leader: Adolf Hitler (see pages 212–13)	Extreme right-wing party formed in 1919. It was anti-republican, anti-Semitic and strongly nationalist. Until 1930 it remained a fringe party with support from the lower middle classes.
German Social Democratic Party (*Sozialdemokratische Partei Deutschlands*, SPD)	Leaders: Friedrich Ebert (see page 104) and Philipp Scheidemann	The moderate wing of the socialist movement, it was very much the party of the working class and the trade unions. It strongly supported parliamentary democracy and was opposed to the revolutionary demands of the more left-wing socialists.
Independent German Social Democratic Party (*Unabhängige Sozialdemokratische Partei Deutschlands*, USPD)	Leaders: Karl Kautsky and Hugo Haase	The USPD broke away from the SPD in April 1917. It included many of the more radical elements of German socialism and, therefore, sought social and political change. About half its members joined the KPD during 1919–20 whilst by 1922 most of the others had returned to the ranks of the SPD.
Centre Party (*Zentrumspartei*, ZP)	Leaders: Matthias Erzberger and Heinrich Brüning (see page 198)	The ZP had been created in the nineteenth century to defend the interests of the Roman Catholic Church. It continued to be the major political voice of Catholicism and enjoyed a broad range of supporters from aristocratic landowners to Christian trade unionists. Most of the ZP was committed to the Republic. From the late 1920s it became more sympathetic to the right wing.

Figure 4.2: *Reichstag* election result January 1919. Turn-out 83 per cent. Total number of seats 423.

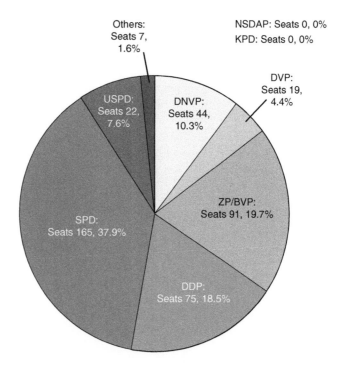

Others: Seats 7, 1.6%

NSDAP: Seats 0, 0%
KPD: Seats 0, 0%

USPD: Seats 22, 7.6%

DNVP: Seats 44, 10.3%

DVP: Seats 19, 4.4%

ZP/BVP: Seats 91, 19.7%

SPD: Seats 165, 37.9%

DDP: Seats 75, 18.5%

However, it should be borne in mind that:

- Although the DNVP gained only 10.3 per cent, it had backing from important conservative supporters, e.g. the landowners, the army officers, industrialists.
- The DVP and its leader, Stresemann, did not support the Weimar Republic in 1919 because they wanted Germany to have a constitutional monarchy.

Key question
How fundamental were the changes brought about by the German Revolution?

What kind of revolution?

By May 1919 a degree of stability had returned to Germany. The revolution had run its course and the Weimar Republic had been established. However, serious doubts remained about the nature and real extent of these revolutionary changes.

Undoubtedly, there existed the possibility of revolution in Germany as the war came to an end. The effects of war and the shock of defeat shook the faith of large numbers of the people in the old order. Imperial Germany could not survive, so Wilhelm II and the other princes were deposed and parliamentary democracy was introduced. These were important changes.

However, in the end, the German Revolution did not go much further than the October reforms and was strictly limited in scope. Society was left almost untouched by these events, for there was no attempt to reform the key institutions:

- The civil service, judiciary and army all remained essentially intact.
- Similarly, the power and influence of Germany's industrial and commercial leaders remained unchanged.
- There were no changes in the structure of big business and land ownership.

Certainly, plans for the improvement of working conditions and the beginnings of a welfare state were outlined by the government, but the SPD leadership hoped that all the changes would follow in the wake of constitutional reform. With hindsight, it seems that more thoroughgoing social and economic changes might well have been a better basis on which to establish democracy. As it was, the divisions on the left played into the hands of the conservative forces. As one historian, M. Hughes, has claimed, 'it is more accurate to talk of a potential revolution which ran away into the sand rather than the genuine article'. Indeed, during the first half of 1919 the increasing reliance of the moderate left on the conservative forces of Imperial Germany became a major factor in German politics. These conservative forces were soon to put into doubt the very survival of Weimar democracy.

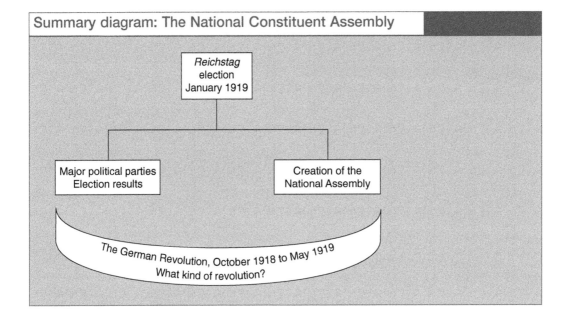

Summary diagram: The National Constituent Assembly

5 | The Key Debate

After the Second World War, when Germany was divided into east and west, two different interpretations about the revolution emerged. These raised the question:

Did Ebert and the SPD leadership betray the German Revolution?

In the 1950s and 1960s most historians in capitalist West Germany (1949–90), such as K.D. Erdmann, assumed that there had only ever been two possible options available to Germany at the end of the war: the people had to choose between a communist dictatorship and a parliamentary republic in the style of Weimar. In this light, Ebert's decisions were portrayed as those of a heroic figure whose actions had saved Germany from Bolshevism.

In contrast, historians in communist East Germany (1949–90) saw the actions of the SPD as betrayal of the left-wing movement. Worse, they felt that Ebert had decided to co-operate with the traditional forces of the army and industry. In their view, the real heroes were the Spartacists who had stuck to their true revolutionary ideas and died on the barricades in Berlin.

Following extensive research in the late 1960s and 1970s, these two traditional interpretations have been questioned and a third one has emerged from historians, such as Kolb and Rürup in West Germany. Close analysis of the workers' councils movement throughout Germany has shown that very few fell under the control of the extreme revolutionary left. The vast majority were led by the SPD with USPD support and it was only after January 1919 that the USPD came to dominate. Thus, it is now generally recognised that the threat from the revolutionary communists was grossly exaggerated. They may well have been vocal in putting forward their revolutionary plans, but their actual base of support was minimal. This evidence has, in turn, led to a reassessment of the German Revolution.

Most historians now argue that although the integrity and sincerity of Ebert and the SPD's leadership remain undoubted, their reading of the political situation was poor. Blinded by their fear of the extreme left, they overestimated the threat from that quarter. This caused them to compromise with the conservative forces of Imperial Germany, rather than asserting their own authority. In that sense, they missed the opportunity to create a solidly based republic built on socialist and democratic principles.

Some key books in the debate
E. Kolb, *The Weimar Republic* (Routledge, 1988).
A.J. Nicholls, *Weimar and the Rise of Hitler* (New York, 2000).
D. Peukert, *The Weimar Republic* (Penguin, 1993).

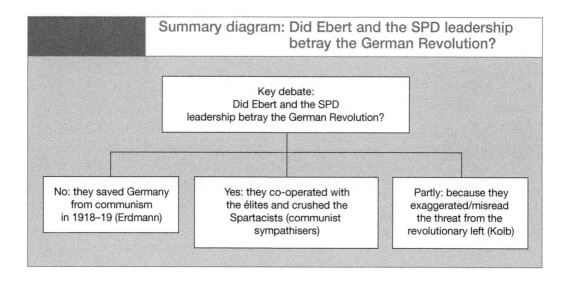

Summary diagram: Did Ebert and the SPD leadership betray the German Revolution?

Key debate:
Did Ebert and the SPD leadership betray the German Revolution?

No: they saved Germany from communism in 1918–19 (Erdmann)

Yes: they co-operated with the élites and crushed the Spartacists (communist sympathisers)

Partly: because they exaggerated/misread the threat from the revolutionary left (Kolb)

5 Weimar's Political Crisis

POINTS TO CONSIDER

In the summer of 1919 two crucial documents were drawn up that influenced the history of the Weimar Republic: the Weimar Constitution which was agreed by the German *Reichstag*, and the Treaty of Versailles which was imposed by the Allies. The importance of each document is examined in three ways:

- The key terms of the documents
- The issues of controversy
- Their significance in the history of Weimar Germany

Although the forces of democracy had successfully established the Weimar Republic, Germany remained in turmoil in the years 1919–23. This chapter concentrates on the extent of Weimar's political problems and the range of political threats it faced. It examines:

- The threats from the extreme left and the extreme right
- Uprisings of the extreme right
- Elections and governments – 'a republic without republicans'

The country also faced fundamental economic problems and these will be the focus of the next chapter.

Key dates

1919	February 6	National Assembly first meeting at Weimar
	June 28	Treaty of Versailles signed
	July 31	Weimar Constitution adopted by the National Assembly
	August 11	Weimar Constitution signed by President Ebert
1920	March	Kapp *putsch*
1921	August 26	Murder of Erzberger
1922	June 24	Murder of Rathenau
1923	Summer	The 'German October' in Saxony
	November 8–9	Munich Beer Hall *putsch*

Key question
What were the significant terms of the Weimar Constitution?

Key dates

National Assembly first meeting at Weimar: 6 February 1919

The Weimar Constitution was adopted by the National Assembly: 31 July 1919

Weimar Constitution signed by President Ebert: 11 August 1919

Key terms

Proportional representation
A system that allocates parliamentary seats in proportion to the total number of votes.

Article 48
Gave the Weimar president the power in an emergency to rule by decree and to override the constitutional rights of the people.

1 | The Weimar Constitution

The key terms of the Constitution

Back in November 1918, Ebert invited the liberal lawyer Hugo Preuss to draw up a new constitution for Germany and a draft was outlined by the time the National Assembly was established in February 1919. Preuss worked closely with a constitutional committee of 28 members over the next six months, though their discussions were deeply overshadowed by the dispute about the Treaty of Versailles (see pages 120–6).

The proposals for the new constitution were influenced by the long-established democratic ideas of Britain and the USA. Nevertheless, Germany's particular circumstances and traditions were not ignored as, for example, in the introduction of **proportional representation** and the creation of a federal structure. Eventually, on 31 July 1919, the *Reichstag* voted strongly in favour of the constitution (for: 262; against: 75) and on 11 August the president ratified it. The main features of the constitution are outlined below and in Figure 5.1 on page 116).

Definition

Germany was declared a 'democratic state' and a republic (all monarchies were ended). It had a federal structure with 17 *Länder* (regional states), e.g. Prussia, Bavaria, Saxony.

President

The people elected the president every seven years. He enjoyed considerable powers, such as:

- The right to dissolve the *Reichstag*.
- The appointment of the Chancellor. (Although the president was not obliged, he tended to choose the Chancellor as the leader of the largest party in the *Reichstag*. In order to form a workable coalition government, it was necessary to negotiate with the leaders of other political parties.)
- The Supreme Commander of the Armed Forces.
- The capacity to rule by decree at a time of national emergency (**Article 48**) and to oversee the *Reichstag*.

But this created a very complex relationship between the powers of the president and the *Reichstag*/Chancellor.

Parliament

There were two houses in the German parliament:

- The *Reichstag* was the main representative assembly and law-making body of the parliament. It consisted of deputies elected every four years on the basis of a system of proportional representation. The PR system allocated members to parliament from the official list of political party candidates. They were distributed on the basis of one member for every 60,000 votes in an electoral district.

- The *Reichsrat* was the less important house in the parliament. It was made up of representatives from all of the 17 state regional governments (*Länder*), which all held local responsibilities such as education, police, etc. But the *Reichsrat* could only initiate or delay proposals, and the *Reichstag* could always overrule it.

Bill of Rights

The constitution also drew up a range of individual rights. It outlined broad freedoms, for example:

- personal liberty and the right to free speech
- censorship was forbidden
- equality before the law of all Germans
- religious freedom (and no State Church was allowed).

In addition to this, the Bill of Rights provided a range of social rights, for example:

- welfare provision, e.g. for housing, the disabled, orphans
- protection of labour.

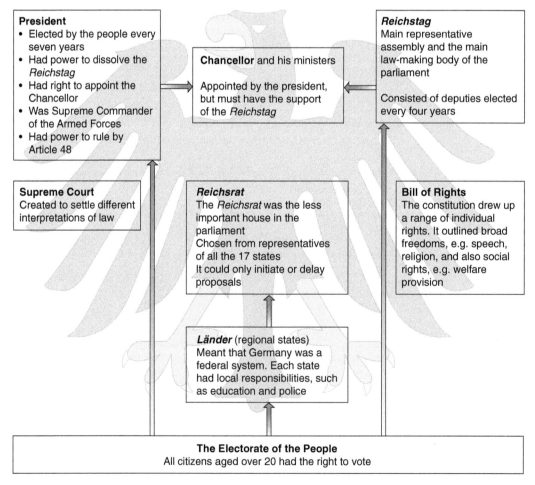

Figure 5.1: The Weimar Constitution.

Supreme Court

In order to settle different interpretations of law, a Supreme Court was created.

Key question
What were the arguments for and against the terms of Weimar Constitution?

The issues of controversy

Since the Weimar Republic lasted only 14 crisis-ridden years, it is hardly surprising that its written constitution has been the focus of considerable attention. Some historians have gone so far as to argue that the real causes of the collapse of the Republic and the success of the Nazis can be found in its clauses. Such claims are based on three aspects of the constitution:

- The introduction of proportional representation.
- The relationship between the president and the *Reichstag* and, in particular, the emergency powers available to the president under Article 48.
- The fact that the traditional institutions of Imperial Germany were allowed to continue.

Proportional representation

The introduction of proportional representation became the focus of criticism after 1945 because, it was argued, it had encouraged the formation of many new, small splinter parties, e.g. the Nazis. This made it more difficult to form and maintain governments.

In Weimar Germany it was virtually impossible for one party to form a majority government, and so coalitions were required – sometimes of three and even four parties. Furthermore, it was argued that all the negotiations and compromises involved in forming governments contributed to the political instability of Weimar. It is for these reasons that many critics of Weimar felt that a voting political system based upon two major parties, like in Britain (or the USA), which favoured the so-called **'first past the post'** model, would have created more political stability.

However, it is difficult to see how an alternative voting system, without proportional representation, could have made for a more effective parliamentary democracy in early twentieth century Germany. The main problem was the difficulty of creating coalitions amongst the main parties, which had been well established in the nineteenth century. The parties were meant to reflect the different political, religious and geographical views and so a system of PR was the only fair way. By comparison, the existence of all the splinter parties was a relatively minor issue.

There is also the view that, after the economic and political crisis of 1929–33 (see pages 189–230), proportional representation encouraged the emergence of political extremism. However, it now seems clear that the changes in the way people voted and the way they changed their allegiance from one party to another were just too volatile to be kept in check. It may also have been the case that a 'first past the post' system would have actually helped the rise of Nazism and communism.

Key term

'First past the post' An electoral system that simply requires the winner to gain one vote more than the second placed candidate. It is also referred to as the plurality system and does not require 50 per cent plus one votes. In a national election it tends to give the most successful party disproportionately more seats than its total vote merits.

The relationship between the president and the *Reichstag*

The relationship created between the *Reichstag* and the president in the Weimar Constitution was meant to have a fair system of checks and balances, but this was very complex.

It was intended to lessen the fears that an unrestricted parliament would become too powerful. Fear of an over-powerful parliament was strong on the right wing, and within liberal circles. It therefore aimed to create a presidency that could provide leadership 'above the parties' and limit the powers of the *Reichstag* (see pages 115–16 and Figure 5.1 on page 116). The president's powers were seen as amounting to those of an *Ersatzkaiser*, a substitute emperor. When the power of the president is compared with the authority of the *Reichstag*, it seems that the attempt to prevent too much power being placed in the hands of one institution resulted in massive power being granted to another. As a result, there was uncertainty in constitutional matters from the start.

The framers of the constitution struggled to keep a balance of power between the president and the *Reichstag*. Was the ultimate source of authority in the democratic republic vested in the representative assembly of the people – the *Reichstag* – or in the popularly elected head of state – the president?

Matters were made more difficult by the powers conferred upon the president by Article 48. This Article provided the head of state with the authority to suspend civil rights in an emergency and restore law and order by the issue of presidential decrees. The intention was to create the means by which government could continue to function in a crisis. However, the effect was to create what the historian Gordon Craig referred to as 'a constitutional anomaly'. Such fears, which were actively expressed by some deputies in the constitutional debate of 1919, later assumed a particular importance during the crisis that brought Hitler to power in 1933. However, it should be remembered that in the crisis of 1923, the presidential powers were used as intended and to very good effect.

The continuity of traditional institutions

Although the Weimar Constitution introduced a wide range of democratic rights and civil liberties, it made no provision to reform the old traditional institutions of Imperial Germany, such as:

- The civil service was well educated and professional, but tended to conform to the conservative values of Imperial Germany.
- The judiciary continued to enjoy its traditional independence under the Weimar Constitution, but the hearts of many judges did not lie with the Weimar Republic. Bluntly, they were biased and tended to favour the extreme right and condemn the extreme left (see page 131).
- The army enjoyed great status and many of the generals were socially linked with the Prussian landowners. It sought to maintain its influence after 1918 and was generally not sympathetic to democratic Germany. It was the only real authority that had military capacity.

- Universities were very proud of their traditional status and generally more sympathetic to the old political ideas and rules.

In Weimar's difficult early years effective use was made of the established professional skills and educated institutions of the state. However, the result was that powerful conservative forces were able to exert great influence in daily life. This was at odds with the left wing's wishes to extend civil rights and to create a modern, democratic society. So, whilst the spirit of the Weimar Constitution was democratic and progressive, the institutions remained dedicated to the values of Imperial Germany.

Key question
Was the Weimar Constitution fatally flawed?

The significance of the Weimar Constitution

With hindsight, it is easy to highlight those parts of the Weimar Constitution that contributed to the ultimate collapse of the Republic. However, it should be remembered that the new constitution was a great improvement upon the previous undemocratic constitution of Imperial Germany and a very large majority voted in favour of it. Indeed, Weimar was initially seen as 'the most advanced democracy in the world'. What the Constitution could not control were the conditions and circumstances in which it had to operate. And the Weimar Republic had other more serious problems than just the Constitution, such as the Treaty of Versailles and its socio-economic problems. As Theodor Heuss, the first president of the German Federal Republic in 1949, said: 'Germany never conquered democracy for herself. Democracy came to Germany … in the wake of defeat.'

Therefore, it seems unrealistic to imagine that any piece of paper could have resolved all Germany's problems after 1918. The Weimar Constitution had weaknesses, but it was not fatally flawed – there were many more serious and fundamental problems within the Weimar Republic.

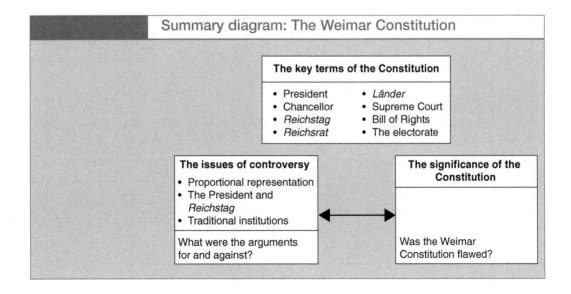

Summary diagram: The Weimar Constitution

The key terms of the Constitution

- President
- Chancellor
- *Reichstag*
- *Reichsrat*
- *Länder*
- Supreme Court
- Bill of Rights
- The electorate

The issues of controversy

- Proportional representation
- The President and *Reichstag*
- Traditional institutions

What were the arguments for and against?

The significance of the Constitution

Was the Weimar Constitution flawed?

2 | The Treaty of Versailles

For most Germans the Paris peace settlement of 1919 was a far more controversial issue than the new constitution. It had been generally assumed among German public opinion that the treaty would result in a fair peace. This was partly because defeat had never really been expected, even as late as the summer of 1918, and partly because it was generally assumed that President Wilson's Fourteen Points would lay the basis of the terms.

However, it soon became clear that the peace treaty would not be open for discussion with Germany's representatives. When the draft terms were presented in May 1919 there was national shock and outrage in Germany. In desperation, the first Weimar government led by Scheidemann resigned. The Allies were not prepared to negotiate, which obliged an embittered *Reichstag* finally to accept the Treaty of Versailles by 237 votes to 138 in June. This was because Germany simply did not have the military capacity to resist. And so, on 28 June 1919, the German representatives, led by Hermann Müller, signed the treaty in the Hall of Mirrors at Versailles near Paris.

The Treaty of Versailles was a compromise, but only in the sense that it was a compromise *between* the Allied powers. So the decisive negotiations were between the so-called 'Big Three':

- Woodrow Wilson, President of the USA
- Georges Clemenceau, Prime Minister of France
- David Lloyd George, Prime Minister of Great Britain.

Woodrow Wilson

He has traditionally been portrayed as an idealist, as he had a strong religious framework. Initially, he had been an academic, but he was drawn into politics when he had campaigned against corruption. At first he had opposed American entry into the war. Once he declared war against Germany in April 1917 he drew up the Fourteen Points in the hope of creating a more just world. His main aims were:

- to bring about international disarmament
- to apply the principle of **self-determination**
- to create a **League of Nations** in order to maintain international peace.

Georges Clemenceau

He was an uncompromising French nationalist. He had been in his country twice when Germany had invaded and he was deeply influenced by the devastation from the war in northern France. He was motivated by revenge and he was determined to gain

Key question
In what ways did the Allies differ over war aims?

Key date

The German government signed the Treaty of Versailles: 28 June 1919

Key terms

Self-determination
The right of people of the same nation to decide their own form of government. In effect, it is the principle of each nation ruling itself. Wilson believed that the application of self-determination was integral to the peace settlement and it would lead to long-term peace.

League of Nations
The international body initiated by President Wilson to encourage disarmament and to prevent war.

Key term

Buffer state
The general idea of separating two rival countries by leaving a space between them. Clemenceau believed that the long-established Franco-German military aggression could be brought to an end by establishing an independent Rhineland state (though this was not implemented because Wilson saw it as against the principle of self-determination).

financial compensation and to satisfy France's security concerns. His main aims were:

- to annex the Rhineland and to create a '**buffer state**'
- to impose the major disarmament of Germany
- to impose heavy reparations in order to weaken Germany
- to get recompense from the damage of the war in order to finance rebuilding.

David Lloyd George

He may be seen as a pragmatist. He was keen to uphold British national interests and initially he played on the idea of revenge. However, he recognised that there would have to be compromise. In particular, he saw the need to restrain Clemenceau's revenge. His main aims were:

- to guarantee British military security – especially, to secure naval supremacy
- to keep communism at bay
- to limit French demands because he feared that excessively weakening Germany would have serious economic consequences for the European economy.

Key question
What were the significant terms of the Treaty of Versailles?

The terms of the Treaty of Versailles

The key terms of the Treaty of Versailles can be listed under the following headings: territorial arrangements, war guilt, reparations, disarmament and maintaining peace.

a) Territorial arrangements

Key terms

Plebiscite
A vote by the people on one specific issue – like a referendum.

Anschluss
Usually translated as 'union'. In the years 1919–38, it referred to the paragraph in the Treaty of Versailles that outlawed any political union between Germany and Austria, although the population was wholly German.

- Eupen-Malmedy. Subject to **plebiscite**, the districts of Eupen and Malmedy to be handed over to Belgium.
- Alsace-Lorraine. Germany to return these provinces to France.
- North Schleswig. Subject to plebiscite, Germany to hand over the North Schleswig.
- West Prussia and Posen. Germany to surrender West Prussia and Posen, thus separating East Prussia from the main part of Germany (creating 'the Polish Corridor').
- Upper Silesia. A plebiscite was to be held in the province and as a result it was divided between Poland and Germany.
- Danzig and Memel. The German cities of Danzig (Gdansk in Polish) and Memel were made international free cities under the control of the League of Nations.
- Austria. The union (*Anschluss*) of Germany with Austria was forbidden.
- Kiel Canal and rivers. All major rivers to be open for all nations and to be run by an international commission.
- Saar area (see 'Reparations' on page 122).
- Rhineland (see 'Disarmament' on page 122).

- Germany's colonies. All German colonies were distributed as **'mandates'**, under control of countries supervised by the League, for example Britain took responsibility for German East Africa.

b) War guilt

Germany was forced to sign the War Guilt clause (Article 231) accepting blame for causing the war and therefore responsibility for all losses and damage:

> Germany accepts the responsibility of Germany and her allies for causing all the loss and damage to which the Allied governments and their peoples have been subjected as a result of the war.

c) Reparations

- Reparations sum to be fixed later by the IARC (Inter-Allied Reparations Commission). In 1921 the sum was fixed at £6600 million.
- Germany to make substantial payments in kind, e.g. coal.
- The Saar to be under the control of the League until 1935, when there was to be a plebiscite. Until then all coal production was to be given to France.

d) Disarmament

- Germany to abolish conscription and to reduce its army to 100,000. No tanks or big guns were allowed.
- The Rhineland was to be demilitarised from the French frontier to a line 32 miles east of the Rhine. (The Rhineland remained part of Germany.)

Key term

Mandates
The name given by the Allies to the system created in the peace settlement for the supervision of all the colonies of Germany (and Turkey) by the League of Nations.

Table 5.1: German losses resulting from the Treaty of Versailles

Type of loss	Loss
Territory	13%
Population	12% (6.5m)
Agricultural production	15%
Iron-ore	48%
Coal	15%

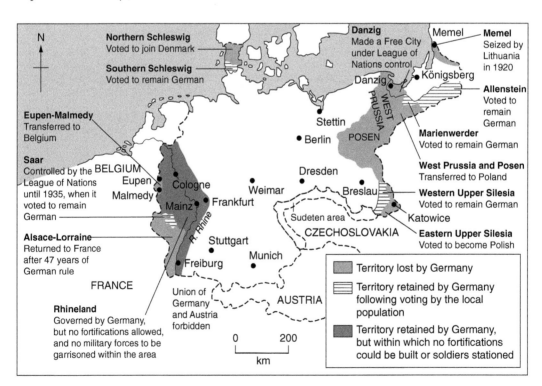

Figure 5.2: The terms of the Treaty of Versailles 1919.

- Germany allowed no military aircraft.
- German navy limited to:
  - six battleships, six cruisers, 12 destroyers, 12 torpedo boats
  - no submarines were allowed.

  (The German fleet surrendered to Britain in 1918, but sank its own ships at Scapa Flow on 28 June 1919.)

e) Maintaining peace

The Treaty also set out the Covenant of the League of Nations, which included the aims and organisation of the League. Germany had to accept the League, but it was initially not allowed to join.

The 'Diktat'

No other political issue produced such total agreement within Weimar Germany as the rejection and condemnation of the Treaty of Versailles. The Treaty's terms were seen as unfair and were simply described as a '*Diktat*'. Germany's main complaints were as follows:

Key question
Why did the Germans view the Treaty as unfair?

Key term

Diktat
A dictated peace. The Germans felt that the Treaty of Versailles was imposed without negotiation.

- The Treaty was considered to be very different from President Wilson's Fourteen Points. Most obviously, many Germans found it impossible to understand how and why the guiding principle of self-determination was *not* applied in a number of cases. They viewed the following areas as 'German', but excluded from the new German state and placed under foreign rule:
  - Austria
  - Danzig
  - Posen and West Prussia
  - Memel
  - Upper Silesia
  - Sudetenland
  - Saar.

  Similarly, the loss of Germany's colonies was not in line with the fifth of Wilson's Fourteen Points, which had called for 'an impartial adjustment of all colonial claims'. Instead, they were passed on to the care of the Allies as mandates.
- Germany found it impossible to accept the War Guilt clause (Article 231), which was the Allies' justification for demanding the payment of reparations. Most Germans argued that Germany could not be held solely responsible for the outbreak of the war. They were convinced that the war of 1914 had been fought for defensive reasons because their country had been threatened by 'encirclement' from the Allies in 1914.
- Germans considered the Allied demand for extensive reparations as totally unreasonable. Worryingly, the actual size of the reparations payment was not stated in the Treaty of Versailles – it was left to be decided at a later date by the IARC. From a German viewpoint this amounted to their being forced to sign a 'blank cheque'.

A cartoon drawn in July 1919 from the German newspaper *Kladderatsch*. It portrays Georges Clemenceau (the French Prime Minister) as a vampire sucking the blood and life from the innocent German maiden.

- The imposition of the disarmament clauses was seen as grossly unfair as Britain and France remained highly armed and made no future commitments to disarm. It seemed as if Germany had been **unilaterally disarmed**, whereas Wilson had spoken in favour of universal disarmament.
- Germany's treatment by the Allies was viewed as undignified and unworthy of a great power. For example, Germany was excluded from the League of Nations but was forced to accept the rules of its Covenant. This simply hardened the views of those Germans who saw the League as a tool of the Allies rather than as a genuine international organisation.

Altogether, the treaty was seen as a *Diktat*. The Allies maintained a military blockade on Germany until the Treaty was signed. This had significant human consequences such as increasing food shortages. Furthermore, the Allies threatened to take further military action if Germany did not co-operate.

Versailles: a more balanced view

In the years 1919–45, most Germans regarded the Treaty of Versailles as a *Diktat*. In Britain, too, there developed a growing sympathy for Germany's position. However, this was not the case in France, where the Treaty was generally condemned as being too lenient. It was only after the Second World War that a more balanced view of the Treaty of Versailles emerged in Europe. As a result, recent historians have tended to view the peacemakers of

Unilateral disarmament
The disarmament of one party. Wilson pushed for general (universal) disarmament after the war, but France and Britain were more suspicious. As a result only Germany had to disarm.

Key term

Key question
To what extent was the Treaty of Versailles motivated by anti-German feeling?

1919 more sympathetically. Earlier German criticisms of the Treaty are no longer as readily accepted as they once were.

Of course, at the Paris peace conferences Allied statesmen were motivated by their own national self-interests, and the representatives of France and Britain were keen to achieve these at the expense of Germany. However, it is now recognised that it was the situation created by the war that shaped the terms of the Treaty and not just anti-German feeling. The aims and objectives of the various Allies differed and achieving agreement was made more difficult by the complicated circumstances of the time. It should be remembered that the Paris peace settlement was not solely concerned with Germany, so Austria-Hungary, Bulgaria and Turkey were forced to sign separate treaties. In addition, other problems had to be dealt with. For example, Britain had national interests to look after in the Middle East as a result of the collapse of the Turkish Empire. At the same time the Allies were concerned by the threat of Soviet Russia and were motivated by a common desire to contain the Bolshevik menace.

In the end, the Treaty of Versailles was a compromise. It was not based on Wilson's Fourteen Points as most Germans thought it would be, but equally it was not nearly so severe as certain sections of Allied opinion had demanded. It should be borne in mind that:

- Clemenceau, the French representative, was forced to give way over most of his country's more extreme demands, such as the creation of an independent Rhineland state and the annexation of the Saar.
- The application of self-determination was not nearly so unfair as many Germans believed:
  - Alsace-Lorraine would have voted to return to France anyway, as it had been French before 1871.
  - Plebiscites were held in Schleswig, Silesia and parts of Prussia to decide their future.
  - Danzig's status under the League was the result of Woodrow Wilson's promise to provide 'Poland with access to the sea'.
  - The eastern frontier provinces of Posen and West Prussia were rather more mixed in ethnic make-up than Germans were prepared to admit (in these provinces Germans predominated in the towns, whereas the Poles did so in the countryside – which made it very difficult to draw a clear frontier line).
  - Austria and Sudetenland had never been part of Germany before 1918, anyway.
- Germany was not physically occupied and, as a result, the real damage was suffered on foreign soil, e.g. France and Belgium.
- In comparison the Treaty of Versailles appeared relatively moderate to the severity of the terms imposed by the Germans on the Russians at the Treaty of Brest-Litovsk in 1918, which annexed large areas of Poland and the Baltic states.

The significance of the Treaty of Versailles

The historical significance of the Treaty of Versailles goes well beyond the debate over its fairness. It raises the important issue of its impact upon the Weimar Republic and whether it acted as a serious handicap to the establishment of long-term political stability in Germany.

Key question
Did the Treaty of Versailles fundamentally weaken Weimar Germany?

The economic consequences of reparations were undoubtedly a genuine concern. The English economist Keynes feared in 1919 that the reparations would fundamentally weaken the economy of Germany with consequences for the whole of Europe. However, Germany's economic potential was still considerable. It had potentially by far the strongest economy in Europe and still had extensive industry and resources. As will be seen later (pages 139–47), the Republic's economic problems cannot be blamed on the burden of reparations alone. And it should also be remembered that by 1932 Germany actually received more in loans under the Dawes Plan (see page 164) than it paid in reparations.

It is not really possible to maintain that the Treaty had weakened Germany politically. In some respects, Germany in 1919 was in a stronger position than in 1914. The great empires of Russia, Austria-Hungary and Turkey had gone, creating a power vacuum in central and eastern Europe that could not be filled at least in the short term by a weak and isolated Soviet Russia or by any other state. In such a situation, cautious diplomacy might have led to the establishment of German power and influence at the heart of Europe.

However, on another level, the Treaty might be considered more to blame because, in the minds of many Germans, it was regarded as the real cause of the country's problems and they really believed that it was totally unfair. In the war German public opinion had been strongly shaped by nationalist propaganda and then deeply shocked by the defeat. Both the Armistice and Versailles were closely linked to the 'stab in the back' myth that the German Army had not really lost the First World War in 1918 (see page 100). It may have been a myth, but it was a very powerful one.

As a result, although the First World War had been pursued by Imperial Germany, it was the new democracy of Weimar that was forced to take the responsibility and the blame for it. Therefore, Weimar democracy was deeply weakened by Versailles, which fuelled the propaganda of the Republic's opponents over the years. Even for sympathetic democrats like Hugo Preuss, Versailles only served to disillusion many into thinking that the gains of the revolution were being undone: '… the German Republic was born out of its terrible defeat … The criminal madness of the Versailles *Diktat* was a shameless blow in the face to such hopes based on international law and political common sense'. In this way the Treaty of Versailles contributed to the internal political and economic difficulties that evolved in Germany after 1919.

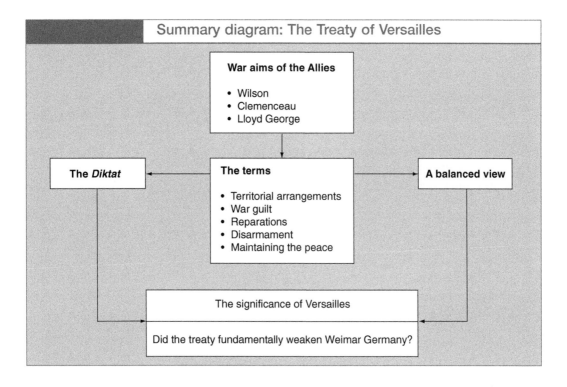

Summary diagram: The Treaty of Versailles

War aims of the Allies

- Wilson
- Clemenceau
- Lloyd George

The *Diktat*

The terms

- Territorial arrangements
- War guilt
- Reparations
- Disarmament
- Maintaining the peace

A balanced view

The significance of Versailles

Did the treaty fundamentally weaken Weimar Germany?

Key question
How serious was the opposition of the extreme left to the Weimar Republic?

3 | The Threat from the Extreme Left

After the German Revolution of 1918–19 the left-wing movement at first remained in a state of confusion:

- The moderate socialists of the SPD were committed to parliamentary democracy.
- The Communists (the KPD) pressed for a workers' revolution.
- The USPD stood for the creation of a radical socialist society, but within a democratic framework.

This situation became clearer when, in 1920, the USPD disbanded and its members joined either the KPD or the SPD. So, from that time there were two left-wing alternative parties, but with fundamental differences.

The KPD believed that the establishment of parliamentary democracy fell a long way short of its real aims. It wanted the revolution to proceed on Marxist lines with the creation of a one-party communist state and the major restructuring of Germany both socially and economically. As a result of the 1917 Russian Revolution, many German communists were encouraged by the political unrest to believe that international revolution would spread throughout Europe.

The KPD's opposition to the Republic was nothing less than a complete rejection of the Weimar system. It was not prepared to be part of the democratic opposition or to work within the parliamentary system to bring about desired changes. The differences between the moderate and extreme left were so basic that there was no chance of political co-operation between them, let alone a coming together into one socialist movement. The extreme left was totally committed to a very different vision of German politics and society, whereas the moderate left was one of the pillars of Weimar democracy.

KPD opposition

The KPD was indeed a reasonable political force in the years 1919–23. It enjoyed the support of 10–15 per cent of the electorate and there were continuous revolutionary disturbances – protests, strikes and uprisings (see Table 5.2 below). However, all these actions by the extreme left gave the impression that Germany was really facing a Bolshevik-inspired '**Red Threat**'. Consequently, as a result of right-wing propaganda, many Germans began to have exaggerated fears about the possibility of impending revolution.

Looking back, it is clear that the extreme left posed much less of a threat to Weimar than was believed at the time. So, despite all the disturbances, the revolutionary left was never really likely to be able to seize political power. The main reasons lie in a combination of their own weaknesses and the effective resistance of the Weimar governments:

- Bad co-ordination. Even during the chaos and uncertainty of 1923, the activities of the extreme left proved incapable of mounting a unified attack on Weimar democracy.
- Poor leadership. The repression it suffered at the hands of the *Freikorps* removed some of its ablest and most spirited leaders, e.g. Liebknecht and Luxemburg (see page 108). The later leadership suffered from internal divisions and disagreements on tactics.
- Concessions. The Weimar governments played on the differences within the extreme left by making concessions

Table 5.2 Major communist uprisings 1919–23

Date	Place	Action	Response
January 1919	Berlin	Spartacist uprising to seize power	Crushed by German army and *Freikorps*
March 1919	Bavaria	Creation of soviet republic	Crushed by the *Freikorps*
March 1920	Ruhr	Formation of the Ruhr Army by 50,000 workers to oppose the Kapp *putsch* (pages 131–3)	Crushed by German Army and *Freikorps*
March 1921	Merseburg and Halle	'March Operation'. Uprising of strikes organised by KPD	Put down by police
Summer 1923	Saxony	'**German October**' A wave of strikes and the creation of an SPD/KPD state government	Overthrown by German army

Key terms

Red Threat
A 'Red' was a loose term used to describe anyone sympathetic to the left. It originated from the Bolshevik use of the red flag in Russia.

German October
The revolutionary uprising in Germany in 1923 is often referred to as the German October, but it is a confusing term. Mass protests started before this, in the summer of 1923, though the uprising did not actually come to a head until October 1923 (which was also emotionally associated with the Bolshevik Revolution in Russia in October 1917).

which split it, e.g. over the Kapp *putsch* in March 1920 (see pages 131–3).
- Repression. The authorities systematically repressed the rebels with considerable brutality.

In the end, the extreme left was just not powerful enough to lead a revolution against the Weimar Republic.

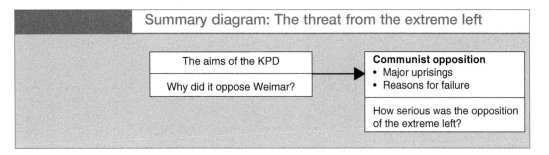

Summary diagram: The threat from the extreme left

The aims of the KPD

Why did it oppose Weimar?

Communist opposition
- Major uprisings
- Reasons for failure

How serious was the opposition of the extreme left?

Key question
What did the extreme right stand for?

4 | The Threat from the Extreme Right

Opposition from the extreme right was very different both in its form and in its extent to that of the extreme left. On the right wing there was a very mixed collection of opponents to the Republic and their resistance found expression in different ways.

The extreme right in theory

In contrast to Marxist socialism, the extreme right did not really have an alternative organised ideology. It was simply drawn together by a growing belief in the following:

- Anti-democracy: it was united by its rejection of the Weimar system and its principles. It aimed to destroy the democratic constitution because it was seen as weak, which it believed had contributed to Germany's problems.
- **Anti-Marxism**: even more despised than democracy was the fear of communism. It was seen as a real threat to traditional values and the ownership of property and wealth – and when Russian communism was established, it reinforced the idea that communism was anti-German.
- Authoritarianism: the extreme right favoured the restoration of some authoritarian, dictatorial regime – though in the early 1920s there was no real consensus on what kind of strong government and leadership would be established.
- Nationalism: nationalism was at the core of the extreme right, but Germany's national pride had been deeply hurt by the events of 1918–19. Not surprisingly, from the time of the Treaty of Versailles, this conservative-nationalist response reinforced the ideas of the 'stab in the back' myth and the '**November criminals**'. The war, it was argued, had been lost not because of any military defeat suffered by the army, but as a result of the betrayal by unpatriotic forces within Germany. These were said to include pacifists, socialists, democrats and Jews. Right-wing

Key terms

Anti-Marxism
Opposition to the ideology of Karl Marx.

November criminals
Those who signed the November Armistice and a term of abuse to vilify all those who supported the democratic republic.

politicians found a whole range of scapegoats to take the blame for German acceptance of the Armistice.

Worse still, these 'November criminals' had been prepared to overthrow the monarchy and establish a republic. To add insult to injury, they had accepted the 'shameful peace' of Versailles. The extreme right accepted such interpretations, distorted as they were. They not only served to remove any responsibility from Imperial Germany, but also acted as a powerful stick with which to beat the leaders of Weimar Germany.

Organisations of the extreme right

The extreme right appeared in various forms. It included a number of political parties and was also the driving force behind the activities of various paramilitary organisations.

Key question
How did the extreme right manifest itself in different ways?

DNVP

The DNVP (German National People's Party) was a coalition of nationalist-minded old imperial conservative parties and included such groups as the Fatherland Party and the Pan-German League. From the very start, it contained extremist and racist elements. Although it was still the party of landowners and industrialists, it had a broad appeal amongst some of the middle classes. It was by far the largest party in the *Reichstag* on the extreme right and was able to poll 15.1 per cent in the 1920 election.

Racist nationalism

The emergence of racist nationalism, or *völkisch* nationalism, was clearly apparent before 1914, but the effects of the war and its aftermath increased its attraction for many on the right. By the early 1920s there were probably about 70 relatively small splinter nationalist parties, which were also racist and anti-Semitic, e.g. the Nazi Party.

Bavaria became a particular haven for such groups, since the regional state government was sufficiently **reactionary** to tolerate them. One such group was the German Workers' Party, originally founded by Anton Drexler. Adolf Hitler joined the party in 1919 and within two years had become its leader. However, during the years 1919–24, regional and policy differences divided such groups and attempts to unify the nationalist right ended in failure. When, in 1923, Hitler and the Nazis attempted to organise an uprising with the Munich Beer Hall *putsch*, it ended in fiasco (see pages 134–5). It was not until the mid-1920s, when Hitler began to bring the different groups together under the leadership of the NSDAP, that a powerful political force was created.

Reactionary
Opposing change and supporting a return to traditional ways.

Paramilitary units
Informal non-legal military squads.

Key terms

Freikorps

The *Freikorps* that flourished in the post-war environment attracted the more brutal elements of German militarism. As a result of the demobilisation of the armed forces there were nearly 200 **paramilitary units** around Germany by 1919.

Key terms

White Terror
The 'Whites' were seen as the opponents (in contrast to the Reds). The 'White Terror' refers to the suppression of the soviet republic in Bavaria in March 1919.

Rapallo Treaty
This was not an alliance, but a treaty of friendship between Germany and Russia.

The *Freikorps* became a law unto themselves and they were employed by the government in a crucial role to suppress the threats from the extreme left. However, as the *Freikorps* was anti-republican and committed to the restoration of authoritarian rule, they had no respect for the Weimar governments. Their bloody actions became known as the '**White Terror**' and showed they were quite prepared to use acts of violence and murder to intimidate others.

Consul Organisation

From 1920 the Weimar governments tried to control the actions of the *Freikorps*, but a new threat emerged from the right wing in the form of political assassination. In the years 1919–22 there were 376 political murders – 22 by the left and 354 by the right. The most notorious terrorist gang was known as the 'Consul Organisation' because it was responsible for the assassination of a number of key republican politicians:

Key dates

The murder of Matthias Erzberger: 26 August 1921

The murder of Walter Rathenau: 24 June 1922

- Matthias Erzberger, Finance Minister 1919–21. Murdered because he was a Catholic and a member of the ZP and had signed the Armistice.
- Walther Rathenau, Foreign Minister, 1921–2 (who drew up the **Rapallo Treaty** with Russia). Murdered because he was Jewish and was committed to democracy.
- Karl Gareis, leader of the USPD. Murdered on 9 June 1921 because he was a committed socialist.

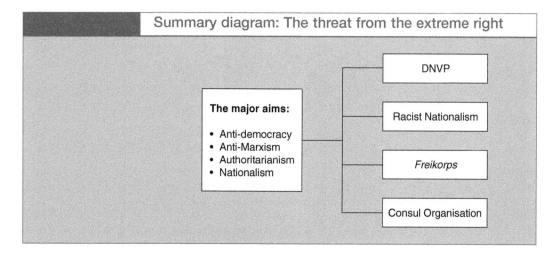

Summary diagram: The threat from the extreme right

The major aims:

- Anti-democracy
- Anti-Marxism
- Authoritarianism
- Nationalism

DNVP

Racist Nationalism

Freikorps

Consul Organisation

Key question
How significant was the Kapp *putsch*?

5 | Extreme Right Uprisings

The Kapp *putsch*

The *Freikorps* played a central role in the first attempt by the extreme right wing to seize power from the constitutional government. This was because by early 1920 there was considerable unease within the ranks of the *Freikorps* at the demands to reduce the size of the German army according to the terms of the Versailles Treaty.

When it was proposed to disband two brigades of the army, the Ehrhardt Marine Brigade and the Baltikum that were stationed in the Berlin area, Wolfgang Kapp (see the profile below) and General Lüttwitz decided to exploit the situation. They encouraged 12,000 troops to march on Berlin and seize the main buildings of the capital virtually unopposed, where they installed a new government.

The Kapp *putsch*: March 1920

Significantly, the German army did not provide any resistance to this *putsch*. In spite of requests from Ebert and the Chancellor to put down the rebellious forces, the army was not prepared to become involved with either side. Although it did not join those involved in the *putsch*, it failed to support the legitimate government. General von Seeckt, the senior officer in the Defence Ministry, spoke for many colleagues when he declared:

> Troops do not fire on troops. So, you perhaps intend, Herr Minister, that a battle be fought before the Brandenburger Tor between troops that have fought side by side against a common enemy? When *Reichswehr* fires on *Reichswehr* all comradeship within the officers' corps will have vanished.

The army's decision to put its own interests before its obligation to defend the government forced the latter to flee the capital and move to Stuttgart. However, the *putsch* collapsed. Before leaving

---

Profile: Wolfgang Kapp 1858–1922

1858	– Born in New York
1870	– Returned to Germany with his family
1886–1920	– Qualified as a doctor of law and then appointed as a Prussian civil servant in various posts
1917	– Helped to found the right-wing German Fatherland Party
1918	– Elected to the *Reichstag*
	– Opposed the abdication of Wilhelm II and remained committed to the restoration of the monarchy
1920	– Collaborated with Lüttwitz to launch the *putsch*. Briefly appointed Chancellor by the leaders of the *putsch*. Fled to Sweden
1922	– Returned to Germany but died while awaiting trial

Kapp has been described as 'a neurotic with delusions' or simply a 'crank' who represented the extreme nationalist-conservative views. He did not play any major part in politics of Imperial Germany until the war, when he helped to form the German Fatherland Party. After the war he campaigned for the restoration of Kaiser Wilhelm, but his *putsch* was a fiasco. Interestingly, some of the men involved in his *putsch* had swastika symbols on their helmets.

Berlin, the SPD members of the government had called for a general strike, which soon paralysed the capital and quickly spread to the rest of the country. After four days, Kapp and his government exerted no real authority and they fled the city.

The aftermath of the Kapp *putsch*

At first sight the collapse of the Kapp *putsch* could be viewed as a major success for the Weimar Republic. In the six days of crisis, it had retained the backing of the people of Berlin and had effectively withstood a major threat from the extreme right. However, what is significant is that the Kapp *putsch* had taken place at all. In this sense, the Kapp *putsch* highlights clearly the weakness of the Weimar Republic. The army's behaviour at the time of the *putsch* was typical of its right-wing attitudes and its lack of sympathy for the Republic. During the months after the *coup*, the government failed to confront this problem.

The army leadership had revealed its unreliability. Yet, amazingly, at the end of that very month Seeckt was appointed Chief of the Army Command (1920–6). He was appointed because he enjoyed the confidence of his fellow officers and ignored the fact that his support for the Republic was at best lukewarm. Under Seeckt's influence, the organisation of the army was remodelled and its status redefined:

- He imposed very strict military discipline and recruited new troops, increasingly at the expense of the *Freikorps*.
- However, he was determined to uphold the independence of the army. He believed it held a privileged position that placed it beyond direct government control. For example, he turned a blind eye to the Versailles disarmament clauses in order to increase the size of the army with more modern weapons.

Many within its ranks believed that the army served some higher purpose to the nation as a whole. It had the right to intervene as it saw fit without regard to its obligations to the Republic. All this suggests that the aftermath of the Kapp *putsch*, the Ebert–Groener Pact (see page 106) and the Constitution's failure to reform the structures of army had made it a '**state within a state**'.

The judiciary also continued with the old political values that had not changed since imperial times. It enjoyed the advantage of maintaining its independence from the Weimar Constitution, but it questioned the legal rights of the new republic and reached some dubious and obviously biased decisions. Those involved in the *putsch* of 1920 never felt the full rigour of the law:

- Kapp died awaiting trial.
- Lüttwitz was granted early retirement.
- Only one of the 705 prosecuted was actually found guilty and sentenced to five years' imprisonment.

Over the years 1919–22 it was clear that the judges were biased and their hearts did not lie with the Weimar Republic:

Key term

State within a state A situation where the authority and government of the state are threatened by a rival power base.

- Out of the 354 right-wing assassins only 28 were found guilty and punished (but no-one was executed).
- Of the 22 left-wing assassins 10 were sentenced to death.

The Munich Beer Hall *putsch*

Although the Munich Beer Hall *putsch* was one of the threats faced by the young republic in the year 1923, the event is also a crucial part of the rise of Hitler and the Nazis. So the details of the events also relate to Chapter 8 on pages 179–80.

In the short term it should be noted that the government of the State of Bavaria was under the control of the ultra-conservative Gustav von Kahr, who blamed most of Germany's problems on the national government in Berlin. Like Hitler, he wished to destroy the republican regime, although his long-term aim was the creation of an independent Bavaria. By October 1923 General von Lossow, the Army's commander in Bavaria, had fallen under von Kahr's spell and had even begun to disobey orders from the Defence Minister from Berlin. So it was both of these ultra-conservatives who plotted with Hitler and the Nazis to 'March on Berlin'.

By the first week of November 1923, Kahr and Lossow, fearing failure, decided to abandon the plan. However, Hitler was not so cautious and preferred to press on rather than lose the

Key question
Who were the plotters and why did they fail?

Key date
The Munich Beer Hall *putsch*:
8–9 November 1923

A cartoon of 1924 derides the judiciary after the trial of Hitler and Ludendorff. The judge simply says 'High treason? Rubbish! The worst we can charge them with is breaking by-laws about entertaining in public.'

Table 5.3: The plotters in the Munich Beer Hall *putsch*

Name	Background/attitude	Involvement
Erich von Ludendorff (retired general)	Took part in Kapp *putsch*. Opposed to democracy (see profile on page 93)	Collaborated with Hitler and supported the *putsch* on 8–9 November
Gustav von Kahr (leader of the Bavarian state government)	Anti-democratic and sympathetic to many of the right-wing extremists. Committed to the restoration of the monarchy in an independent Bavaria	Planned with Hitler and Lossow to seize power, but became wary. Forced to co-operate with his rally on 8 November, although did not support the *putsch*
Otto von Lossow (Commander of the Bavarian section of the German army)	Despised Weimar democracy and supported authoritarian rule. Very conservative	Planned with Hitler and Kahr to seize power, but became wary. Forced to co-operate in the rally on 8 November, though did not support the *putsch*
Adolf Hitler (leader of the Nazi Party)	Extremist: anti-Semitic, anti-democratic and anti-communist. Backed by the Nazi SA (see profile on pages 212–13)	Planned and wholly committed to seizing power. Forced the hands of Kahr and Lossow and carried on with the *putsch*
Hans von Seeckt (General, Chief of the Army Command, 1920–6)	Unsympathetic to democracy and keen to preserve the interests of the army, but suspicious of Hitler and the Nazis (see pages 132–3)	Initially ambiguous attitude in early November. But in the crisis he used his powers to command the armed forces to resist the *putsch*.

opportunity. On 8 November Hitler, together with his Nazi supporters, stormed into and took control of a large rally, which von Kahr was addressing in one of Munich's beer halls, and declared a 'national revolution'. Under pressure, Kahr and Lossow co-operated and agreed to proceed with the uprising, but in reality they had lost their nerve when Seeckt used his powers to command the armed forces to resist the *putsch*. So when, on the next day, the Nazis attempted to take Munich they had insufficient support and the Bavarian police easily crushed the *putsch*. Fourteen Nazis were killed and Hitler was arrested on a charge of treason.

Key question
How significant was the Munich Beer Hall *putsch*?

The aftermath of the Munich Beer Hall *putsch*

On one level the inglorious result of the Nazi *putsch* was encouraging for Weimar democracy. It withstood a dangerous threat in what was a difficult year. Most significantly, Seeckt and the army did not throw in their lot with the Nazis – which upset Hitler so much that he described him as a 'lackey of the Weimar Republic'. However, once again it was the dealings of the judiciary that raised so much concern:

- Hitler was sentenced to a mere five years (the minimum stipulation for treason). His imprisonment at Landsberg provided quite reasonable conditions and he was released after less than 10 months.
- Ludendorff was acquitted on the grounds that although he had been present at the time of the *putsch*, he was there 'by accident'!

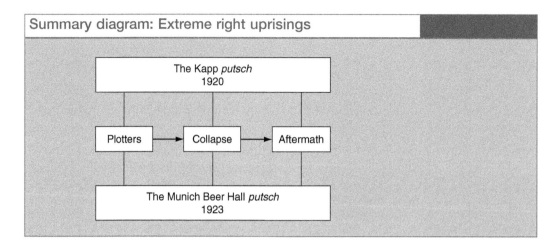

Summary diagram: Extreme right uprisings

The Kapp *putsch* 1920

Plotters → Collapse → Aftermath

The Munich Beer Hall *putsch* 1923

6 | Weimar Democracy: A Republic Without Republicans

Key question
What was the greatest threat to Weimar democracy?

The optimism of the first election of the Republic gave way to concerns in the election of June 1920. The results can be seen in Table 5.4 and they raise several key points:

- The combined support for the three main democratic parties declined dramatically:
  - 1919: 76.1 per cent
  - 1920: 48.0 per cent.
  (The figures do not include the DVP under the leadership of Stresemann which voted against the Weimar Constitution at first, but became committed to the Republic from 1921.)
- The support for each of the pro-democratic parties declined:
  - the SPD declined sharply from 37.9 to 21.7 per cent
  - the DDP declined catastrophically from 18.5 to 8.3 per cent
  - the ZP dropped down slightly from 19.75 to 18.0 per cent.
- The support for the extreme left and right increased, especially the DNVP:
  - the DNVP increased from 10.3 to 15.1 per cent
  - the KPD/USPD increased from 7.6 to 20.0 per cent.

Weimar governments

The Weimar Republic not only faced overt opposition from both the extremes but also its democratic supporters struggled with

Table 5.4: *Reichstag* election results 1919–20 (see major political parties on page 110)

	Turn-out	NSDAP	DNVP	DVP	ZP/BVP	DDP	SPD	USPD/KPD	Others
January 1919									
Seats	423	–	44	19	91	75	165	22	7
Per cent	83		10.3	4.4	19.7	18.5	37.9	7.6	1.6
June 1920									
Seats	459	–	71	65	85	39	102	88	9
Per cent	79.2		15.1	13.9	18.0	8.3	21.2	20.0	2.9

the practical problem of creating and maintaining workable government coalitions. In the four years 1919–23 Weimar had six governments – the longest of which lasted just 18 months (see Table 5.5).

Table 5.5: Governments of the Weimar Republic 1919–23

Period in office	Chancellor	Make-up of the coalition
1919	Philipp Scheidemann	SPD, ZP, DDP
1919–20	Gustav Bauer	SPD, ZP, DDP
1920	Hermann Müller	SPD, Centre, DDP
1920–1	Konstantin Fehrenbach	ZP, DDP, DVP
1921–2	Joseph Wirth	SPD, DDP, ZP
1922–3	Wilhelm Cuno	ZP, DDP, DVP

Conclusion

The success of the democratic parties in the *Reichstag* elections of January 1919 at first disguised some of Weimar's fundamental problems in its political structure. But opposition to the Republic ranged from indifference to brutal violence and, as early as 1920, democratic support for Weimar began to switch to the extremes. This is shown by the results of the first election after the Treaty of Versailles.

The extent of the opposition from the extreme right to democracy was not always appreciated. Instead, President Ebert and the Weimar governments overestimated the threat from the extreme left and they came to rely on the forces of reaction for justice and law and order. This was partly because the conservative forces successfully exploited the image of the left as a powerful threat. So, in many respects, it was the persistence of the old attitudes in the major traditional national institutions that represented the greatest long-term threat to the Republic. The violent forces of counter-revolution, as shown by the *putsches* of Kapp and Hitler, were too weak and disorganised to seize power in the early years. But the danger of the extreme right was actually insidious; it was the real growing threat to Weimar democracy.

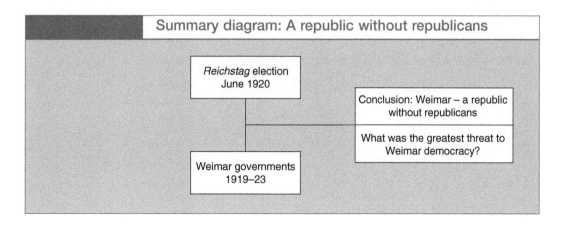

Summary diagram: A republic without republicans

Study Guide: A2 Question

'By May 1919 the German revolution had brought about remarkably little change in Germany.' How far do you agree with this judgement?

Exam tips

The cross-references are intended to take you straight to the material that will help you to answer the question.

This question asks you to evaluate the extent of change in Germany resulting from the German revolution. To assess change, you need a clear idea of what was different and what had remained the same six months after the declaration of the republic. You should also re-read Chapters 1 and 2 before tackling this question.

Some examples of change are:

- the abdication of the Kaiser (page 102)
- the creation of the National Constituent Assembly and the commitment to the creation of a parliamentary democracy (pages 109–12)
- the promise to create a welfare state and improved working conditions (pages 107–8, 116 and 152).

Some of the ways the German Revolution was limited are:

- Ebert's government's overreliance on the army and the *Freikorps* (pages 106–8 and 132–3)
- the failure to change the ownership of land and industry (pages 106–7 and 118).

To reach a conclusion on 'extent' of change, consider the weight of these differences. Do you see the things which remained the same as significant? Have much the same groups retained much the same amount of power? Or do the changes go deeper than that?

The question also requires you to address one further element: 'remarkably little change'. This means that you need to go further than an evaluation of the amount of change which took place. To address 'remarkably' you need to ask yourself how much change was likely or possible. In view of strength of the revolutionary potential of 1918, is it surprising that there was not more change? Or, in view of the strength of conservative forces in Germany, would you challenge the view that the amount of change was 'remarkably' little even if you consider that there was little change?

6 The Great Inflation

POINTS TO CONSIDER
1923 became known as the year of the Great Inflation, when Germany's money became totally worthless. For Germans living in the Weimar Republic it was a difficult time for them to understand and it resulted in a further serious loss of confidence in the government. Therefore, to appreciate the significance of the period it is important to consider the main themes:

- The causes of the inflation – long term, medium term and short term
- The consequences of the inflation
- Stresemann's 100 days and the end of the crisis

Key dates

1921	May	IARC (Inter-Allied Reparations Commission) fixed reparations at £6600 million (132 billion gold marks)
1923	January	Franco-Belgian occupation of the Ruhr Passive resistance proclaimed
	Jan.–Nov.	Period of hyper-inflation
	August	Stresemann made Chancellor of Germany
	Aug.–Nov.	Stresemann's 100 days
	December	Introduction of *Rentenmark*
1924	April	Dawes Plan proposed and accepted

1 | The Causes of the German Inflation

Germany's growing economic problems came to a head in 1923 when prices soared and money values spiralled down. This is often referred to as **hyper-inflation**. However, the crises of that year blinded many to the fact that prices had been rising since the early months of the war. Many Germans glibly assumed it was a result of the Treaty of Versailles and particularly the reparations. Still more unthinking explanations simply blamed it on the financial greed and corruption of the Jews.

However, with hindsight it is clear that the fundamental cause of the inflation was the huge increase in the amount of paper money in circulation, resulting from the government's printing more and

Key question
Why did Germany suffer hyper-inflation?

Key term

Hyper-inflation
Prices spiralled out of control because the government increased the amount of money being printed. As a result, it displaced the whole economy.

more notes to pay off the interest on its massive debts. The causes of the Great Inflation can be divided into three phases:

- Long term – the military demands of the First World War (1914–18) led to an enormous increase in financial costs.
- Medium term – the costs of introducing social reforms and welfare and the pressure to satisfy the demands for reparation payments from 1921.
- Short term – the French occupation of the Ruhr in 1923 resulted in crisis and the government of Cuno encouraged a policy of '**passive resistance**'.

Long term

Not surprisingly, Germany had made no financial provision for a long, drawn-out war. However, despite the increasing cost of the war, the Kaiser's government had decided, for political reasons, against increases in taxation. Instead, it had borrowed massive sums by selling 'war bonds' to the public. When this proved insufficient from 1916, it simply allowed the national debt to grow bigger and bigger.

The result of Imperial Germany's financial policies was that by the end of 1918 only 16 per cent of war expenditure had been raised from taxation – 84 per cent had been borrowed.

Another factor was that the war years had seen almost full employment. This was because the economy had concentrated on the supply of military weapons. But, since production was necessarily military based, it did not satisfy the requirements of the civilian consumers. Consequently, the high demand for, and the shortage of, consumer goods began to push prices up.

Victory would doubtless have allowed Imperial Germany to settle its debts by claiming reparations from the Allies, but defeat meant the reverse. The Weimar Republic had to cope with the massive costs of war. By 1919, Germany's finances were described by Volker Berghahn as 'an unholy mess'.

Medium term

The government of the Weimar Republic (like any government with a large deficit) could control inflation only by narrowing the gap between the government's income and expenditure through:

- increasing taxation in order to raises its income
- cutting government spending to reduce its expenditure.

However, in view of Germany's domestic situation neither of these options was particularly attractive, as both would alienate the people and cause political and social difficulties, such as increased unemployment and industrial decline.

Consequently, from 1919 the Weimar government guided by Erzberger, the Finance Minister (see page 97), extensively increased taxation on profits, wealth and income. However, it decided not to go so far as aiming to **balance the budget**. It decided to adopt a policy of deficit financing in the belief that it would:

Key terms

Passive resistance
Refusal to work with occupying forces.

Balanced budget
A financial programme in which a government does not spend more than it raises in revenue.

- maintain the demand for goods and, thereby, create work
- overcome the problems of demobilising millions of returning troops
- cover the cost of public spending on an extensive welfare state, e.g. health insurance, housing and benefits for the disabled
- reduce the real value of the national debt.

Key date

The IARC (Inter-Allied Reparations Commission) fixed the sum for reparations at £6600 million (132 billion gold marks): May 1921

Deficit financing means planning to increase the nation's debt by reducing taxation in order to give the people more money to spend and so increase the demand for goods and thereby create work. The government believed that this would enable Germany to overcome the problems of demobilisation – a booming economy would ensure there were plenty of jobs for the returning soldiers and sailors – and also reduce the real value of the national debt. Unfortunately, an essential part of this policy was to allow inflation to continue.

The reparations issue should be seen as one contributory factor to the inflation. It was certainly not the primary cause. Nevertheless, the sum drawn up by the Reparations Commission added to the economic burden facing the Weimar government

Key term

Hard currency
A currency that the market considers to be strong because its value does not depreciate. In the 1920s the hardest currency was the US dollar.

because the reparation payments had to be in **hard currency**, like dollars and gold (not inflated German marks). In order to pay their reparations, the Weimar governments proceeded to print larger quantities of marks and sell them to obtain the stronger currencies of other countries. This was not a solution. It was merely a short-term measure that had serious consequences. The mark went into sharp decline and inflation climbed even higher (see Table 6.1).

Table 6.1: The Great Inflation: exchange rate and wholesale prices

The Great Inflation	Exchange rate of German marks against the dollar	Wholesale price index. The index is created from a scale of prices starting with 1 for 1914
1914 July	4.2	1
1919 January	8.9	2
1920 January	14.0	4
1921 January	64.9	14
1922 January	191.8	37
1923 January	17,792	2,785
1923 July	353,412	74,787
1923 September	98,860,000	23,949,000
1923 November	200,000,000,000	750,000,000,000

Short term

Germany had already been allowed to postpone several instalments of her reparations payments in early 1922, but an attempt to resolve the crisis on an international level by calling the Genoa Economic Conference was ill fated. When, in July 1922, the German government made another request for a 'holiday' from making reparations payments, the final stage of the country's inflationary crisis set in.

The French government, at this time led by Raymond Poincaré, suspected German intentions and was determined to secure what was seen as France's rightful claims. Therefore, when in December 1922 the Reparations Commission declared Germany to be in default, Poincaré ordered French and Belgian troops to occupy the Ruhr, the industrial heartland of Germany. In the next few months the inflationary spiral ran out of control – hyper-inflation.

The government, led by Wilhelm Cuno, embarked on a policy of 'passive resistance' and in a way the invasion did help to unite the German people. It urged the workers to go on strike and refuse to co-operate with the French authorities, although it also promised to carry on paying their wages. At the same time, the government was unable to collect taxes from the Ruhr area and the French prevented the delivery of coal to the rest of Germany, thus forcing the necessary stocks of fuel to be imported.

In this situation, the government's finances collapsed and the mark fell to worthless levels. By autumn 1923, it cost more to print a bank note than the note was worth and the *Reichsbank* was forced to use newspaper presses to produce sufficient money. The German currency ceased to have any real value and the German people had to resort to barter (see Table 6.2).

Key dates

Franco-Belgian occupation of the Ruhr: January 1923

'Passive resistance' in Ruhr against French and Belgian soldiers: 13 January 1923

Period of hyper-inflation: January–November 1923

Table 6.2: Prices in the Great Inflation (in German marks)

Items for sale in	1913	Summer 1923	November 1923
1 kg of bread	0.29	1,200	428,000,000,000
1 kg of butter	2.70	26,000	6,000,000,000,000
1 kg of beef	1.75	18,800	5,600,000,000,000
1 pair of shoes	12.00	1,000,000	32,000,000,000,000

Conclusion

The fundamental cause of the German Inflation is to be found in the mismanagement of Germany's finances from 1914 onwards. Certainly, the inflationary spiral did not increase at an even rate and there were short periods, as in the spring of 1920 and the winter of 1920–1, when it did actually slacken. However, at no time was there willingness by the various German governments to bring spending and borrowing back within reasonable limits.

Until the end of 1918 the cost of waging war was the excuse, but in the immediate post-war period the high levels of debt were allowed to continue. It has been argued by some that the inflation remained quite modest in the years 1914–22 and perhaps acceptable in view of all the various difficulties facing the new government. However, the payment of reparations from 1921 simply added to an already desperate situation and the government found it more convenient to print money than to tackle the basic problems facing the economy.

By the end of 1922 hyper-inflation had set in. Cuno's government made no effort to deal with the situation. Indeed, it could be said that Cuno deliberately exacerbated the economic crisis and played on the nationalist fervour brought by the popular decision to encourage 'passive resistance'. It was only in August 1923, when the German economy was on the verge of complete collapse, that a new coalition government was formed under Gustav Stresemann. He found the will to introduce an economic policy which was aimed at controlling the amount of money in circulation.

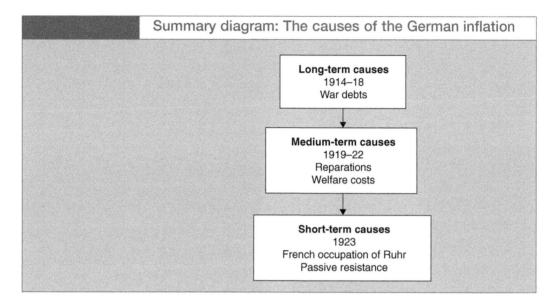

Summary diagram: The causes of the German inflation

Long-term causes
1914–18
War debts

Medium-term causes
1919–22
Reparations
Welfare costs

Short-term causes
1923
French occupation of Ruhr
Passive resistance

Key question
Why did some
Germans lose and
some win?

2 | The Consequences of the Great Inflation

It has been claimed that the worst consequence of the inflation was the damage done to the German middle class. Stresemann himself said as much in 1927. Later on in the 1930s it was generally assumed that the reason a large proportion of the middle class voted for the Nazis was because of their economic suffering in 1923. In the light of recent historical research, such assumptions have come to be questioned and a much more complex interpretation has emerged about the impact of the inflation on the whole of society.

The key to understanding who gained and who lost during the period of the hyper-inflation lies in considering each individual's savings and their amount of debt. However, it was not always clearly linked to class differences. So what did this mean in practice?

The real winners were those sections of the community who were able to pay off their debts, mortgages and loans with inflated and worthless money. This obviously worked to the advantage of such groups as businessmen and homeowners, which included members of the middle class. Those who recognised the situation for what it was exploited it by making massive gains from buying up property from those financially desperate. Some businessmen profited from the situation by borrowing cheaply and investing in new industrial enterprises. Amongst these, one of the most notorious examples was Hugo Stinnes who, by the end of 1923, controlled 20 per cent of German industry.

At the other extreme were those who depended on their savings. Any German who had money invested in bank accounts with interest rates found their real value had eroded. Most famously, millions who had bought and invested in war bonds now could not get their money back. The bonds were worth nothing. Those living on fixed incomes, such as pensioners, found themselves in a similar plight. Their savings quickly lost value, since any increase was wiped out by inflation (see Table 6.3).

Table 6.3: Financial winners and losers

Financial winners and losers	Explanation of gains or losses
Mortgage holders	Borrowed money was easily paid off in valueless money
Savers	Money invested was eroded
Exporters	Sales to foreign countries were attractive because of the rate of exchange
Those on fixed incomes	Income declined in real terms dramatically
Recipients of welfare	Depended on charity or state. Payments fell behind the inflation rate
Long-term renters/landlords	Income was fixed in the long term and so it declined in real terms
The German State	Large parts of the government debt were paid off in valueless money (but not reparations)

The human consequences

The material impact of the hyper-inflation has recently been the subject of considerable historical research in Germany and, as a result, our understanding of this period has been greatly increased and many previous conclusions have been revised. However, you should remember that the following discussion of the effects of the hyper-inflation on whole classes deals with broad categories, e.g. region and age, rather than individual examples. Two people from the same social class could be affected in very different ways depending on their individual circumstances.

Key question
Who were the winners and the losers?

Peasants

In the countryside the peasants coped reasonably well as food remained in demand. They depended less on money for the provision of the necessities of life as they were more self-sufficient.

Mittelstand

Shopkeepers and craftsmen also seem to have done reasonably good business, especially if they were prepared to exploit the demands of the market.

Children playing with blocks of worthless banknotes in 1923.

Industrial workers

Workers' real wages and standard of living improved until 1922. It was in the chaos of 1923 that, when the trade unions were unable to negotiate wage settlements for their members, wages could not keep pace with the rate of inflation and a very real decline took place. However, as they had fewer savings, they lost proportionally less than those living on saved income. Unemployment did go up to 4.1 per cent in 1923, but it was still at a relatively low level.

Civil servants

The fate of public employees is probably the most difficult to analyse. Their income fell sharply in the years 1914–20, but they made real gains in 1921–2. They suffered again in the chaos of 1923 because they depended on fixed salaries, which fell in value before the end of each month. They tended to gain – if they were buying a property on a mortgage – but many had been attracted to buy the war bonds and so lost out.

Retired

The old generally suffered badly because they depended on fixed pensions and savings.

Businessmen

Generally, they did well because they bought up property with worthless money and they paid off mortgages. They also benefited if they made sales to foreign countries, as the rate of exchange was very attractive.

Other social effects

By merely listing the financial statistics of the Great Inflation, there is a danger of overlooking the very real human dimension. As early as February 1923 the health minister warned:

> ... we do have a preliminary mortality rate for towns with 100,000 or more inhabitants. After having fallen in 1920–1, it has climbed again for the year 1921–2, rising from 12.6 to 13.4 per thousand inhabitants ... thus, oedema [an unpleasant medical condition which occurs when water accumulates in parts of the body] is reappearing, this so-called war dropsy, which is a consequence of a bad and overly watery diet. There are increases in stomach disorders and food poisoning, which are the result of eating spoiled foods. There are complaints of the appearance of scurvy, which is a consequence of an unbalanced and improper diet. From various parts of the Reich, reports are coming in about an increase in suicides ... More and more often one finds 'old age' and 'weakness' listed in the official records as the cause of death; these are equivalent to death through hunger.

Even more telling than the health minister's description about Germany's declining health were the possible effects on behaviour, as people began to resort to desperate solutions:

- a decline in law and order and an increase in crime
- a decline in 'morality', for example, more prostitution
- a growth in suicides
- an increase in prejudice and a tendency to find scapegoats, e.g. Jews.

It has often been suggested that such social problems contributed to people's lack of faith in the republican system. The connection is difficult to prove, as it is not easy to assess the importance of morality and religious codes in past societies. However, it would be foolish to dismiss out of hand their effects upon German society and its traditional set of values. At the very least, the loss of some old values led to increased tensions. Even more significantly, when another crisis developed at the end of the decade, the people's confidence in the ability of Weimar to maintain social stability was eventually lost. In that sense the inflation of 1923 was not the reason for the Weimar Republic's decline, but it caused psychological damage that continued to affect the Republic in future years.

Key question
In what other ways did the Great Inflation affect people's lives?

Key question
Was the Great
Inflation a disaster?

Conclusion

Traditionally, the German inflation has been portrayed as a catastrophe with damaging consequences that paved the way for the collapse of the Weimar Republic and the rise of Nazism. However, from the 1980s some have perceived the event differently.

The economic historian Holtfrerich maintains that in the years up to the end of 1922 Weimar's economic policy amounted to a 'rational strategy … in the national interest'. His interpretation is that by not reducing the budget deficits, the Weimar Republic was able to maintain economic growth and increase production. He argues that the German economy compared favourably with other European economies that also went into recession in 1920–1:

- Low unemployment. Whereas Britain had an unemployment rate of 17 per cent in 1921, Germany had nearly full employment with only 1.8 per cent unemployed.
- Rising wage levels. The real wages of industrial workers increased between 1918 and 1922.
- Growing foreign investment. Foreigners' capital, particularly from the USA, provided an important stimulus to economic activity.
- Industrial production. This nearly doubled from 1919 to 1922 (albeit from a low base because of the war).

Holtfrerich does not accept that the policy was a disaster. In fact, he sees it as the only way that could have ensured the survival of the Weimar Republic. He argues that, in the early years of 1921–2, any policy that required cutting back spending would have resulted in the most terrible economic and social consequences – and perhaps even the collapse of the new democracy. In this sense the inflation up to 1923 was actually beneficial.

This interpretation remains controversial and many have found it difficult to accept. Holtfrerich has been criticised for drawing an artificial line at 1922 – as if the years up to 1922 were those of modest and 'good' inflation, whereas the year 1923 marked the start of hyper-inflation with the problems arising from that date. This seems a rather doubtful way of looking at the overall development of the Great Inflation, bearing in mind the long-term build-up and the nature of its causes. It also tends to separate the inflation from the drastic measures that were eventually required to solve it. Finally, an assessment of the Great Inflation must consider other important factors, such as the social and psychological. There is always a danger for economic historians to rely largely on a study of economic and financial data.

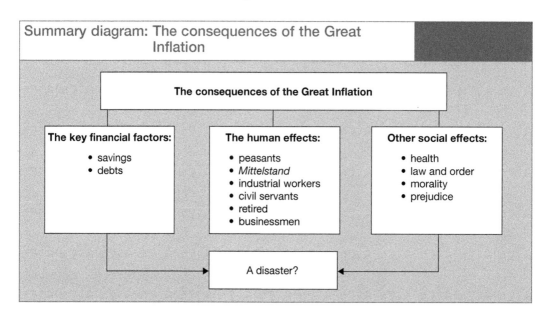

Summary diagram: The consequences of the Great Inflation

The consequences of the Great Inflation

The key financial factors:
- savings
- debts

The human effects:
- peasants
- *Mittelstand*
- industrial workers
- civil servants
- retired
- businessmen

Other social effects:
- health
- law and order
- morality
- prejudice

A disaster?

3 | Stresemann's 100 Days

In the summer of 1923 the problems facing the Weimar Republic came to a head and it seemed close to collapse:

- The German currency had collapsed and hyper-inflation had set in.
- French and Belgian troops were occupying the Ruhr.
- The German government had no clear policy on the occupation, except for 'passive resistance'.
- There were various left-wing political disturbances across the country – in Saxony the creation of an SPD/KPD regional state government resulted in an attempted communist uprising (page 128).
- The ultra-conservative state government in Bavaria was defying the national government. This finally resulted in the Munich Beer Hall *putsch* (see page 134).

Yet, only a few months later a semblance of calm and normality returned. The Weimar Republic's remarkable survival illustrates the telling comment of the historian Peukert that even 1923 shows 'there are no entirely hopeless situations in history'.

Stresemann's achievements

It is important to recognise that, during the summer of 1923, things had just been allowed to slide under the Chancellor, Cuno. Nevertheless, the appointment of Gustav Stresemann as Chancellor in August 1923 resulted in the emergence of a politician who was actually prepared to take difficult political decisions. Stresemann led a broad coalition of DVP, DDP, ZP and SPD and aimed to resolve Germany's economic plight and also tackle the problem of her weakness internationally.

Key question
How did the Weimar Republic survive the crisis of 1923?

Key dates

Stresemann appointed Chancellor: 12 August 1923

Stresemann's 100 days of leadership: August–November 1923

Within a few weeks Stresemann made a series of crucial initiatives:

- First, in September, he called off the 'passive resistance' in the Ruhr and promised to resume the payment of reparations. He needed to conciliate the French in order to evoke some sympathy for Germany's economic and international position.
- Under the guidance of Finance Minister, Hans Luther, the government's expenditure was sharply cut in order to reduce the deficit. Over 700,000 public employees were sacked.
- He appointed the leading financial expert Hjalmar Schacht to oversee the introduction of a new German currency. In December 1923 the trillions of old German marks were replaced and a new stable currency, the *Rentenmark*, was established.
- He evoked some sympathy from the Allies for Germany by the 'miracle of the *Rentenmark*' and his conciliatory policy. He therefore asked the Allies to hold an international conference to consider Germany's economic plight and, as a result, the Dawes Committee was established. Its report, the Dawes Plan, was published in April 1924. It did not reduce the overall reparations bill, but for the first five years it fixed the payments in accordance with Germany's ability to pay.
- The extremists of the left and the right were defeated (pages 128 and 135).

Key dates

Introduction of the *Rentenmark*: December 1923

Dawes Plan proposed and accepted: April 1924

The survival of Weimar

Although Stresemann's resolute action in tackling the problems might help to explain why the years of crisis came to an end, on its own it does not help us to understand why the Weimar Republic was able to come through. The Republic's survival in 1923 was in marked contrast to its collapse 10 years later when challenged by the Nazis.

Why, then, did the Republic not collapse during the crisis-ridden months before Stresemann's emergence on the political scene? This is a difficult question to answer, though the following factors provide clues:

- Popular anger was directed more towards the French and the Allies than towards the Weimar Republic itself.
- Despite the effects of inflation, workers did not suffer to the same extent as they did during the mass unemployment of the 1930s.
- Similarly, employers tended to show less hostility to the Republic in its early years than they did in the early 1930s at the start of the depression.
- Some businessmen did very well out of the inflation, which made them tolerant of the Republic.

If these suggestions about public attitudes towards the Republic are correct, then it seems that, although there was distress and disillusionment in 1923, hostility to the Weimar Republic had not yet reached unbearable levels – as it was to do 10 years later.

Moreover, in 1923 there was no obvious political alternative to Weimar. The extreme left had not really recovered from its divisions and suppression in the years 1918–21 and, in its isolated position, it did not enjoy enough support to overthrow Weimar.

The extreme right, too, was not yet strong enough. It was similarly divided and had no clear plans. The failure of the Kapp *putsch* served as a clear warning of the dangers of taking hasty action and was possibly the reason why the army made no move in 1923.

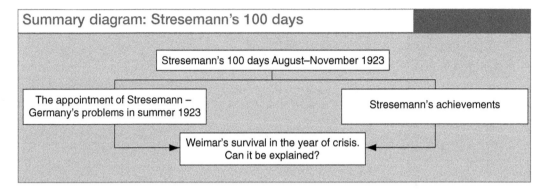

Summary diagram: Stresemann's 100 days

Stresemann's 100 days August–November 1923

The appointment of Stresemann – Germany's problems in summer 1923

Stresemann's achievements

Weimar's survival in the year of crisis. Can it be explained?

Weimar: The Years of Stability 1924–9

Key dates

1922		Treaty of Rapallo
1923–9		Stresemann as Foreign Minister
1924	April	Dawes Plan
1925		Hindenburg elected president
	October	Locarno Conference
1928	May	Müller's Grand Coalition
	August	Kellogg-Briand Pact
	October	Hugenberg leader of DNVP
1929		Young Plan
	October	Death of Stresemann
	October	Wall Street Crash

Key term

Great Depression
The severe economic crisis of 1929–33 that was marked by mass unemployment, falling prices and a lack of spending.

1 | The Economic Recovery

It is often claimed that after the hyper-inflation, the introduction of the new currency – the *Rentenmark* – and the measures brought about by the Dawes Plan ushered in five years of economic growth and affluence. Certainly the period stands out between the economic chaos of 1922–3 and the **Great Depression** of 1929–33. So, for many Germans looking back from the end of the 1920s, it seemed as if Germany had made a remarkable recovery.

Key question
What were the strengths of the German economy?

The strengths of the German economy

In spite of the loss of resources as a result of the Treaty of Versailles, heavy industry was able to recover reasonably quickly and, by 1928, production levels reached those of 1913. This was the result of the use of more efficient methods of production, particularly in coal-mining and steel manufacture, and also because of increased investment. Foreign bankers were particularly attracted by Germany's high interest rates.

At the same time, German industry had the advantage of being able to lower costs because of the growing number of cartels, which had better purchasing power than smaller industries. For example, *IG Farben*, the chemicals giant, became the largest manufacturing enterprise in Europe, whilst *Vereinigte Stahlwerke* combined the coal, iron and steel interests of Germany's great industrial companies and grew to control nearly half of all production.

Between 1925 and 1929, German exports rose by 40 per cent. Such economic progress brought social benefits as well. Hourly wage rates rose every year from 1924 to 1930 and by as much as 5–10 per cent in 1927 and 1928.

The benefits of social welfare

There were striking improvements in the provision of social welfare. The principles of a welfare state were written into the new Weimar Constitution and in the early 1920s generous pensions and sickness benefits were introduced. In 1927, a compulsory unemployment insurance covering 17 million workers was created, which was the largest scheme of its kind in the world. In addition, state subsidies were provided for the construction of local amenities such as parks, schools, sports facilities and especially council housing. All these developments, alongside the more obvious signs of wealth, such as the increasing number of cars and the growth of the cinema industry, supported the view that the Weimar Republic's economy was enjoying boom conditions. However, it should be borne in mind that the social costs had economic implications.

The weaknesses in the German economy

From the statistics for 1924–9 it is easy to get an impression of the 'golden twenties'. However, the actual rate of German recovery was unclear:

Key question
Was the Weimar economy fundamentally weak?

- There was economic growth, but it was uneven, and in 1926 production actually declined. In overseas trade, the value of imports always exceeded that of exports.
- Unemployment never fell below 1.3 million in this period. And even before the effects of America's financial crisis began to be felt (see pages 190–2), the number of unemployed workers averaged 1.9 million in 1929.
- In agriculture, grain production was still only three-quarters of its 1913 figure and farmers, many of whom were in debt, faced falling incomes. By the late 1920s, income per head in agriculture was 44 per cent below the national average.

Fundamental economic problems

The economic indicators listed above suggest that the German economy had fundamental problems in this period and it is therefore important to appreciate the broader view by looking at the following points.

- World economic conditions did not favour Germany. Traditionally, Germany had relied on its ability to export to achieve economic growth, but world trade did not return to pre-war levels. German exports were hindered by protective tariffs in many parts of the world. By the Treaty of Versailles, they were also handicapped by the loss of valuable resources in territories, such as Alsace-Lorraine and Silesia (see pages 121–2). German agriculture also found itself in difficulties because of world economic conditions. The fall in world prices from the mid-1920s placed a great strain on farmers, who made up one-third of the German population. Support in the form of government financial aid and tariffs could only partially help to reduce the problems. This decline in income reduced the spending power of a large section of the population and this led to a fall in demand within the economy as a whole.
- The changing balance of the population. From the mid-1920s, there were more school leavers because of the high pre-war birth rate. The available workforce increased from 32.4 million in 1925 to 33.4 million in 1931. This meant that, even without a recession, there was always likely to be an increase in unemployment in Germany.
- Savings and investment discouraged. Savers had lost a great deal of money in the Great Inflation and, after 1924, there was less enthusiasm to invest money again. As a result, the German economy came to rely on investors from abroad, for example the USA, who were attracted by the prospect of higher interest rates than those in their own countries. Germany's economic well-being became ever more dependent on foreign investment.
- Government finances raised concern. Although the government succeeded in balancing the budget in 1924, from 1925 it continually ran into debt. It continued to spend increasing sums of money and by 1928 public expenditure had reached 26 per cent of GNP, which was double the pre-war figure. The government found it difficult to encourage domestic savings and was forced to rely on international loans. Such a situation did not provide the basis for solid future economic growth.

Key debate

In the late 1970s a vigorous argument developed on the performance of the German economy in the period 1924–9, which has raised an important question among economic historians:

Was the Weimar economy a fundamentally sick economy?

The economic historian Karl Borchardt was the first to argue that, during the years 1925–9, Germany was living well beyond its means and that public spending was out of control. He maintained that the government intervention in the **labour market** showed an over-sympathetic attitude towards the trade unions since wage levels were rising without being matched by increases in production.

Borchardt also argued that the higher contributions required from employers towards social insurance both increased production costs and left less money available for investment, as well as making employers less willing to take on workers. This slowed economic growth. By 1927–8, the prospect of falling profits had so badly affected business that there were already signs that the 'points were set to depression'. In his assessment, the Weimar economy was 'an abnormal, in fact a sick economy which could not possibly have gone on in the same way, even if the world depression had not occurred'.

Holtfrerich thought differently. He threw doubt on Borchardt's view that excessive wage increases were at the heart of Weimar's economic problems and he did not blame trade union greed. Instead, he believed that the real cause lay with the business leaders who discouraged industrial and agricultural investment. Consequently, growth remained at low levels and there was no means of creating new jobs. Holtfrerich concluded that the German economy was not in a chronic condition, but only temporarily 'off the rails'.

All this evidence suggests that before the start of the depression in 1929 the problems of the German economy were hidden by the flood of foreign capital and by the development of an extensive social welfare system. However, it was clear that the German economy was already in a very poor state and it seems safe to offer several key conclusions:

- The German economy's dependence on foreign loans made it liable to suffer from any problems that arose in the world economy.
- Investment was too low to encourage growth.
- The cost of the welfare state could be met only by the government's taking on increasing debts.
- Various sectors of the German economy had actually started to slow down from 1927 and the agricultural sector faced serious problems from the mid-1920s.

Whether this amounts to proof of Borchardt's view of a 'sick' economy is controversial, and to assess what might have happened without a world economic crisis can only be guesswork. However, it is interesting that Stresemann wrote in 1928: 'Germany is dancing on a volcano. If the short-term credits are called in, a large section of our economy would collapse.' So, on balance, the evidence suggests that by 1929 the republic was already facing serious difficulties and was heading for an economic crisis. In that sense, the German economy faced a 'crisis before the crisis', when the USA's financial collapse in October 1929 added to an already grave situation.

Key term

Labour market
Comprises the supply of labour (those looking for work) and the demand for labour from employers. These two forces within the labour market determine wage rates.

Some key books in the debate
K. Borchardt, *Perspectives on Modern German Economic History and Policy* (Cambridge, 1991).
I. Kershaw (ed.) *Weimar: Why Did German Democracy Fail?* (London, 1990).

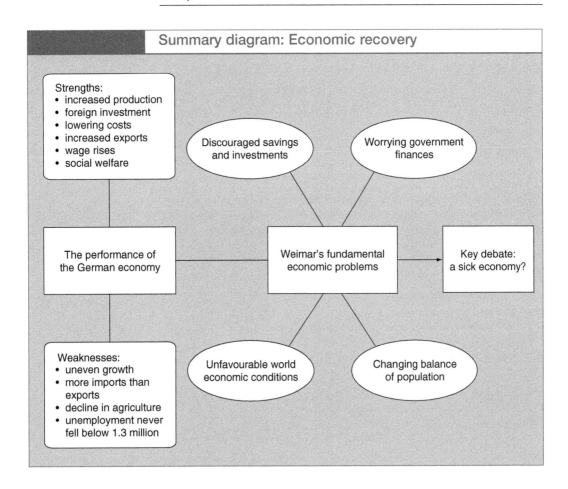

Summary diagram: Economic recovery

Strengths:
- increased production
- foreign investment
- lowering costs
- increased exports
- wage rises
- social welfare

Discouraged savings and investments

Worrying government finances

The performance of the German economy

Weimar's fundamental economic problems

Key debate: a sick economy?

Weaknesses:
- uneven growth
- more imports than exports
- decline in agriculture
- unemployment never fell below 1.3 million

Unfavourable world economic conditions

Changing balance of population

Key question
Did the general election results of 1924–8 reflect optimism about the Weimar Republic among German voters?

Key date
Müller's 'Grand Coalition' formed: May 1928

2 | Political Stability

The election results during the middle years of the Weimar Republic gave grounds for cautious optimism about its survival (see Table 7.1). The extremist parties of both left and right lost ground and altogether they polled less than 30 per cent of the votes cast. The DNVP peaked in December 1924 with 103 seats (20.5 per cent of the vote) and fell back to 73 (14.2 per cent) in May 1928. The Nazis lost ground in both elections and were reduced to only 12 seats (2.6 per cent) by 1928. The KPD, although recovering slightly by 1928 with 54 seats (10.6 per cent), remained below their performance of May 1924 and well below the combined votes gained by the KPD and USPD in June 1920 (see page 156).

Table 7.1: Weimar *Reichstag* election results 1924 and 1928 (see major political parties on page 110)

	Turn-out	NSDAP	DNVP	DVP	ZP/BVP	DDP	SPD	KPD	Others
May 1924									
Seats	472	32	95	45	81	28	100	62	29
Per cent	74.4	6.5	19.5	9.2	15.6	6.3	20.5	12.6	10.3
December 1924									
Seats	493	14	103	51	88	32	131	45	29
Per cent	78.8	3.0	20.5	10.1	17.3	4.9	26.0	9.0	7.8
May 1928									
Seats	491	12	73	45	78	25	153	54	51
Per cent	75.6	2.6	14.2	8.7	15.2	5.7	29.8	10.8	14.0

In comparison, the parties sympathetic to the Republic maintained their share of the vote and the SPD made substantial gains, winning 153 seats (29.8 per cent) in 1928. As a result, following the 1928 election, a 'Grand Coalition' of the SPD, DDP, DVP and Centre was formed under Hermann Müller, the leader of the SPD. It enjoyed the support of over 60 per cent of the *Reichstag* and it seemed as if democracy was at last beginning to emerge in Weimar politics.

Coalition politics

The election of 1928 must not be regarded as typical in Weimar history, and it should not hide the continuing basic weaknesses of the German parliamentary system. These included not only the problems created by proportional representation (see page 117), but also the ongoing difficulty of creating and maintaining coalitions from the various parties. In such a situation each party tended to put its own self-interests before those of the government.

The parties tended to reflect their traditional interests; in particular, religion and class. So attempts to widen their appeal made little progress. As a result, the differences between the main parties meant that opportunities to form workable coalitions were very limited.

Key question
Why did the political parties find it so difficult to co-operate?

- There was never any possibility of a coalition including both the SPD and the DNVP because the former believed in parliamentary democracy whereas the latter fundamentally rejected the Weimar political system.
- The Communists, KPD, remained totally isolated.
- A right–centre coalition of Centre, DVP and DNVP created a situation in which the parties tended to agree on domestic issues, but disagree on foreign affairs.
- On the other hand, a broad coalition of SPD, DDP, DVP and Centre meant that these parties agreed on foreign policy, but differed on domestic issues.
- A minority government of the political centre, including the DDP, DVP and Centre, could only exist by seeking support from either the left or right. It was impossible to create a coalition

with a parliamentary majority that could also consistently agree on both domestic and foreign policy.

In this situation, there was little chance of democratic government being able to establish lasting political stability. Of the seven governments between 1923 and 1930 (see Table 7.2), only two had majorities and the longest survived for just 21 months. In fact, the only reason governments lasted as long as they did was that the opposition parties were also unable or unwilling to unite. More often than not, it was conflicts within the parties that formed the coalition governments that led them to collapse.

Table 7.2: Governments of the Weimar Republic 1923–30

Period in office	Chancellor	Make-up of the coalition
1923–4	Wilhelm Marx	Centre, DDP, DVP
1924–5	Wilhelm Marx	Centre, DDP, DVP
1925	Hans Luther	Centre, DVP, DNVP
1926	Hans Luther	Centre, DDP, DVP
1926	Wilhelm Marx	Centre, DDP, DVP
1927–8	Wilhelm Marx	Centre, DDP, DNVP
1928–30	Hermann Müller	SPD, DDP, Centre, DVP

The responsibility of the parties

The attitude of the Weimar Republic's political parties towards parliamentary government was irresponsible. This may well have been a legacy from the imperial years. In that time the parties had expressed their own narrow interests in the knowledge that it was the Kaiser who ultimately decided policy. However, in the 1920s, parliamentary democracy needed the political parties to show a more responsible attitude towards government. The evidence suggests that no such attitude existed, even in the most stable period of the Republic's history.

Key question
In what ways was the SPD divided?

The SPD

Until 1932 the SPD remained the largest party in the *Reichstag*. However, although firm in its support of the Republic, the party was divided between its desire to uphold the interests of the working class and its commitment to democracy. Some members, and especially those connected with the trade unions, feared that joining coalitions with other parties would lead to a weakening of their principles. Others, the more moderate, wanted to participate in government in order to influence it. At the same time, the party was hindered by the old argument between those committed to a more extreme left-wing socialist programme and those who favoured moderate, gradual reform.

As a result, during the middle years of the Republic the SPD did not join any of the fragile government coalitions. This obviously weakened the power base of those democratic coalitions from 1924 to 1928. The SPD remained the strongest party during those years: although it was committed to democracy, it was not prepared to take on the responsibility of government until 1928.

The Centre Party

It therefore fell to the Centre Party to provide real political leadership in Weimar politics. The ZP electoral support was solid and the party participated in all the coalition governments from 1919 to 1932 by taking ministerial posts. However, its support did not increase because its appeal was restricted to traditional Catholic areas. Further, its social and economic policies which aimed at bridging the gaps between the classes led to internal quarrels.

In the early years, such differences had been put to one side under the strong left-wing leadership of Matthias Erzberger and Josef Wirth. However, during the 1920s, the party moved decisively to the right and the divisions within the party widened. In 1928, the leadership eventually passed to Ludwig Kaas and Heinrich Brüning, who appealed more to the conservative partners of the coalition than to the liberal or social democratic elements. This was a worrying sign both for the future of the Centre Party and for Germany herself.

> **Key question**
> What were the limitations of the Centre Party?

The liberal parties

The position of the German liberals was not a really strong one. The DDP and DVP joined in all the coalition governments of this period and in Gustav Stresemann, the leader of the DVP, they possessed the Republic's only really capable statesman. However, this hid some worrying trends. Their share of the vote, though constant in the mid-1920s, had nearly halved since 1919–20, when it had been between 22 and 23 per cent.

The reasons for the liberals' eventual collapse after 1930 were already established beforehand. This decline was largely a result of the divisions within both parties. The DDP lacked clear leadership and its membership was involved in internal bickering over policy. The DVP was also divided and, despite Stresemann's efforts to bring unity to the party, this remained a source of conflict. It is not really surprising that moves to bring about some kind of united liberal party came to nothing. As a result, German liberalism failed to gain popular support; and after 1929 its position declined dramatically.

> **Key question**
> What were the weaknesses of the German liberal parties?

The DNVP

Since 1919, the DNVP had been totally opposed to the Republic and it had refused to take part in government. In electoral terms, it had enjoyed considerable success, and in December 1924, gained 103 seats (20.5 per cent). However, as the Republic began to recover after the 1923 crisis (see pages 148–9), it became increasingly clear that the DNVP's hopes of restoring a more right-wing government were diminishing. The continuous opposition policy meant that the party had no real power and achieved nothing. Some influential groups within the DNVP realised that if they were to have any influence on government policy, then the party had to be prepared to participate in government. As a result, in 1925 and 1927, the DNVP joined

> **Key question**
> How did the DNVP change over time?

Profile: Alfred Hugenberg 1865–1951

1865	– Born in Hanover
1894	– Founder of Pan-German League
1920	– Reichstag DNVP deputy
1927	– Leader of UFA, Germany's largest film company
1928	– Leader of DNVP until 1933
1929	– Campaigned against the Young Plan
1931	– Joined the Harzburg Front against Brüning (see page 194)
1933	– Member of Hitler's coalition, but replaced in June and had no political influence in the Nazi years
1946–51	– Interned by the British and died in 1951

As a leading financier, Hugenburg was a conservative-nationalist strongly opposed to the Weimar Republic from the outset. He used his massive wealth to back the DNVP and the campaigns against reparations and the Versailles Treaty. Once he became leader of the party he began to fund Hitler and in 1931–3 his political and financial power were instrumental in Hitler's rise to power. He lost his political power and influence when Hitler established the Nazi dictatorship in mid-1933.

government coalitions. This more sympathetic attitude towards the Weimar Republic was an encouraging development.

However, that more conciliatory policy was not popular with all groups within the party. When, in the 1928 election, the DNVP vote fell by a quarter, the more extreme right wing asserted its influence. Significantly, it elected Alfred Hugenberg, an extreme nationalist, as the new leader (see profile above). Hugenberg was Germany's greatest media tycoon: he owned 150 newspapers and a publishing house, and had interests in the film industry. He utterly rejected the idea of a republic based on parliamentary democracy and he used all his resources to promote his political message. The DNVP reverted to a programme of total opposition to the Republic and refused to be involved in government. A year later, his party was working closely with the Nazis against the Young Plan (see pages 167 and 194).

Key date
Hugenberg leader of DNVP: October 1928

President Hindenburg

A presidential election was due in 1925. It was assumed that President Friedrich Ebert would be re-elected. So his unexpected death in February 1925 created political problems. There was no clear successor in the first round of the election and so a second round was held. It did result in the choice of Hindenburg as president, but the figures clearly underlined the divisions in German society (see Table 7.3).

Key question
Was the appointment of Hindenburg as president a good or a bad sign for Weimar democracy?

The appointment of President Hindenburg has remained controversial. On the one hand, on Hindenburg's coming to power there was no immediate swing to the right. The new president proved totally loyal to the constitution and carried out his presidential duties with correctness. Those nationalists who had hoped that his election might lead to the restoration of the monarchy, or the creation of a military-type regime, were disappointed. Indeed, it has been argued that Hindenburg as president acted as a true substitute kaiser or **Ersatzkaiser** (so although Wilhelm II had abdicated and Germany had lost its monarchy, Hindenburg was seen by monarchists as, in effect, fulfilling the role of sovereign). In that sense, the status of Hindenburg as president at last gave Weimar some respectability in conservative circles.

On the other hand, it is difficult to ignore the pitfalls resulting from the appointment of an old man. In his heart, Hindenburg had no real sympathy for the Republic or its values. Those around him were mainly made up of anti-republican figures, many of them from the military. He preferred to include the DNVP in government and, if possible, to exclude the SPD. From the start, Hindenburg's view was that the government should move towards the right, although it was really only after 1929 that the serious implications of his outlook became fully apparent for Weimar democracy. As the historian A.J. Nicholls put it: 'he refused to betray the republic, but he did not rally the people to its banner'.

The limitations of the political system

During this period the parliamentary and party political system failed to make any real progress. It just coped as best it could. Government carried out its work but with only limited success. There was no *putsch* from left or right and the anti-republican extremists were contained. Law and order were restored and the activities of the various paramilitary groups were limited.

However, these were only minor and very negative successes and, despite the good intentions of certain individuals and groups, there were no signs of any real strengthening of the political structure. Stable government had not been established. This is not surprising when it is noted that one coalition government collapsed in 1926 over a minor issue about the use of the national flag and the old imperial flag. Another government fell over the creation of religious schools.

Even more significant for the future was the growing contempt and cynicism shown by the people towards party politics. This was particularly connected with the negotiating and bargaining involved in the creation of most coalitions. The turn-out of the elections declined in the mid-1920s compared to 1919 and 1920. There was also an increasing growth of small fringe parties. The apparent stability of these years was really a deception, a mirage. It misled some people into believing that a genuine basis for lasting stable government had been achieved. It had not.

Key date
Hindenburg elected president: 1925

Key term
Ersatzkaiser
Means 'substitute emperor'. After Marshal Hindenburg was elected president, he provided the *ersatzkaiser* figure required by the respectable right wing – he was a conservative, a nationalist and a military hero.

Key question
Was Weimar's political recovery a 'false stability'?

Table 7.3: Presidential election, second round, 26 April 1925

Candidate (party)	Votes (millions)	Percentage
Paul von Hindenburg (DNVP)	14.6	48
Wilhelm Marx (ZP)	13.7	45
Ernst Thälmann (KPD)	1.9	6

Profile: Paul von Hindenburg 1847–1934

1847	–	Born of a Prussian noble family in Posen
1859	–	Joined the Prussian army and fought in the Franco-Prussian War 1870–1
1911	–	Retired with the rank of General
1914	–	Recalled at start of First World War and won the victory of the Battle of Tannenberg
1916	–	Promoted to Field Marshal and military dictator in 1916–18
1918	–	Accepted the defeat of Germany and retired again
1925	–	Elected President of Germany
1930–2	–	Appointed Brüning, Papen and Schleicher as Chancellors
1932	–	Re-elected President
1933	–	Persuaded to appoint Hitler as Chancellor
1934	–	Death. Granted a national funeral

Hindenburg was regularly promoted, but his career was seen as 'steady rather than exceptional'. In 1914, he was recalled from retirement and his management of the campaign on the Eastern Front earned him distinction. However, Hindenburg did not have great military skills and was outshone in his partnership with Ludendorff. During the years 1916–18, the two men were effectively the military dictators of Germany.

Although Hindenburg was President of Germany (1925–34) he only accepted the post reluctantly. He was not a democrat and looked forward to the return of the monarchy. Nevertheless, he took up the responsibility of his office and performed his duties correctly. From 1930 his political significance increased in the growing political and economic crisis. As President, he was responsible for the appointment of all the Chancellors from 1930 to 1934, although he became a crucial player in the political intrigue of the competing forces. Given his authority, Hindenburg must be held ultimately responsible for the events that ended with the appointment of Hitler, but he was very old and easily influenced by Papen and Schleicher. He had no respect for Hitler, but he did not have the will and determination to make a stand against Nazism.

Summary diagram: Political stability

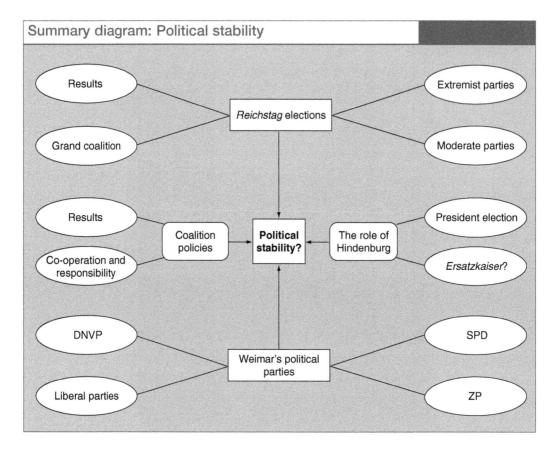

3 | Gustav Stresemann's Achievements

Before 1921–2, there was little to suggest that Stresemann was to become the mainstay of Weimar democracy. In the years before 1914 his nationalism found expression in his support of the Kaiser's *Weltpolitik* and from the start of the First World War, Stresemann was an ardent supporter of the *Siegfriede*. He campaigned for 'unrestricted submarine warfare' and opposed supporters of peace in 1917 (page 97).

By 1918 his support for the military regime and the Treaty of Brest-Litovsk had earned him the title of 'Ludendorff's young man' (see page 86). Indeed, when the war ended, Stresemann was excluded from the new liberal party, the DDP, and he formed his own party, the DVP. At first, it was hostile to the 1918 revolution and the Republic and campaigned for the restoration of the monarchy.

Turning point

Indeed, it was only after the failed Kapp *putsch* and the murders of Erzberger and Rathenau (page 131) that Stresemann led his party into adopting a more sympathetic approach towards the Weimar Republic. His sudden change of heart has provided plenty of evidence for those critics who have regarded his support of the Weimar Republic as sham. This charge is not entirely fair.

Key question
How did Stresemann's career change and develop?

Despite the conservatism of his early years, Stresemann's subsequent career shows that he was a committed supporter of constitutional government.

Stresemann's ideal was a constitutional monarchy. But that was not to be. By 1921 he had become convinced that the Republic and its constitution provided Germany with its only chance of preventing the dictatorship of either left or right. This was his realistic assessment of the situation and why he was referred to as a *Vernunftrepublikaner*, a rational republican, rather than a convinced one.

Stresemann's aims

Key question
What were Stresemann's aims and objectives?

From the time he became responsible for foreign affairs at the height of the 1923 crisis, Stresemann's foreign policy was shaped by his deep understanding of the domestic and international situations. He recognised, unlike many nationalists, that Germany had been militarily defeated and not simply 'stabbed in the back'. He also rejected the solutions of those hardliners who failed to understand the circumstances that had brought Germany to its knees in 1923.

Key term

Vernunftrepublikaner 'A rational republican' – used in the 1920s to define those people who really wanted Germany to have a constitutional monarchy but who, out of necessity, came to support the democratic Weimar Republic.

Stresemann's main aims were to free Germany from the limitations of Versailles and to restore his country to the status of a great power. Offensive action was ruled out by Stresemann and so his only choice therefore was diplomacy. As he himself once remarked, he was backed up only by the power of German cultural traditions and the German economy. So, at first, he worked towards his main aims in the 1920s by pursuing the following objectives:

- To recognise that France did rightly have security concerns and that France also controlled the balance of power on the continent. He regarded Franco-German friendship as essential to solving outstanding problems.
- To play on Germany's vital importance to world trade in order to earn the goodwill and co-operation of Britain and the USA. The sympathy of the USA was also vital so as to attract American investment into the German economy.
- To maintain the Rapallo Treaty-based friendship with the USSR. He rejected out of hand those 'hardliners' who desired an alliance with Soviet Russia and described them as the 'maddest of foreign policy makers'. Stresemann's strategy was in the tradition of Wirth's fulfilment.
- To encourage co-operation and peace, particularly with the Western powers. This was in the best interests of Germany to make it the leading power in Europe once again.

Key date

Treaty of Rapallo: 1922

Stresemann and foreign affairs 1923–9
The Dawes Plan

Key question
What were the strengths and weaknesses of the Dawes Plan?

The starting point of Stresemann's foreign policy was the issue of reparations. As Chancellor, he had called off 'passive resistance' and agreed to resume the payment of reparations. The result of this was the US-backed Dawes Plan (see Figure 7.1 on page 164),

---

THE DAWES PLAN 1924

Acceptance of German reorganisation of the German currency
- One new *Rentenmark* was to be worth one billion of the old marks.
- The setting up of a German national bank, the *Reichsbank*, under Allied supervision.

An international loan of 800 million gold marks to aid German economic recovery
- The loan was to be financed mainly by the USA.

New arrangements for the payment of reparations
- Payment to be made annually at a fixed scale over a longer period.

Figure 7.1: The Dawes Plan.

The US-backed Dawes Plan was accepted by the German government: April 1924

Key date

which has been described as 'a victory for financial realism'. Despite opposition from the right wing it was accepted in April 1924.

Although the Dawes Plan left the actual sum to be paid unchanged, the monthly instalments over the first five years were calculated according to Germany's capacity to pay. Furthermore, it provided for a large loan to Germany to aid economic recovery. For Stresemann, its advantages were many:

- For the first time since the First World War, Germany's economic problems received international recognition.
- Germany gained credit for the cash-starved German economy by means of the loan and subsequent investments.
- It resulted in a French promise to evacuate the Ruhr during 1925.

In the short term, the Dawes Plan was a success. The German economy was not weakened, since it received twice as much capital from abroad as it paid out in reparations. The mere fact that reparations were being paid regularly contributed to the improved relations between France and Germany during these years. However, the whole system was dangerously dependent on the continuation of American loans, as can be seen in Figure 7.2. In attempting to break out of the crisis of 1923, Stresemann had linked Germany's fortunes to powerful external forces, which had dramatic effects after 1929.

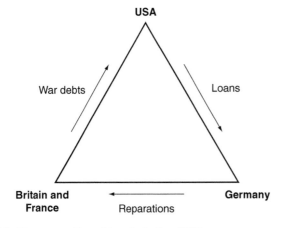

Figure 7.2: The reparations triangle in the 1920s.

Key question
Why were the
Locarno treaties so
significant?

Key date

Locarno Pact: the
conference was held
in October 1925 and
the treaties were
signed in December

Key terms

Alliance
An agreement where
members promise to
support the other(s),
if one or more of
them is attacked.

**Mutual guarantee
agreement**
An agreement
between states on a
particular issue, but
not an alliance.

Demilitarisation
The removal of
military personnel,
weaponry or forts.
The Rhineland
demilitarised zone
was outlined by the
Treaty of Versailles.

Arbitration treaty
An agreement to
accept the decision
by a third party to
settle a conflict.

The Locarno Pact

The ending of the occupation of the Ruhr and the introduction of the Dawes Plan showed that the Great Powers were prepared to take Germany's interests seriously. However, Stresemann continued to fear that Anglo-French friendship could lead to a military **alliance**. In order to counter this concern, Stresemann proposed an international security pact for Germany's western frontiers. Although France was at first hesitant, Britain and the USA both backed the idea. This formed the basis for the Locarno Pact.

In October 1925 a series of treaties was signed which became known as the Locarno Pact. The main points were:

- A **mutual guarantee agreement** accepted the Franco-German and Belgian-German borders. These terms were guaranteed by Britain and Italy. All five countries renounced the use of force, except in self-defence.
- The **demilitarisation** of the Rhineland was recognised as permanent.
- The **arbitration treaties** between Germany, Poland and Czechoslovakia agreed to settle future disputes peacefully – but the existing frontiers were not accepted as final.

To see the territories affected by the Treaty of Locarno, refer to the map, Figure 5.2 on page 122.

The Locarno treaties represented an important diplomatic development. Germany was freed from its isolation by the Allies and was again treated as an equal partner. Stresemann had achieved a great deal at Locarno at very little cost.

He had confirmed the existing frontiers in the west, since Germany was in no position to change the situation. In so doing he had also limited France's freedom of action since the occupation of the Ruhr or the possible annexation of the Rhineland was no longer possible. Moreover, by establishing the beginnings of a solid basis for Franco-German understanding, Stresemann had lessened France's need to find allies in eastern Europe. The Poles viewed the treaties as a major setback, since Stresemann had deliberately refused to confirm the frontiers in the east.

Further diplomatic progress

Stresemann hoped that further advances would follow Locarno, such as the restoration of full German rule over the Saar and the Rhineland, a reduction in reparations, and a revision of the eastern frontier. However, although there was further diplomatic progress in the years 1926–30 it remained limited:

- Germany had originally been excluded from the League of Nations (see page 123) but, in 1926, she was invited to join the League and was immediately recognised as a permanent member of the Council of the League.
- Two years later, in 1928, Germany signed the Kellogg-Briand Pact, a declaration that outlawed 'war as an instrument of

Profile: Gustav Stresemann 1878–1929

1878	– Born in Berlin, the son of a publican and brewer
1900	– Graduated from Berlin University in Political Economy and went into business
1907	– Elected the youngest member of *Reichstag* at 29
1914–18	– Nationalist and supporter of the *Siegfriede*
1919	– Formed the DVP and became its leader, 1919–29 Initially opposed the creation of the Weimar Republic
1921	– Decided to work with the Weimar Republic
1923	– Chancellor of Germany
1923–9	– Foreign Minister in all governments. Major successes included: Dawes Plan (1924), Locarno Pact (1925), German entry into League of Nations (1926), Kellogg-Briand Pact (1928) and Young Plan (1929)
1926	– Awarded the Nobel Peace Prize
1929	– Died

With a very successful business career, Stresemann joined the old National Liberals and was elected in 1907 to the *Reichstag* as a committed monarchist and nationalist. He supported *Weltpolitik* and in the war Stresemann came to be an ardent supporter of the *Siegfriede* and the expansionist policies. As a result, he was forced to leave his old party.

Stresemann was appalled by Germany's defeat and the Treaty of Versailles and in his heart he remained a monarchist and hoped to create a constitutional monarchy. So, in 1919, he formed the DVP and opposed the Weimar Republic. However, by 1921 he came to recognise the political reality and finally committed himself and his party to the Republic.

In the 1923 crisis Stresemann was made Chancellor, and it is generally recognised by historians that it marked the climax of his career. All the problems were confronted: the occupation of the Ruhr, the hyper-inflation and the opposition from left- and right-wing extremists. So, although his term in office lasted for just three months it laid the basis for the recovery 1924–9.

Stresemann was Foreign Minister in all the Weimar governments, of 1923–9, and was the 'main architect of republican foreign policy' (Kolb). Most significantly, he showed a strength of character and a realism which allowed him to negotiate with the Allies. Stresemann achieved a great deal in securing Germany's international position. Nevertheless, he failed to generate real domestic support for Weimar. It is questionable whether he could have saved the Weimar Republic from Nazism.

Key dates

Stresemann as
Foreign Minister:
1923–9

Kellogg-Briand Pact:
August 1928

Young Plan: 1929

national policy'. Although of no real practical effect it showed that Germany was working with 68 nations.

- In 1929 the Allies agreed to evacuate the Rhineland earlier than intended, in return for a final settlement of the reparations issue. The result was the Young Plan, which further revised the scheme of payments. Germany now agreed to continue to pay reparations until 1988, although the total sum was reduced to £1850 million, only one-quarter of the figure demanded in 1921 (see page 122).

The Treaty of Berlin

Key question
How was Stresemann able to reach agreements with both the USSR and the West?

Although Stresemann viewed friendship with the West as his priority, he was not prepared to drop the Rapallo Treaty. He was still determined to stay on good terms with the USSR. As a result, the two countries signed the Treaty of Berlin in April 1926 in order to continue the basis of a good Russo-German relationship. This was not double-dealing by Stresemann, but was simply a recognition that Germany's defence needs in the heart of Europe meant that she had to have understanding with both the East and the West. The treaty with the USSR therefore reduced strategic fears on Germany's Eastern Front and placed even more pressure on Poland to give way to German demands for frontier changes. It also opened up the possibility of a large commercial market and increased military co-operation.

'He looks to the right, he looks to the left – he will save me.' A German cartoon drawn in 1923 portrays Stresemann as the guardian angel of the young republic. However, it is worth noting that the little boy is the German Michael – a stereotype for the naïve German.

Key debate

In 1926 Stresemann was awarded the Nobel Peace Prize (along with his French counterpart Aristide Briand). Just three years later, at the age of 51, he died suddenly of a heart attack. However, the emergence of the Weimar Republic's only statesman of quality has always been the focus of controversy. He has been regarded as both a fanatical nationalist and a 'great European' working for international reconciliation. He has been praised for his staunch support of parliamentary government, but condemned for pretending to be a democrat. He has also been portrayed as an idealist on the one hand and an opportunist on the other. So the key question remains:

Death of Gustav Stresemann in the same month as the Wall Street Crash: October 1929

Key date

Did Stresemann fail or succeed?

Stresemann achieved a great deal in a short time to change both Germany's domestic and international positions. Moreover, the improvement had been achieved by peaceful methods. When one also considers the dire situation inherited in 1923 with forces stacked against him, it is perhaps not surprising that his policy has been described by the leading historian E. Kolb, as 'astonishingly successful', a perception upheld by the English historian Jonathan Wright in 2004, who entitled his biography *Stresemann: Weimar's Greatest Statesman*.

However, it should be borne in mind that the circumstances in the years 1924–9 were working strongly in Stresemann's favour. Walsdorff, in 1971, is more critical of Stresemann for failing to achieve his fundamental aims to revise Versailles. He argues, first, that Stresemann overestimated his ability to establish friendly relations with other powers. Secondly, he suggests that the limits and slow pace of the changes had come to a dead end – and there was no hint of any revision of the Polish frontier.

Despite these debates historians agree in one sense that Stresemann's policies failed because he did not generate real domestic support for Weimar. The right wing was always totally against 'fulfilment' and, although a minority, they became increasingly loud and influential in their criticism. They were also connected with powerful groups in society and, by the time of Stresemann's death, the nationalist opposition was already mobilising itself against the Young Plan. Even more significantly, it seems that the silent majority had not really been won over by Stresemann's policy of conciliation. Consequently, his policy had not had enough time to establish itself and to generate sufficient support to survive the difficult circumstances of the 1930s.

Some key books in the debate
E. Kolb, The *Weimar Republic* (London, 1988).
J. Wright, *Stresemann: Weimar's Greatest Statesman* (Oxford, 2002).

Summary diagram: Gustav Stresemann and Weimar foreign policy

Personal background: formative years and his turning point → Stresemann's foreign policy aims ← Background of German foreign policy

Stresemann's work

| Reparations Dawes Plan Young Plan | Locarno Pact 1925 | League of Nations 1926 | Treaty of Berlin 1926 | Kellogg-Briand Pact 1928 | Allied occupation ended 1929 |

Key debate: did Stresemann succeed or fail?

Key question
Why were the 1920s a culturally rich period?

4 | Weimar Culture

The Weimar years witnessed a radical cultural reaction to the turmoil that followed the war and defeat. Whereas the Germany of the Second Reich had been conservative, authoritarian and conformist, in contrast, the Weimar Republic was a liberal society that upheld **toleration** and reduced censorship. These factors contributed to the label of the 'golden years', as described by William Shirer, the European correspondent of the American newspaper, the *Chicago Tribune*:

> A wonderful ferment was working in Germany. Life seemed more free, more modern, more exciting than in any place I had ever seen. Nowhere else did the arts or the intellectual life seem so lively … In contemporary writing, painting, architecture, in music and drama, there were new currents and fine talents.

More broadly, the period was also one of dramatic changes in communication and the media, for this decade saw the emergence of film, radio and the car.

The new cultural ferment

The term generally used to reflect the cultural developments in Weimar Germany was *Neue Sachlichkeit*. It can be translated as 'new practicality' or '**new functionalism**', which means essentially a desire to show reality and objectivity. These words are best explained by looking at some of the major examples of different art forms.

Key terms

Toleration
Acceptance of alternative political, religious and cultural views.

New functionalism
A form of art that developed in post-war Germany which tried to express reality with a more objective view of the world.

Key question
What was *Neue Sachlichkeit* and how did it express itself?

Art

Artists in favour of the 'new objectivity' broke away from the traditional nostalgia of the nineteenth century. They wanted to understand ordinary people in everyday life – and by their art they aimed to comment on the state of society. This approach was epitomised by Georg Grosz and Otto Dix whose paintings and caricatures had strong political and social messages.

Architecture and design

One of the most striking artistic developments in Weimar Germany was the Bauhaus school led by the architect Walter Gropius, which was established in 1919 in the town of Weimar itself. The Bauhaus movement was a new style that influenced all aspects of design. Its approach was functional and it emphasised the close relationship between art and technology, which is underlined by its motto 'Art and Technology – a new unity'.

Literature

It is impossible to categorise the rich range of writing which emerged in Weimar Germany. Not all writers were **expressionists** influenced by the *Neue Sachlichkeit*. For example, the celebrated Thomas Mann, who won the Nobel Prize for literature, was not part of that movement. In fact, the big sellers were the authors who wrote traditional nostalgic literature – such as Hans Grimm. In the more *avant garde* style were the works of Arnold Zweig and Peter Lampel, who explored a range of social issues growing out of the distress and misery of working people in the big cities. Two particular books to be remembered are: the pacifist *All Quiet on the Western Front*, published in 1928 by Erich Maria von Remarque, an ex-soldier critical of the First World War; and *Berlin Alexanderplatz*, written by Alfred Döblin, which examined the life of a worker in Weimar society.

Expressionism
An art form which suggests that the artist transforms reality to express a personal outlook.

Avant garde
A general term suggesting new ideas and styles in art.

Key terms

A painting from 1927 by the German artist Otto Dix. Dix's war service deeply influenced his experiences and this piece underlines the contrast between the good-life of the affluent and the seedier side of the poor and disabled.

The *Weißenhofsiedlung* was built on the Killesberg in Stuttgart in 1927. It is one of the best examples of the 'new architecture' in Germany and formed part of the exhibition *Die Wohnung* ('The flat') organised by the German *Werkbund*.

Theatre

In drama, *Neue Sachlichkeit* developed into what was called *Zeittheater* (theatre of the time) which introduced new dramatic methods often with explicit left-wing sympathies – and were most evident in the plays of Bertolt Brecht and Erwin Piscator. They used innovative techniques such as banners, slogans, film and slides, and adopted controversial methods to portray characters' behaviour in their everyday lives.

Key question
In what ways did Weimar culture reach out to ordinary people?

Mass culture

The 1920s were a time of dramatic changes that saw the emergence of a modern mass culture. Germany was no exception. It saw the development of mass communication methods and international influences, especially from the USA, such as jazz music and consumerism.

Film

During the 1920s, the German film industry became the most advanced in Europe. German film-makers were well respected for their high-quality work; most notable of the films of the time were:

- *Metropolis* (1927) by Fritz Lang
- *Fridericus Rex* (*King Frederick the Great*) (1922)
- *Blue Angel* (1930), with the young actress Marlene Dietrich.

However, although the German film market was very much dominated by the organisation UFA, run by Alfred Hugenberg (see page 159), from the mid-1920s American 'movies' quickly made an exceptional impact. The popular appeal of the comedy of Charlie Chaplin shows that Weimar culture was part an international mass culture and was not exclusively German.

Radio
Radio also emerged very rapidly as another mass medium. The German Radio Company was established in 1923 and by 1932, despite the depression, one in four Germans owned a radio.

Cabaret
Berlin had a vibrant nightlife. Cabaret clubs opened up with a permissiveness that mocked the conventions of the old Germany: satirical comedy, jazz music, and women dancers (and even wrestlers) with varying degrees of nudity.

The conflict of cultures
There were some respected conservative intellectuals, like Arthur Möller and Oswald Spengler, who condemned democratic and industrial society. Moreover, many of the writers in the 1920s opposed pacifism and proudly glorified the sacrifices of the First World War. Berlin was definitely not typical of all Germany, but it left a very powerful impression – both positive and negative. Some could enjoy and appreciate the cultural experimentation, but most Germans were horrified by what they saw as the decline in established moral and cultural standards. It has also been suggested that Weimar culture never established a genuinely tolerant attitude. The *avant garde* and the conservatives were clearly at odds with each other. More significantly, both sides took advantage of the freedoms and permissiveness of Weimar liberalism to criticise it, while not being genuinely tolerant or sympathetic towards each other. Weimar society was become increasingly **polarised** before the onset of the political and economic crisis in 1929.

Key question
Who reacted against *Neue Sachlichkeit* and why?

Polarisation
The division of society into distinctly opposite views (the comparison is to the north and south poles).

Key term

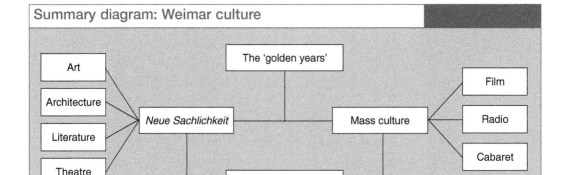

Summary diagram: Weimar culture

Key question
Were the years
1924–9 deceptively
stable?

5 | Weimar 1924–9: An Overview

The years 1924–9 marked the high point of the Weimar Republic. By comparison with the periods before and after, these years do appear stable. The real increase in prosperity experienced by many, and the cultural vitality of the period, gave support to the view that these years were indeed the 'golden years'. However, historians have generally tended to question this stability because it was in fact limited in scope. This is the reason why the historian Peukert describes these years as a 'deceptive stability'.

An unstable economy

Germany's economic recovery was built on unstable foundations that created a false idea of prosperity. Problems persisted in the economy and they were temporarily hidden only by an increasing reliance on credit from abroad. In this way Germany's economy became tied up with powerful external forces over which it had no control. Hindsight now allows historians to see that, in the late 1920s, any disruption to the world's trade or finance markets was bound to have a particularly damaging effect on the uncertain German economy.

A divided society

German society was still divided by deep class differences as well as by regional and religious differences that inhibited national agreement and harmony. The war and the years of crisis that followed had left bitterness, fear and resentment between employers and their workers. Following the introduction of the state scheme for settling disputes in 1924, its procedure was used as a matter of course, whereas the intention had been that it would be the exception, not the rule. As a result, there was arbitration in some 76,000 industrial disputes between 1924 and 1932.

In 1928, workers were locked out from their place of work in the Ruhr ironworks when the employers refused to accept the arbitration award. It was the most serious industrial confrontation of the Weimar period. A compromise solution was achieved, but it showed the extent of the bitterness of industrial relations even before the start of the world depression.

Political division

Tension was also evident in the political sphere where the parliamentary system had failed to build on the changes of 1918. The original ideals of the Constitution had not been developed and there was little sign that the system had produced a stable and mature system. In particular, the main democratic parties had still not recognised the necessity of working together in a spirit of compromise. It was not so much the weaknesses of the Constitution, but the failure to establish a shared political outlook that led to its instability.

Foreign affairs

Even the successes of Stresemann in the field of foreign affairs were offset by the fact that significant numbers of his fellow countrymen rejected his policy out of hand and pressed for a more hardline approach.

In reality, the middle years of the Weimar Republic were stable only in comparison with the periods before and after. Weimar's condition suggested that the fundamental problems inherited from war and the years of crisis had not been resolved. They persisted, so that when the crisis set in during 1929–30 the Weimar Republic did not prove strong enough to withstand the storm.

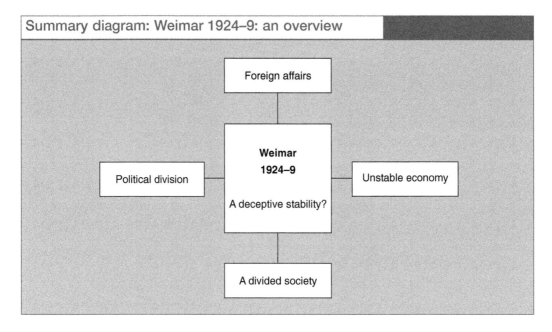

Summary diagram: Weimar 1924–9: an overview

8 The Early Years of the Nazis 1919–29

POINTS TO CONSIDER
In the 1920s Hitler and the Nazi Party enjoyed a rather chequered history and they did not made any real political impact until the onset of the Great Depression. However, Nazism did take root. The purpose of this chapter is to examine the role of the Nazis in 1920s' Germany through the following themes:

- The personal background of Adolf Hitler and the creation of the Nazi Party
- The Munich Beer Hall *putsch*
- Nazi ideas
- Mixed fortunes of Nazism in the 1920s

Key dates

1919		Creation of German Workers' Party (DAP) by Anton Drexler
1920	February	Party name changed to NSDAP (National Socialist German Workers' Party)
	February	25-Points party programme drawn up by Drexler and Hitler
1923	November 8–9	Beer Hall *putsch* in Munich
1924		Hitler in Landsberg prison *Mein Kampf* written
1925	February 27	NSDAP refounded in Munich
1926	February 14	Bamberg Conference: Hitler's leadership re-established
1928	May	*Reichstag* election result

1 | Adolf Hitler and the Creation of the Nazi Party

Hitler's early years

Key question
How did Hitler become involved in politics?

There was little in the background of Adolf Hitler (1889–1945) to suggest that he would become a powerful political figure. Hitler was born at Braunau-am-Inn in 1889 in what was then the Austro-Hungarian Empire. He failed to impress at school, and after the death of his parents he moved to Vienna in 1907. There he applied unsuccessfully for a place as a student at the Academy of Fine Arts. For the next six years he led an aimless and unhappy existence in the poorer districts of the city. It was not until he joined the Bavarian Regiment on the outbreak of war in 1914 that he found a real purpose in life. He served bravely throughout the war and was awarded the Iron Cross First Class.

When the war ended he was in hospital recovering from a British gas attack. By the time he had returned to Bavaria in early 1919 he had already framed in his mind the core of what was to become National Socialism:

- fervent German nationalism
- support of authoritarianism and opposition to democracy and socialism
- a racially inspired view of society which exhibited itself most obviously in a rabid anti-Semitism and a veneration of the German *Volk* as the master race.

Such a mixture of ideas in a man whose personal life was much of a mystery – he had no close family and few real friends – has excited some historians to resort to psychological analysis leading to extraordinary speculation. Did his anti-Semitism originate from contracting syphilis from a Jewish prostitute? Could his authoritarian attitude be explained by his upbringing at the hands of an old and repressive father? Such psychological diagnoses – and there are many – may interest the student, but the supporting evidence for such explanations is at best flimsy. As a result, the conclusions reached are highly speculative and do not really help to explain the key question of how and why Hitler became such an influential political force.

The creation and emergence of the Nazi Party

It was because of his committed right-wing attitudes that Hitler was employed in the politically charged atmosphere of 1919 as a kind of spy by the political department of the Bavarian section of the German army. One of his investigations brought him into contact with the DAP (*Deutsche Arbeiterpartei* – German Workers' Party) which was not a movement of the revolutionary left, as Hitler had assumed on hearing its name, but one committed to nationalism, anti-Semitism and **anti-capitalism**. Hitler joined the tiny party and immediately became a member of its committee. His energy, oratory and propaganda skills soon made an impact on the small group and it was Hitler who, with the party's founder, Anton Drexler, drew up the party's 25-points programme in February 1920 (see Figure 8.1 on page 177). At the same time, it was agreed to change the party's name to the NSDAP, the National Socialist German Workers' Party. (For analysis of Nazi ideology, see pages 181–4.)

By mid-1921 Hitler was the driving-force behind the party. Although he still held only the post of propaganda chief, it was his powerful speeches that had impressed local audiences and had helped to increase party membership to 3300. He had encouraged the creation of the armed squads to protect party

Key question
How significant was the NSDAP by 1922?

Key date
Creation of the German Workers' Party (DAP) by Anton Drexler: 1919

Key term
Anti-capitalism
Rejects the economic system based upon private property and profit. Early Nazi ideas laid stress upon preventing the exploitation of workers and suggesting social reforms.

Key dates

Name of the DAP party changed to NSDAP (National Socialist German Workers' Party): February 1920

Party's programme of 25 points drawn up by Drexler and Hitler: February 1920

1. We demand the union of all Germans in a Greater Germany on the basis of the right of national self-determination.

2. We demand equality of rights for the German People in its dealings with other nations, and the revocation of the peace treaties of Versailles and Saint Germain.

3. We demand land and territory (colonies) to feed our people and to settle our surplus population.

4. Only members of the *Volk* (nation) may be citizens of the State. Only those of German blood, whatever their creed may be members of the nation. Accordingly no Jew may be a member of the nation.

7. We demand that the State shall make it its primary duty to provide a livelihood for its citizens. If it should prove impossible to feed the entire population, non-citizens must be deported from the Reich.

10. It must be the first duty of every citizen to perform physical or mental work. The activities of the individual must not clash with the general interest, but must proceed within the framework of the community and be for the general good.

14. We demand profit sharing in large industrial enterprises.

18. We demand the ruthless prosecution of those whose activities are injurious to the common interest. Common criminals, usurers, profiteers must be punished with death, whatever their creed or race.

25. We demand the creation of a strong central power of the *Reich*.

Figure 8.1: Extracts from the 25 points of the programme of the German Workers' Party.

meetings and to intimidate the opposition, especially the communists. It was his development of early propaganda techniques – the Nazi salute, the swastika, the uniform – that had done so much to give the party a clear and recognisable identity.

Alarmed by Hitler's increasing domination of the party, Drexler and some other members of the committee tried to limit his influence. However, it was here, for the first time, that Hitler showed his political ability to manoeuvre and to gamble. He was by far the most influential speaker and the party knew it, so, shrewdly, he offered to resign. In the ensuing power struggle he was quickly able to mobilise support at two meetings in July 1921. He was invited back in glory. Embarrassed, Drexler resigned and Hitler became chairman and *Führer* (leader) of the party.

Having gained supreme control over the party in Munich, Hitler aimed to subordinate all the other right-wing groups under his party's leadership and certainly, in the years 1921–3, the party was strengthened by a number of significant developments:

- The armed squads were organised and set up as the **SA** in 1921 as a paramilitary unit led by Ernst Röhm (see page 236). It was now used to organise planned thuggery and violence. Most

Key term

SA
Sturm Abteilung became known in English as the Stormtroopers. They were also referred to as the Brownshirts after the colour of the uniform. They supported the radical socialist aspects of Nazism.

notoriously, the conflict in the town of Coburg degenerated into a pitched battle between the communists and the SA, but it showed how politically vital it was to win to control of the streets.

- The party established its first newspaper in 1921, the *Völkischer Beobachter* (the *People's Observer*).
- In 1922 Hitler won the backing of Julius Streicher, who previously had run a rival right-wing party in northern Bavaria. Streicher also published his own newspaper, *Der Stürmer*, which was overtly anti-Semitic with a range of seedy articles devoted to sex and violence.
- Hitler was also fortunate to win the support of the influential Hermann Göring, who joined the party in 1922 (see page 285). He was born into a Bavarian landowning family, while his wife was a leading Swedish aristocrat. They made many very helpful social contacts in Munich, which gave Hitler and Nazism respectability.

By 1923, the party had a membership of about 20,000. Hitler certainly enjoyed an impressive personal reputation and, as a result, Nazism successfully established an influential role on the extreme right in Bavaria. However, despite Nazi efforts, it still proved difficult to control all the radical right-wing political groups, which remained independent organisations across Germany. The Nazi Party was still very much a fringe party, limited to the region of Bavaria.

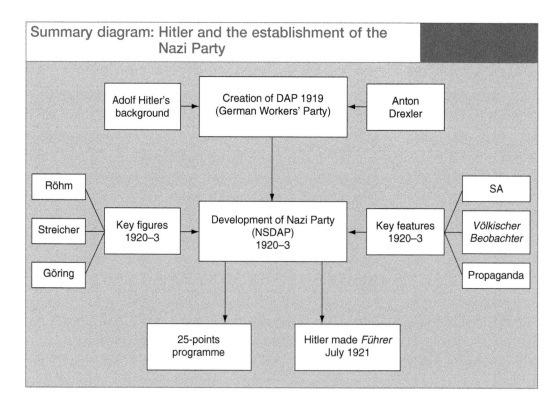

Summary diagram: Hitler and the establishment of the Nazi Party

Key question
How did Hitler manage to turn the failure of the Munich Beer Hall *putsch* to his advantage?

Key date

The Beer Hall *putsch* in Munich:
8–9 November 1923

2 | The Beer Hall *Putsch* 1923

The successful take-over of power by Mussolini in Italy in October 1922, combined with the developing internal crisis in Germany, convinced Hitler that the opportunity to seize power had arrived. Indeed, a leading Nazi introduced Hitler at one of his speeches in Munich by saying: 'Germany's Mussolini is called Adolf Hitler'. However, the Nazis were far too weak on their own to stage any kind of political take-over and Hitler himself was still seen merely as a 'drummer' who could stir up the masses for the national movement. It was the need for allies which led Hitler into negotiations with Kahr and the Bavarian State Government and the Bavarian section of the German army under Lossow (see pages 134–5).

It was with these two men that Hitler plotted to 'March on Berlin' (in the style of Mussolini's *coup* which, only the previous year, had become known as the 'March on Rome'). They aimed to mobilise all the military forces from Bavaria – including sections of the German army, the police, the SA and other paramilitaries – and then, by closing in on Berlin, to seize national power. With hindsight, Hitler's plan was unrealistic and doomed because:

- he grossly overestimated the level of public support for a *putsch* – despite the problems faced by Weimar's democratic government in 1923
- he showed a lack of real planning
- he relied too heavily on the promise of support of Ludendorff
- most significantly, at the eleventh hour, Kahr and Lossow, fearing failure, decided to hold back.

A photograph of the main leaders of the Beer Hall *putsch* posing before the trial in February 1924. Frick (A), Ludendorff (B), Hitler (C), and Röhm (D) can be identified by the letters.

Hitler was not so cautious and preferred to press on rather than lose the opportunity. On 8 November, when Kahr was addressing a large audience in one of Munich's beer halls, Hitler and the Nazis took control of the meeting, declared a 'national revolution' and forced Kahr and Lossow to support it. The next day Hitler, Göring, Streicher, Röhm, Himmler (and Ludendorff) marched into the city of Munich with 2000 SA men, but they had no real military backing, and the attempted take-over of Munich was easily crushed by the Bavarian police. Fourteen Nazis were killed and Hitler was arrested on a charge of treason.

The consequences

In many respects the *putsch* was a farce. Hitler and the *putschists* were arrested and charged with treason and the NSADP itself was banned. However, Hitler gained significant political advantages from the episode:

- He turned his trial into a great propaganda success both for himself and for the Nazi cause. He played on all his rhetorical skills and evoked admiration for his patriotism. For the first time he made himself a national figure.
- He won the respect of many other right-wing nationalists for having had the courage to act.
- The leniency of his sentence – five years, the minimum stipulated by the Weimar Constitution and actually reduced to 10 months – seemed like an act of encouragement on the part of the judiciary.
- He used his months in prison to write and to reassess his political strategy (see below), including dictating **Mein Kampf**.

Key date

Hitler imprisoned in Landsberg prison; *Mein Kampf* written: 1924

Key term

Mein Kampf
'My struggle'. The book written by Hitler in 1924, which expresses his political ideas.

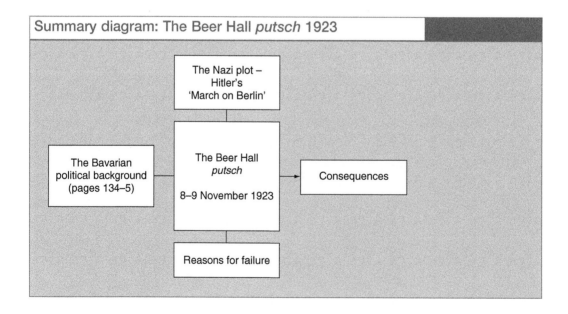

Summary diagram: The Beer Hall *putsch* 1923

The Nazi plot – Hitler's 'March on Berlin'

The Bavarian political background (pages 134–5)

The Beer Hall *putsch*
8–9 November 1923

Consequences

Reasons for failure

Key question
What were the main elements of Nazi thinking?

3 | Nazi Ideas

Nazism always emphasised the importance of action over thought. However, whilst in Landsberg prison, Hitler dictated the first part of *Mein Kampf* which, in the following years, became the bible of National Socialism. Together with the 25-points programme of 1920, it provides the basic framework of Hitler's ideology and of Nazism itself.

Racism

Hitler's ideas were built on his concept of race and had been deeply shaped by Social Darwinism (see page 15). He therefore argued that life was a struggle between races, just as animals fought for food and territory in the wild. Furthermore, he considered it vital to maintain racial purity, so that the blood of the weak would not undermine the strong.

It was a crude philosophy, which appears even more simplistic when Hitler's analysis of the races is considered. The *Herrenvolk* (master-race) was the Aryan race and was exemplified by the Germans. It was the task of the Aryan to remain pure and to dominate the inferior races, such as the Jews and the Slavs. In the following extract from *Mein Kampf* Hitler writes:

> The adulteration of the blood and racial deterioration conditioned thereby are the only causes that account for the decline of ancient civilisations; for it is never by war that nations are ruined, but by the loss of their powers of resistance, which are exclusively a characteristic of pure racial blood. In this world everything that is not of sound stock is like chaff. Every historical event in the world is nothing more nor less than a manifestation of the instinct of racial self-preservation, whether for weal or woe [for better or for worse].

(See also the 25-points programme, page 177: points 4 and 7.)

Anti-democracy

In Hitler's opinion there was no realistic alternative to strong dictatorial government. Ever since his years in Vienna he had viewed parliamentary democracy as weak and ineffective. It went against the German historical traditions of militarism and the power of the state. Furthermore, it encouraged the development of an even greater evil, communism.

More specifically, Hitler saw Weimar democracy as a betrayal. In his eyes, it was the democratic and socialist politicians of 1918, 'the November criminals', who had stabbed the German army in the back, by accepting the armistice and establishing the Republic (pages 100–2). Since then Germany had lurched from crisis to crisis.

In place of democracy Hitler wanted an all-embracing one-party state that would be run on the *Führerprinzip*, which rejected representative government and liberal values. Thus, the masses in society were to be controlled for the common good, but an individual leader was to be chosen in order to rouse the nation

Key term

Führerprinzip
'The leadership principle'. Hitler upheld the idea of a one-party state, built on an all-powerful leader.

into action, and to take the necessary decisions. (See also the 25-points programme, page 177: point 25.)

Nationalism

A crucial element in Nazi thinking was an aggressive nationalism, which developed out of the particular circumstances of Germany's recent history. The armistice of 1918 and the subsequent Treaty of Versailles had to be overturned, and the lost territories had to be restored to Germany (see pages 121–2). But Hitler's nationalism called for more than a mere restoration of the 1914 frontiers. It meant the creation of an empire (*Reich*) to include all those members of the German *Volk* who lived beyond the frontiers of the Kaiser's Germany: the Austrian Germans; the Germans in the Sudetenland; the German communities along the Baltic coast; all were to be included within the borderlands of Germany.

Yet, Hitler's nationalist aims did not end there. He dreamed of a Greater Germany, a superpower, capable of competing with the British Empire and the USA. Such an objective could be achieved only by territorial expansion on a grand scale. This was the basis of Hitler's demand for *Lebensraum* for Germany. Only by the conquest of Poland, the Ukraine and Russia could Germany obtain the raw materials, cheap labour and food supplies so necessary for continental supremacy. The creation of his 'New Order' in eastern Europe also held one other great attraction: namely, the destruction of the USSR, the centre of world communism.

In *Mein Kampf* Hitler wrote:

> The German people must be assured the territorial area which is necessary for it to exist on earth ... People of the same blood should be in the same Reich. The German people will have no right to engage in a colonial policy until they shall have brought all their children together in one state. When the territory of the Reich embraces all the Germans and finds itself unable to assure them a livelihood, only then can the moral right arise, from the need of the people, to acquire foreign territory ... Germany will either become a World Power or will not continue to exist at all. ... The future goal of our foreign policy ought to be an Eastern policy, which will have in view the acquisition of such territory as is necessary for our German people.

(See also the 25-points programme, page 177: points 1, 2 and 3.)

The socialist aspect of Nazism

A number of points in the 1920 programme demanded socialist reforms and, for a long time, there existed a faction within the party that emphasised the anti-capitalist aspect of Nazism, for example:

- profit-sharing in large industrial enterprises
- the extensive development of insurance for old age
- the nationalisation of all businesses.

Hitler accepted these points in the early years because he recognised their popular appeal but he never showed any real commitment to such ideas. As a result they were the cause of important differences within the party and were not really dropped until Hitler had fully established his dominant position by 1934. (See also the 25-points programme, page 177: points 10, 14 and 15.)

What Hitler and Goebbels later began to promote was the concept of the *Volksgemeinschaft* (people's community). This remained the vaguest element of the Nazi ideology, and is therefore difficult to define precisely. First, it was intended to overcome the old differences of class, religion and politics. But secondly, it aimed to bring about a new collective national identity by encouraging people to work together for the benefit of the nation and by promoting 'German values'. Such a system could of course only benefit those who racially belonged to the German *Volk* and who willingly accepted the loss of individual freedoms in an authoritarian system.

Key term

Volksgemeinschaft
'A people's community'.
Nazism stressed the development of a harmonious, socially unified and racially pure community.

Key question
Was Nazism an original German ideology?

The ideology of National Socialism

Early historians and biographers of Hitler simply saw him as a cynical opportunist motivated by the pursuit of power. Others have now generally come to view him as a committed political leader influenced by certain key ideas that he used to lay the basis of a consistent Nazi programme.

However, to describe Hitler's thinking, or Nazism, as an ideology is really to flatter it. An 'ideology' suggests a coherent thought-through system or theory of ideas, as found, for example, in Marxism. Nazism lacked coherence and was intellectually superficial and simplistic. It was not genuinely a rational system of thought. It was merely a collection of ideas which grew out of the Age of Enlightenment and the spirit of German Romanticism. It was not in any positive sense original – every aspect of Hitler's thinking was to be found in the nationalist and racist writings of the nineteenth century:

- His nationalism was an outgrowth of the fervour generated in the years leading up to Germany's unification of 1871.
- His idea of an all-German *Reich* was a simple repetition of the demands for the 'Greater Germany' made by those German nationalists who criticised the limits of the 1871 unification.
- Even the imperialism of *Lebensraum* had already found expression in the programme of 'Germanisation' supported by those writers who saw the German race as somehow superior.
- The growing veneration for the *Volk* had gone hand-in-hand with the development of racist ideas, and in particular of anti-Semitism.

Thus, even before Hitler and other leading Nazis were born, the core of what would become Nazism was already current in political circles. It was to be found in the cheap and vulgar pamphlets sold to the masses in the large cities; in the political programme of respectable pressure groups, such as the

Pan-German League; within the corridors of Germany's great universities; and in the creative works of certain cultural figures, such as the composer Richard Wagner.

However, despite these links, one must avoid labelling Nazi ideology as the logical result of German intellectual thinking. It is all too easy to emphasise those elements that prove the linkage theory, whilst ignoring the host of other evidence that points to entirely different views, e.g. the strong socialist tradition in Germany. Moreover, it is well to remember that a number of countries, but especially Britain and France, also witnessed the propagation of very similar ideas at this time. In that sense, nationalism and racism were an outgrowth of nineteenth-century European history. Nazi ideology may not have been original, but it should not therefore be assumed that it was an inevitable result of Germany's past.

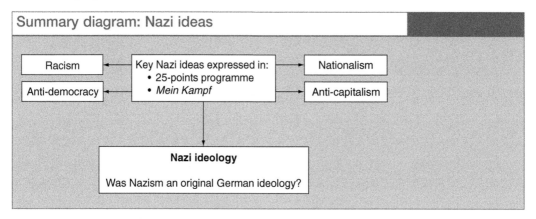

Summary diagram: Nazi ideas

4 | Nazi Fortunes in the 1920s

When Hitler left prison in December 1924 the future for Nazism looked bleak. The party was in disarray; its leading members were split into factions and the membership was in decline. More significantly, the atmosphere of crisis that had prevailed in the early years of the Republic had given way to a period of political and economic calm (see pages 151–5). Nevertheless, the party was officially refounded on 27 February 1925 and at the same time Hitler wrote a lengthy editorial for the *Völkischer Beobachter* with the heading 'A new beginning'.

Strategy and leadership

In Landsberg prison Hitler, reflecting on the failure of the 1923 *putsch*, became convinced of two vital points:

- He must establish his own absolute control over the party.
- An armed *coup* was no longer an appropriate tactic and the only sure way to succeed was to work within the Weimar Constitution and to gain power by legal means. Such a policy of legality would necessitate the creation of a party structure geared to gaining success in the elections. As Hitler himself said in prison in 1924:

Key question
In what ways was the Nazi Party revitalised?

NSDAP refounded in Munich: 27 February 1925

Bamberg Conference: Hitler's leadership re-established: 14 February 1926

Key dates

... we shall have to hold our noses and enter the *Reichstag* against the Catholic and Marxist deputies. If out-voting them takes longer than our shooting them, at least the result will be guaranteed by their own constitution. Any lawful process is slow.

However, the party remained deeply divided in a number of ways:

- Not everyone agreed with the new policy of legality.
- Traditional regional hostilities continued to exist, particularly between the party's power base in Bavaria and the branches in northern Germany.
- Most importantly, policy differences had got worse between the nationalist and anti-capitalist wings of the party (see pages 182–3).

For over a year Hitler struggled with this internal friction. The problem was highlighted by the power and influence of Gregor Strasser and also his brother Otto. Gregor Strasser joined the NSDAP in 1920 and stood loyally next to Hitler in the Munich *putsch*, but he epitomised the opposing standpoint within the party. He favoured the more socialist anti-capitalist policies for the workers and he was in effect the leader of the movement in northern Germany.

Eventually, in February 1926, the differences within the party came to a head at a special party conference in Bamberg. On the one hand it was a significant victory for Hitler, as he mobilised sufficient support to re-establish his supremacy. The Nazi Party

---

Profile: Gregor Strasser 1892–1934

1892	– Born in Bavaria
1914–18	– Served in the First World War
1920	– Joined the NSDAP and supported the anti-capitalist 'left-wing' socialist faction
1923	– Took part in the Munich *putsch*
1926	– Defeated by Hitler over party leadership at the Bamberg Conference, but he continued to criticise Hitler's policies
1926–32	– Responsible for building the mass movement of the party
	– Led the NSDAP in northern Germany
1932	– Offered the post of vice-chancellor by Schleicher (see page 219–20). Expelled from the party
1934	– Murdered in the SA purge (see page 237)

The significance of Gregor Strasser in the rise of Nazism must not be forgotten – he was, in effect, second to Hitler until 1932. He was always a supporter of the anti-capitalist 'left-wing' socialist faction, and became disillusioned when Hitler courted big business. He was an inspiring speaker, but also an excellent administrator and moulded the party into a mass movement. (He worked closely with his brother until Otto left the party in 1930.)

was to be run according to the *Führerprinzip* and there was to be no place for disagreements. On the other hand, the party declared that the original 25 points of the programme with its socialist elements remained unchangeable. So, although Hitler had cleverly outmanoeuvred his greatest threat and he had re-established a degree of unity within the party, there were still significant rivalries and differences.

The creation of the party structure

The most significant development in the years before the depression lay in the reorganisation of the party structure. The whole of Germany was divided into regions (*Gaue*), which reflected the electoral geography of Weimar's system of proportional representation. The control of each region was put in the hands of a **Gauleiter**, who had the responsibility of creating district (*Kreis*) and branch (*Ort*) groups. In this way a vertical party structure was created throughout Germany, which did not detract from Hitler's own position of authority as leader.

Perhaps the most renowned of the *Gauleiters* was the holder of the Berlin post, Joseph Goebbels. Goebbels had originally been a sympathiser of Strasser's socialist ideas, but from 1926 he gave his support to Hitler and was rewarded as Berlin *Gauleiter* with the responsibility for winning over the capital, a left-wing stronghold of the SPD. He showed a real interest in propaganda and created the newspaper *Der Angriff* (*The Attack*), but was not appointed chief of party propaganda until 1930 (see his profile on page 263).

The Nazis also founded a number of new associated Nazi organisations that were geared to appeal to the specific interests of particular groups of Germans. Among these were:

- The Hitler Youth
- The Nazi Teachers' Association
- Union of Nazi Lawyers
- The Order of German Women.

Gregor Strasser was mainly responsible for building up an efficient party structure and this was reflected in its increasing membership during these years (see Table 8.1).

One other significant initiative in these years was the creation of the **SS**. It was set up in 1925 as an élite body of black-shirted guards, sworn to absolute obedience to the *Führer*. In 1929 it had only 200 members. At first, it was just Hitler's personal bodyguard though, when it was placed under the control of Himmler later that year, it soon developed its own identity.

Table 8.1: NSDAP membership

Year	Numbers
1925	27,000
1926	49,000
1927	72,000
1928	108,000

Key question
How strong was the
Nazi Party by the end
of the 1920s?

The *Reichstag* election of May 1928

By 1928 it can be seen clearly that the party had made progress
and was really an effective political machine, most obviously
because:

- the structure was effectively organised
- the membership had increased four-fold since 1925
- Hitler's leadership was authoritative and secure (despite the
  ongoing challenge from the Strasser faction).

As a result, the Nazi Party had also successfully taken over many
of the other right-wing racist groups in Germany.

Such advances, however, could not compensate for Nazi
disappointment after the *Reichstag* election in May 1928. When
the votes were counted, the party had won only 2.6 per cent
of the vote and a mere 12 seats (see page 156). It seemed as if
Hitler's policy of legality had failed to bring political success,
whereas in the favourable socio-economic circumstances Weimar
democracy had managed to stabilise its political position. So,
Nazism may have taken root, but there was no real sign that it
could flourish in Germany.

If this evidence confirmed the belief of many that Hitler was
nothing more than an eccentric without the personal leadership
to establish a really broad national appeal, there was just one
telling sign. In the election, the party made significant gains in
the northern part of Germany among the rural and middle and
lower middle classes of areas such as Schleswig-Holstein.

This trend was reflected in the regional state elections of 1929,
which suggested that the fall in agricultural prices was beginning
to cause discontent – demonstrations and protests were giving
way to bankruptcies and violence. Most significantly, in the
province of Thuringia, in central Germany, the Nazi Party trebled
its vote and broke the 10 per cent barrier for the first time,
recording 11.3 per cent. Such figures suggested that the Nazis
could exploit the increasingly difficult economic times of the
Great Depression.

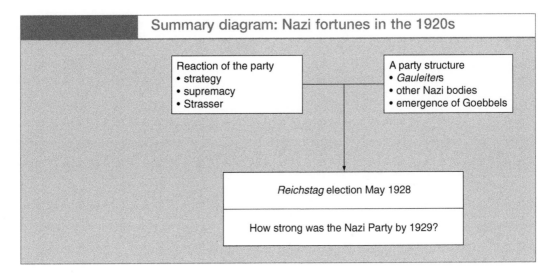

Summary diagram: Nazi fortunes in the 1920s

Reaction of the party
- strategy
- supremacy
- Strasser

A party structure
- *Gauleiters*
- other Nazi bodies
- emergence of Goebbels

Reichstag election May 1928

How strong was the Nazi Party by 1929?

Study Guide: A2 Question

'No more than a fringe irritant in German politics.' How far do you agree with this view of the strength of the Nazi Party in the years 1920–9?

Exam tips

The cross-references are intended to take you straight to the material that will help you to answer the question.

Before tacking this question, you should also re-read Chapters 5 and 8.

This question is requiring you to make an overall judgement about whether the Nazi Party can be dismissed as a political force in the 1920s. In coming to a judgement, you will need to consider the evidence of the party's weaknesses and limitations – and also the evidence which suggests its potential to challenge the political system.

Weaknesses might include:

- limitations of the party in the early years and the failure of the *putsch* (pages 134–5 and 179–80)
- party disarray and division 1924–5 (page 184)
- recovery and stability in Weimar Germany making the possibility of challenge less likely (Chapter 7).

A counter-argument might consider the restructuring of the party and the growth in membership (pages 184–6) to the extent that it could be considered an 'effective political machine' by 1928.

A key element of your argument should hinge on the position in 1928–9, where the evidence points in both directions and gives you the opportunity to argue a case. Note the lack of success in the 1928 election, but also see the comments which suggest that the Nazi Party was gaining significant electoral support in key areas and among key groups (page 187).

9 The Decline of Weimar and the Rise of Nazism 1929–32

POINTS TO CONSIDER

Weimar faced pressures before 1929, but the Wall Street Crash, in the same month as Stresemann died, ushered in the Great Depression that precipitated a political and economic crisis in Germany. This chapter examines the collapse of the Weimar Republic and the emergence of the Nazis. Its main themes are:

- The effects of the world economic crisis on Germany
- The breakdown of parliamentary government
- The advent of presidential government under Brüning, 1930–2
- The appointment of Papen as Chancellor
- The death of the Weimar Republic

The next chapter of this book will concentrate on how and why Hitler was appointed Chancellor in 1933.

Key dates

1929	October	Wall Street Crash
1930	March	Resignation of Müller's government
		Brüning appointed Chancellor
		Young Plan approved by the *Reichstag*
	September	*Reichstag* election: Nazis emerged as second largest party
	December	Brüning's economic measures imposed by presidential decree
1931	July	Five leading German banks failed
	October	Formation of Harzburg Front
1932	January	Unemployment peaked at 6.1 million
	April	Re-election of Hindenburg as President of Germany
	May	Brüning resigned
		Papen appointed Chancellor
	July	*Reichstag* election: Nazis emerged as largest party

1 | The Impact of the World Economic Crisis on Germany

Key question
Did the Wall Street Crash cause the economic crisis in Germany?

The Wall Street Crash: October 1929

Key date

Germany undoubtedly felt the world economic crisis particularly badly. It suffered the consequences of the Wall Street Crash – the collapse of share prices on the New York Stock Exchange in October 1929 – more than any other country. US loans and investment ceased and demands quickly followed for the repayment of previous short-term loans. Also, the crisis caused a further decline in the price of food and raw materials as the industrialised nations reduced their imports. As demand for exports collapsed, so world trade slumped and German industry could no longer pay its way. Without overseas loans and with its export trade falling, prices and wages fell and bankruptcies increased.

Table 9.1: Economic effects of the world economic crisis on Germany

Economic effects	Key features
Trade Slump in world trade. Demand for German exports fell rapidly, e.g. steel, machinery and chemicals	Exports value fell by 55 per cent 1929 = £630m 1932 = £280m
Employment Workers laid off – mass unemployment	Number of registered unemployed (annual averages) 1929 = 1.8m 1932 = 5.6m
Industry Industrial production declined sharply	Production: (1928 = 100) 1929 = 100 1932 = 58
Agriculture Wages and incomes fell sharply. Many farms sold off	Agricultural prices (1913 = 100) 1927 = 138 1932 = 77
Finance Banking sector dislocated by loss of confidence	Five major banks collapsed in 1931 50,000 businesses bankrupted

However, it is all too easy to put Germany's economic crisis down to the Wall Street Crash. It should be borne in mind that there were fundamental weaknesses in the German economy *before* the crash:

- The balance of trade was in the red, i.e. in debt.
- The number of unemployed averaged 1.9 million in 1929.
- Many farmers were already in debt and had been facing falling incomes since 1927.
- Government finances from 1925 were continually run in deficit.

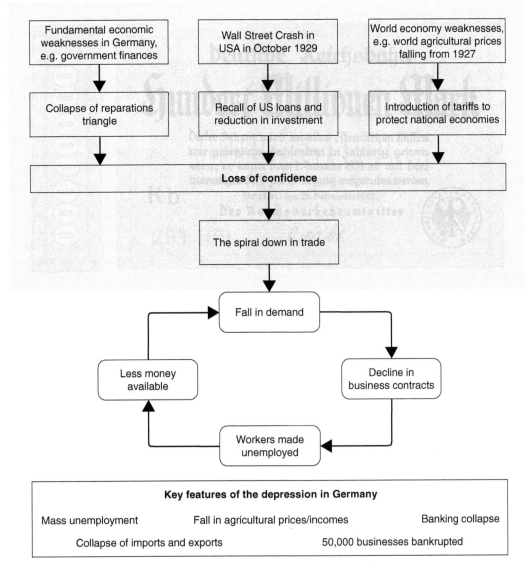

Figure 9.1: Germany in the Great Depression: causes and consequences of the world economic crisis.

The world economic crisis therefore should really be seen as simply the final blow that wrecked the Weimar economy, not the fundamental cause of its crash.

The human effects of the Great Depression

Key question
How did the economic crisis affect the German people's lives?

During the winter of 1929–30, unemployment rose above two million and only 12 months after the crash, it had reached three million. By January 1932 it stood at 6.1 million, and did not substantially fall until the spring of 1933. On their own, such figures can provide only a limited understanding of the effects of depression of this magnitude. Unemployment figures do not take

A camp for the unemployed and homeless in Berlin. Because there were so many poor people, large camps of tents were set up. These camps gave the impression of orderliness: numbered tents in neat rows with names, like streets.

into account those who did not register or the extent of part-time working throughout German industry.

Above all, statistics fail to convey the extent of the human suffering that was the consequence of this disaster because the depression in Germany affected virtually everyone; few families escaped its effects.

Many manual industrial workers, both skilled and unskilled, faced the prospect of long-term unemployment and the impossible task of trying to feed families and keep homes warm on limited social security benefits.

Nor were such problems limited to the working class. Among the middle classes, from small shopkeepers to the well-qualified professionals in law and medicine, people struggled to survive in a world where there was little demand for their goods and services. For such people, the decline in their economic position and the onset of poverty were made more difficult by the loss of pride and respectability.

The situation in the countryside was no better than in the towns. As world demand fell further, the agricultural depression deepened, leading to widespread rural poverty. For some tenant farmers there was even the ultimate humiliation of being evicted from their homes, which had often been in their families for generations.

In the more prosperous times we live in today, it is difficult to appreciate the scale of the suffering that struck German people in the early 1930s. The city of Cologne could not pay the interest on its debts, banks closed their doors and, in Berlin, large crowds of unemployed youngsters were kept occupied with open-air games of chess and cards. To many ordinary respectable Germans it seemed as if society itself was breaking down uncontrollably. It is

Unemployment peaked at 6.1 million: January 1932

Key date

not surprising that many people lost faith in the Weimar Republic, which seemed to offer no end to the misery, and began to see salvation in the solutions offered by political extremists. This was why the economic crisis in Germany quickly degenerated into a more obvious political crisis.

The political implications

Key question
Why did the economic crisis turn into a political one?

The impact of the depression in Germany was certainly more severe than in either Britain or France, but was on a par with the USA. In Germany, one worker in three was unemployed in 1933 and industrial production 1929–32 fell by 42 per cent. In the USA, the comparable figures were one in four and 46 per cent.

However, in Germany the economic crisis quickly became a political crisis, because a lack of confidence in democracy weakened the republic's position in its hour of need. Britain, France and the USA were all well-established democracies whose citizens may have lost faith in their governments, but not in the system. Taken together these two points suggest that the Great Depression hastened the end of the Weimar Republic, because the infant democracy had become associated with economic failure.

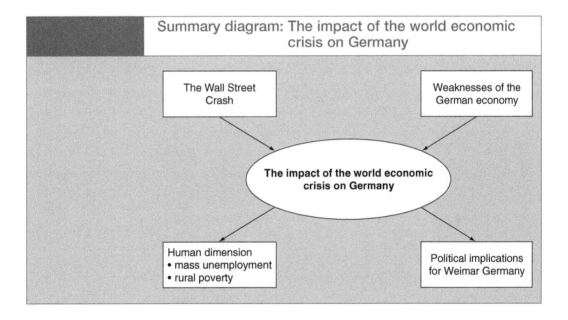

Summary diagram: The impact of the world economic crisis on Germany

The Wall Street Crash

Weaknesses of the German economy

The impact of the world economic crisis on Germany

Human dimension
• mass unemployment
• rural poverty

Political implications for Weimar Germany

2 | The Breakdown of Parliamentary Government

Key question
How and why did the Young Plan increase political exposure for the Nazis?

At the very time when unity and firm government were required to tackle the economic crisis Hermann Müller's Grand Coalition, formed after the general election of May 1928 (see page 156), was assailed by the re-emergence of the emotive issue of reparations.

The Dawes Plan (1924) successfully overcame the reparations crisis of the early 1920s by rescheduling payments based on Germany's capacity to pay but was seen as a temporary measure until Germany regained its economic strength (see pages 151–5). In early 1929 the IARC (Inter-Allied Reparations Commission) formed a committee of international financiers chaired by the US banker Owen Young. Its report in June 1929 suggested that Germany should pay until 1988 but reduced the final sum to £1850 million (only one-quarter of the figure demanded in 1921). After some negotiation by Stresemann, the German government accepted the Young Plan shortly before Stresemann's death.

However, in right-wing circles in Germany, Stresemann's diplomatic achievement was seen as yet another betrayal of national interests to the Allies. To the right wing, any payment of reparations was based upon the 'lie' of Germany's war guilt (Article 231 of the Treaty of Versailles) and the new scheme had, therefore, to be opposed. A national committee, led by the new DNVP leader, Alfred Hugenberg, was formed to fight the Young Plan (see page 167). Hugenberg was also Germany's greatest media tycoon with the means to promote his message and he generated support from a wide variety of right-wing nationalist factions.

This '**National Opposition**' drafted a *Law against the Enslavement of the German People*, which denounced any payment of reparations and demanded the punishment of any minister agreeing to it. The proposal gained enough signatures to invoke a national referendum in December 1929. The National Opposition won only 5.8 million votes, a long way short of the 21 million required by the constitution for success, but its campaign stirred nationalist emotions, focusing opposition on the democratic government at a vital time. It had also brought together many right-wing opponents of the Republic. For Hitler, the campaign showed clear-cut benefits:

- The party membership grew to 130,000 by end of 1929.
- Nazism really gained a national standing for the first time.
- The main party rally at Nuremberg had been a great propaganda success on a much more grandiose scale than any before.
- Hitler made influential political contacts on the extreme right wing.
- It brought the opportunity of having access to Hugenberg's media empire.

The collapse of Müller's Grand Coalition

Müller's coalition government successfully withstood the attack from the 'National Opposition'. However, it was not so successful in dealing with its own internal divisions. Müller, a Social Democrat, struggled to hold the coalition together but, not surprisingly, it was an issue of finance which finally brought down the government in March 1930.

The sharp increase in unemployment had created a large deficit in the new national insurance scheme, and the four major parties in the coalition could not agree on how to tackle it. The SPD, as the political supporters of the trade unions, wanted to

Key dates

Young Plan approved by *Reichstag:* March 1930

Resignation of Müller's government: March 1930

Brüning appointed Chancellor: March 1930

Key term

National Opposition
A title given to various political forces that united to campaign against Weimar. It included the DNVP, the Nazis, the Pan-German League and the *Stahlhelm* – an organisation of ex-soldiers. The 'National Opposition' opposed reparation payments.

Key question
Why could the Grand Coalition not agree?

increase the contributions and to maintain the levels of welfare payments. The DVP, on the other hand, had strong ties with big business and insisted on reducing benefits. Müller could no longer maintain a majority and he had no option but to tender the resignation of his government.

The appointment of Heinrich Brüning

Key question
How was parliamentary government weakened by the leadership of Heinrich Brüning?

President Hindenburg made Heinrich Brüning Chancellor. At first sight, this appeared an obvious choice, since he was the parliamentary leader of the ZP, the second largest party in the *Reichstag*. However, Brüning's appointment marked a crucial step towards the end of true parliamentary government. This was for two reasons.

First, because he was manoeuvred into office by a select circle of political intriguers, who surrounded the ageing Hindenburg:

- Otto Meissner, the president's State Secretary
- Oskar von Hindenburg, the president's son
- Major General Kurt von Schleicher, a leading general (see profile on page 219).

All three were conservative-nationalists with no real faith in the democratic process. Instead, they looked to the President and the emergency powers of Article 48 of the constitution (see pages 115 and 118) as a means of creating a more authoritarian government. In Brüning, they saw a respectable, conservative figure, who could offer firm leadership.

Secondly, Brüning's response to the growing economic crisis led to a political constitutional crisis. He proposed cuts in government expenditure to achieve a balanced budget and avoid reviving inflation. However, the budget was rejected in the *Reichstag* by 256 votes to 193 in July 1930. When, despite this, Brüning put the proposals into effect by means of an emergency decree, signed by the President according to Article 48, the *Reichstag* challenged the decree's legality and voted for its withdrawal. Deadlock had been reached. Brüning, therefore, asked Hindenburg to dissolve the *Reichstag* and to call an election for September 1930.

Nazi breakthrough

Key question
Why was the 1930 *Reichstag* election so significant?

Key date
Reichstag election – Nazis emerged as second largest party in *Reichstag*: September 1930

Brüning had hoped that in the developing crisis the people would be encouraged to support the parties of the centre-right from which a coalition could be formed. However, the election results proved him wrong and the real beneficiary was the Nazi Party, which increased its vote from 810,000 to a staggering 6,409,600 (see Table 9.2).

The key features about the performance of the political parties are as follows:

- Nazis: With 107 seats and 18.3 per cent, the NSDAP became the second largest political party in Germany.
- Nationalists: The vote of the DNVP was halved from 14.2 per cent to 7 per cent, largely benefiting the Nazis.
- Middle-class democratic parties: The DDP and the DVP lost 20 seats between them.

Table 9.2: *Reichstag* election results for 1928 and 1930 (see major political parties on page 110)

	Turn-out	NSDAP	DNVP	DVP	ZP/BVP	DDP	SPD	USPD/KPD	Others
May 1928									
Seats	491	12	73	45	78	25	153	54	51
Per cent	75.6	2.6	14.2	8.7	15.2	4.9	29.8	10.8	14.0
September 1930									
Seats	577	107	41	30	87	20	143	77	72
Per cent	82.0	18.3	7.0	4.5	14.8	3.8	24.5	13.1	13.8

- Left-wing parties: The vote of the SPD declined from 29.8 per cent to 24.5 per cent, though in contrast the vote of the KPD increased from 10.8 per cent to 13.1 per cent.

Because the result of the 1928 *Reichstag* election had been so disappointing, not even Hitler could have expected the dramatic gains of 1930. Nevertheless, there are several key factors to explain the Nazi breakthrough:

- Since 1928 the Nazi leaders had deliberately directed their propaganda at rural and middle-class/lower middle-class audiences. Nazi gains were at the expense of the DNVP, DVP and DDP.
- Nazi success cannot just be explained by these 'protest votes'. Nearly half of the Nazi seats were won by the party attracting 'new' voters:
  - The electorate had grown by 1.8 million since the previous election because a new generation of voters had been added to the roll.
  - The turn-out had increased from 75.6 per cent to 82 per cent.

The Nazis seem to have picked up a fair proportion of young first-time voters, and also persuaded many people who had not previously voted to support them.

The implications of the 1930 *Reichstag* election were profound. Left and right extremes had made extensive gains against the pro-democratic parties, making it very difficult for proper democratic parliamentary government to function.

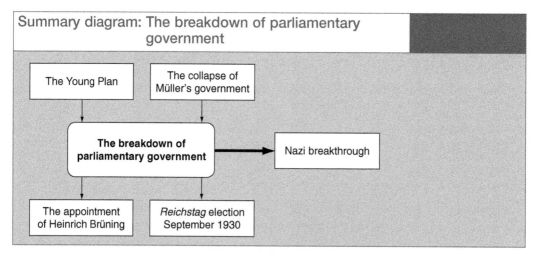

Summary diagram: The breakdown of parliamentary government

3 | Brüning: Presidential Government

Key question
Was Brüning simply a victim of the circumstances?

Brüning's political position after the election was undoubtedly very difficult. His plan to reinforce his parliamentary support from the centre–right had not succeeded. Instead, he faced the committed opposition of the more powerful extremes of left and right. However, he was not dismissed as Chancellor. Brüning still enjoyed the support of Hindenburg and the SPD decided to 'tolerate' his cabinet. So, although the SPD did not join the government, given the threat now facing the Republic from the extremists it was not prepared to defeat the emergency decrees by the use of Article 48.

In this way, true parliamentary democracy gave way to 'presidential government' with some backing from the *Reichstag*. From 1930–2 Brüning remained as Chancellor and he governed Germany by the use of Article 48 through President Hindenburg. He was almost a semi-dictator, as can be seen from his growing use of presidential decrees (see Table 9.3).

Table 9.3: Presidential government 1930–2

	1930	1931	1932
Presidential decree laws (Article 48)	5	44	66
Reichstag laws	98	34	5
Sitting days of the *Reichstag*	94	42	13

Economic policy

Key question
Was Brüning economically incompetent?

Brüning's economic policy was at least consistent. Throughout his two years in office his major aims were imposed by presidential decree:

- To balance the budget.
- To prevent renewed inflation.
- To get rid of the burden of German reparations.

And so, his policy's main measures were:

- To cut spending drastically.
- To raise taxes.

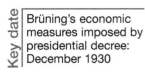

Key date
Brüning's economic measures imposed by presidential decree: December 1930

This clearly lowered demand and it led to a worsening of the slump. Most obviously, there was a large increase in the number of unemployed and a serious decline in the welfare state provision. Soon he was mocked with the title 'the Hunger Chancellor'.

Many historians have condemned Brüning's economic regime of sticking to his policy of reducing expenditure, for seriously worsening the situation and making possible the rise of the Nazis. He was criticised particularly for his failure to introduce economic measures in the summer of 1931, such as work creation schemes in the construction industry and the reduction of agricultural subsidies. These might have lessened the worst effects of the depression during 1932.

However, it could be argued that Brüning had no real alternatives to his economic policy. This was because the German economy had *entered* the depression with such severe weaknesses from the 1920s (see pages 153–4) that economic failure was unavoidable. So, it could be argued that no Chancellor would have been able to expand the economy and Brüning was at the mercy of other forces.

Brüning's fall from power

In the spring of 1932, Hindenburg's first seven-year term of office as President came to an end. Brüning committed himself to securing the old man's re-election and after frenetic campaigning Hindenburg was re-elected on the second ballot. He gained 19.3 million votes (53 per cent) compared with Hitler's 13.4 million (36.8 per cent). However, it was a negative victory. Hindenburg had only been chosen because he was the only alternative between Hitler and the KPD candidate, Ernst Thälmann. Also, Hitler had doubled the Nazi vote, despite losing, and had

Key question
Why did Hindenburg force Brüning to resign?

Profile: Heinrich Brüning 1885–1970

1885	– Born into a Catholic trading family
1904–11	– Attended Munich University and awarded a Ph.D. in economics
1915–18	– Volunteer in the war and won the Iron Cross, first class
1924–33	– Elected to the *Reichstag* as an ZP deputy
1929	– Chosen as ZP leader
1930	– Appointed Chancellor by Hindenburg
	– Tried to pass the budget, but rejected by *Reichstag*. This resulted in the *Reichstag* election of September 1930
1932	– Proposed land reform of the Prussian estates
	– Dismissed by Hindenburg in May
1934	– Fled to the Netherlands and emigrated to the USA
1970	– Died in the USA

In his heart, Brüning remained a monarchist and he hoped to change the constitution to make it a more authoritarian system. However, although he was opposed to the Nazis his policies and decisions have been heavily criticised because:

- He called for the *Reichstag* election in September 1930 and misread the political consequences.
- He remained committed to the economic programme of balancing the budget, which resulted in enormous economic and political pressures.
- He relied on Hindenburg for the emergency decrees – and he failed to recognise his overdependence on the president.

In his defence, it may be claimed that he was a man of integrity and a victim of exceptional circumstances. His reputation is overshadowed by the later development of the Nazi dictatorship.

projected an even more powerful personal image. Moreover, Hindenburg showed no real gratitude to Brüning and, at the end of May 1932, the president forced his Chancellor to resign by refusing to sign any more emergency decrees. Why was this?

Banking crisis

Key dates

Five leading German banks failed: July 1931

Formation of Harzburg Front: October 1931

Re-election of Hindenburg as president of Germany: April 1932

Brüning resigned. Papen appointed Chancellor: May 1932

In June 1931, the collapse of a major bank, the Danat, and several others, revived fears of financial crisis. By the end of the year unemployment was approaching five million people and there were demonstrations in the streets. In October 1931 the 'National Opposition' (see page 194) was reborn as the Harzburg Front. This coalition of right-wing political, military and economic forces demanded the resignation of Brüning and a new election. It arranged a massive rally to denounce Brüning, but in the winter of 1931–2 the Chancellor still enjoyed Hindenburg's support.

Land reform

Brüning planned to turn some *Junker* estates in east Prussia into 600,000 allotments for unemployed workers. This displeased Hindenburg, himself a *Junker*. Landowners saw it as a threat to their property interests and dubbed it 'agrarian bolshevism'.

Intrigue

Brüning's land policy spurred on the right wingers, led by Kurt von Schleicher. Schleicher persuaded Hindenburg to force the Chancellor's resignation at the end of May 1932 and to create a right-wing government.

One might be tempted to view Brüning as an innocent sacrifice who was removed by Hindenburg without consultation with the *Reichstag*. However, it should be borne in mind that he had only survived as Chancellor because he enjoyed the personal backing of the President. Brüning had agreed with the creation of presidential government based on Article 48 of the constitution, but he was not astute enough to recognise the precarious nature of his own position. He depended solely on retaining the confidence of the President so he was vulnerable to the intrigue of the presidential court.

Assessment of Brüning

Key question
Was Brüning a failure?

Brüning was an honest, hard-working and honourable man who failed. He was not really a committed democrat, but neither was he sympathetic to Nazism, and it is very important to remember that last point. In many respects, Brüning was making good progress towards his aims, when he was dismissed:

• He succeeded in ending the payment of reparations.
• He sympathised with the reduction of the democratic powers of the *Reichstag*.

However:

• He was not clever enough to appreciate how dangerous and unstable the economic crisis had become in Germany by 1932.

- Neither did he realise how insecure was his own position. For as long as Brüning retained the confidence of Hindenburg, presidential government protected his position.

With no real hope of improvement in the economic crisis, it is not surprising that large sections of the population looked to the Nazis to save the situation. Brüning would have nothing to do with Hitler and the Nazis and he continued to uphold the rule of law. Sadly, presidential rule had accustomed Germany again to rule by decree. In this way democracy was undermined and the way was cleared for more extreme political parties to assume power. In the end, it is hard to escape the conclusion that Brüning's chancellorship was a dismal failure, and, in view of the Nazi tyranny that was soon to come, a tragic one.

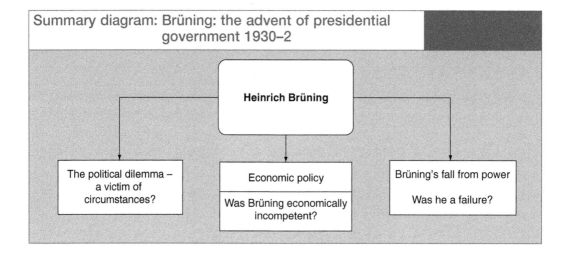

Summary diagram: Brüning: the advent of presidential government 1930–2

Heinrich Brüning

The political dilemma – a victim of circumstances?

Economic policy
Was Brüning economically incompetent?

Brüning's fall from power
Was he a failure?

4 | From Brüning to Papen

Key question
What was Papen's political aim?

Schleicher now sought to use his influence with Hindenburg by recommending Franz von Papen as the new Chancellor. If many greeted the choice of Papen with disbelief, it was his very lack of ability which appealed to Schleicher, who saw the opportunity to influence events more directly through him. As an aristocrat, Papen had good connections with high society; as a Catholic he was a member of the Centre Party, although his political views mirrored those of the nationalists. His outlook quickly formed the basis for a close friendship with Hindenburg.

Papen was politically ambitious, but his understanding and experience of politics was limited (he did not even hold a seat in the *Reichstag*). The new cabinet was called a non-party government of 'national concentration', although it was soon nicknamed the 'Cabinet of Barons'. It was a presidential government dominated by aristocratic landowners and industrialists – and many were not even members of the *Reichstag*. In order to strengthen the government, Papen and Schleicher wanted to secure political support from the Nazis. Hitler agreed not to oppose the new government in return for two concessions:

- The dissolution of the *Reichstag* and the calling of fresh elections.
- The end of a government ban on the SA and SS, introduced after violence during the presidential campaign.

Papen and Schleicher hoped that this agreement with the Nazis would result in the creation of a right-wing authoritarian government with some popular support in the form of the Nazis. The *Reichstag* was therefore dissolved and an election was arranged for 31 July 1932.

Key question
Why was the
Reichstag election of
July 1932 so
politically significant?

Reichstag election: July 1932

The election campaign was brutal, as street violence once again took hold in the large cities. In the month of July alone 86 people died as a result of political fights.

Such bloodshed gave Schleicher and Papen the excuse to abolish the most powerful regional state government in Germany, Prussia. This government of Prussia had long been a coalition of the SPD and the ZP and had been the focus of right-wing resentment since 1919. On 20 July 1932, it was simply removed by Papen who declared a state of emergency and appointed

---

Profile: Franz von Papen 1879–1969

1879	– Born into a Catholic aristocratic family
1913–18	– Cavalry officer and diplomat
1921	– Elected to the Prussian *Land* as ZP member
1932	– Appointed Chancellor in May to head his 'Cabinet of Barons'
	– Dissolved the *Reichstag*, with serious consequences
	– Removed the Prussian state government and appointed himself as Reich Commissioner of Prussia
	– Personally defeated by a massive vote of no confidence in the *Reichstag*
	– Dismissed in November, but schemed to replace Schleicher in order to recover his power
1933	– Appointed in January as vice-chancellor in Hitler's coalition
1934	– Resigned after the Night of Long Knives
1934–44	– German ambassador in Austria and Turkey
1946	– Found not guilty of war crimes in the Nuremberg trials
1969	– Lived privately until his death

Papen had limited political experience and was really out of his depth. His advance was mainly due to his connections with the aristocracy, the Catholic Church and big business. He was always a monarchist and a nationalist (although nominally a member of ZP). As Chancellor, he aspired to undo the Weimar Constitution and was quite happy to rule by presidential decrees and to denounce the state government of Prussia. Despite his failings, he pursued his personal ambitions and was quickly outmanoeuvred by Hitler.

Table 9.4: *Reichstag* election results 1928–32 (see major political parties on page 110)

	Turn-out	NSDAP	DNVP	DVP	ZP/BVP	DDP	SPD	KPD	Others
May 1928									
Seats	491	12	73	45	78	25	153	54	51
Per cent	75.6	2.6	14.2	8.7	15.2	4.9	29.8	10.8	14.0
September 1930									
Seats	577	107	41	30	87	20	143	77	72
Per cent	82.0	18.3	7.0	4.5	14.8	3.8	24.5	13.1	13.8
July 1932									
Seats	608	230	37	7	97	4	133	89	11
Per cent	84.1	37.3	5.9	1.2	15.7	1.0	21.6	14.3	2.9

himself as Reich Commissioner of Prussia. This was of immense significance:

- It was an arbitrary and unconstitutional act.
- It replaced a parliamentary system with a presidential authoritarian government.
- Democrats – especially the SPD and the trade unions – gave in without any real opposition. Their passive response shows how far the forces of democracy had lost the initiative.

Many on the right wing congratulated Papen on the Prussian *coup*. However, it did not win him any additional electoral support. When the election results came in, it was again the Nazis who had cause to celebrate. They had polled 13.7 million votes and had won 230 seats. Hitler led by far the largest party in Germany and constitutionally he had every right to form a government.

It is worth bearing in mind the following key features about the performance of the political parties:

- Nazis: With 230 seats and 37.3 per cent the NSDAP became the largest political party in Germany.
- Nationalists: The vote of the DNVP fell further to 5.9 per cent.
- Middle-class democratic parties: The DDP and the DVP collapsed disastrously. They polled only 2.2 per cent of the vote and gained just 11 seats between them.
- Left-wing parties: The vote of the SPD declined further to 21.6 per cent, though in contrast the vote of the KPD increased to 14.3 per cent.

Key date

Nazis emerged as the largest party in the *Reichstag* election: July 1932

In electoral terms the gains of the Nazis could be explained by:

- the collapse of the DDP and DVP vote
- the decline of the DNVP
- a small percentage of disgruntled workers changing from SPD to NSDAP
- the support for the 'other parties' falling from 13.8 per cent to 2.9 per cent, which suggests that their loyalty transferred to the Nazis

Table 9.5: Germany's governments 1928–33

Chancellors	Dates in office	Type of government
Hermann Müller (SPD)	May 1928– March 1930	Parliamentary government. A coalition cabinet of SPD, ZP, DDP, DVP
Heinrich Brüning (ZP)	March 1930– May 1932	Presidential government dependent on emergency decrees. A coalition cabinet from political centre and right
Franz von Papen (ZP, but very right wing)	May 1932– December 1932	Presidential government dependent on emergency decrees. Many non-party cabinet members
General Kurt von Schleicher (Non-party)	December 1932– January 1933	Presidential government dependent on emergency decrees. Many non-party cabinet members
Adolf Hitler (NSDAP)	1933–45	Coalition cabinet of NSDAP and DNVP, but gave way to Nazi dictatorship

- the turnout increasing to 84 per cent which indicated the same trend as September 1930 that the party was attracting even more 'new voters'.

Two further points worth remembering about the *Reichstag* election of July 1932 are:

- Only 39.5 per cent voted for the main pro-democratic parties.
- Added together, the percentage of votes for the KPD and NSDAP combined to 51.6 per cent.

These two political facts are telling indeed. The German people had voted to reject democracy.

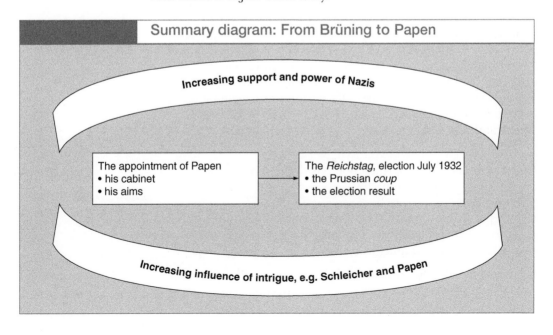

Summary diagram: From Brüning to Papen

Increasing support and power of Nazis

The appointment of Papen
- his cabinet
- his aims

→

The *Reichstag*, election July 1932
- the Prussian *coup*
- the election result

Increasing influence of intrigue, e.g. Schleicher and Papen

5 | The Death of the Weimar Republic

Key question
Why did Weimar democracy fail?

It is now clear that Weimar democracy was really dead before the establishment of the Nazi dictatorship in early 1933 (see pages 222–6). The problem for the historian is trying to determine when Weimar democracy expired and why.

Three major themes stand out as fundamental weaknesses of the Weimar Republic.

(i) The hostility of Germany's vested interests

From the start, the Weimar Republic faced the hostility of Germany's established élites. Following military defeat and the threat of revolution, this opposition was at first limited. However, the fact that so many key figures in German society and business rejected democracy was a major problem for Weimar. They worked against the interests of Weimar and hoped to restore authoritarian government. This was a powerful handicap to the successful development of the Republic in the 1920s and, in the 1930s, it became a decisive factor in its final collapse.

(ii) Ongoing economic problems

The Republic was also troubled by an almost continuous economic crisis that affected all levels of society. It inherited the enormous costs of the First World War followed by the burden of post-war reconstruction, Allied reparations and the heavy expense of the new welfare benefits. So, even though the inflation crisis of 1923 was overcome, problems in the economy were disguised by US loans and remained unresolved. These were to have dramatic consequences with the onset of the world economic crisis in 1929.

(iii) Limited base of popular support

Weimar democracy never enjoyed widespread political support. There was never total acceptance of, and confidence in, its system and its values. From the Republic's birth its narrow base of popular support was caught between the extremes of left and right. But, as time went by, Weimar's claims to be the legitimate government became increasingly open to question. Sadly, Weimar democracy was associated with defeat and the humiliation of the Treaty of Versailles, reparations, inflation, and now unemployment. Its reputation was further damaged by the crisis of 1922–3. Significantly, even the mainstays of the Weimar Republic had weaknesses:

- The main parties of German liberalism, the DDP and DVP, were losing support from 1924.
- The ZP and DNVP were both moving to the political right.
- Even the loyalty and the commitment of the SPD to democracy has to be balanced against its failure to join the coalitions in the mid-1920s and its conflict with its left-wing partner, the KPD.

In short, a sizeable proportion of the German population never had faith in the existing constitutional arrangements and, as the years passed, more were looking for change.

To some historians, Weimar had been a gamble with no chance of success. For others, the Republic continued to offer the hope of democratic survival right until mid-1932, when the Nazis became the largest party in the July *Reichstag* election. However, the manner of Brüning's appointment and his decision to rule by emergency decree created a particular system of presidential government. This fundamentally undermined the Weimar system and was soon followed by the electoral breakthrough of the Nazis. From this time, democracy's chance of surviving was very slim, although it lived on with ever increasing weakness before it reached its demise in July 1932. However, in truth, democratic rule in Weimar Germany was doomed from the summer of 1930.

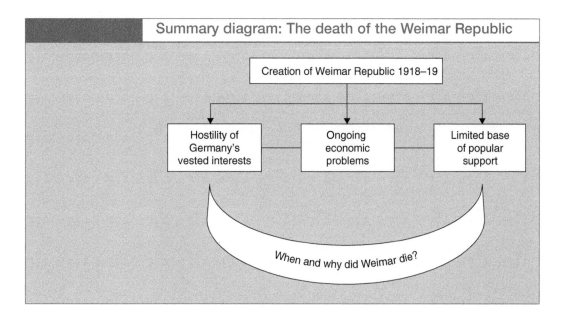

Summary diagram: The death of the Weimar Republic

Creation of Weimar Republic 1918–19

Hostility of Germany's vested interests

Ongoing economic problems

Limited base of popular support

When and why did Weimar die?

Study Guide: A2 Question

'It had fundamental weaknesses and these meant that it remained a fragile institution throughout the period 1919–32.' How far do you agree with this opinion of the Weimar Republic?

Exam tips

Before tacking this question, you should also re-read Chapters 5 and 7.

This question requires you to examine two aspects of the statement: whether the Weimar Republic was' fundamentally weak' and whether, as a result, it was 'fragile throughout the period'.

You should examine aspects which could be classified as fundamental weaknesses:

- instability in the political system
- economic weaknesses
- opposition within sections of German society.

How serious and constant were these weaknesses? Consider whether the successes of the years 1924–9 allow you to challenge the concept of fragility. If you view the post-1929 period as representing a set of exceptional circumstances, then you may choose to argue against the validity of the statement 'throughout the period'. Or you may choose to regard the later period as revealing inherent weaknesses which had always made a collapse likely.

In coming to a conclusion, you should take account of the evidence that:

- the world economic crisis can be seen as simply the final blow that wrecked the economy, rather than the fundamental cause of its crash
- a lack of confidence in democracy fatally weakened the Republic's position in the ensuing crisis.

10 The Nazi Road to Dictatorship 1932–3

POINTS TO CONSIDER

Although Weimar democracy was, in effect, dead by the summer of 1932, it should not be assumed that Hitler's appointment was inevitable. The purpose of this chapter is to consider two questions that are inextricably linked: 'Why did Hitler and the Nazis become so politically powerful?' and 'Why was Weimar Germany replaced by a Nazi dictatorship?' The main themes covered are:

- The creation of a Nazi mass movement: Who voted for the Nazis and why?
- Nazi political methods: Propaganda and violence
- Political intrigue: The appointment of Hitler as Chancellor
- The establishment of the Nazi dictatorship, January–March 1933
- Key debate: Why did the Weimar Republic collapse and why did it give way to Hitler and Nazism?

Key dates

1932	July	*Reichstag* election: Nazis won 230 seats (37.3 per cent)
	September	*Reichstag* passed a massive vote of no confidence in Papen's government (512 votes to 42)
	November	*Reichstag* election: Nazi vote dropped to 33.1 per cent, winning 196 seats
	December	Papen dismissed as Chancellor and replaced by Schleicher
1933	January 30	Schleicher dismissed and Hitler appointed as Chancellor
	February 27	*Reichstag* Fire: communists blamed
	March 5	Final *Reichstag* elections according to Weimar Constitution
	March 21	The 'Day of Potsdam'
	March 23	Enabling Law passed

1 | The Creation of a Nazi Mass Movement

Key question
Who voted for the
Nazis?

The point is often made that Hitler and the Nazis never gained an overall majority in *Reichstag* elections. However, such an occurrence was unlikely because of the number of political parties in Weimar Germany and the operation of the proportional representation system. Considering this, Nazi electoral achievements by July 1932 were very impressive. The 13,745,000 voters who had supported them represented 37.3 per cent of the electorate, thus making Hitler's party the largest in the *Reichstag*. Only one other party on one other occasion had polled more: the SPD in the revolutionary atmosphere of January 1919. Nazism had become a mass movement with which millions identified and, as such, it laid the foundations for Hitler's coming to power in January 1933. Who were these Nazi voters and why were they attracted to the Nazi cause?

Reichstag election:
Nazis won 230 seats
(37.3 per cent): July
1932

Key date

The results of the elections 1928–32 show the changing balance of the political parties (see pages 198 and 202), although really these figures on their own are limited in what they show us about the nature of Nazi support. However, the graph and table in Figure 10.1 reveal a number of significant points about the kind of people who actually voted for the Nazis.

From this it seems fairly clear that the Nazis made extensive gains from those parties with a middle-class and/or a Protestant identity. However, it is also apparent that the Catholic parties, the Communist Party and, to a large extent, the Social Democrats were able to withstand the Nazi advances.

Geography and denomination

These political trends are reflected in the geographical base of Nazi support, which was generally higher in the north and east of the country and lower in the south and west. Across the North German Plain, from East Prussia to Schleswig-Holstein, the Nazis gained their best results and this seems to reflect the significance of two important factors – religion and the degree of urbanisation.

In the predominantly Catholic areas (see Figure 10.2) the Nazi breakthrough was less marked, whereas the more Protestant regions were more likely to vote Nazi. Likewise, the Nazis fared less well in the large industrial cities, but gained greater support in the more rural communities and in residential suburbs.

The Nazi vote was at its lowest in the Catholic cities of the west, such as Cologne and Düsseldorf. It was at its highest in the Protestant countryside of the north and north-east, such as Schleswig-Holstein and Pomerania. Therefore, Bavaria, a strongly Catholic region, and the birthplace of Nazism, had one of the lowest Nazi votes. Such a picture does not of course take into account the exceptions created by local circumstances. For instance, parts of the province of Silesia, although mainly Catholic and urbanised, still recorded a very high Nazi vote. This was probably the result of nationalist passions generated in a border province, which had lost half its land to Poland.

Figure 10.1:
Percentage of vote gained by each major political grouping in the four *Reichstag* elections 1928–32.

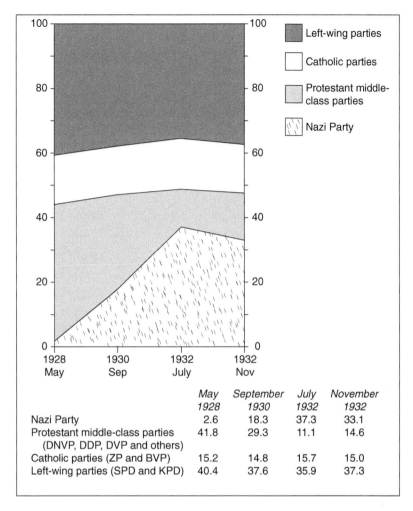

	May *1928*	*September* *1930*	*July* *1932*	*November* *1932*
Nazi Party	2.6	18.3	37.3	33.1
Protestant middle-class parties (DNVP, DDP, DVP and others)	41.8	29.3	11.1	14.6
Catholic parties (ZP and BVP)	15.2	14.8	15.7	15.0
Left-wing parties (SPD and KPD)	40.4	37.6	35.9	37.3

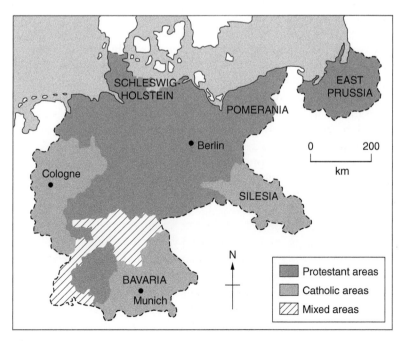

Figure 10.2:
Electoral split by religion.

Class

Nazi voters also reflected the rural/urban division in terms of their social groupings. It seems that the Nazis tended to win a higher proportion of support from:

- the peasants and farmers
- the '*Mittelstand*' (the lower middle classes, e.g. artisans, craftsmen and shopkeepers)
- the established middle classes, e.g. teachers, **white-collar workers**, public employees.

This tendency is shown in the figures of the Nazi Party's membership lists, which can be seen in Figure 10.3.

From this it is clear that a significantly higher proportion of the middle-class subsections tended to join the Nazi Party than the other classes, i.e. government officials/employees, self-employed, white-collar workers. However, it is worth bearing in mind two other points. First, although the working class did join the Nazi Party in smaller proportions, it was still the largest section in the NSDAP. Secondly, although the peasants tended to vote for the Nazis, the figures show they did not join the NSDAP in the same proportion.

The appeal of Nazism

It is clear that more of the Protestants and the middle classes voted for Nazism in proportion to their percentage in German society. The real question is: why were Catholics or socialists not so readily drawn to voting for the Nazis?

- First, both of them represented well-established ideologies in their own right and both opposed Nazism on an intellectual level.
- Secondly, the organisational strength of each movement provided an effective counter to Nazi propaganda. For socialism, there was the trade union structure. For Catholicism, there was the Church hierarchy, extending right down to the local parish priest.
- Thirdly, both movements had suffered under the Imperial German regime. As so often happens, persecution strengthened commitment. It was, therefore, much harder for the Nazis to break down the established loyalties of working-class and Catholic communities and their traditional '**associationism**', or identity, remained strong. In contrast, the Protestants, the farmers and the middle classes had no such loyalties. They were therefore more likely to accept the Nazi message.

The 'politics of anxiety'

What was common among many Nazi voters was their lack of faith in, and identity with, the Weimar system. They believed that their traditional role and status in society was under threat. For many of the middle classes (see Figure 10.3) the crisis of 1929–33 was merely the climax of a series of disasters since 1918. Hitler

Key terms

White-collar workers
Workers not involved in manual labour.

Associationism
Having a strong identity or affiliation with a particular group.

Key question
Why were the Protestants, the middle classes and the young more attracted to Nazism?

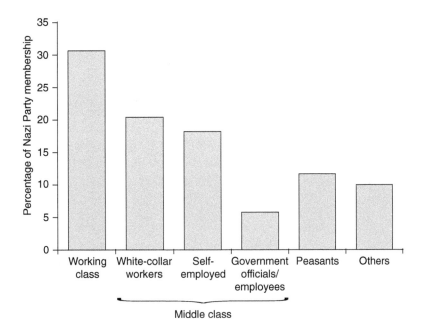

Figure 10.3: Nazi Party members in 1932.

Table 10.1: German society as a whole in 1933 (%)

Working class	Middle class			Peasants	Others
	White-collar workers	Self-employed	Government officials/ employees		
46.3	12.4	9.6	4.8	20.7	6.2

was able to exploit what is termed 'the politics of anxiety', as expressed by the historian T. Childers in his book *The Nazi Voter*:

> [By 1930] the NSDAP had become a unique phenomenon in German electoral politics, a catch-all party of protest, whose constituents, while drawn primarily from the middle class electorate were united above all by a profound contempt for the existing political and economic system.

In this way Hitler seemed able to offer to many Germans an escape from overwhelming crisis and a return to former days.

The young
Another clearly identifiable group of Nazi supporters was the youth of Germany. The Depression hit at the moment when young adults from the pre-war baby-boom came of age and, however good their qualifications were, many had little chance of finding work. In a study of Nazi Party membership, 41.3 per cent of those who joined before 1933 had been born between 1904 and 1913, despite this age group representing only 25.3 per cent

Profile: Adolf Hitler 1889–1945

1889	–	Born at Braunau-am-Inn, Austria
1905	–	Left school with no real qualifications
1907–13	–	Lived as a dropout in Vienna and moved to Munich
1914	–	Joined the German army and awarded the Iron Cross, first class in 1918
1919	–	Joined the DAP led by Drexler
1920	–	Drew up the party's 25-points programme with Drexler; the Party was renamed the NSDAP
1921	–	Appointed leader of the party
1923	–	Beer Hall *putsch* in Munich on 8–9 November
	–	Found guilty of treason and sentenced to five years, reduced to nine months. Wrote *Mein Kampf*
1925	–	NSDAP refounded at Munich
1925–33	–	Restructured the party and committed the party to a 'legality policy'
1930	–	Nazi breakthrough in September in the *Reichstag* election: 107 seats won
1933	–	Appointed Chancellor of coalition government by Hindenburg on 30 January
	–	Given dictatorial powers by the Enabling Law
1934	–	Ordered the purge of the SA, known as the Night of the Long Knives
	–	Combined the posts of Chancellor and President on the death of Hindenburg on 2 August. Thereafter, referred to as *Der Führer*
1937	–	Hossbach Conference
1938	–	Blomberg–Fritsch crisis. Purge of army generals and other leading conservatives
1939	–	Ordered the invasion of Poland on 1 September (resulting in the declaration of war by Britain and France)
1941	–	Ordered the invasion of the USSR on 22 June
	–	Declared war on the USA on 11 December after Japanese attack on 7 December
1944	–	Stauffenberg Bomb Plot
1945	–	Committed suicide in the ruins of Berlin on 30 April

Hitler's outlook on life was shaped by his unhappy years in Vienna (1907–13) when he failed to become an art student. It was here, too, that the core of his political ideas was firmly established: anti-Semitism, German nationalism, anti-democracy and anti-Marxism. Hitler found a real purpose in the war. His nationalism and the camaraderie of the troops gave him direction, but the shock of Germany's surrender confirmed all his prejudices.

Hitler in 1919 was drawn to the NSDAP, just one of many ultra-right-wing racist parties in post-war Germany, which remained a fringe political party in Bavaria in the 1920s. The depression created the environment in which Hitler could exploit his political skills: his charisma, his speeches and his advanced use of propaganda. Nevertheless, although he emerged by 1932 as the leader of the largest party, he was only invited to be Chancellor in January 1933 when he joined a coalition with other nationalists and conservatives.

Hitler established his dictatorship with immense speed and was given unlimited powers. He was portrayed as the all-powerful dictator, but there has been considerable debate about his real direction of daily affairs (see pages 241–4). Nevertheless, it is fair to conclude that Hitler's leadership controlled German events:

- by creating a one-party state (see pages 231–4)
- by supporting the racial policy that culminated in the genocide of the Jews (see pages 316–21 and 341–4)
- by pursuing an expansionist foreign policy – *Lebensraum* (see pages 330–5).

Below the surface, Hitler's regime was chaotic; but the cult of the *Führer* was upheld by Goebbels' propaganda machine as well as by the diplomatic and military successes from 1935–41. However, the winter of 1942–3 marked the 'turn of the tide' and Hitler, increasingly deluding himself, refused to consider surrender. It was only when the Soviet army closed in on the ruins of Berlin that the spell of the *Führer*'s power was finally broken – by his own suicide in the bunker on 30 April 1945.

of the total population. Equally striking, of the young adults aged 20–30 who became members of political parties, 61 per cent joined the Nazis. Thus, it was the young who filled the ranks of the SA – often unemployed, disillusioned with traditional politics and without hope for the future. They saw Nazism as a movement for change, not a search for respectability. Equally, the SA activities gave them something to do. All ages were prepared to vote for the Nazis, but the younger members of society were actually more likely to become involved by joining the party.

Key question
Why has Nazism been described as a 'people's party'?

Nazism: the people's party

The previous analysis should not obscure the fact that the Nazis still boasted a broader cross-section of supporters than any other political party. Unlike most of the other parties, the Nazis were not limited by regional, religious or class ties. So, by 1932 it is fair to say that the NSDAP had become Germany's first genuine *Volkspartei* or broad-based people's party. This point was made in a recent study of voting habits that suggests the Nazis became a mass party only by making inroads into the working-class vote. Hitler therefore succeeded in appealing to *all* sections of German society; it is simply that those from Protestant, rural and middle-class backgrounds supported in much greater numbers.

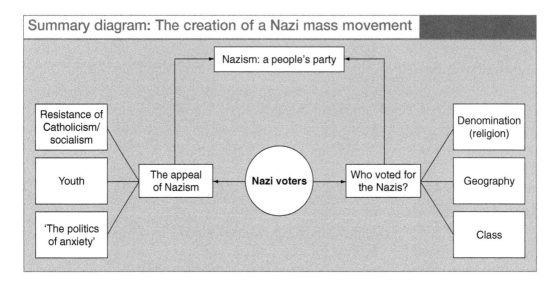

Summary diagram: The creation of a Nazi mass movement

2 | Nazi Political Methods

It would be wrong to assume that voters for the Nazi Party were simply won over by the appeal of a radical political ideology at a time of economic crisis. There were still various fringe parties on the extreme right, which publicised similar messages. What made the Nazis stand out for the voters was their revolutionary political style. Or, to use present-day jargon, it was the presentation and packaging of the party and its programme.

Propaganda

From his earliest days in politics Hitler had shown an uncanny, but cynical awareness of the power of propaganda. In 1924 in *Mein Kampf* he had written:

Key question
What were the main aims of Nazi propaganda?

> The receptive powers of the masses are very restricted, and their understanding is feeble. On the other hand, they quickly forget. Such being the case, all-effective propaganda must be confined to a few bare essentials and those must be expressed as far as possible in stereotyped formulas. These slogans should be persistently repeated until the very last individual has come to grasp the idea that has been put forward.

Such thinking was to remain the basis of Nazi propaganda, and there can be little doubt that its implementation in the years 1929–33 played a vital part in Nazi success.

The whole process of Nazi propaganda was highly organised. From April 1930 Joseph Goebbels was promoted and put in complete charge of the party's propaganda machine, which reached right down to branch level. In this way, information and instructions could be sent out from party headquarters and adapted to local circumstances. It also allowed the party to target its money and its efforts in the key electoral districts. Finally, it encouraged feedback from the grass roots, so that particularly effective ideas could be put into practice elsewhere.

Key question
In what ways did
Goebbels develop
propaganda?

Canvassing

Posters and leaflets had always played an important role in Nazi electioneering, but Goebbels was able to initiate a new approach. He practised mass politics on a grand scale. The electorate was deluged with material that had a range of propaganda techniques and an increasingly sophisticated application. He showed a subtlety and an understanding of psychology, which we now associate with advertising agencies.

Goebbels correctly recognised the need to direct propaganda according to people's social and economic interests. Specific leaflets were produced for different social groups, and Nazi speakers paid particular attention to the worries and concerns of the individual clubs and societies they addressed. In this way, the Nazi propaganda message was tailored to fit a whole range of people. For example:

- To appeal to farmers and peasants by offering special benefits to offset the collapse of agricultural prices.
- To appeal to the unemployed and the industrial workers by aiming to overcome the depression and offering 'Bread' and 'Work'.
- To appeal to the *Mittelstand*, for example, by limiting the control of large department stores.
- To appease the industrialists by playing down the fear of nationalisation and the state control of the economy.

Technology

Modern technology was also exploited. Loudspeakers, radio, film and records were all used. Expensive cars and aeroplanes were hired, not only for the practical purpose of transporting Hitler quickly to as many places as possible, but also to project a statesman-like image. In 1932, three major speaking programmes were organised for Hitler called 'Flight over Germany'. At a local level the political message was projected by the party arranging social events and entertainments: sports, concerts and fairs.

Mass suggestion

Key term

Mass suggestion
A psychological
term suggesting
that large groups of
people can be
unified simply by
the atmosphere of
the occasion. Hitler
and Goebbels used
their speeches and
large rallies to
particularly good
effect.

However, it was in the organisation of the mass rallies that the Nazis showed their mastery of propaganda. The intention was to create an atmosphere so emotional that all members of the crowd would succumb to the collective will. This is the idea of '**mass suggestion**' and every kind of device was used to heighten the effect: uniforms, torches, music, salutes, flags, songs and anthems, and speeches from leading personalities. Many people have since described how they were converted as a result of such meetings.

Scapegoats and unifying themes

In order to project itself as a mass people's party, Nazism tried to embrace and bring together many of the disparate elements in Germany. This was partly achieved by Goebbels, who showed an astute ability to play on social and psychological factors in Nazi propaganda. Three key unifying themes dominated Nazi propaganda:

- The *Führer* cult. Hitler was portrayed as a messiah-type figure, who could offer strong authoritarian leadership and a vision for Nazi Germany's future.
- The *Volksgemeinschaft* (national community). To appeal to the people for the development of a unifying idea, regardless of class.
- German nationalism. To play on German nationalism and to exploit the discontent since the First World War. To make Germany great again.

Through these themes, Nazi propaganda successfully portrayed itself as both revolutionary and reactionary. The party aimed to destroy the Republic, while at the same time promising a return to a glorious bygone age.

In addition, Nazism cynically played on the idea of 'scapegoats'. It focused on several identifiable groups, which were denounced and blamed for Germany's suffering:

- The 'November criminals'. The politicians responsible for the Armistice and the creation of the Republic became representative of all aspects associated with Weimar democracy.
- Communists. By playing on the fears of communism – the KPD was a sizeable party of 13–17 per cent in 1930–2 – and the increasing threat of communist USSR.

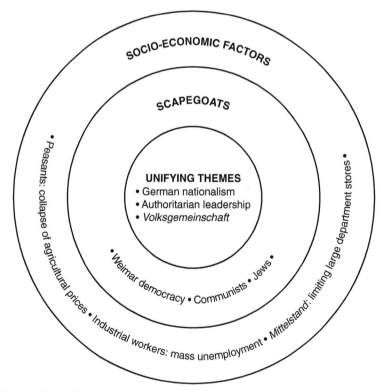

Figure 10.4: Nazi propaganda.

- Jews. It was easy to exploit the long-established history of anti-Semitism in Europe as a whole, and in Germany in particular.

Key question
Did SA violence advance the rise of Nazism?

Violence

There was one other strand to the political style of this Nazi revolution: the systematic encouragement and use of violence. Weimar politics had been a bloody affair from the start, but the growth of the SA and SS unleashed an unprecedented wave of violence, persecution and intimidation.

The growth of unemployment resulted in a phenomenal expansion of the SA, led by Röhm, in 1921–3 and 1930–4. Understandably, many people joined as members of the SA out of desperation, for food and accommodation, although much of it was just thuggery. The SA mainly was responsible for the violence against the opposition, especially the communists. All this helped to destabilise the already difficult situation in Germany and, in the wake of the presidential election (see page 198), the SA was actually banned for three months. However, it was restored by the new Chancellor, Papen, in June 1932. So, during the campaign of July 1932, there were 461 political riots in Prussia alone: battles between communists and Nazis on 10 July left 10 people dead; a week later, 19 died after the Nazis marched through a working-class suburb of Hamburg.

Such violent activities were encouraged by the Nazi leadership, as control of the streets was seen as essential to the expansion of Nazi power. The ballot box of democracy remained merely a means to an end, and, therefore, other non-democratic tactics were considered legitimate in the quest for power. The Nazis poured scorn on rational discussion and fair play. For them the end did justify the means. For their democratic opponents, there was the dilemma of how to resist those who exploited the freedoms of a democratic society merely to undermine it.

The Stennes' revolt

Despite the Nazi violence, Hitler became increasingly keen to maintain the policy of legality. He felt it was important to keep discipline, so he could maintain the image of a party that could offer firm and ordered government. The SA had generally supported the radical socialist aspects of Nazism, and yet Hitler was concerned increasingly with appealing to the middle-class conservative Nazi voters. The most serious disagreement between the SA and the party leadership has become known as the Stennes' revolt in February 1931.

Walther Stennes, the leader of the Berlin SA, rebelled against the orders of Hitler and Goebbels to act legally and to limit the violence. Hitler defeated the revolt with a small purge, but it underlined the fact that the relationship between the party leadership and the SA was at times very difficult. These differences were not really resolved until the infamous **Night of the Long Knives** in 1934 (see pages 235–9).

Key term

Night of the Long Knives
A crucial turning point when Hitler arranged for the SS to purge the SA leadership and murder about 200 victims, including Ernst Röhm, Gregor Strasser and Kurt von Schleicher.

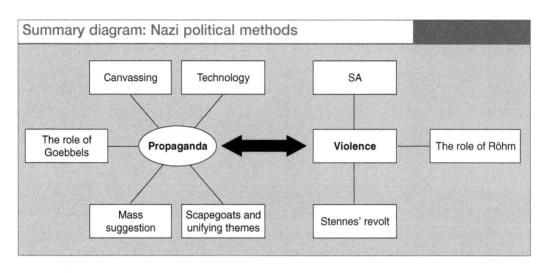

Summary diagram: Nazi political methods

Canvassing — Technology — SA

The role of Goebbels — **Propaganda** ⬌ **Violence** — The role of Röhm

Mass suggestion — Scapegoats and unifying themes — Stennes' revolt

3 | Political Intrigue, July 1932 to January 1933

Key question
Why did Papen fail to prevent Hitler's coming to power?

The political strength of the Nazi Party following the July 1932 *Reichstag* elections was beyond doubt (see pages 208–13). However, there still remained the problem for Hitler of how to translate this popular following into real power. He was determined to take nothing less than the post of Chancellor for himself. This was unacceptable to both Schleicher and Papen, who were keen to have Nazis in the cabinet, but only in positions of limited power. Therefore, the meeting between Hitler, Papen and Hindenburg on 13 August ended in deadlock.

Papen's failure

As long as Papen retained the sympathy of Hindenburg, Hitler's ambitions would remain frustrated. Indeed, a leading historian, Jeremy Noakes, describes the period from August to December 1932 as 'the months of crisis' for the Nazis, since 'it appeared the policy of legality had led to a cul-de-sac'. Party morale declined and some of the wilder SA members again became increasingly restless.

Reichstag passed a massive vote of no confidence in Papen's government (512 votes to 42): September 1932

Reichstag election: Nazi vote dropped to 33.1 per cent, winning 196 seats: November 1932

Key dates

On the other hand, Papen was humiliated when on 12 September the *Reichstag* passed a massive vote of no confidence in Papen's government (512 votes to 42). Consequently, he dissolved the new *Reichstag* and called for yet another election. In some respects Papen's reading of the situation was sound. The Nazis were short of money, their morale was low and the electorate was growing tired of repeated elections. These factors undoubtedly contributed to the fall in the Nazi vote on 6 November to 11.7 million (33.1 per cent), which gave them 196 seats. However, Papen's tactics had not achieved their desired end, since the fundamental problem of overcoming the lack of majority *Reichstag* support for his cabinet remained. Hitler stood firm: he would not join the government except as Chancellor.

In his frustration, Papen began to consider a drastic alternative: the dissolution of the *Reichstag*, the declaration of martial law and the establishment of a presidential dictatorship. However, such a plan was completely opposed by Schleicher, who found Papen's growing political desperation and his friendship with President Hindenburg additional causes for concern. Schleicher still believed that the popular support for the Nazis could not be ignored, and that Papen's plan would give rise to civil commotion and perhaps civil war. When he informed Hindenburg of the army's lack of confidence in Papen, the President was forced, unwillingly, to demand the resignation of his friendly Chancellor.

Key date

Papen dismissed as Chancellor and replaced by Schleicher: December 1932

Key question

Why did Schleicher fail to prevent Hitler's coming to power?

Schleicher's failure

Schleicher at last came out into the open. Over the previous two years he had been happy to play his role behind the scenes, but he now decided to become the dominant player, when he gained the favour of Hindenburg and was appointed Chancellor on 2 December. Schleicher's aims, rather ambitiously, were to achieve political stability and restore national confidence by creating a more broadly based government. He had a two-pronged strategy:

- First, to gain some support from elements of the political left, especially the trade unions, by suggesting a programme of public works.
- Secondly, to split the Nazis and attract the more socialist wing of the Nazi Party, under Gregor Strasser, by offering him the position of vice-chancellor.

With these objectives Schleicher, therefore, intended to project himself as the Chancellor of national reconciliation. However, his political manoeuvres came to nothing.

Profile: Kurt von Schleicher 1882–1934

1882	– Born in Brandenburg, Prussia
1900–18	– Professional soldier. Also made two close friends with Papen and Hindenburg
1919–32	– Worked in the German civil service in the Defence Ministry
1932	– Appointed Defence Minister in Papen's presidential government
	– Appointed Chancellor of Germany in December
1933	– Dismissed by Hindenburg on 28 January
1934	– Murdered in the Night of the Long Knives

Schleicher was a shadowy figure, yet, had an important influence in the years 1930–3 (his name translated from German is 'Sneaker' or 'Creeper'). He really preferred to exert political power behind the scenes and he did not take any high-ranking post until June 1932. Nevertheless, he was undoubtedly the 'fixer', who set up the appointments of Brüning and Papen and then finally contrived his own chancellorship. As an army general, his primary aim was to preserve the interests of the German army, but in the end he was unable to control the intrigue – and a year later he lost his own life.

First, the trade unions remained deeply suspicious of his motives and, encouraged by their political masters from the SPD, they broke off negotiations. Moreover, the idea of public works alienated some of the landowners and businessmen. Secondly, although Schleicher's strategy to offer Strasser the post of vice-chancellor was a very clever one, in the end it did not work. Strasser himself responded positively to Schleicher's overtures and he was keen to accept the post, but the fundamental differences between Hitler and Strasser led to a massive row. Hitler retained the loyalty of the party's leadership and Strasser was left isolated and promptly forced to resign from the party. Nevertheless, the incident had been a major blow to party morale and tensions remained high in the last few weeks of 1932, as the prospect of achieving power seemed to drift away.

Hitler's success

Hitler's fortunes did not begin to take a more favourable turn until the first week of 1933. Papen had never forgiven Schleicher for dropping him. Papen was determined to regain political office and he recognised he could only achieve this by convincing

Key question
Why did President Hindenburg eventually appoint Hitler as Chancellor?

Nazi parade celebrating Hitler's appointment as Chancellor near the Brandenburg Gate during the evening of 30 January 1933.

Hindenburg that he could muster majority support in the *Reichstag*. Consequently, secret contacts were made with Nazi leaders, which culminated in a meeting on 4 January 1933 between Papen and Hitler. Here it was agreed in essence that Hitler should head a Nazi–Nationalist coalition government with Papen as vice-chancellor.

Backstage intrigue to unseat Schleicher now took over. Papen looked for support for his plan from major landowners, leaders of industry and the army. It was only now that the conservative establishment thought that they had identified an escape from the threat of communism and the dangerous intrigues of Schleicher. But, above all, Papen had to convince the president himself. Hindenburg, undoubtedly encouraged by his son, Oskar, and his state secretary, Meissner, eventually gave in. Schleicher had failed in his attempt to bring stability. In fact, he had only succeeded in frightening the powerful vested interests with his ambitious plans. Hindenburg, therefore, heeded the advice of Papen to make Hitler Chancellor of a coalition government, secure in the knowledge that those traditional conservatives and nationalists would control the Nazis. On 28 January 1933, Hindenburg withdrew his support for Schleicher as Chancellor.

It was only in this situation that Hindenburg finally agreed, on the suggestion of Papen, to appoint Hitler as Chancellor in the mistaken belief Hitler could be controlled and used in the interests of the conservative establishment. Papen believed that Hitler would be a chancellor in chains and so two days later, on 30 January 1933, Hindenburg agreed to sanction the creation of a Nazi–Nationalist coalition.

Key date

Schleicher dismissed and Hitler appointed as Chancellor:
30 January 1933

Summary diagram: Political intrigue, July 1932 to January 1933

Reasons for Papen's failure
• increased support for extremists
• vote of no confidence
• dissolution of *Reichstag*
• doubts of Schleicher

Political intrigue

Reasons for Schleicher's failure
• doubts of trade unions
• suspicion of landowners
• businessmen
• isolation of Strasser

Hitler's appointment – why?
In the end support from:
• Papen
• Hindenburg
• landowners
• leaders of industry
• army

4 | The Nazi 'Legal Revolution', January–March 1933

Although Hitler had been appointed Chancellor, his power was by no means absolute. Hindenburg had not been prepared to support Hitler's appointment until he had been satisfied that the Chancellor's power would remain limited. Such was Papen's confidence about Hitler's restricted room for manoeuvre that he boasted to a friend, 'In two months we'll have pushed Hitler into a corner so hard that he'll be squeaking.'

The limitations of Hitler as Chancellor

At first sight, the confidence of the conservatives seemed to be justified, since Hitler's position was weak in purely constitutional terms:

Key question
What were the political constraints on Hitler?

- There were only two other Nazis in the cabinet of 12: Wilhelm Frick as Minister of the Interior, and Hermann Göring as a minister without portfolio (a minister with no specific responsibility) (see profile, page 285). There were, therefore, nine other non-Nazi members of the cabinet, all from conservative-nationalist backgrounds, such as the army, industry and landowners.
- Hitler's coalition government did not have a majority in the *Reichstag*, suggesting that it would be difficult for the Nazis to introduce any dramatic legislation.
- The Chancellor's post, as the previous 12 months had clearly shown, was dependent on the whim of President Hindenburg, and he openly resented Hitler. Hindenburg had made Hitler Chancellor but he could as easily sack him.

Hitler was very much aware of the potential power of the army and the trade unions. He could not alienate these forces, which could break his government. The army could arrange a military *coup* or the trade unions could organise a general strike, as they had done in 1920 (see pages 132–3).

Hitler's strengths

Within two months, the above weaknesses were shown not to be real limitations when Hitler became a dictator. Moreover, power was to be achieved by carrying on with the policy of legality which the party had pursued since 1925. Hitler already possessed several key strengths when he became Chancellor:

Key question
What were Hitler's main political strengths?

- He was the leader of the largest political party in Germany, which was why the policy of ignoring him had not worked. During 1932 it had only led to the ineffectual governments of Papen and Schleicher. Therefore, political realism forced the conservatives to work with him. They probably needed him more than he needed them. The alternative to Hitler was civil war or a communist *coup* – or so it seemed to many people at the time.
- More importantly, the Nazi Party had now gained access to the resources of the state. For example, Göring (see page 285) not

only had a place in the cabinet but was also Minister of the Interior in Prussia, with responsibility for the police. It was a responsibility that he used blatantly to harass opponents, while ignoring Nazi crimes. Goebbels (see page 263), likewise, exploited the propaganda opportunities on behalf of the Nazis. 'The struggle is a light one now', he confided in his diary, '...since we are able to employ all the means of the state. Radio and press are at our disposal.'

- Above all, however, Hitler was a masterly political tactician. He was determined to achieve absolute power for himself whereas Papen was really politically naïve. It soon became clear that 'Papen's political puppet' was too clever to be strung along by a motley collection of ageing conservatives.

The *Reichstag* election, 5 March 1933

Key question
How did Hitler create a dictatorship in two months?

Hitler lost no time in removing his strings. Within 24 hours of his appointment as Chancellor, new *Reichstag* elections had been called. He felt new elections would not only increase the Nazi vote, but also enhance his own status.

The campaign for the final *Reichstag* elections held according to the Weimar Constitution had few of the characteristics expected of a democracy: violence and terror dominated with meetings of the socialists and communists being regularly broken up by the Nazis. In Prussia, Göring used his authority to enrol an extra 50,000 into the police; nearly all were members of the SA and SS. Altogether 69 people died during the five-week campaign.

The Nazis also used the atmosphere of hate and fear to great effect in their election propaganda. Hitler set the tone in his 'Appeal to the German People' of 31 January 1933. He blamed the prevailing poor economic conditions on democratic government and the terrorist activities of the communists. He cultivated the idea of the government as a 'national uprising' determined to restore Germany's pride and unity. In this way he played on the deepest desires of many Germans, but never committed himself to the details of a political and economic programme.

Another key difference in this election campaign was the improved Nazi financial situation. At a meeting on 20 February with 20 leading industrialists, Hitler was promised three million *Reichsmarks*. With such financial backing and Goebbels' exploitation of the media, the Nazis were confident of securing a parliamentary majority.

The *Reichstag* Fire

As the campaign moved towards its climax, one further bizarre episode strengthened the Nazi hand. On 27 February the *Reichstag* building was set on fire, and a young Dutch communist, van der Lubbe, was arrested in incriminating circumstances. At the time, it was believed by many that the incident was a Nazi plot to support the claims of a communist *coup*, and thereby to justify Nazi repression. However, to this day the episode has defied satisfactory explanation. A major investigation in 1962

'Not the most comfortable seat.' A US cartoon drawn soon after Hitler's appointment as Chancellor. What does it suggest about Hitler's political position at that time?

concluded that van der Lubbe had acted alone; a further 18 years later the West Berlin authorities posthumously acquitted him; whereas the recent biography of Hitler by Ian Kershaw remains convinced that van der Lubbe acted on his own in a series of three attempted arsons within a few weeks. So, it is probable that the true explanation will never be known. The real significance of the *Reichstag* Fire is the cynical way it was exploited by the Nazis to their advantage.

On the next day, 28 February, Frick drew up, and Hindenburg signed, the 'Decree for the Protection of People and State'. In a few short clauses most civil and political liberties were suspended and the power of central government was strengthened. The

Reichstag Fire: communists blamed: 27 February 1933

Final *Reichstag* elections according to Weimar Constitution: 5 March 1933

Key dates

justification for the decree was the threat posed by the communists. Following this, in the final week of the election campaign, hundreds of anti-Nazis were arrested, and the violence reached new heights.

Election result

In this atmosphere of fear, Germany went to the polls on 5 March. The election had a very high turnout of 88 per cent – a figure this high suggests the influence and intimidation of the SA, corruption by officials and an increased government control of the radio.

Somewhat surprisingly, the Nazis increased their vote from 33.1 per cent to only 43.9 per cent, thereby securing 288 seats. Hitler could claim a majority in the new *Reichstag* only with the help of the 52 seats won by the Nationalists. It was not only disappointing; it was also a political blow, since any change in the existing Weimar Constitution required a two-thirds majority in the *Reichstag*.

The Enabling Law, March 1933

Despite this constitutional hurdle, Hitler decided to propose to the new *Reichstag* an Enabling Law that would effectively do away with parliamentary procedure and legislation and which would instead transfer full powers to the Chancellor and his government for four years. In this way the dictatorship would be grounded in legality. However, the successful passage of the law depended on gaining the support or abstention of some of the other major political parties in order to get a two-thirds majority.

A further problem was that the momentum built up within the lower ranks of the Nazi Party was proving increasingly difficult for Hitler to contain in the regional areas. Members were impatiently taking the law into their own hands and this gave the impression of a '**revolution from below**'. It threatened to destroy Hitler's image of legality, and antagonise the conservative vested interests and his DNVP coalition partners. Such was his concern that a grandiose act of reassurance was arranged. On 21 March, at Potsdam Garrison Church, Goebbels orchestrated the ceremony to celebrate the opening of the *Reichstag*. In the presence of Hindenburg, the Crown Prince (the son of Kaiser Wilhelm II) and many of the army's leading generals, Hitler symbolically aligned National Socialism with the forces of the old Germany.

Two days later the new *Reichstag* met in the Kroll Opera House to consider the Enabling Law, and on this occasion the Nazis revealed a very different image. The communists (those not already in prison) were refused admittance, while the deputies in attendance faced a barrage of intimidation from the ranks of the SA who surrounded the building.

However, the Nazis still required a two-thirds majority to pass the law and, on the assumption that the Social Democrats would vote against, they needed the backing of the Centre Party. Hitler thus promised in his speech of 23 March to respect the rights of the Catholic Church and to uphold religious and moral values. These were false promises, which the ZP deputies deceived

Key term

Revolution from below
The radical elements in the party, e.g. the SA, that wanted to direct the Nazi revolution from a more local level rather than from the leadership in Berlin.

Key dates

The 'Day of Potsdam': 21 March 1933

Enabling Law passed: 23 March 1933

themselves into believing. In the end only the Social Democrats voted against, and the Enabling Law was passed by 444 to 94 votes.

Germany had succumbed to what Karl Bracher, a leading German scholar, has called 'legal revolution'. Within the space of a few weeks Hitler had legally dismantled the Weimar Constitution. The way was now open for him to create a one-party totalitarian dictatorship.

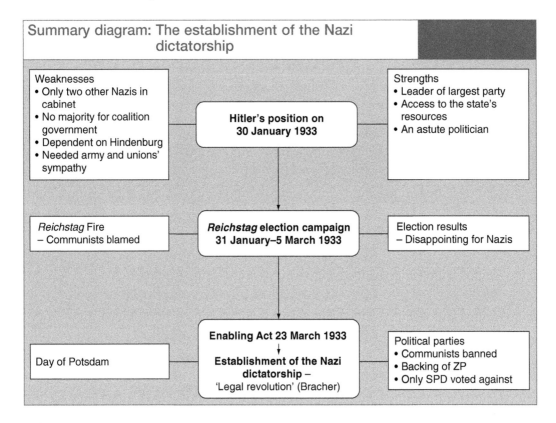

Summary diagram: The establishment of the Nazi dictatorship

Weaknesses
- Only two other Nazis in cabinet
- No majority for coalition government
- Dependent on Hindenburg
- Needed army and unions' sympathy

Hitler's position on 30 January 1933

Strengths
- Leader of largest party
- Access to the state's resources
- An astute politician

Reichstag Fire – Communists blamed

***Reichstag* election campaign 31 January–5 March 1933**

Election results – Disappointing for Nazis

Day of Potsdam

Enabling Act 23 March 1933
↓
Establishment of the Nazi dictatorship –
'Legal revolution' (Bracher)

Political parties
- Communists banned
- Backing of ZP
- Only SPD voted against

5 | The Key Debate

The rise of Hitler and the Nazis stands as one of the most controversial and intriguing historical debates. One key question continues to dominate the discussion:

Why did the Weimar Republic collapse and why did it give way to Hitler and Nazism?

Historians have various different interpretations.

Left-wing Marxists: Nazism, the result of crisis capitalism

In the 1930s many left-wing analysts sought to explain the unexpected rise of Nazism (and the rise of fascism in Italy). They came to believe that there was a close connection between the rise of Nazism and the crisis of capitalism faced by Germany in 1929–33. Consequently, big business lost faith in the Weimar Republic and supported the Nazis, who were seen as mere 'agents' for the controlling capitalists who sought to satisfy their desire for profits.

Anti-German determinists: Hitler, the inevitable result of German history

However, left-wing arguments were matched by some equally unquestioning views outside Germany. Clearly, anti-German feelings can be put down to the requirements of wartime propaganda in Britain. Nevertheless, some academic historians after the war portrayed Nazism as the natural product of German history. The renowned English historian A.J.P. Taylor wrote in *The Course of German History* in 1945:

> It was no more a mistake for the German people to end up with Hitler than it is an accident when a river flows into the sea.

The culmination of this kind of **anti-German determinist** view was probably reached with the publication in 1959 of William Shirer's *Rise and Fall of the Third Reich*. This monumental work, written by an American journalist who had worked as a correspondent in Germany between 1926 and 1941, had a profound impact on the general public. In it he explained how Nazism was 'but a logical continuation of German history'. He argued that Germany's political evolution, its cultural and intellectual heritage and the people's national character all contributed to the inevitable success of Hitler.

Gerhard Ritter: Nazism, the result in Germany of a 'moral crisis' in Europe

Not surprisingly, the implicit anti-German sentiments were not kindly received in Germany, especially among those intellectuals who had opposed Hitler. As a consequence, there emerged in the post-war decade in West Germany a school of thought that emphasised the 'moral crisis of European society'. It was epitomised above all by the writings of Gerhard Ritter, who focused on the European circumstances in which Nazism had emerged. In his view, it was hard to believe that Germany's great traditions, such as the power of the Prussian state, or its rich cultural history could have contributed to the emergence of Hitler. Instead, Ritter emphasised the events and developments since 1914 in Europe as a whole. It was the shock given to the traditional European order by the First World War that created the appropriate environment for the emergence of Nazism. The decline in religion and standards of morality, a tendency towards corruption and materialism and the emergence of mass democracy were all exploited by Hitler to satisfy his desire for power.

Key term

Anti-German determinist
Believes that the collapse of Weimar democracy and the rise of Nazi dictatorship were bound to happen because of Germany's long-term history and the national character of its people.

Structuralists: Nazism, a response to Germany's social and economic 'structures'

The 1960s witnessed the beginning of a phenomenal growth in research on the Third Reich, partly due to the practical reason that the German archives in the hands of the Western Allies had been made available. By the late 1960s and early 1970s, historians, such as Martin Broszat and Hans Mommsen, had started to exert a major influence on our understanding of the rise of Hitler and the Third Reich and their approach has been dubbed 'structuralist'.

In essence, the structuralist interpretation emphasises Germany's continuities from the 1850s to 1945. It argues that Germany had remained dominated by authoritarian forces in Germany's society and economy, such as the armed services and the bureaucracy, and had not really developed democratic institutions. As a result, the power and influence of such conservative vested interests continued to dominate Germany – even after the creation of the Weimar Republic – and therefore, these conservatives sympathised with the Nazi movement, which provided the means to uphold a right-wing authoritarian regime.

Intentionalists: Nazism, a result of Hitler's ideology and his evil genius

However, some historians have continued to argue that there is no escape from the central importance of Hitler the individual in the Nazi seizure of power. Indeed, '**intentionalists**', such as Klaus Hildebrand and Eberhard Jäckel, believe that the personality and ideology of Hitler remain so essential that Nazism can really be directly equated with the term Hitlerism. This is because although the intentionalists accept the special circumstances created by Germany's history, they emphasise the indispensable role of the individual, Hitler.

> **Intentionalists** Interpret history by emphasising the role (intentions) of people who shape history.
>
> *Key term*

Kershaw: Hitler's coming to power – the result of miscalculation

This latest interpretation has arisen as a result of the recently published biography by Ian Kershaw, arguably the leading British historian of Nazi Germany. However, he is keen to stress that his book goes well beyond the framework of mere biography and tries to balance the role of structuralist and intentionalist interpretations. Most significantly, he emphasises that the appointment of Hitler was not inevitable until the very last moment – 11 o'clock on 30 January 1933. Hitler's appointment as Chancellor was the result of a series of miscalculations and if Brüning, Papen, Schleicher or Hindenburg had made just one different crucial decision in 1930–3, history would have been very different. In that way Kershaw shows that Hitler's 'path ought to have been blocked long before the final drama'.

Conclusion

The Great Depression transformed the Nazis into a mass movement. Admittedly, 63 per cent of Germans never voted for them, but 37 per cent of the electorate did, so that the Nazis became by far the strongest party in a multi-party democracy. The Depression had led to such profound social and economic hardship that it created an environment of discontent, which was easily exploited by the Nazis' style of political activity. Indeed, it must be questionable whether Hitler would have become a national political figure without the severity of that economic downturn. However, his mixture of racist, nationalist and anti-democratic ideas was readily received by a broad spectrum of German people, and especially by the disgruntled middle classes.

Yet, other extreme right-wing groups with similar ideas and conditions did not enjoy similar success. This is partially explained by the impressive manner in which the Nazi message was communicated: the use of modern propaganda techniques, the violent exploitation of scapegoats – especially Jews and communists – and the well-organised structure of the party apparatus. All these factors undoubtedly helped but, in terms of electoral appeal, it is impossible to ignore the powerful impact of Hitler himself as a charismatic leader with a cult following. Furthermore, he exhibited a quite extraordinary political acumen and ruthlessness when he was involved in the detail of political infighting.

Nevertheless, the huge popular following of the Nazis, which helped to undermine the continued operation of democracy, was insufficient on its own to give Hitler power. In the final analysis, it was the mutual recognition by Hitler and the representatives of the traditional leaders of the army, the landowners and heavy industry that they needed each other, which led to Hitler's appointment as Chancellor of a coalition government on 30 January 1933. Ever since September 1930 every government had been forced to resort almost continuously to the use of presidential emergency decrees because they lacked a popular mandate.

In the chaos of 1932 the only other realistic alternative to including the Nazis in the government was some kind of military regime – a presidential dictatorship backed by the army, perhaps. However, that, too, would have faced similar difficulties. Indeed, by failing to satisfy the extreme left and the extreme right there would have been a very real possibility of civil war. A coalition with Hitler's Nazis, therefore, provided the conservative élites with both mass support and some alluring promises: a vigorous attack on Germany's political left wing; and rearmament as a precursor to economic and political expansion abroad. For Hitler, the inclusion of Papen and Hugenberg gave his cabinet an air of conservative respectability.

In the end, Hitler became Chancellor because the political forces of the left and centre were too divided and too weak, and because the conservative right wing was prepared to accept him as a partner in government in the mistaken belief that he could be tamed. With hindsight, it can be seen that 30 January 1933 was decisive. The dictatorship did not start technically until the completion of the 'legal revolution' in February–March 1933, but Hitler was already entrenched in power and, as one historian has claimed, now he 'could only be removed by an earthquake'.

Some key books in the debate

M. Broszat, *Hitler and the Collapse of Weimar Germany* (Berg, 1987).
Richard J. Evans, *The Coming of the Third Reich* (Penguin, 2004).
Ian Kershaw, *Hitler 1889–1936: Hubris* (Allen Lane, 2001).
Ian Kershaw (ed.), *Weimar: Why Did German Democracy Fail?* (Weidenfeld & Nicolson, 1990).
A.J. Nicholls, *Weimar and the Rise of Hitler* (Palgrave Macmillan, 2000).
G. Ritter, *The Third Reich* (Weidenfeld & Nicolson, 1955).
A.J.P. Taylor, *The Course of German History* (Methuen, 1961).

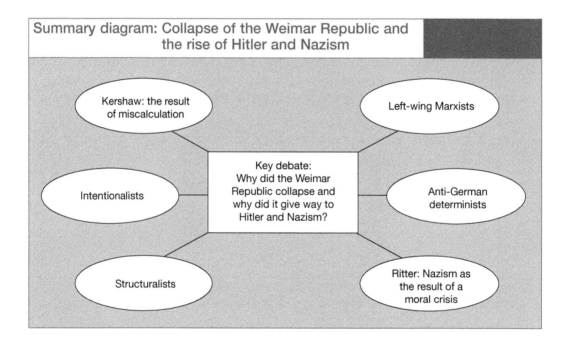

Summary diagram: Collapse of the Weimar Republic and the rise of Hitler and Nazism

Kershaw: the result of miscalculation

Left-wing Marxists

Intentionalists

Key debate: Why did the Weimar Republic collapse and why did it give way to Hitler and Nazism?

Anti-German determinists

Structuralists

Ritter: Nazism as the result of a moral crisis

11 The Political Structure of the Third Reich 1933–9

POINTS TO CONSIDER
It is possible to assume that the consolidation of power in 1933–4 created a tightly structured dictatorship in the Third Reich, but, in fact, it became a very complex system of forces which changed over time. Therefore, the following main themes need to be considered:

• Consolidation
• A 'second revolution'
• The role of Hitler
• The party and the state
• The apparatus of the police state
• Propaganda and censorship
• The German army
• Key debate: Was Nazi Germany a chaotic polycracy or a state efficient to the *Führer*'s will?

Key dates

1933	March 15	Creation of the Ministry of Popular Enlightenment and Propaganda under Josef Goebbels
1933	July 14	All political opposition to NSDAP declared illegal
1934	June 30	Night of the Long Knives
1934	August 2	Hitler merged posts of Chancellor and President to become *Führer*
1936	June	Appointment of Heinrich Himmler as Chief of the German Police
1938	February	Forced resignation of Field Marshal Blomberg and General Fritsch. Purge of army leadership
1939	September	Creation of RSHA

1 | Consolidation

The Enabling Law was the constitutional foundation stone of the Third Reich. In purely legal terms the Weimar Constitution was not dissolved until 1945, and the Enabling Law provided a legal basis for the dictatorship which evolved from 1933 (see page 225). The intolerance and violence used by the Nazis to gain power could now be used as tools of government by the dictatorship of Hitler and the party.

Gleichschaltung

The degeneration of Weimar's democracy into the Nazi state system is usually referred to as *Gleichschaltung* or co-ordination. It applied to the Nazifying of German society and structures and specifically to the establishment of the dictatorship, 1933–4. To some extent it was generated by the power and freedom exploited by the SA at the local level – a 'revolution from below'. But it was also directed by the Nazi leadership from the political centre in Berlin – a 'revolution from above'. These two political forces attempted to 'co-ordinate' as many aspects of German life as possible along Nazi lines, although differences over the exact long-term goals of National Socialism laid the basis for future conflict within the party (see pages 234–41).

Co-ordination has been viewed rather neatly as the 'merging' of German society with party associations and institutions in an attempt to Nazify the life of Germany. At first, many of these Nazi creations had to live alongside existing bodies, but they gradually replaced them. In this way, much of Germany's educational and social life became increasingly controlled (see Chapter 13). However, in the spring and summer of 1933 the priority of the Nazi leadership was to secure its political supremacy through the 'co-ordination' of the federal states, the political parties and the independent trade unions – agencies which were at odds with Nazi political aspirations.

Key question
What was *Gleichschaltung*?

Key term

Gleichschaltung
'Bringing into line' or 'co-ordination'.

Main features of co-ordination
The regional states (*Länder*)

The regions had a very strong tradition in Germany history (see pages 3 and 115–16). This contradicted Nazi desires to create a fully unified country. Nazi activists had already exploited the climate of February–March 1933 to intimidate opponents and to infiltrate federal governments. Indeed, their 'political success' rapidly degenerated into terror and violence that seemed even beyond the control of Hitler, who called for restraint because he was afraid of losing the support of the conservatives. The situation was resolved in three legal stages:

Key question
In what ways did Nazism achieve co-ordination?

- First, a law of 31 March 1933 dissolved regional parliaments (*Landtage*) and reformed them with acceptable majorities, allowing the Nazis to dominate regional state governments.
- Secondly, a law of 7 April 1933 created Reich Governors (*Reichstatthalter*) who more often than not were the local party *Gauleiters* with full powers.
- Finally, in January 1934 regional parliaments were abolished. The governments of all the states were subordinated to the Ministry of the Interior in Berlin central government.

By early 1934 the federal principle of government was as good as dead. Even the Nazi Reich governors existed simply 'to execute the will of the supreme leadership of the Reich'.

The trade unions

Germany's trade union movement was powerful because of its mass membership and its strong connections with socialism and Catholicism. In 1920 it had clearly shown its industrial muscle when a general strike defeated the Kapp *putsch* (see page 132). German organised labour was hostile to Nazism so posed a major threat to the stability of the Nazi state.

Yet, by May 1933 it was a spent force. The depression had already severely weakened it by reducing membership and lessening the will to resist. However, the trade union leaders deluded themselves that they could work with the Nazis and thereby preserve a degree of independence and at least the structure of trade unionism. Their hope was that:

- in the short term, trade unionism would continue to serve its social role to help members
- in the long term, it could provide the framework for development in the post-Nazi era.

However, the labour movement was deceived by the Nazis.

The Nazis surprisingly declared 1 May (the traditional day of celebration for international socialist labour) a national holiday, which gave the impression to the trade unions that perhaps there was some scope for co-operation. This proved to be the briefest of illusions. On the following day, trade union premises were occupied by the SA and SS, union funds were confiscated and many of the leaders were arrested and sent to the early concentration camps, such as Dachau.

Independent trade unions were then banned and in their place all German workers' organisations were absorbed into the German Labour Front (*Deutscher Arbeitsfront*, DAF), led by Robert Ley. DAF became the largest organisation in Nazi Germany with 22 million members, but it acted more as an instrument of control than as a genuine representative body of workers' interests and concerns (see pages 293–5). Also, it lacked the most fundamental right to negotiate wages and conditions of work. So, by the end of 1933, the power of the German labour movement had been decisively broken.

Political parties

Gleichschaltung could never allow the existence of other political parties. Nazism openly rejected democracy and any concessions to alternative opinions. Instead, it aspired to establish authoritarian rule within a one-party state. This was not difficult to achieve:

- The Communists had been outlawed since the *Reichstag* Fire (see pages 223–5).
- Soon after the destruction of the trade unions the assets of the Social Democrats were seized and they were then officially banned on 22 June.
- Most of the major remaining parties willingly agreed to dissolve themselves in the course of late June 1933 – even the

Key date

All political opposition to NSDAP declared illegal: 14 July 1933

Nationalists (previously coalition partners to the Nazis)
obligingly accepted.
- Finally, the Catholic Centre Party decided to give up the
struggle and followed suit on 5 July 1933.

Thus, there was no opposition to the decree of 14 July that
formally proclaimed the Nazi Party as the only legal political
party in Germany.

Success of *Gleichschaltung* in 1933

By the end of 1933 the process of *Gleichschaltung* was well
advanced in many areas of public life in Germany, although far
from complete. In particular, it had made no impression on the
role and influence of the churches, the army and big business.
Also, the civil service and education had only been partially
co-ordinated. This was mainly due to Hitler's determination to
shape events through the 'revolution from above' and to avoid
antagonising such powerful vested interests. Yet, there were many
in the lower ranks of the party who had contributed to the
'revolution from below' and who now wanted to extend the
process of *Gleichschaltung*. It was this internal party conflict which
laid the basis for the bloody events of June 1934.

Key question
How advanced was
the process of Nazi
co-ordination by the
end of 1933?

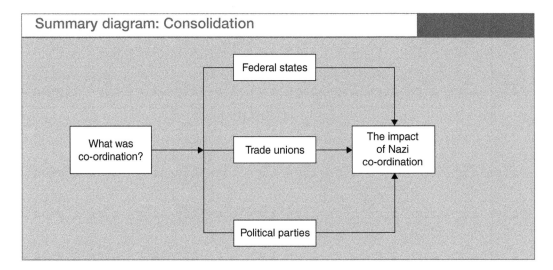

Summary diagram: Consolidation

Federal states

What was
co-ordination?

Trade unions

The impact
of Nazi
co-ordination

Political parties

2 | A 'Second Revolution'

Within six months of coming to power Hitler had indeed turned
Germany into a one-party dictatorship. However, in a speech on
6 July 1933 to the Reich Governors, Hitler warned of the dangers
of a permanent state of revolution. He therefore formally
declared an end to the revolution and demanded that 'the stream
of revolution must be guided into the safe channel of evolution'.

Hitler was caught in a political dilemma. He was increasingly
concerned that the behaviour of party activists was beyond his
control. This was likely to create embarrassment in his relations
with the more conservative forces whose support he still depended

Key question
What exactly was the
political dilemma
faced by Hitler?

on, e.g. big business, civil service and, above all, the army. Hitler's speech amounted to a clear-cut demand for the party to accept the realities of political compromise and the necessity of change from above.

The position of the SA

However, Hitler's appeal failed to have the desired effect. If anything, it reinforced the fears of many party members that the Nazi leadership was prepared to dilute National Socialist ideology. Such concerns came in particular from within the ranks of the SA giving rise to calls for a '**second revolution**'.

Key term

Second revolution
Refers to the aims of the SA, led by Ernst Röhm, which wanted social and economic reforms and the creation of a 'people's army' – merging the German army and the SA. The aims of 'a second revolution' were more attractive to 'left-wing socialist Nazis' or 'radical Nazis', who did not sympathise with the German conservative forces.

Table 11.1: SA membership 1931–4

	1931	1932	1933	1934
Membership figures	100,000	291,000	425,000	3,000,000

SA membership grew at first because of the large number of unemployed young men, but from 1933 many joined as a way to advance themselves.

The SA represented the radical, left wing of the Nazi Party and to a large extent it reflected a more working-class membership, often young and unemployed. It placed far more emphasis on the socialist elements of the party programme than Hitler ever did and saw no need to hold back simply to satisfy the élites. After its vital role in winning the political battle on the streets before 1933, many members were embittered and frustrated over the limited nature of the Nazi revolution. They were also disappointed by their own lack of personal gain from this acquisition of power.

Such views were epitomised by the SA leader, Ernst Röhm, who openly called for a genuine 'National Socialist Revolution'. Röhm was increasingly disillusioned by the politics of his old friend Hitler and recognised that the developing confrontation would decide the future role of the SA in the Nazi state. In a private interview in early 1934 with a local party boss, Rauschning, Röhm gave vent to his feelings and his ideas:

> Adolf is a swine. He will give us all away. He only associates with the reactionaries now ... Getting matey with the East Prussian generals. They're his cronies now ... Adolf knows exactly what I want. I've told him often enough. Not a second edition of the old imperial army.

Röhm did not want SA marches and rallies to degenerate into a mere propaganda show now that the street-fighting was over. He wanted to amalgamate the army and the SA into a people's militia – of which he would be the commander.

The power struggle between the SA and the army

However, Röhm's plan was anathema to the German army which saw its traditional role and status directly threatened. Hitler was

Profile: Ernst Röhm 1887–1934

1887	– Born in Munich
1914–18	– Served in the First World War and reached the rank of captain
1919	– Joined the *Freikorps* and joined the Nazi Party
1921	– Helped to form the SA and was leader in 1921–3
1923	– Participated in the Munich Beer Hall *putsch*
1924	– Initially jailed, but soon released on probation
1925–30	– Left for Bolivia as a military adviser to the army
1930–4	– Returned to Germany at Hitler's request and resumed SA leadership
1933	– Invited to join the cabinet
1934	– Arrested and murdered in the Night of the Long Knives

Röhm was always a controversial character. He was an open homosexual and a heavy drinker, and enjoyed the blood and violence of war and political street battles, yet, he had turned the SA into a powerful force by 1931. He was one of Hitler's closest friends in the years 1919–34, which partially explains why Hitler found it so painful to destroy the SA and its leader.

Röhm was committed to pursue a 'second revolution' that reflected the reforms of the 'left-wing socialist Nazis' or 'radical Nazis'. He did not sympathise with the conservative forces in Germany and aimed to create a 'people's army' by merging the German army and the SA. This fundamental difference culminated in the Night of the Long Knives and his own death.

therefore caught between two powerful, but rival, forces. Both could create considerable political difficulties for him.

The SA consisted of three million committed Nazis with his oldest political friend leading it. It had fought for Hitler in the 1923 Munich *putsch* and in the battle of the streets, 1930–3. The SA was far larger than the army, but the army was the one organisation that could unseat Hitler. The officer class was suspicious of Hitler and had close social ties with many of the powerful interests, e.g. civil service and *Junkers*. Moreover, the army alone possessed the military skills vital to the success of his foreign policy aims. However large, the SA could never match the discipline and professional expertise of the army.

Political realities dictated that Hitler had to retain the backing of the army but, in the winter of 1933–4, he was still loath to engineer a showdown with his old friend, Röhm. He tried to conciliate Röhm by bringing him into the cabinet. He also called a meeting in February between the leaders of the army, the SA and the SS to seek an agreement about the role of each within the Nazi state. However, the tension did not ease. Röhm and the SA resented Hitler's apparent acceptance of the privileged position of the army, while the unrestrained actions and ill-discipline of the SA increased dissatisfaction among the generals.

The Night of the Long Knives

Key question
When and why did the political conflict come to a head?

The developing crisis came to a head in April 1934 when it became apparent that President Hindenburg did not have much longer to live. The implications of this were profound as Hitler wanted to assume the presidency without opposition. He certainly did not want a contested election, and had no sympathy for those who wanted to restore the monarchy. Hitler's hand was forced by the need to secure the army's backing for his succession to Hindenburg.

The support of the army had become the key to the survival of Hitler's regime in the short term, while in the long term it offered the means to fulfil his ambitions in foreign affairs. Any personal loyalty Hitler felt for Röhm and the SA was finally put to one side. The army desired their elimination and an end to the talk of a 'second revolution' and a 'people's militia'. By agreeing to this, Hitler could gain the favour of the army generals, secure his personal position and remove an increasingly embarrassing millstone from around his neck.

Without primary written evidence it is difficult to establish the exact details of the events in June 1934. However, it seems highly probable that, at a meeting on the battleship *Deutschland* in April 1934, Hitler and the two leading generals, Blomberg and Fritsch, came to an agreed position against Röhm and the SA. Furthermore, influential figures within the Nazi Party, in particular Göring and Himmler, were also manoeuvring behind the scenes. They were aiming for a similar outcome in order to further their own ambitions by removing a powerful rival. Given all that, Hitler probably did not decide to make his crucial move to solve the problem of the SA until mid-June when Vice-Chancellor Papen gave a speech calling for an end to SA excesses and criticised the policy of co-ordination. Not surprisingly, these words caused a real stir and were seen as a clear challenge. Hitler now recognised that he had to satisfy the conservative forces – and that meant destroying the power of the SA immediately.

Key date
Night of the Long Knives: 30 June 1934

On 30 June 1934, the Night of the Long Knives, Hitler eliminated the SA as a political and military force once and for all. Röhm and the main leaders of the SA were shot by members of the SS, although the weapons and transport were actually provided by the army. There was no resistance of any substance. In addition, various old scores were settled: Schleicher, the former Chancellor, and Strasser, the leader of the radical socialist wing of the Nazi Party, were both killed. Altogether it is estimated that 200 people were murdered.

From a very different perspective, on 5 July 1934 the *Völkischer Beobachter (People's Observer)*, the Nazi newspaper, reported on the cabinet meeting held two days earlier:

> Defence Minister General Blomberg thanked the *Führer* in the name of the cabinet and the army for his determined and courageous action, by which he had saved the German people from civil war ....

The *Reich* cabinet then approved a law on measures for the self-defence of the state. Its single paragraph reads: 'The measures taken on 30 June and 1 and 2 July to suppress the acts of high treason are legal, being necessary for the self-defence of the state.'

The significance of the Night of Long Knives

It would be difficult to overestimate the significance of the Night of the Long Knives. In one bloody action Hitler overcame the radical left in his own party, and neutralised the conservative right of traditional Germany. By the summer of 1934, the effects of the purge could be seen clearly:

Key question
How significant was the Night of the Long Knives?

- The German army had endorsed the Nazi regime, as shown by Blomberg's public vote of thanks to Hitler on 1 July. German soldiers agreed to take a personal oath of loyalty to Hitler rather than to the state.

A cartoon/photomontage published by the German communist John Heartfield in July 1934. The image is of a Stormtrooper who has been murdered on Hitler's order in the Night of the Long Knives. What is ironic about his Heil Hitler salute?

- The SA was virtually disarmed and played no further political role in the Nazi state. Thereafter its major role was to attend propaganda rallies as a showpiece force, just as Röhm had feared.
- More ominously for the future, the incident marked the emergence of the SS. German generals had feared the SA, but they failed to recognise the SS as the party's élite institution of terror.
- Above all, Hitler had secured his own personal political supremacy. His decisions and actions were accepted, so in effect he had managed to legalise murder. He told the *Reichstag* that 'in this hour, I was responsible for the fate of the German nation and thereby the supreme judge'. From that moment, it was clear that the Nazi regime was not a traditional authoritarian one, like Imperial Germany 1871–1918; it was a personal dictatorship with frightening power.

Key date
Hitler combined the offices of Chancellor and President to become *Führer*: 2 August 1934

When Hindenburg died on 2 August there was no political crisis. Hitler merged the offices of Chancellor and President, and took the new official title of *Führer*. The Nazi regime had been stabilised and the threat of a 'second revolution' had been completely removed.

Key question
In what ways did the Nazis consolidate their power between 1933 and 1934?

The Nazi revolution

The Nazis effectively established a dictatorship between 1933 and 1934 by the following key factors:

- *Terror*. The Nazis used violence – increasingly without legal restriction, e.g. the arrest of the communists and the Night of the Long Knives. Nazi organisations also employed violence at a local level to intimidate opposition.
- *Legality*. The use of law by the Nazis gave a legal justification for the development of the regime, e.g. the Emergency Decree of 28 February 1933, the Enabling Law, the dissolution of the parties.
- *Deception*. Hitler misled powerful groups in order to destroy them, e.g. the trade unions and the SA.
- *Propaganda*. The Nazis successfully cultivated powerful images – especially when Goebbels took on responsibility for the Propaganda Ministry. Myths were developed about Hitler as a respectable statesman, e.g. the Day of Potsdam (see page 225).
- *Weaknesses of the opposition*. In the early Weimar years, the left had considerable potential power, but it became divided between the Social Democrats and the Communists – and was marred by the economic problems of the depression.
- *Sympathy of the conservative right*. Many of the traditional vested interests, e.g. the army and the civil service, were not wholly committed to Weimar and they really sympathised with a more right-wing authoritarian regime. They accepted the Night of the Long Knives.

Conclusion

All too often, the term 'revolution' is used for effect and with scant regard for its real meaning. The term means a fundamental change – an overturning of existing conditions. If Germany had undergone a 'political revolution' in the course of 1933–4, the evidence must support the idea that there was a decisive break in the country's political development.

Key question
Did Germany undergo a political revolution in the years 1933–4?

Arguments for

At first sight the regime created by the Nazis by the end of 1934 seems the very opposite of the Weimar Republic. However, Weimar democracy had ceased to function effectively well before Hitler became Chancellor. The strength of the anti-democratic forces had threatened the young democracy from the very start, so that it was never able to establish strong roots. Yet, even by comparison with pre-1918 Germany, the Nazi regime had wrought fundamental changes:

- the destruction of the **autonomy** of the federal states
- the intolerance shown towards any kind of political opposition
- the reduction of the *Reichstag* to complete impotence.

Autonomy
The right of self-government.

Key term

So *Gleichschaltung* decisively affected political traditions which had been key features of Imperial Germany 1871–1918. Thus it is reasonable to view the events of 1933–4 as a 'political revolution', since the Nazis had turned their backs quite categorically on the federal and constitutional values which had even influenced an authoritarian regime like Imperial Germany.

Arguments against

However, there were elements of continuity. At the time of Hindenburg's death, major forces within Germany were still independent of the Nazi regime; namely, the army, big business and the civil service. One might even include the Christian Churches, although they did not carry the same degree of political weight.

Hitler's willingness to enter into political partnership with these representatives of the old Germany had encouraged Röhm and the SA to demand a 'second revolution'. The elimination of the power of the SA in the Night of the Long Knives suggests that Hitler's claim for a 'national revolution' had just been an attractive slogan.

In reality this 'revolution' was strictly limited in scope. It involved political compromise and had not introduced any fundamental social or economic change. In this sense, one could suggest that the early years of the Nazi regime were merely a continuation of the socio-economic forces which had dominated Germany since 1871.

Certainly, this would seem to be a fair assessment of the situation until late 1934. However, the true revolutionary extent of the regime can only be fully assessed by considering the political, social and economic developments that took place in Germany throughout the entire period of the Third Reich. These will be the key points of the next few sections and chapters.

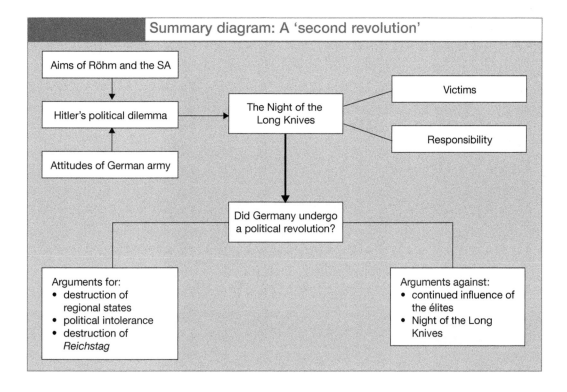

Summary diagram: A 'second revolution'

- Aims of Röhm and the SA
- Hitler's political dilemma
- Attitudes of German army
- The Night of the Long Knives
  - Victims
  - Responsibility
- Did Germany undergo a political revolution?

Arguments for:
- destruction of regional states
- political intolerance
- destruction of *Reichstag*

Arguments against:
- continued influence of the élites
- Night of the Long Knives

Key question
What was the role of Hitler in Nazi Germany?

3 | The Role of Hitler

In theory, Hitler's power was unlimited. Nazi Germany was a one-party state and Hitler was undisputed leader of that party. In addition, after the death of Hindenburg in August 1934, the *Law concerning the Head of State of the German Reich* combined the posts of President and Chancellor. Constitutionally, Hitler was also Commander-in-Chief of all the armed services. (This image of Hitler was very much presented in the poster on page 242: *Ein Volk, Ein Reich, Ein Führer.*)

'*Führer* power'

However, if one studies contemporary documents, such as this extract from a leading Nazi theorist, E. Huber, it is clear that Hitler's personal dictatorship was portrayed in more than purely legal terms:

> If we wish to define political power in the *völkisch Reich* correctly, we must not speak of 'state power' but of '*Führer* power'. For it is not the state as an impersonal entity which is the source of political power, but rather political power is given to the *Führer* as the executor of the nation's common will. '*Führer* power' is comprehensive and total: it unites within itself all means of creative political activity: it embraces all spheres of national life.

Huber's grandiose theoretical claims for '*Führer* power' could not mask basic practical problems. First, there was no all-embracing constitution in the Third Reich. The government and law of Nazi

A poster of Adolf Hitler.

Germany emerged over time in a haphazard fashion. Secondly, there was (and is) no way one individual could ever be in control of all aspects of government. Thus, Hitler was still dependent upon sympathetic subordinates to put policy decisions into effect. And thirdly, Hitler's own personality and attitude towards government were mixed and not conducive to strong and effective leadership.

Hitler's character

Hitler certainly appeared as the charismatic and dynamic leader. His magnetic command of an audience enabled him to play on 'mass suggestion'; he portrayed himself as the ordinary man with the vision, will-power and determination to transform the country.

However, this was an image perpetuated by the propaganda machine and, once in government, Hitler's true character revealed itself, as is shown in the memoirs of one of his retinue:

> Hitler normally appeared shortly before lunch ... When Hitler stayed
> at Obersalzberg it was even worse. There he never left his room
> before 2.00p.m. He spent most afternoons taking a walk, in the
> evening straight after dinner, there were films ... He disliked the
> study of documents. I have sometimes secured decisions from him
> without his ever asking to see the relevant files. He took the view
> that many things sorted themselves out on their own if one did not
> interfere ... He let people tell him the things he wanted to hear,
> everything else he rejected. One still sometimes hears the view that
> Hitler would have done the right thing if people surrounding him
> had not kept him wrongly informed. Hitler refused to let himself be
> informed ... How can one tell someone the truth who immediately
> gets angry when the facts do not suit him?

Hitler liked to cultivate the image of the artist and really he was
quite lazy. This was accentuated further by Hitler's lifestyle: his
unusual sleeping hours; his long periods of absence from Berlin
when he stayed in the Bavarian Alps; his tendency to become
immersed in pet projects such as architectural plans.
Furthermore, as he got older he became neurotic and moody as
was demonstrated in his obsession with his health and medical
symptoms, both real and imagined.

Hitler was not well-educated and had no experience for any
role in government or administration. As cynics say, Hitler's first
real job was his appointment as Chancellor. He followed no real
working routine, he loathed paperwork and disliked the formality
of committees in which issues were discussed. He glibly believed
that mere will-power was the solution to most problems.

Hitler's leadership

Surprisingly, Hitler was not even very decisive when it came to
making a choice. Although he was presented to the world as the
all-powerful dictator, he never showed any inclination to
co-ordinate government. For example, the role of the cabinet
declined quite markedly after 1934. In 1933 the cabinet met
72 times, but only four times in 1936 and the last official cabinet
meeting was held in February 1938. Consequently, rivalry between
the various factions of the party and state was rife and decision-
making became, more often than not, the result of the *Führer*'s
whim or an informal conversation rather than rational clear-cut
chains of command.

Despite everything, Hitler still played a decisive role in the
development of the Third Reich, as will be further discussed on
pages 268–71. In his research, Kershaw has outlined an
interpretation of Hitler's style of rule as one of 'charismatic
domination'. In his words, 'Hitler's personalised form of rule
invited initiatives from below and offered such initiatives backing,
so long as they were in line with his broadly defined goals.'
Kershaw suggests that:

• Hitler was crucial because he was still responsible for the
  overall Nazi dream.

- He had no real effective opposition to his aims.
- Although the government structure was chaotic, Hitler did not get lost in the detail of the day-to-day government.
- He generated an environment in which his followers carried out his presumed intentions. In this way, others willingly took the responsibility 'to work towards the *Führer*'.

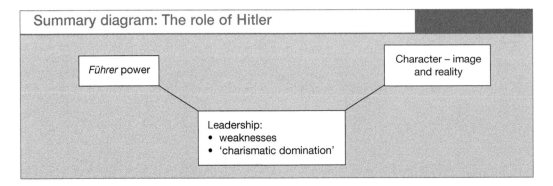

Summary diagram: The role of Hitler

Führer power

Character – image and reality

Leadership:
- weaknesses
- 'charismatic domination'

4 | The Party and the State

Key question
Why was the relationship between the party and the state unclear?

By July 1933, Germany had become a one-party state, in which the Nazi Party claimed sole political authority. Nazi **totalitarian** claims, reinforced by a powerful propaganda machine, deceived many people at the time into thinking that Nazism was a clear and well-ordered system of government. The reality was very different. Fundamentally, this was because the exact relationship between the structure of the party on the one hand and the apparatus of the German state on the other was never clarified satisfactorily. It meant that there was much confusion between the two forces in Nazi government and this clash has been given the term **dualism**.

The revolutionary elements within the party wanted party control of the civil service in order to smash the traditional organs of government and to create a new kind of Germany. However, there seem to have been three reasons why the Nazi leadership did not do this:

- Many recognised that the bureaucracy of the German state was well established and staffed by educated and effective people. Initially, therefore, there was no drastic purge of the state apparatus. The *Law for the Restoration of the Professional Civil Service* of April 1933 only called for the removal of Jews and well-recognised opponents of the regime (see page 317).
- Another factor which emerged during 1933 after the Nazi consolidation of power was a vast increase in party membership. It increased three-fold 1933–5 as people jumped on the bandwagon. The so-called '**March converts**' tended to dilute the influence of the earlier Nazis, further weakening the radical cutting edge of the party apparatus within the regime.
- Finally, Hitler remained unclear on the issue of the party and the state. The *Law to ensure the Unity of Party and State* issued in

Key terms

Totalitarian
A system of government in which all power is centralised and does not allow any rival authorities.

Dualism
A government system in which two forces co-exist, e.g. the Nazi Party and the German state (and the Communist Party and the Soviet state).

March converts
Those who joined the NSDAP immediately after the consolidation of power in January–March 1933.

December 1933 proclaimed that the party 'is inseparably linked with the state', but the explanation was so vague as to be meaningless. Two months later, Hitler declared that the party's principal responsibilities were to implement government measures and to organise propaganda and indoctrination. Yet, in September 1934, he told the party congress that 'it is not the state which commands us but rather we who command the state', and a year later he specifically declared that the party would assume responsibility for those tasks which the state failed to fulfil. Hitler's ambiguity on this issue is partially explained by the political unrest of these years and by the need to placate numerous interest groups and it was not really ever resolved.

Dualism: state institutions

Key question
How did the state institutions develop under the Third Reich?

In the German state the term for a 'civil servant' was a very broad one, it included most of the following categories, including teachers. Generally, the state bureaucracy was unsympathetic to Weimar, but was loyal to the institutions of the state. Only five per cent of the civil servants were purged and, as time passed, more and more joined the party until it became compulsory in 1939.

Reich Chancellery
The Reich Chancellery was responsible for co-ordinating government and, as the role of the cabinet declined from 1934, the Chancellery became increasingly important. Its head was Hans-Heinrich Lammers and he played a pivotal role because he:

- drew up all government legislation
- became the vital link between Hitler and all other organisations, so he in effect controlled all the flow of information.

But even as a very organised bureaucrat Lammers found it impossible to co-ordinate effectively the growing number of organisations.

Government ministries
Ministries, such as transport, education and economics, were run by leading civil servants. They were generally very conservative, most notably the Foreign Office. They were under pressure in the late 1930s from growing Nazi institutions: for example, the Economics Ministry was affected by the Four-Year Plan and the Foreign Office lost its position of supreme control to the so-called **Ribbentrop Bureau**. Very significantly the aristocrat Neurath was replaced in 1938 as Foreign Minister by the Nazi Joachim von Ribbentrop. More Nazi officials were then brought in.

Judiciary
In the 1920s the judiciary was hostile to the Weimar Republic. It had been ultra-conservative and in notorious cases it was biased against the left and in favour of the right. So, on one level the judiciary was reasonably content to work with the regime. Judges

Key term

Ribbentrop Bureau
Name given to the office created by Joachim von Ribbentrop, who ran his own personal 'bureau' to oversee foreign affairs.

Profile: Hans Heinrich Lammers 1879–1962

1879   – Born in Silesia, Germany
1921–33   – Worked as a civil servant in the Ministry of Interior
1932   – Joined the NSDAP
1933–45   – Head of the Reich Chancellery
1940   – Appointed to the honorary rank of an SS general
1945   – Sentenced to 20 years' imprisonment at war trials
1952   – Released in 1952 and died in Düsseldorf in 1962

Lammers had long enjoyed a senior post as a civil servant in the Ministry of Interior and he served as Head of the Reich Chancellery throughout the Nazi years. In effect he became the most powerful bureaucrat in the Third Reich and personally close to Hitler. His significance was that he:

- gave legal advice
- served as a link between Hitler and the bureaucracy
- became politically more powerful in co-operation with Bormann and Keitel, who became known as the 'Council of Three'.

---

and lawyers were 'co-ordinated' (see pages 231–4), although not many were replaced. In fact, until 1941, the Justice Minister, Franz Gürtner, was not a Nazi.

However, the judiciary was not immune from Nazi interference and over the years it felt the ever-increasing power of the Nazi organisations. First of all, the structure of new courts enabled the Nazis to get round the established system of justice:

- In 1933 Special Courts were set up to try political offences without a jury.
- In 1934 the People's Court was established to try cases of **high treason** with a jury composed specifically of Nazi Party members (7000 out of the 16,000 cases resulted in a death sentence in 1934–45).

Secondly, all legal authorities lost influence to the arbitrary power of the SS-Police system who increasingly behaved above the law (see pages 251–6). The decree *Nacht und Nebel* **(Night and Fog)** of 1941 gave the SS-Police system the right to imprison without question any person thought to be dangerous. In that way, although the traditional role of the judiciary in the state continued to function, it was severely subverted.

Regional state governments

By early 1934 *Gleichschaltung* had destroyed the federal principle of government (see page 232). The Nazi Reich Governors existed only 'to execute the will of the supreme leadership of the *Reich*', who more often than not were the local party *Gauleiters* with full powers (although their role within the party structure was certainly not clear – see pages 248–50).

Key terms

High treason
The crime of betraying one's country, especially by attempting to overthrow the leader or government.

Nacht und Nebel
(Night and Fog)
Name given to a decree by Hitler in December 1941 to seize any person thought to be dangerous. They should vanish into *Nacht und Nebel*.

German judges swearing the oath to serve Germany and Hitler in the Berlin State Opera House.

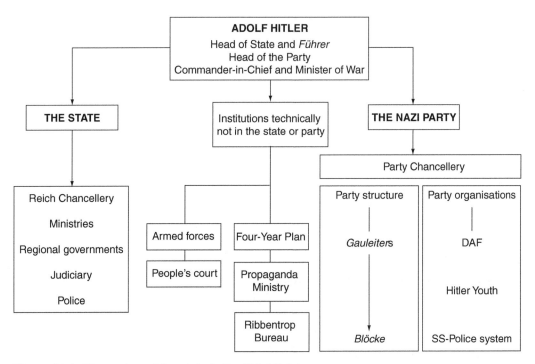

Figure 11.1: The party and the state in the Third Reich.

Dualism: party institutions

The role and shape of the Nazi Party was determined by its background and composition. Its organisation had been created and had evolved in order to *gain* political power and it had proved remarkably well designed for this purpose. However, the party had to find a new role from 1933 and yet it was by no means a unified structure and not really geared to the task of government. The party's problems were caused by the following:

Key question
How did the Nazi Party's institutions develop under the Third Reich?

- Up to 1933 it had developed out of the need to attract support from different sections of society and it consisted of a mass of specialist organisations, such as the Hitler Youth, the SA and the NS Teachers' League. Once in power, such groups were keen to uphold and advance their own particular interests.
- The party became increasingly splintered. Various other organisations of dubious political position were created and some institutions were caught between the state and the party. For example, Goebbels' propaganda machine was a newly formed ministry and the Four-Year Plan Office was an added response to the economic crisis of 1936 (see pages 283–5).
- The actual membership and administrative structure of the party was established on the basis of the *Führerprinzip* in a major hierarchy, but it did not really work in terms of effective government. The system led to the dominating role of the *Gauleiters* in the regions who believed that their only allegiance was to Hitler. As a result, they endeavoured to preserve their own interests and tended to resist the authorities of both the state and the party (see Figure 11.2 below).

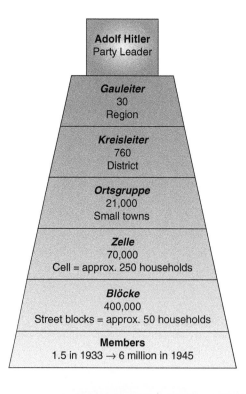

Figure 11.2: Nazi Party structure and leadership.

Profile: Rudolph Hess 1894–1987

1894	– Born in Alexandria, Egypt
1914–18	– Served in the First World War
1920	– Early member of the party and secretary to Hitler
1923–4	– Took part in Munich *putsch* and helped Hitler to write *Mein Kampf* while in prison at Landsberg
1933–41	– Deputy leader of the party. Appointed to various posts, e.g. minister without portfolio
1941	– Flew to Scotland on his own initiative to negotiate peace and interned by British authorities
1946	– Sentenced to life imprisonment at the Nuremberg trials
1987	– Committed suicide in Spandau Prison, Berlin

Hess may have been deputy leader of the party, but he was actually of limited abilities and did not exert any real power. He was well known for his absolute loyalty to Hitler. Most significantly in the 1930s he did contribute, alongside Bormann, to developing a more influential party bureaucracy, although the scheme was limited by the nature of the Third Reich political structure.

In one way the position of the party certainly did improve over the years. This was mainly because Rudolf Hess, Deputy *Führer*, was granted special powers and developed a party bureaucracy in the mid-1930s. In 1935 he was given the right to vet the appointment and promotion of all civil servants, and to oversee the drafting of all legislation. By 1939 it had become compulsory for all civil servants to be party members. In this way, the foundations were laid for increasing party supervision.

The other key figure in the changing fortunes of the party was Martin Bormann, a skilled and hard-working administrator with great personal ambition. Working alongside Hess, he correctly analysed the problems confronting the party and created two new departments with the deliberate aim of strengthening the party's position (and thereby his own):

- The Department for Internal Party Affairs, which had the task of exerting discipline within the party structure.
- The Department for Affairs of State, which aimed to secure party supremacy over the state.

The trend continued in the war years, especially from 1941 after Hess's flight to Scotland. Bormann was then put in charge of the party chancellery and thereafter, by constant meddling, by sheer perseverance and by maintaining good personal relations with Hitler, Bormann effectively advanced the party's fortunes. By 1943, when he officially became Hitler's Secretary, and thus secured direct access to the *Führer*, Bormann had constructed an immensely strong power-base for himself.

Profile: Martin Bormann 1900–45

1900	– Born at Halberstadt in Saxony, Germany
1918	– Dropped out of school and joined the army
1919–20	– Joined the Rossbach *Freikorps*
1924	– Found guilty of murder, but only served one year
1927	– Joined the Nazi Party
1928	– Made *Gauleiter* of Thuringia
1933	– Chief-of-staff to Hess with responsibility to organise the party
1941	– Head of the party chancellery after Hess's departure
1943	– Became Hitler's secretary
	– Formed the 'Council of Three' with Keitel and Lammers
1945	– Died trying to escape from Berlin

Despite his limited education and his brutal background, Bormann became a workaholic bureaucrat at the heart of the party administrative machine. He quietly played an important part with Hess in improving the influence of the party's bureaucracy over the state in the years 1933–9, but his personal power increased markedly from 1941 after the departure of Hess. Bormann played a significant role because he:

- was a radical Nazi and advanced the racial policy against the Jews and the campaign against the Christian Churches
- became a manipulator who advanced the interests of the party machine and himself. He used his position to block access to Hitler from other leading Nazis (part of the reason why relations between him and Himmler and Göring were so poor).

Conclusion

Under Bormann's influence the party became more than merely an organisation geared to seizing power. It strengthened its position in relation to the traditional apparatus of the state. Undoubtedly, it was one of the key power blocs within Nazi Germany, and its influence continued to be felt until the very end. However:

- The party bureaucracy had to compete strenuously for influence over the established state institutions, and the latter were never destroyed, even if they were significantly constrained.
- The internal divisions and rivalries within the party itself were never overcome.
- The independence of the *Gauleiters* was one of the main obstacles to control.

Consequently, the Nazi Party never became an all-pervasive dominating instrument like the Communist Party in Soviet Russia. Therefore the next section examines a number of other power blocs.

Key question
Which lost out: the party or the state?

Summary diagram: The party and the state

Dualism
- -
The problem of the relationship
between state and party

State institutions:
- Reich Chancellery (Lammers)
- government ministries
- judiciary
- regional state governments

Party institutions:
- specialist organisations
- *Gauleiters*
- Hess
- Bormann

Which lost out: the party or the state?

Key question
How did the SS
emerge?

5 | The Apparatus of the Police State

Amid all the confusion of the state and party structure an organisation emerged which became the mainstay of the Third Reich: the SS. The SS developed an identity and structure of its own which kept it separate from the state and yet, through its dominance of police matters, linked it with the state.

The emergence of Himmler and the SS

The SS had been formed in 1925 as an élite bodyguard for Hitler, but it remained a relatively minor section of the SA, with only 250 members, until Himmler became its leader in 1929. By 1933 the SS numbered 52,000, and it had established a reputation for blind obedience and total commitment to the Nazi cause.

Himmler had also created in 1931 a special security service, **SD** (*Sicherheitsdienst*), to act as the party's own internal security police. In 1933–4 he assumed control of all the police in the *Länder*, including the **Gestapo** in Prussia. Thus, Hitler turned to Himmler's SS to carry out the purge of June 1934 (see pages 237–8). The loyalty and brutal efficiency of the SS on the Night of the Long Knives had its rewards, for it now became an independent organisation within the party. In 1936 all police powers were unified under Himmler's control as 'Reichsführer SS and Chief of all German Police', including the *Gestapo*. In 1939 all party and state police organisations involving police and security matters were amalgamated into the **RSHA**, overseen by Himmler but actually co-ordinated by his deputy, Heydrich (see profile on page 343).

Key dates
Appointment of
Heinrich Himmler as
Chief of the German
Police: June 1936

Creation of RSHA:
September 1939

Key terms

SD
Security service.

Gestapo
Secret State Police –
*Geheime Staats
Polizei.*

RSHA
Reich Security
Office, which
amalgamated all
police and security
organisations.

Profile: Heinrich Himmler 1900–45

1900 – Born in Munich
1917–18 – Joined the cadets, but did not face action in the war
1919–22 – Studied agriculture at technical college
1923 – Joined the Nazi Party and took part in Beer Hall *putsch*
1929 – Appointed leader of the SS
1934 – Arranged the purge of the SA on 30 June
1936 – Given responsibility as '*Reichsführer* SS and Chief of all German Police'
1939 – Made Commissar of the Strengthening of the German Nationhood. Formed the RSHA
1943 – Appointed Minister of Interior (replacing Frick)
1944 – Appointed as Commander-in-Chief of the Home Army
1945 – Arrested by the British, but committed suicide before trial

Himmler was in many respects a non-descript uninspiring character who before 1929 achieved little in his work or in the party. Yet, with a reputation for an organised, obsessive, hard-working style, he became the leader of the brutally efficient SS machine which really held the Third Reich together. His responsibility for the purge in the Night of the Long Knives was his turning point. From then on, Himmler's political power continued to increase until the collapse of the Third Reich. He must therefore take responsibility for:

- the development and control of the apparatus of terror which by surveillance and repression created the system of control
- the pursuit of his aim to create a German master-race and the development of élite institutions like *Ordensburgen* and the *Lebensborn* (see pages 301 and 313)
- the extermination of Jews and Gypsies in concentration camps
- the exploitation of all the occupied lands for slave labour and arms production
- the development of the *Waffen* SS as an élite military force that matched the might of the German army by the end of the war.

The SS-Police system which had been created, therefore, served four main functions:

- Intelligence gathering by the SD. It was responsible for all intelligence and security and was controlled by its leader Heydrich, but still part of the SS. All its responsibilities grew as occupied lands spread.
- Policing by the *Gestapo* and the **Kripo**. The *Kripo* was responsible for the maintenance of general law and order e.g. dealing with asocials and thieves. In 1936 the *Kripo* was linked with the *Gestapo*. The *Gestapo* was the key policing organisation for upholding the regime by using surveillance and repression. It had a reputation for brutality and it could arrest and detain

Kripo
Criminal police responsible for the maintenance of general law and order.

Key term

anyone without trial, although its thoroughness and effectiveness have been questioned (see pages 254–5).

- Disciplining the opposition. Torture chambers and concentration camps were created early in 1933 to deal with political opponents – mainly socialists and communists. In 1936 the number of inmates was still limited to about 6000. Thereafter this increased dramatically when, using Dachau as the model, the Nazis began to formalise their system of concentration camps. They then started to round up anyone who did not conform – asocials, beggars, gypsies – and the numbers grew to 21,000 by 1939.
- Military action by the first units of the **Waffen** SS. Up to 1938 it consisted of about 14,000 soldiers in three units, but it was racially pure, fanatically loyal and committed to Nazi ideology. From 1938 its influence grew rapidly. This was affected by the weakening of the German army in the Blomberg–Fritsch crisis (see page 265) and also by the more anti-Semitic policies (see pages 318–20).

It is important to keep in perspective the importance of the SS in 1933–9. Its power had definitely been established. The take-over of territories in 1939 began the creation of the '**New Order**' and the expansion of the influence of the SS.

The SS state

As *Reichsführer* SS, Himmler controlled a massive police apparatus answerable only to Hitler. The SS system grew into a key power bloc in the Third Reich. It became, in the words of E. Kogon,

Key terms

Waffen SS
The armed SS: the number of *Waffen* SS armed divisions grew during the war from three to 35.

New Order
A phrase given by the Nazis to the economic, political and racial integration of Europe under the Third Reich.

Key question
How powerful was the SS?

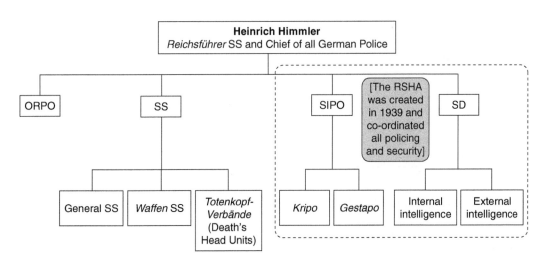

Figure 11.3: The SS-Police system in 1939.

a 'state within a state'. It was a huge vested interest, which numbered 250,000 in 1939 and had begun to eclipse other interest groups in terms of power and influence. The onset of war accentuated this. As German troops gained control over more and more areas of Europe, the power of the SS was inevitably enhanced:

- *Security*. All responsibilities of policing and intelligence expanded as occupied lands spread. The job of internal security became much greater and SS officers were granted severe powers to crush opposition.
- *Military*. The *Waffen* SS increased from three divisions in 1939 to 35 in 1945, which developed into a 'second army': committed, brutal and militarily highly rated. By 1944 the SS was so powerful it rivalled the power of the German army.
- *Economy*. The SS became responsible for the creation of the 'New Order' in the occupied lands of eastern Europe. Such a scheme provided opportunities for plunder and power on a massive scale, which members of the SS exploited to the full. By the end of the war the SS had created a massive commercial organisation of over 150 firms, which exploited slave labour to extract raw materials and to manufacture textiles, armaments and household goods.
- *Ideology and race*. The racial policy of extermination and resettlement was pursued with vigour and the system of concentration camps was widely established and run by the SS Death's Head Units (see also Chapter 14, pages 341–2). The various 'inferior' races were even used for their economic value.

The SS was not immune to the rivalries and arguments which typified Nazi Germany. Disagreements often arose, particularly with local *Gauleiters* and the governors of the occupied territories. However, the SS state under Himmler not only preserved the Nazi regime through its brutal, repressive and often arbitrary policies of law enforcement, but gradually extended its influence. In this way it evolved over time to become the key power group in the Third Reich.

Key debate

Although it has been generally accepted that the SS developed into the key power in the Third Reich, its influence over people's everyday life has been questioned. Historians have therefore asked:

Did the *Gestapo* really control the people?

Traditionally, the *Gestapo* was seen as representing the all-knowing totalitarian police state. This view was actually cultivated by the *Gestapo* itself, by the Allied propagandists during the war and by many post-war films. This interpretation was largely upheld in academic circles, most notably in the standard work *The History of the Gestapo* by Jacques Delarue in 1962. He entitled one chapter 'The *Gestapo* is everywhere' and then wrote: 'Never before, in no other land and at no other time, had an organisation attained such a comprehensive penetration [of society], possessed such power and reached such a degree of "completeness" in its ability to arouse terror and horror, as well as in its actual effectiveness.'

However, many local social studies of Germany have led to an influential reinterpretation. The German historians Mallman and Paul, and the US historian Gellately, have drawn attention to the limits of the *Gestapo*'s policing by revealing that:

- The manpower of the *Gestapo* was limited: only 40,000 agents for the whole of Germany. Large cities, like Frankfurt or Hamburg, with about half a million people, were policed by just about 40–50 agents.
- Most *Gestapo* work was actually prompted by public informers: between 50 per cent and 80 per cent in different areas. Much information and many denunciations were mere gossip, which generated enormous paperwork for limited return.
- The *Gestapo* had relatively few 'top agents', so it coped by over-relying on the work of the *Kripo*.

Key term	**Revisionist**
	In general terms it is the aim to modify or change something. In this context, it refers specifically to a historian who changes a well-established interpretation.

More recently the US historian Eric Johnson has tried to put the latest **revisionist** views into perspective through his case study of the Rhineland. He accepts the limitations of the *Gestapo*, and argues that it did not impose a climate of terror on ordinary Germans. Instead it concentrated on surveillance and repression of specific enemies: the political left, Jews and, to a lesser extent, religious groups and asocials. Controversially, he claims the Nazis and the German population formed a grim 'pact': the population turned a blind eye to the *Gestapo*'s persecution and, in return, the Nazis overlooked minor transgressions of the law by ordinary Germans.

The oppression of Jews began early in Hitler's regime. Especially persecuted were the *Ostjuden* (Jews from eastern Europe, who had settled in Germany). Here, plainclothes *Gestapo* agents take Jews into custody.

Some key books in the debate
R. Gellately, *Gestapo and German Society* (Oxford, 1990).
Eric Johnson, *Nazi Terror: The Gestapo, Jews and Ordinary Germans* (Basic Books, 2000).
K.M. Mallmann and G. Paul, 'Omniscient, omnipotent and omnipresent: Gestapo society and resistance' in D. Crew (ed.), *Nazi and German Society, 1933–45* (Routledge, 1994).

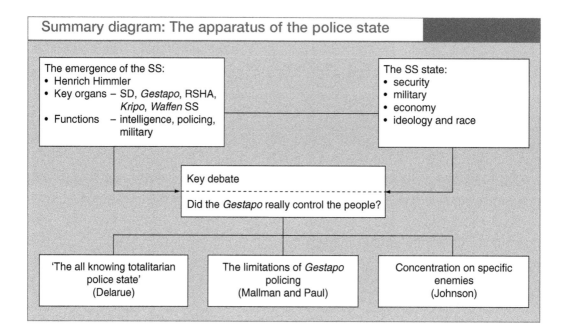

Summary diagram: The apparatus of the police state

The emergence of the SS:
• Henrich Himmler
• Key organs – SD, *Gestapo*, RSHA, *Kripo*, *Waffen* SS
• Functions – intelligence, policing, military

The SS state:
• security
• military
• economy
• ideology and race

Key debate

Did the *Gestapo* really control the people?

'The all knowing totalitarian police state'
(Delarue)

The limitations of *Gestapo* policing
(Mallman and Paul)

Concentration on specific enemies
(Johnson)

6 | Propaganda and Censorship

Goebbels stated at his first press conference on the creation of the Ministry of Popular Enlightenment and Propaganda:

> I view the first task of the new ministry as being to establish co-ordination between the government and the whole people … If the means achieves the end, the means is good. Whether it always satisfies stringent aesthetic criteria or not is immaterial.

Considerable resources were directed towards the development of the propaganda machine in order to achieve the following aims:

• to glorify the regime
• to spread the Nazi ideology and values (and by implication to censor the unacceptable)
• to win over the people and to integrate the nation's diverse elements.

All the means of public communication were brought under state control.

Key question
How did Nazi propaganda use the media?

Key date

Creation of the Ministry of Popular Enlightenment and Propaganda under Josef Goebbels: 15 March 1933

Radio

Goebbels (and Hitler) had always recognised the effectiveness of the spoken word over the written and they had already begun to use new technology during the election campaigns of 1932–3. Up until this time, German broadcasting had been organised by regional states. Once in power, Goebbels efficiently brought all broadcasting under Nazi control by the creation of the Reich Radio Company. Furthermore, he arranged the dismissal of 13 per cent of the staff on political and racial grounds, and replaced them with his own men. He told his broadcasters in March 1933:

> I am placing a major responsibility in your hands, for you have in your hands the most modern instrument in existence for influencing the masses. By this instrument you are the creators of public opinion.

Yet, control of broadcasting was of little propaganda value unless the people had the means to receive it. In 1932 less than 25 per cent of German households owned a wireless, although that was quite a high figure compared to the rest of the world. Consequently, the Nazi government arranged the production of a cheap set, the People's Receiver (*Volksempfänger*). Radio was a new and dynamic medium and access increased markedly. By 1939, 70 per cent of German homes had a radio – the highest national figure in the world – and it became a medium of mass communication controlled completely by the regime.

Broadcasting was also directed at public places. The installation of loudspeakers in restaurants and cafés, factories and offices made them all into venues for collective listening. 'Radio wardens' were even appointed, whose duty it was to co-ordinate the listening process.

Press

Control of the press was not so easily achieved by Goebbels. Germany had over 4700 daily newspapers in 1933 – a result of the strong regional identities which still existed in a state that had only been unified in 1871. All were papers owned privately, and traditionally owed no loyalty to central government; their loyalty was to their regional publishing company.

Various measures were taken to achieve Nazi control:

- The Nazi publishing house, Eher Verlag, bought up numerous newspapers, so that by 1939 it controlled two-thirds of the German press.
- The various news agencies were merged into one, the state-controlled DNB, which vetted news material before it got to journalists.
- Goebbels introduced a daily press conference at the Propaganda Ministry to provide guidance on editorial policy.
- The so-called Editors' Law of October 1933 made newspaper content the sole responsibility of the editor, who had to satisfy the requirements of the Propaganda Ministry or face the

appropriate consequences. Thus, as one historian has explained, 'There was no need for censorship because the editor's most important function was that of censor.'

To a large extent, the Nazis succeeded in muzzling the press so that even the internationally renowned *Frankfurter Zeitung* was forced to close in 1943, whereas the circulation of the party's official newspaper, *Völkisher Beobachter*, continued to grow after 1933, reaching 1.7 million by 1944. However, the price of that success was the evolution of bland and sterile journalism, which undoubtedly contributed to a 10 per cent decline in newspaper circulation before 1939.

The Berlin Olympics

The 1936 Olympic Games were awarded to Berlin in 1931, well before Hitler and the Nazis had come to power. Yet, despite Hitler's initial doubts, Goebbels was determined to exploit them as a propaganda 'gold-mine'. Initially, he saw the games as a means to present Nazi propaganda aims (see pages 181–4 and 260), but with several important caveats:

- They were not only to glorify the regime for the German people, but also for millions of people across the world, who would see Germany as the centre of attention.
- They were trying to spread Nazi ideological themes, without causing international upset. So, for example, many anti-Jewish posters and newspapers were played down.

Everything was done to present a positive image of the 'new Germany'. Over 42 million *Reichsmarks* were spent on the 325-acre Olympics sports complex and the gigantic Olympic stadium was built of natural stone in the classical style, the original modernist plan having been rejected. It could seat 110,000 spectators and at the time it was the world's largest stadium. The new Berlin Olympic Village was also a prototype for future games with excellent facilities.

Not surprisingly, the Nazi government was meticulous in overseeing all the media preparations:

- *Radio*. Twenty transmitting vans were put at the disposal of the foreign media along with 300 microphones. Radio broadcasts at the Olympics were given in 28 different languages.
- *Film*. The Nazis promoted and financed filming by the director Leni Riefenstahl. She brought 33 camera operators to the Olympics and shot over a million feet of film. It took her 18 months to edit the material into a four-hour film, *Olympia*, which was released in two parts beginning in April 1938.
- *TV*. Television was in its early stages, but the games prompted a significant technical development. Broadcasts of the games were made and seen by 150,000 people in 28 public television rooms in Berlin, although the image quality was variable.

The Nazi ideal of the tall, blond, blue-eyed Aryan race was epitomised by the athlete Eifrig lighting the torch at the start of the games in the Olympic stadium.

Siegfried Eifrig lights the Olympic flame to mark the start of the 1936 Games.

On the sports front, Germany successfully finished top of the medal table, gaining 89 medals with the Americans coming in second with 56. However, the Nazi dream was marred by the success of the black American athlete Jesse Owens, who won four gold medals in the 100 m, 200 m, long jump and 4 by 100 m relay. Hitler showed his displeasure by refusing to present him with his medal.

Overall, the Berlin Olympics were a major success for the Nazis, who gained praise for their excellent management and impressive spectacle, as was recognised by the US correspondent William Shirer:

> ... I'm afraid the Nazis have succeeded with their propaganda. First, the Nazis have run the games on a lavish scale never before experienced, and this has appealed to the athletes. Second, the Nazis have put up a very good front for the general visitors, especially the big businessmen.

Nazi ritual

One final aspect of the Goebbels propaganda machine was the deliberate attempt to create a new kind of social ritual. The *Heil Hitler* greeting, the Nazi salute, the **Horst Wessel** anthem and the preponderance of militaristic uniforms were all intended to strengthen the individual's identity with the regime. This was further encouraged by the establishment of a series of public festivals to commemorate historic days in the Nazi calendar (see Table 11.2).

Table 11.2: Historic days in the Nazi calendar

30 January	The seizure of power (1933)
24 February	Party Foundation Day (1925)
16 March	Heroes' Remembrance Day (war dead)
20 April	Hitler's birthday
1 May	National Day of Labour
Second Sunday in May	Mothering Sunday
21 June	Summer solstice
Second Sunday of July	German culture
September	Nuremberg party rally
October	Harvest festival
9 November	The Munich *putsch* (1923)
Winter solstice	Pagan festival to counter Christmas

Culture

Nazi culture was no longer to be promoted merely as 'art for art's sake'. Rather, it was to serve the purpose of moulding public opinion, and, with this in mind, the Reich Chamber of Culture was supervised by the Propaganda Ministry. Germany's cultural life during the Third Reich was simply to be another means of achieving censorship and indoctrination, although Goebbels expressed it in more pompous language:

> What we are aiming for is more than a revolt. Our historic mission is to transform the very spirit itself to the extent that people and things are brought into a new relationship with one another.

Culture was therefore 'co-ordinated' by means of the Reich Chamber of Culture, established in 1933, which made provision for seven sub-chambers: fine arts, music, the theatre, the press, radio, literature and films. In this way, just as anyone in the media had no option but to toe the party line, so all those involved in cultural activities had to be accountable for their creativity. Nazi culture was dominated by a number of key themes reflecting the usual ideological prejudices:

- anti-Semitism
- militarism and the glorification of war
- nationalism and the supremacy of the Aryan race
- the cult of the *Führer* and the power of absolutism
- **anti-modernism** and the theme of 'Blood and Soil'
- neo-paganism and a rejection of traditional Christian values.

Key question
How did Nazism try to create a new social ritual?

Key question
What was the purpose of Nazi culture?

Key terms

Horst Wessel
A young Nazi stormtrooper killed in a fight with communists in 1930. The song he wrote became a Nazi marching song and later virtually became an alternative national anthem.

Anti-modernism
Strand of opinion which rejects, objects to, or is highly critical of changes to society and culture brought about by technological advancement.

Key question
In what ways did the Nazis shape German culture?

Music

The world of music managed to cope reasonably well in the Nazi environment, partly because of its less obvious political overtones. Also, Germany's rich classical tradition from the works of Bach to Beethoven was proudly exploited by the regime. However, Mahler and Mendelssohn, both great Jewish composers, were banned, as were most modern musical trends. The new wave of modern classical composers, Schoenberg and Hindemith, were disparaged for their atonal music. Also the new 'genres' of jazz and dance-band were respectively labelled 'negroid' and 'decadent'.

Literature

Over 2500 of Germany's writers left their homeland during the years 1933–45. This fact alone is a reflection of how sadly German writers and dramatists viewed the new cultural atmosphere. Among those who left were:

- Thomas Mann, the author and Nobel Prize winner, who was a democrat and an old-fashioned liberal
- Bertolt Brecht, the prestigious modern playwright, who was a communist
- Erich Maria Remarque, the author of *All Quiet on the Western Front*, who was a pacifist.

Their place was taken by a lesser literary group, who either sympathised with the regime or accepted the limitations. It is difficult to identify a single book, play or poem written during the Third Reich, and officially blessed by the regime, which has stood the test of time.

Actors, like the musicians, tended to content themselves with productions of the classics – Schiller, Goethe (and Shakespeare) – in the knowledge that such plays were politically acceptable and in the best traditions of German theatre.

Visual arts

The visual arts were also effectively limited by the Nazi constraints. Modern schools of art were held in total contempt and Weimar's rich cultural awakening was rejected as degenerate and symbolic of the moral and political decline of Germany under a system of parliamentary democracy. Thus, the following were severely censored:

Key term

New objectivity
Artists in favour of the 'new objectivity' broke away from the traditional romantic nostalgia of the nineteenth century.

- **'New objectivity'** artists, like Georg Grosz and Otto Dix, as their paintings had strong political and social messages (see page 170).
- The Bauhaus style started by Walter Gropius with its emphasis on the close relationship between art and technology (see page 170).

The modern styles of art were resented by Nazism so much that in July 1937 two contrasting art exhibitions were launched entitled 'Degenerate Art' and 'Great German Art'. The first one was deliberately held up to be mocked and many of the pieces were destroyed; the second one glorified all the major Nazi themes of *Volksgemeinschaft* and celebrated classic styles and traditional nineteenth century romanticism. Most admired were:

- the sculptor Arno Breker
- the architect Albert Speer, who drew up many of the great plans for rebuilding the German cities and oversaw the 1936 Berlin Olympics stadium
- the artists Adolf Ziegler and Hermann Hoyer.

Cinema

Only in the field of film can it be said that the Nazi regime made a genuine cultural contribution. Germany's cinematic reputation had been established in the 1920s and a degree of continuity was maintained, as many of the major film studios were in the hands of nationalist sympathisers. However, Jewish film actors and directors such as Fritz Lang were removed and then decided to leave Germany. Perhaps the most famous German *émigrée* was Marlene Dietrich, who swiftly established a new career in Hollywood.

Goebbels recognised the importance of expanding the film industry, not only as as a means of propaganda, but also as an entertainment form; this explains why, out of 1097 feature films produced between 1933 and 1945, only 96 were specifically at the request of the Propaganda Ministry. The films can be divided into three types:

- Overt propaganda, e.g. *The Eternal Jew* (*Ewige Jude*), a tasteless, racist film that portrayed Jews like rats, and *Hitlerjunge Queux*, based on the story of a Nazi murdered by communists.
- Pure escapism, e.g. *The Adventures of Baron von Münchhausen*, a comedy based on an old German legend which gives the baron the powers of immortality.
- Emotive nationalism, e.g. *Olympia*, Leni Riefenstahl's docu-drama of the Berlin Olympics, *Triumph of the Will*, her film about the 1934 Nuremberg rally, and *Kolberg*, an epic produced in the last year of the war, which played on the national opposition to Napoleon. These last two films are still held in high regard by film buffs for their use of subtle cinematic techniques despite the clear underlying political messages.

Conclusion

Control of the press and radio was Goebbels' major objective, but he gradually took control of film, music, literature and art. However, it is very difficult for historians to assess the effectiveness of Nazi propaganda. This clearly has implications for the whole thorny issue of public opinion, which is considered on pages 321–7. Historians initially assumed rather too glibly that Nazi propaganda was successful because it was possible to highlight the way Goebbels exploited all the means for propaganda: photographs, party rallies, sport, festivals. This view was underlined by Herzstein's book in the 1960s *The War that Hitler Won*. However, more recent research from oral history of

Key question
How effective was Nazi propaganda and censorship?

Profile: Josef Goebbels 1897–1945

1897	– Born in the Rhineland and slightly disabled
1917–21	– Attended Heidelberg University
1924	– Joined the Nazi Party and supported the radical faction
1926	– Broke with Strasser and sided with Hitler
	– Hitler appointed him as *Gauleiter* of Berlin
1927	– Created the Nazi newspaper *Der Angriff*
1930	– Put in charge of party propaganda
1933–45	– Joined the cabinet and appointed Minister of Public Enlightenment and Propaganda
	– Encouraged the burning of 'un-German books'
1938	– An affair with the actress Lída Baarová undermined his position
	– Issued the orders for the anti-Semitic attacks of *Kristallnacht* in November
1943	– Called for 'total war' to rouse the nation after the defeat at Stalingrad
1945	– Committed suicide in a pact with his wife after poisoning their children

Goebbels was a man from a humble background with many talents who became one of the few intellectuals in the Nazi leadership. However, he suffered from a strong inferiority complex over his physical limitations and he became an embittered and committed anti-Semite.

As propaganda chief of the party, he played a crucial role in exploiting every possible method to sell the Nazi image in the elections, 1930–3. And as Minister of Propaganda, he developed propaganda techniques that were frighteningly ahead of their time. Unscrupulous and amoral in his methods, he was mainly responsible for:

- advancing the idea of Nazi totalitarianism
- censoring all non-Nazi culture and media
- promoting all the main ideological ideas of Nazism.

Goebbels was a very highly skilled orator and he remained a central figure until the final collapse of the regime, although other leading Nazis, such as Göring and Ribbentrop, distrusted him. His rivals also exploited his many love affairs to undermine his position and he became quite politically isolated in the years 1938–42. But with his personal leadership and his organisational skills he played an important part in the last two years of the war in making the nation ready for total war:

- He organised help for people in the bombed cities.
- He gave the orders to put down the July Bomb Plot (see pages 335–6).
- He maintained civilian morale, e.g. by visiting bombed cities (unlike Hitler).
- He took the responsibility to mobilise the last efforts to resist the Allied advance.

local studies has raised serious doubts about its effectiveness and tended to show that the degree of success of propaganda varied according to different purposes. Very generally it is felt that propaganda succeeded in the sense that it:

- cultivated the 'Hitler myth' of him as an all-powerful leader
- strengthened the regime after Germany's economic and political crisis, 1929–33
- appealed effectively to reinforce established family values and German nationalism.

On the other hand, propaganda failed more markedly in its attempt:

- to denounce the Christian Churches
- to seduce the working classes away from their established identity through the ideal of *Volksgemeinschaft*
- to develop a distinctive Nazi culture.

Such points give backing to the view that the propaganda machine was of secondary importance compared to the power and influence of the SS-Police system in upholding the Third Reich.

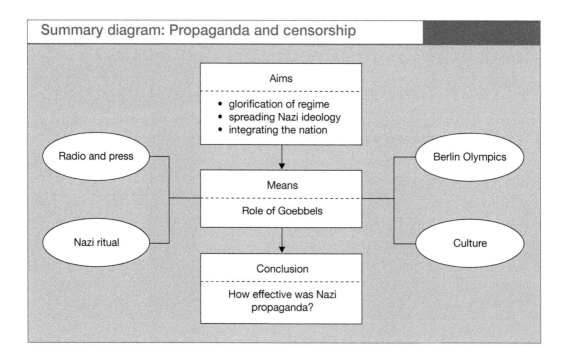

Summary diagram: Propaganda and censorship

7 | The German Army

Key question
To what extent did the German army co-operate with the Nazi regime?

Despite its suspicion of Nazism, the army accepted the Nazi accession to power and co-operated in the manoeuvrings which led to the Night of the Long Knives (see pages 234–9). Moreover, the generals were confident that they had gained the upper hand when Hitler agreed to the destruction of his own SA. Ironically, they believed that now the radical element within Nazism had been removed they could make the Nazi state work for them.

However, the army only succeeded in preserving its influence in the short term by a compromise which was fatal in the long term. This is most clearly shown by the new oath of loyalty demanded by Hitler of all soldiers, and accepted by Field Marshal von Blomberg, the Defence Minister, and General von Fritsch, the Commander-in-Chief of the Army:

> I swear by God this sacred oath: that I will render unconditional obedience to the *Führer* of the German Reich and people, Adolf Hitler, the Supreme Commander of the Armed Forces, and will be ready as a brave soldier to risk my life at any time for this oath.

For a German soldier, bound by discipline and obedience, such words marked a commitment which made any future resistance an act of the most serious treachery.

In the years 1934–7 the relationship between the Nazi state and the army remained cordial. The generals were encouraged by:

- the expansion of the rearmament programme from 1935
- Hitler's reintroduction of conscription in March 1935, thereby increasing the size of the army to 550,000
- the diplomatic successes over the Saar (1935) and the Rhineland (1936).

Blomberg even issued a number of military decrees in an attempt to adjust army training according to Nazi ideology and to elevate the *Führer*. Yet, Blomberg and the army leaders deceived themselves into believing that its independent position was being preserved. In fact, the power of the SS was growing fast, while Hitler had little respect for the conservative attitudes held by many army officers. It was merely political realism which held him back from involvement in army affairs until 1938.

The Blomberg–Fritsch crisis 1937–8

Key question
Why was the Blomberg–Fritsch crisis so significant?

The balance between the army and Hitler changed in the winter of 1937–8 after the so-called Hossbach conference meeting on 5 November 1937. In this meeting Hitler outlined to Germany's chiefs of the armed forces his foreign policy aims for military expansion. Blomberg and Fritsch, in particular, were both seriously concerned by Hitler's talk of war and conquest especially bearing in mind Germany's state of military unpreparedness. Their doubts further convinced Hitler that the army leadership was spineless, and in February 1938 both men were forced out of

Key date
Forced resignation of Field Marshal Blomberg and General Fritsch. Purge of army leadership: February 1938

office after revelations about their private lives. Blomberg had just married for the second time, with Hitler as principal witness, but it subsequently became known that his wife had a criminal record for theft and prostitution. Fritsch was accused falsely of homosexual offences on evidence conveniently produced by Himmler.

This sordid episode provided Hitler with the perfect opportunity to subordinate the army. He abolished the post of Defence Minister and took the title Commander-in-Chief and Minister of War himself. Day-to-day leadership of all armed forces was given to the High Command, the *Oberkommando der Wehrmacht* (OKW), headed by a loyal and subservient General Keitel. The new Commander-in-Chief of the Army was General Brauchitsch, who was another willing supporter of the regime. Also, a further 16 generals were retired and 44 transferred. At the same time Foreign Minister Neurath was replaced by the Nazi Ribbentrop. In the words of Feuchtwanger:

> It was a crisis of the regime not unlike the Night of the Long Knives in 1934, although this time there was no bloodshed. Again Hitler was the undisputed winner and the national-conservative élites who had helped him into the saddle, suffered a further loss of influence.

From 1938 the army's ability to shape political developments in Germany was drastically reduced. At first Hitler had correctly recognised the need to work with the army leadership, but by

---

Profile: Werner von Blomberg 1878–1946

1878	– Born in Pomerania
1914–18	– Served in the First World War and joined the General Staff
1920–33	– Served various military posts
1933	– Appointed by Hitler as Minister of Defence
1935–8	– War Minister and Commander-in-Chief of armed forces
1938	– Remarried to his new, young wife Erna Grün
	– Forced to resign
1938–46	– Lived privately. Died awaiting the Nuremberg trials

Blomberg's significance is as a member of the conservative faction that supported Hitler. Convinced that Hitler was the authoritarian leader who would restore German power, he backed the destruction of the SA in the purge. He then played a vital role in persuading the army generals to take the oath of loyalty. Blomberg's doubts about Hitler's foreign policy emerged from 1936 over the occupation of the Rhineland and the Hossbach conference. This led to his removal from office in 1938, which suited Göring and Himmler because they resented the man's influence.

Figure 11.4: Hitler's increasing power and the armed forces.

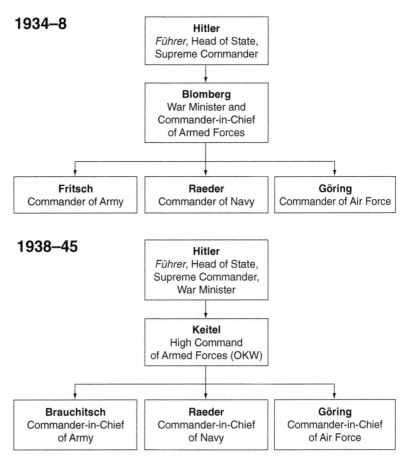

1934–8

Hitler
Führer, Head of State, Supreme Commander

Blomberg
War Minister and Commander-in-Chief of Armed Forces

Fritsch	Raeder	Göring
Commander of Army	Commander of Navy	Commander of Air Force

1938–45

Hitler
Führer, Head of State, Supreme Commander, War Minister

Keitel
High Command of Armed Forces (OKW)

Brauchitsch	Raeder	Göring
Commander-in-Chief of Army	Commander-in-Chief of Navy	Commander-in-Chief of Air Force

early 1938 he was strong enough to mould it more closely to his requirements. The army was not without power, but it had been tamed to serve its new master. It still remained the one institution with the technical means of striking successfully at the regime. For example, in the summer of 1938 a plan was drawn up by General Beck to arrest Hitler if a full-scale European war broke out over the Czech crisis. It came to nothing because Hitler was proved right.

Conclusion

Generally, historians have not been sympathetic to the role played by the German army. It is difficult to avoid the conclusion that the army leadership played a naïve and inept political game. Conditioned by their traditions of obedience, loyalty and patriotism, and encouraged by the authoritarian position of the Third Reich, the army became a vital pillar of the Nazi regime in the early years. Even when its own power to influence events had been drastically reduced in 1938 and the full implications of Nazi rule became apparent during the war, the army's leaders could not escape from their political and moral dilemma. From 1938 to 1942 Nazi diplomatic and military policy was so successful that it effectively ruined the plans of any doubting officers.

Once war began in 1939, resistance was not only unpatriotic but actually treasonable. Only by early 1943, when the military situation had changed dramatically, did a growing number of generals come to believe that the war could not be won and opposition started to grow.

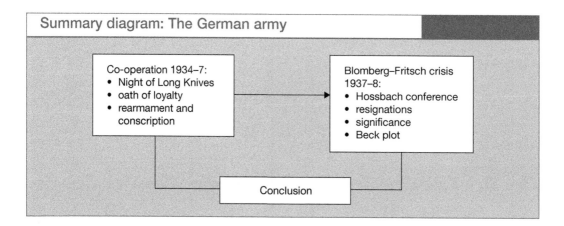

Summary diagram: The German army

Co-operation 1934–7:
- Night of Long Knives
- oath of loyalty
- rearmament and conscription

Blomberg–Fritsch crisis 1937–8:
- Hossbach conference
- resignations
- significance
- Beck plot

Conclusion

8 | The Key Debate

The debate about the political structure of the Third Reich stands at the heart of nearly all aspects of Nazi Germany, but it leaves one key question:

> Was Nazi Germany a chaotic polycracy or a state efficient to the *Führer*'s will?

Historians have various different interpretations.

Nazi Germany: a model of totalitarianism

The concept of totalitarianism was studied by George Orwell in the late 1940s, in the aftermath of Nazism and the shadow of the new Cold War with Stalin's USSR. In his futuristic novel *Nineteen Eighty-Four* he portrayed a political system and a society which became a 'model' of totalitarianism. There was no place for the individual. Every aspect of life was controlled by the party, which in turn was dominated by the all-pervasive personality of 'Big Brother'.

In the 1950s a number of historians and political scientists began to interpret the Nazi regime as an example of the totalitarian model. According to such interpretations there were no fundamental differences between the regimes of Fascist Italy, Nazi Germany and Soviet Russia. Indeed, Carl Friedrich's analysis went so far as to identify six major features common to totalitarian dictatorships:

- an official ideology
- a single mass party
- terroristic control by the police

- monopolistic control over the media
- a monopoly of arms
- central control of the economy.

The idea of Nazism as a form of totalitarianism held great weight in the 1950s, but is now less readily accepted. The term is still used to describe Hitler's regime, but is somewhat misleading. It was a product of the Cold War, when liberal Western historians rather too readily assumed close similarities between Hitler's Germany and Stalin's Russia. Nazi Germany was not the single, all-powerful structure suggested by the term totalitarian, so that definition can be criticised on two major counts. First, although Germany was a one-party state, the Nazi Party did not have the same degree of organisation and unity as the communists in the USSR. Secondly, the Nazis never established a centralised control over the economy, again in direct contrast to the situation in the USSR.

Hitler the strong dictator: the intentionalist interpretation

The so-called 'intentionalist' approach has continued to maintain that Hitler still played the vital role in the development of the Third Reich. In a telling phrase N. Rich wrote: 'The point cannot be stressed too strongly. Hitler was master in the Third Reich'; and many continue to uphold this view.

Intentionalists do not deny that there was division and confusion in Hitler's regime. However, they believe that it was the result of a deliberate policy of 'divide and rule' on the part of Hitler. Moreover, they claim that this strategy was successful in maintaining the *Führer*'s own political authority. Hitler took the responsibility for taking the 'big' decisions which shaped the direction of Nazi Germany, e.g. foreign policy. Moreover, although there were other power bases within the party, Hitler preserved his own authority by tolerating only key Nazis, who were personally loyal, for example Himmler. Finally, he hired and fired both Nazis and non-Nazis whom he could use. For example, Schacht had considerable freedom of manoeuvre for a time, but was removed when he no longer conformed. These views are outlined by Bracher and Jäckel. For such historians Nazism was in essence Hitlerism and all the vital developments of the Third Reich grew from Hitler and his 'blueprint for power'.

The Third Reich: a polycracy

The 1960s witnessed the beginning of a remarkable growth in research into the Third Reich partly due to the practical reason that the German archives in the hands of the Western Allies had been made readily available. By the late 1960s and early 1970s, historians, such as Broszat and Mommsen, had started to exert a major influence in their analysis of the structure of the Third Reich; hence their approach has been dubbed 'structuralist'.

They believe that the Nazi regime really just evolved from the pressure of the circumstances and not from Hitler's dominant role. In fact, Hitler's personal weaknesses and limitations led to poor leadership. He was considered incapable of making effective decisions and, as a result, the government lacked clear direction. He was not able to keep the tensions in the economy and the state under control. Moreover, he was never able to control the other powerful institutions, for example, the army and the civil service. Finally, the leading Nazis exerted their own influence for their own objectives and frequently Hitler did not intervene. Indeed, Mommsen even goes as far as to describe Hitler as 'unwilling to take decisions, frequently uncertain, exclusively concerned with upholding his prestige and personal authority, influenced in the strongest fashion by his current entourage, in some respects a weak dictator'.

This is why structuralists have seen the Third Reich in its power structure as a 'polycracy', which became an alliance of different overlapping power groups. Although they did not always agree; they were dependent on each other and prepared to work with together as partners in power. The most important of these blocs would seem to have been the Nazi Party itself, the SS-Police system and the army, big business and the higher levels of the state bureaucracy.

Conclusion

In the early years, Hitler and the Nazi were heavily dependent on the sympathy of the army and big business so they did not attempt to control them directly because they feared alienating them. Indeed, the destruction of the SA in 1934 was driven by the need to satisfy those traditional vested interests, and was a blow to radical Nazis. At this stage the SS-Police system was relatively limited. The rearmament programme and the early moves in foreign policy acted as a powerful focus of common interest: profits for industry and the restoration of prestige for the army.

All this changed during 1936–8. Hitler's personal political position was by this time much stronger and was ruthlessly supported by the emerging power of Himmler's SS-Police system. Hitler was therefore less restricted by the need for political compromise and he could pursue his aims more vigorously. Consequently, the economic crisis of 1936 led to the disappearance of Schacht and the introduction of the Four-Year Plan under Göring. This development represented a major shift in the balance of political power away from big business as a whole, although it was strongly supported by the electrochemicals sector because of its links with arms production. Although the army had sided with the Nazi leadership in 1936, it was severely weakened two years later by the purge of major generals after Blomberg and Fritsch had expressed their doubts about the direction of Hitler's foreign policy.

By 1938, therefore, big business, the army and other élites had been reduced to the role of junior partners in the Third Reich's power structure. This weakening of their positions was to continue in subsequent years, although at first the army gained great status from the military victories from 1939. From 1939, the power and influence of the SS-Police system grew to become the dominant power bloc, so much so that some historians have gone so far as to refer to it as the emergence of the 'SS state'. This also coincided with the weakening of the traditional élites within the state bureaucracy, as the party apparatus began to exert a greater influence.

Structuralist historians have certainly succeeded in highlighting a lack of planning and organisation on Hitler's part, so that it is now generally appreciated that divisions and rivalries were rife in the government of the Third Reich. The leading Nazis headed their own institutional empires and their aims and interests often brought them into conflict with each other. For example, the economy from 1936 was in the hands of several major wrangling leaders and their offices:

- Göring as the director of the Four-Year Plan
- Schacht as President of the Reichsbank
- Funk as Minister of the Economics
- Ley in charge of DAF.

On top of this there were personality clashes which led to personal rivalries and ambitions at the expense of efficient government. Most notably, Bormann and Himmler despised each other, and Göring and Goebbels were barely on speaking terms.

Yet, despite all this talk of individual and institutional confrontation, it is difficult to ignore the importance of Hitler or to accept the view of him as a 'weak dictator' (except perhaps in the last few months of his life). In a telling phrase the historian Noakes writes: 'Perhaps, the most outstanding characteristic of the political system of the Third Reich was its lack of formal structure.' Hitler created the party and headed a regime built on the principle of authoritarian leadership. It is impossible to pinpoint any major domestic development which was contrary to Hitler's wishes. In Kershaw's words, 'Hitler's personalised form of rule invited initiatives from below and offered such initiatives backing, so long as they were in line with his broadly defined goals.' In this way Hitler's personality and ideology led to a dramatic radicalisation of policy in the key spheres, such as:

- politically, by the creation of a one-party state brutally upheld by the SS-Police system
- a reorientation (reshaping) of society by the application of racial laws, followed by a policy of genocide
- and finally, in the field of foreign policy, by the drive towards a German (Aryan) world hegemony.

It is hard to envisage all these developments without Hitler at the helm. It is also surely indicative that the SS-Police system emerged as the dominant power bloc and its guiding principle from the start had been unquestioning obedience to the will of the *Führer*.

Some key books in the debate

K.D. Bracher, *The German Dictatorship* (Penguin, 1973).

M. Broszat, *The Hitler State* (London, 1981).

C.J. Friedrich and Z. Brzezinski, *Totalitarian Dictatorship and Autocracy* (Harvard University Press, 1956).

I. Kershaw, *The Nazi Dictatorship: Problems and Perspectives of Interpretation* (London, 1993).

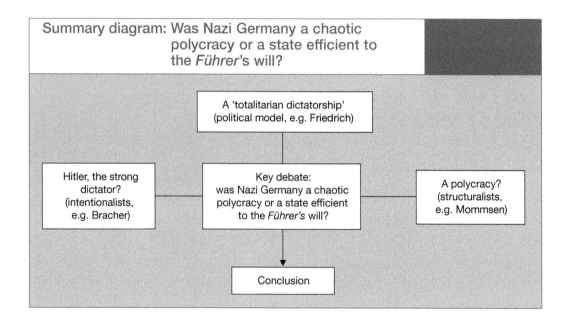

Summary diagram: Was Nazi Germany a chaotic polycracy or a state efficient to the *Führer*'s will?

Study Guide: A2 Question

How far do you agree with the view that, in the years 1934–9, Hitler was not in control of the Third Reich? Explain your answer, using Sources 1–3 and your own knowledge of the issues related to this controversy.

Source 1

From: Ian Kershaw, The Hitler Myth: Image and Reality, *published in 1984.*

The adoration of Hitler by millions of German people, who otherwise might have been only marginally committed to Nazism, meant that the person of the *Führer* became the focal point of the Nazi system of rule. With Hitler's massive personal popularity, the regime could repeatedly call upon plebiscites for support. This legitimised its actions at home and abroad, defused opposition and boosted the independence of the Nazi leadership from the traditional national-conservative élites, who had imagined they would keep Hitler in check. Hitler's popularity sustained the frenetic and increasingly dangerous momentum of Nazi rule. Most important of all, Hitler's huge platform of popularity made his own power position ever more unassailable, and made possible the process by which his personal ideological obsessions became translated into attainable reality.

Source 2

From: Edgar Feuchtwanger, Hitler's Germany, *published in 2000.*

Hitler often refused to take decisions, especially when a decision might damage his popularity, and left his subordinates to thrash these out. He gave those men who were close to him conflicting responsibilities, which often resulted in a state of near anarchy. Some have argued that Hitler was a weak dictator, but this really does not stand up for he could take any decision he wanted to and took some of his major decisions without much consultation. He had little need for the tactic of divide and rule, for none of the other leading Nazis ever challenged his supremacy. The very fact that he had removed himself from day-to-day decisions of government made him the central figure of the Third Reich. It meant that he could take key decisions without having to go through a time-consuming and confusing process of bureaucratic consultation. The Third Reich was not so much a totalitarian state but more a chaotic system of rival empires.

Source 3

From: Tim Mason, Nazism, Fascism and the Working Class, *published in 1995.*

Personally, Hitler had a preference for creating new organs of state to carry out specific projects. He had a preference, too, for choosing 'the right man for the job' and giving him the powers to carry it out, regardless; and there is no doubt that he carefully sought out men who were loyal to, and dependent upon, him for all top positions in the regime. More importantly, his personal popularity was a source of power. However, while this shielded Hitler against ultimate contradictions by ministers and generals, it was not much help in the practical business of selecting goals, reaching decisions and making policy. Hitler's sense of dependence upon his own popularity was so great that the cult of the *Führer* may well have contributed to government inaction in domestic affairs. Hitler was certainly careful not to associate himself with any measure that he thought might be unpopular. In this sense Hitler can be seen to have been a 'weak dictator'.

Exam tips

The cross-references are intended to take you straight to the material that will help you to answer the question.

You are asked to use the sources and your own knowledge in answering this question. The sources raise issues for you and can be used as the core of your plan. They contain points for and against the stated claim. Make sure you have identified all the issues raised by the sources, and then add in your own knowledge, both to make more of the issues in the sources (add depth to the coverage) and to add new points (extend the range covered). In the advice given below, links are made to the relevant pages where information can be found.

Your answers will be stronger if you cross-refer between the sources rather than treating them separately. Begin with just one of the sources, highlight the relevant issues in it (it may help to give them a separate colour or number), and then link to each of the other sources by number or colour code.

For example, you could identify four issues in Source 3: two are done for you:

1. Hitler's personal popularity was a source of power.
2. Hitler was a weak dictator in not being prepared to associate himself with unpopular decisions.

Now sort your list into two columns of points which support and which challenge the statement and then go on to Source 2.

Source 2 has material relating to these issues. What direct links can you find which confirm, modify or challenge a point made by Mason in Source 3? One is done for you:

- Feuchtwanger agrees that Hitler refused to take decisions which might damage his popularity; however, he challenges the idea in Source 3 that this made Hitler a weak dictator, since 'he could take any decision he wanted to'.

However:

- Feuchtwanger emphasises the 'conflicting responsibilities' of Hitler's subordinates. He comments on a 'state of near anarchy' and a 'chaotic system of rival empires'. Is this is an issue to which Mason refers? If so link it by colour/number.

Now go through the same process of analysis and linkage with the views of Kershaw in Source 1.

Essentially the three sources deal with issues which relate to:

- the personal popularity of the *Führer*
- the divisions within government
- and the extent to which Hitler was actually in control.

You can expand on each of these from your own knowledge (Chapters 11 and 13), linking points directly to the precise issues raised by the sources.

An additional point you could make relates to the role of Himmler and the SS in strengthening Hitler's position and holding the Third Reich together (pages 251–6). Which of your colour-coded or numbered issues does this relate to?

Ultimately you will need to reach a conclusion. Be prepared to enter into the debate. There is not a right answer here. It is clear that historians debate the issue. This is an opportunity for you to decide what the balance of the evidence appears to suggest, drawing on the arguments advanced by historians.

12 The Nazi Economy 1933–9

POINTS TO CONSIDER

The purpose of this chapter is to consider Nazi economic policies and their effects on the performance of the Nazi economy over the years 1933–9. The economy went through various stages and to appreciate the significance of these, it is important to consider the following main themes:

- The economic recovery of Germany 1933–6
- The introduction of the Four-Year Plan 1936–9
- The role of big business
- Key debate: Did Germany have a war economy in peacetime?

Key dates

1933	March	Appointment of Schacht as President of the *Reichsbank*
1934	July	Appointment of Schacht as Minister of Economics
	September	New Plan introduced
1936	October	Four-Year Plan established under Göring
1937	November	Resignation of Schacht as Minister of Economics

1 | Economic Recovery 1933–6

The sheer scale of the world economic depression that began in 1929 meant that Germany undoubtedly suffered in a particularly savage way (see page 190–2). In the years before 1933 Hitler had been careful not to become tied down to the details of an economic policy. He even told his cabinet in February 1933 to 'avoid all detailed statements concerning an economic programme of the government'. Nevertheless, Hitler was also politically astute enough to realise that his position depended on bringing Germany out of depression.

Schacht's economic strategy

In the early years, Nazi economic policy was under the control of Hjalmar Schacht, President of the *Reichsbank* (1933–9) and Minister of Economics (1934–7). This reflected the need of the

Key question
How did Schacht's policies stimulate economic recovery?

Key date

Appointment of Schacht as President of the *Reichsbank*: March 1933

Nazi leadership to work with the powerful forces of big business. Schacht was already a respected international financier because of his leading role in the creation of the new currency in the wake of the 1923 hyper-inflation.

It is certainly true that the economic depression reached its low-point in the winter of 1932–3 and that afterwards the trade cycle began to improve. This undoubtedly worked to the political and economic advantage of the Nazis. Nevertheless, there was no single, easy 'quick fix' solution. The heart of economic recovery lay in the major revival of public investment led, for the most part, by the state itself which embarked on a large-scale increase in its own spending in an effort to stimulate demand and raise national income. So, under Schacht's guidance and influence, deficit financing was adopted through a range of economic measures.

Banking and the control of capital

Initially, because the German banking system had been so fundamentally weakened, the state increasingly assumed greater responsibility for the control of capital within the economy. It then proceeded to set interest rates at a lower level and to reschedule the large-scale debts of local authorities.

Assistance for farming and small businesses

Particular financial benefits were given to groups, such as farmers and small businesses. This not only stimulated economic growth, it also rewarded some of the most sympathetic supporters of the Nazis in the 1930–3 elections. Some of the measures included (see also pages 295–7):

- tariffs on imported produce were maintained in order to protect German farmers
- subsidies were given by the Reich Food Estate, as part of a nationally planned agricultural system
- the Reich Entailed Farm Law tried to offer more security of land ownership to small farmers: debts were reduced by tax concessions and lower interest rates
- giving allowances to encourage the rehiring of domestic servants
- the allocation of grants for house repairs.

State investment: public works

However, of the greatest significance was the direct spending by the state on a range of investment projects. In June 1933 the Law to Reduce Unemployment was renewed and expanded (from a scheme which had originally been started by Papen in 1932) and the RAD (*Reicharbeitsdienst*, Reich Labour Service) was expanded to employ 19–25 year olds. For a long time most historians assumed that rearmament was the main focus of investment, but the figures for public expenditure show that this was initially spread among rearmament, construction and transportation. So the investment in the first three years was directed towards work creation schemes such as:

- reforestation
- land reclamation
- motorisation: the policy of developing the vehicle industry and the building of improved roads, e.g. the *autobahnen* (motorways)
- building: especially the expansion of the housing sector and public buildings.

The cumulative effect of these policies was to triple public investment between 1933 and 1936 and to increase government expenditure by nearly 70 per cent over the same period. By early 1936 the economic recovery was well advanced and then emphasis began to turn even more towards rearmament.

Table 12.1: Public investment and expenditure in billions of *Reichsmark* (RM) 1928–36

	1928	1932	1933	1934	1935	1936
Total public investment	6.6	2.2	2.5	4.6	6.4	8.1
Total government expenditure	11.7	8.6	9.4	12.8	13.9	15.8

Table 12.2: Public expenditure by category in billions of *Reichsmark* (RM) 1928–36

	1928	1932	1933	1934	1935	1936
Construction	2.7	0.9	1.7	3.5	4.9	5.4
Rearmament	0.7	0.7	1.8	3.0	5.4	10.2
Transportation	2.6	0.8	1.3	1.8	2.1	2.4

As a result of these strategies, there was a dramatic growth in jobs. From the registered peak of six million unemployed in January 1932, the official figure of 1936 showed it had declined to 2.1 million. For those many Germans who had been desperately out of work, it seemed as if the Nazi economic policy was to be welcomed. Even in other democratic countries scarred by mass unemployment, observers abroad admired Germany's achievement of job creation.

Table 12.3: Unemployment and production in Germany 1928–36

	1928	1929	1930	1931	1932	1933	1934	1935	1936
Unemployment (millions)	1.4	1.8	3.1	4.5	5.6	4.8	2.7	2.2	1.6
Industrial production (1928 =100)	100	100	87	70	58	66	83	96	107

Unemployed men (with shovels) enrol for work on an autobahn in September 1933.

Yet, even in 1936, the government public deficit certainly did not run out of control, since Schacht maintained taxes at a relatively high level and encouraged private savings in state savings banks. Of course, it must be remembered that all this took place as the world economy began to recover and Schacht was aided by the natural upturn in the business cycle after its low-point in winter 1932. Nevertheless, it is difficult to believe that such a marked turn-around in investment and employment could have been achieved without Nazi economic policy.

The balance of payments problem

Key question
Why was Germany's balance of trade problem so significant?

Germany made an impressive economic recovery between 1933 and 1936, but two underlying worries remained:

- the fear that a rapid increase in demand would rekindle inflation
- the fear that a rapid increase in demand would lead to the emergence of a balance of trade deficit.

Key date

Appointment of Schacht as Minister of Economics: July 1934

In fact, the problem of inflation never actually materialised, partly because there was a lack of demand in the economy, but also because the regime established strict controls over prices and wages. This had been helped by the abolition of the trade unions in May 1933 (see page 233). On the other hand, what was to be a recurring balance of payments problem emerged for the first time in the summer of 1934. This was a consequence of Germany's importing more raw materials while failing to increase its exports. Its gold and foreign currency reserves were also low.

The balance of payments problem was not merely an economic issue, for it carried with it large-scale political implications. If

Germany was so short of foreign currency, which sector of the economy was to have priority in spending the money? The early Economics Minister, Schmitt, wanted to try to reduce unemployment further by manufacturing more consumer goods for public consumption, e.g. textiles. However, powerful voices in the armed forces and big business were already demanding more resources for major programmes, e.g. rearmament (see Table 12.2 on page 278).

Hitler could not ignore such pressure, especially as this economic problem coincided with the political dilemma over the

The first autobahn was not initiated by the Nazis, but was prompted by the mayor of Cologne, Adenauer; the stretch from Cologne to Bonn was opened in 1932. Nevertheless, 3000 km of motorway roads were developed by the end of the 1930s and the onset of the war. They served as an economic stimulus, but were also politically used as a propagandist tool. Their military value has been doubted.

SA (see pages 235–9). Consequently, Schmitt's policy was rejected and he was removed, thereby allowing Schacht to combine the offices of Minister of Economics and President of the *Reichsbank*.

Schacht's 'New Plan'

By the law of 3 July, Schacht was given dictatorial powers over the economy, which he then used to introduce the 'New Plan' of September 1934. This provided for a comprehensive control by the government of all aspects of trade, tariffs, capital and currency exchange in an attempt to prevent excessive imports. From that time the government decided which imports were to be allowed or disapproved. For example, imports of raw cotton and wool were substantially cut, whereas metals were permitted in order to satisfy the demands of heavy industry.

The economic priorities were set by a series of measures:

- **Bilateral trade treaties**. Schacht tried to promote trade and save foreign exchange by signing bilateral trade treaties, especially with the countries of south-east Europe, e.g. Romania and Yugoslavia. These often took the form of straightforward barter agreements (thus avoiding the necessity of formal currency exchange). In this way Germany began to exert a powerful economic influence over the Balkans long before it obtained military and political control.
- The *Reichsmark* currency. Germany agreed to purchase raw materials from all countries it traded with on the condition that *Reichsmarks* could only be used to buy back German goods (at one time it is estimated that the German *Reichsmark* had 237 different values depending on the country and the circumstances!).
- Mefo bills. Mefo were special government money bills (like a credit note) designed by Schacht. They were issued by the *Reichsbank* and guaranteed by the government as payment for goods and were then held for up to five years earning four per cent interest per annum. The main purpose of Mefo bills was that they successfully disguised government spending.

Schacht was never a member of the Nazi Party, but he was drawn into the Nazi movement and the regime. His proven economic skills earned him respect both in and outside the party and it was he who laid the foundations for economic recovery. By mid-1936:

- unemployment had fallen to 1.5 million
- industrial production had increased by 60 per cent since 1933
- GNP had grown over the same period by 40 per cent.

However, such successes disguised fundamental structural weaknesses which came to a head in the second half of 1936 over the future direction of the German economy.

Key question
How did Schacht try to resolve the problem?

Key date
New Plan introduced: September 1934

Key term
Bilateral trade treaty
A trade agreement between two countries or parties.

Profile: Hjalmar Schacht 1877–1970

1877	– Born in North Schleswig, Germany
1916	– Appointed director of the National Bank
1923	– Set up the new currency, *Rentenmark*, and then made President of the *Reichsbank* (see page 149)
1930	– Resigned as President of the *Reichsbank* in protest at the Young Plan
1931	– Became sympathetic to Nazism and agreed to raise money for the Nazi Party through his contacts in banking and industry
1933	– Reappointed as President of the *Reichsbank*
1934	– Appointed as Minister of Economics. Drew up and oversaw the New Plan to control all capital and trade
1937	– Increasingly lost influence and resigned as Minster of Economics
1939	– Resigned as President of the *Reichsbank* in protest at Nazi economic policy
1939–43	– Remained in the government, but in private he became increasingly disaffected with the Nazi regime. In contact with the anti-Nazi resistance
1945–6	– Charged at the Nuremberg trials, but acquitted
1950–63	– Private financial consultant to the government of many countries
1970	– Died

Schacht was an economic genius. He built his reputation on the way he stabilised the German economy through the creation of the new currency, the *Rentenmark*, in 1923. He served as President of the *Reichsbank* to all the Weimar governments 1923–30, but he was a strong nationalist and eventually resigned over the Young Plan.

Schacht was increasingly taken in by Hitler's political programme. From 1930, his influence went through three clear stages:

- He played a vital role in encouraging big business to finance the rise of the Nazis and he backed Hitler's appointment.
- In the years 1933–6 Schacht was in effect economic dictator of Germany and it was he who shaped Germany's economic recovery by deficit financing and the New Plan of 1934.
- However, he disagreed with the emphasis on rearmament in the Four-Year Plan and after 1936 his influence declined.

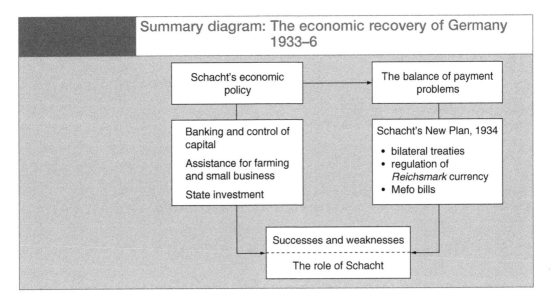

Summary diagram: The economic recovery of Germany 1933–6

Schacht's economic policy → The balance of payment problems

Banking and control of capital

Assistance for farming and small business

State investment

Schacht's New Plan, 1934
- bilateral treaties
- regulation of *Reichsmark* currency
- Mefo bills

Successes and weaknesses
- - - - - - - - - - - - - - -
The role of Schacht

Key question
What was the main purpose of the Four-Year Plan?

2 | The Implementation of the Four-Year Plan 1936

In many respects, as Schacht himself was only too aware, he had merely hidden the balance of payments problem by a series of clever financial tricks. And, despite his apparent sympathy for deficit financing, Schacht believed that a combination of a budget deficit and a balance of payments deficit could not be maintained indefinitely. In early 1936 it became clear to him that, as the demands for rearmament and consumption of goods increased, the German balance of payments would go deeply into the red. He therefore suggested a reduction in arms expenditure in order to increase the production of industrial goods which at least could be exported so as to earn foreign exchange. Such a solution had its supporters, especially among industries geared to exporting, e.g. electronics and tool-making. However, it was unacceptable to the armed forces and to the Nazi leadership. By the mid-1930s, then, this debate was popularly summed up by the question: should the economy concentrate on producing '**guns or butter**'?

Key term

Guns or butter
A phrase used to highlight the controversial economic choice between rearmament and consumer goods.

The aims and objectives of the plan

Most significantly, Hitler himself expressed his position in a secret memorandum in August 1936. This has been seen as one of the most significant documents of Nazi history, as it provides a clear insight into Hitler's war aims and the development of the Nazi economy. He concluded by writing:

> There has been time enough in four years to find out what we cannot do. Now we have to carry out what we can do. I thus set the following tasks.
> (i) The German armed forces must be operational within four years
> (ii) The German economy must be fit for war within four years.

Key date

Four-Year Plan established under Göring: October 1936

The politico-economic crisis of 1936 was resolved by the introduction of the Four-Year Plan under the control of Hermann

Göring who, in October of that year, was appointed 'Plenipotentiary of the Four-Year Plan'. Its aims were clearly to expand rearmament and autarky to make Germany as self-sufficient as possible in food and industrial production. In order to achieve this, the plan highlighted a number of objectives:

- To regulate imports and exports, so as to prioritise strategic sectors, e.g. chemicals and metals at the expense of agricultural imports.
- To control the key sectors of the labour force, so as to prevent price inflation, e.g. the creation of a Reich Price Commissioner and increased work direction by DAF (see pages 293–5).
- To increase the production of raw materials, so as to reduce the financial cost of importing vital goods, e.g. steel, iron and aluminium.
- To develop *ersatz* (substitute) products, e.g. oil (from coal) and artificial rubber (buna).
- To increase agricultural production, so as to avoid imported foodstuffs, e.g. grants for fertilisers and machinery.

The effects of the Four-Year Plan

The decision to implement the Four-Year Plan marked an important turning point in the Nazi regime. Nazi control over the German economy became much tighter, as Schacht described in his own book written in 1949:

> … On December 17th 1936, Göring informed a meeting of big industrialists that it was no longer a question of producing economically, but simply of producing. And as far as getting hold of foreign exchange was concerned it was quite immaterial whether the provisions of the law were complied with or not … Göring's policy of recklessly exploiting Germany's economic substance necessarily brought me into more and more acute conflict with him, and for his part he exploited his powers, with Hitler and the party behind him, to counter my activity as Minister of Economics to an ever-increasing extent.

Schacht had no real respect for Göring, who had no economic expertise and who deliberately and increasingly ignored Schacht's advice. Schacht recognised that that his influence was on the wane and eventually in November 1937 he resigned. He was replaced by the weak Walther Funk, although from this time Göring himself became the real economic dictator.

The success of the plan was mixed over the years (see Table 12.4). On the one hand, production of a number of key materials, such as aluminium and explosives, had expanded greatly, or at least at a reasonable rate. On the other hand, it fell a long way short of the targets in the vital commodities of rubber and oil, while arms production never reached the levels desired by the armed forces and Hitler. All in all, the Four-Year Plan had succeeded in the sense that Germany's reliance on imports had not increased. However, this still meant that when war did break out Germany was dependent on foreign supplies for one-third of its raw materials.

Key question
Why was the creation of the Four-Year Plan so significant?

Resignation of Schacht as Minister of Economics: November 1937

Key date

Profile: Hermann Göring 1893–1946

1893	– Born in Bavaria, the son of the governor of German South West Africa
1914–18	– Served in the First World War as a pilot officer
1922	– Dropped out of university and joined the party as an SA commander
1923	– Took part in the Munich *putsch* and was injured
1928	– Elected to the *Reichstag*
1933	– Joined Hitler's cabinet as minister without portfolio
	– Exploited the *Reichstag* Fire to discredit the communists
	– Organised the terror to impose the dictatorship and to uphold co-ordination
1934	– Helped to organise the Night of Long Knives
1935	– Commander-in-Chief of the new *Luftwaffe* (airforce)
1936	– Appointed Plenipotentiary of the Four-Year Plan
1939	– Named as Hitler's successor at the height of his power
1940–5	– Retained most of his offices, but became increasingly isolated within the leadership and his influence declined
1946	– Committed suicide before the hour of his execution at the Nuremberg trials

Göring played a crucial role in the rise of Nazism and during the early years of the Third Reich. He came from a well-to-do family and with this status and the contacts provided by his aristocratic first wife he was able to give Nazism a more respectable image in high society. He was popular because of his witty and charming conversation, but he became increasingly resented for his ambition and greed.

Göring's approach was uncompromising and brutal. During 1933–4 he organised the infiltration of the German police with the SA and SS and willingly used violence and murder in the terror to secure Nazi power. He was deeply involved in the *Reichstag* Fire (see page 223) and the Night of the Long Knives (see page 237). From 1936 he became in effect economic dictator, although after the failures of the *Luftwaffe* to win the Battle of Britain in 1940, his influence sharply declined.

Table 12.4: The Four-Year Plan launched in 1936

Commodity (in thousands of tons)	Four-Year Plan target	Actual output for 1936	Actual output for 1938	Actual output for 1942
Oil	13,830	1,790	2,340	6,260
Aluminium	273	98	166	260
Rubber (buna)	120	0.7	5	96
Explosives	223	18	45	300
Steel	24,000	19,216	22,656	20,480
Hard coal	213,000	158,400	186,186	166,059

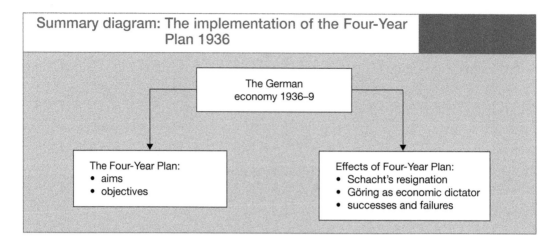

Summary diagram: The implementation of the Four-Year Plan 1936

The German economy 1936–9

The Four-Year Plan:
• aims
• objectives

Effects of Four-Year Plan:
• Schacht's resignation
• Göring as economic dictator
• successes and failures

3 | The Role of Big Business

Key question
Why did big business benefit?

From 1933 the position of the business community began to improve. Helped by the upturn in world trade, and encouraged by the Nazi destruction of the free trade unions and by its economic programme, a commercial recovery occurred. Despite the increasing range of government controls, the financial gains were impressive. The value of German industry steadily increased, as shown by the following:

• The share price index increased from 41 points in 1932 to 106 in 1940, while annual dividends to investors grew from an average 2.83 per cent to 6.6 per cent over the same period.
• The improvement in salaries of management from an average RM3700 in 1934 to RM5420 in 1938 also reflected the economic growth.
• Moreover, the annexations of lands from 1938 and then the onset of the war provided enormous opportunities for taking over foreign property, land and companies.

However, it would be wrong to see big business as a uniform interest group. Different sectors were affected by the changing circumstances in different ways. Small business was squeezed out by the power of big business, whose support was more crucial in the creation of new jobs. It was the building and the giant coal and steel industries which initially prospered most, while consumer goods' production remained relatively depressed. So in the first few years of Nazi rule, big business was able to exert an influence – particularly through the role of Schacht. It maintained a privileged position in its own sphere, just as the army generals did in the military field (see also pages 265–6).

The Four-Year Plan in 1936 marked an important development. Schacht and the leaders of heavy industry urged a reduction of rearmament and an increased emphasis on consumer goods and exports. However, this was a fatal error of political judgement which brought about the downfall of Schacht and the end of heavy industry's supremacy. Instead, Göring, as director of the Four-Year Plan, was now in control and the only groups with real influence were in the electrics–chemicals sector because of their crucial role in rearmament:

- In the chemical industry IG Farben led the way with its development of synthetic substitutes.
- The electrical industry was dominated by Siemens.

Most telling of all was the subservient position of the so-called 'Ruhr barons' of heavy industry in coal and steel. When they refused to co-operate, Göring nationalised the iron-ore deposits and created a new state firm, the Reichswerke Hermann Göring, to exploit them. From 1936, the divisions in big business meant that the needs of the economy were determined by political decisions, especially those in foreign and military policy. Private property always remained in private hands, but the free market and business independence gave way to state regulation. On the whole business accepted the controls of the political leadership, fearing that resistance to state interference would weaken their situation further.

Perhaps, this was because the material benefits were on the whole just too attractive. Profits generally continued to grow until the end of the war and this was reason enough to work with the regime, although they were never directly in charge of policy. From 1936 this was clearly determined by the Nazi leadership. In a mocking simile Grunberger writes:

> German business can be likened to the conductor of a runaway bus, who has no control over the actions of the driver, but keeps collecting the passengers' fares right up to the final crash.

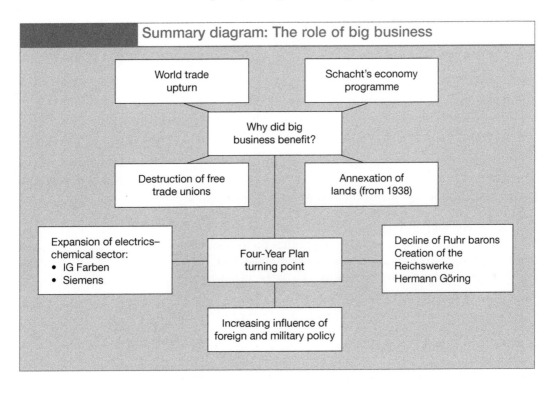

Summary diagram: The role of big business

4 | The Key Debate

From the very start, the Nazi economy was the focus of historical controversy because it was closely linked with the Nazi dictatorship and the onset of war from 1939. Among historians at the heart of the economic analysis there lies one important question:

Did Germany have a war economy in peacetime?

Klein

The research of B.H. Klein in the 1950s led him to argue that Germany's economic mobilisation was actually limited in the early years of the war. He claimed that Nazi economic policy was deliberately connected with the military strategy of *Blitzkrieg*. In his view, Hitler and the armed forces recognised Germany's precarious position over the production of raw materials, and consequently developed the strategy of short wars. This would avoid the economic strain of 'total war' and also it had the political advantage of not reducing the production of consumer goods excessively. In that way, Germany seemed to have both 'guns and butter'. Klein argued that pre-1939 civilian consumption remained comfortable and not limited and that the 'the scale of Germany's economic mobilisation for war was quite modest'. Indeed, he claimed, it was not until after the defeat at Stalingrad in the winter of 1942–3 (see page 334) that a 'total war economy' began in earnest.

Milward

Klein's basic thesis proved to be very influential, although it was somewhat modified in the mid-1960s by A. Milward. He accepted that *Blitzkrieg* was meant to avoid total war, but he also pointed out that 'no nation had ever previously spent so vast a sum on preparations for war'. Moreover, he suggested that it was the German failure to take Moscow at the end of 1941 (see page 334) which was the real economic turning point. By spring 1942 the German economic machine was ready for the **war of attrition** (see page 337).

Mason

In contrast, the **Marxist historian** Tim Mason from the 1970s has argued that the Nazi economy was in fact under increasing strain from 1937. He believes that Hitler's war aims were clearly driving the pace of rearmament to such an extent that the economy was put under tremendous pressures and it was in danger of expanding too quickly and overheating. He particularly points out economic indicators that:

- There were growing shortages, in such areas as raw materials, food and consumer goods.
- There were labour shortages, especially the skilled, which tended to increase wages.

Key terms

Blitzkrieg
Literally 'lightning war'. It was the name of the military strategy developed to avoid static war. It was based on the use of dive-bombers, paratroopers and motorised infantry.

War of attrition
A long, drawn-out war aimed at wearing down the enemy.

Marxist historians
A school of historians who believe that history has been deeply shaped by economic circumstances. They are influenced by the ideology of the philosopher Karl Marx.

- The balance of trade was going further into the red and becoming increasingly difficult to finance.
- The government expenditure and deficit were expanding and becoming increasingly difficult to finance.

Most significantly, Mason argues that that all these pressures were contributing to significant social discontent among the working class. He goes so far as to suggest that by 1939 the situation was so serious that Hitler embarked on the war as the only way out of Germany's domestic economic dilemma.

Overy

However, Richard Overy has rejected the traditional opinions. This is because Overy, although still an economic historian, has come to be influenced by the work of diplomatic historians, who see Hitler stumbling unintentionally into a major European war in September 1939. Overy has argued forcefully that Hitler had always envisaged a great conflict for world power and that this necessitated the transformation of the economy to the demands of total war. However, his preparations for this kind of war were not intended to be finished until 1943. The war with Poland in 1939 was meant to be a local war which Hitler wrongly believed would not involve Britain and France. The premature outbreak of continental conflict inevitably found the German economy only partially mobilised.

Overy, therefore, believes that the underlying principles of Nazi economic policy were abundantly clear from 1936. The German economy had been unashamedly directed towards war preparation, so that two-thirds of all German investment went into war-related projects:

- Full employment was achieved, but over a quarter of the workforce was involved in rearmament.
- Levels of government expenditure more than doubled in the same period with the result that the government debt increased accordingly.
- In the last full year of peace 17 per cent of Germany's GNP went on military expenditure (compared to eight per cent in Britain and one per cent in the USA).

According to such a view then, the German economy by 1939 was already an economy dominated by the preparations for war, though this did not yet amount to the full-scale mobilisation required of total war, since total war was not envisaged until about 1943. In a thought-provoking conclusion Overy suggested:

> … If war had been postponed until 1943–5 as Hitler had hoped, then Germany would have been much better prepared, and would also have had rockets, jet aircraft, inter-continental bombers, perhaps even atomic weapons. Though Britain and France did not

know it, declaring war in 1939 prevented Germany from becoming the super-power Hitler wanted. The drive for total war became instead *Blitzkrieg* by default.

Germany therefore found itself at war in September 1939 really because of diplomatic miscalculation. The German economy in 1939 was still a long way short of being fully mobilised, but it was certainly on more of a war footing than Britain or France.

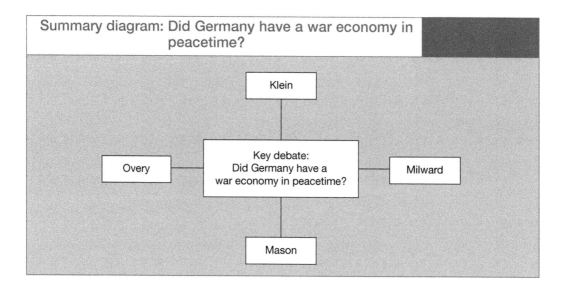

Summary diagram: Did Germany have a war economy in peacetime?

Some key books in the debate

B.H. Klein, *Germany's Economic Preparations for War* (Harvard, 1959).
T.W. Mason, *Social Policy in the Third Reich* (Oxford, 1992).
A.S. Milward, *The German Economy at War* (London, 1965).
R.J. Overy, *The Nazi Economic Recovery, 1932–1938* (Cambridge, 1996).

13 Nazi Society 1933–9

POINTS TO CONSIDER

The purpose of this chapter is to consider Nazi social aims and policies and their effects on the Nazi regime. It will introduce the concept of *Volksgemeinschaft*, which is essential to understanding German society, and will examine the following themes of German social history:

- The Nazi *Volksgemeinschaft*
- Social groups
- Education and youth
- Religion
- Women and the family
- Outsiders
- Nazi anti-Semitism

The following questions arise from these themes. Did the *Volksgemeinschaft* fundamentally change German society? How popular was the Nazi regime?

Key dates

1933	April 1	First official boycott of Jewish shops and professions
	May	Creation of German Labour Front
	July	Concordat signed with the Papacy
1934		Reich Ministry of Education created – control of education was taken away from *Länder*
		Creation of the Confessional Church
1935	September 15	Nuremberg Race Laws introduced
1937		Papal encyclical, *Mit Brennender Sorge*, issued
1938	November 9–10	*Kristallnacht*, anti-Jewish pogrom
1939		Creation of the Reich Central Office for Jewish Emigration

1 | The Nazi *Volksgemeinschaft*

Key question
What was the purpose of the Nazis in promoting the idea of the *Volksgemeinschaft*?

When Nazi ideology developed in the 1920s it was based on three key elements: racism, nationalism and authoritarianism (see pages 181–4). However, Hitler always claimed that National Socialism was more than just a political ideology. It aimed to transform German society. It rejected the values of communism, liberalism and Christianity and in their place upheld the concept of *Volksgemeinschaft*.

Volksgemeinschaft was probably the vaguest element of Nazi ideology so is difficult to define precisely. Historians are divided between those who see it as a 'pseudo-ideology' built on image alone, and those who see it as a more concrete movement with genuine support. The essential purpose of the *Volksgemeinschaft* was to overcome the old German divisions of class, religion and politics and to bring about a new collective national identity by encouraging people to work together. This new social mentality aimed to bring together the disparate elements and to create a German society built on the Nazi ideas of race and struggle, uniting traditional German values with the new ideology. The ideal German image was that of the classic peasant working on the soil in the rural community; this was exemplified in the Nazi concept of 'Blood and Soil' (*Blut und Boden*) and by upholding the traditional roles of the two sexes.

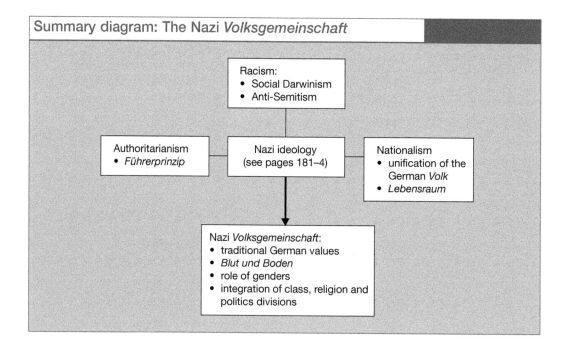

Summary diagram: The Nazi *Volksgemeinschaft*

Racism:
- Social Darwinism
- Anti-Semitism

Authoritarianism
- *Führerprinzip*

Nazi ideology
(see pages 181–4)

Nationalism
- unification of the German *Volk*
- *Lebensraum*

Nazi *Volksgemeinschaft*:
- traditional German values
- *Blut und Boden*
- role of genders
- integration of class, religion and politics divisions

2 | Social Groups

Before the war it really did seem to many Germans as if the Nazis' revival of the economy had pulled their country out of the economic quagmire. However, in material terms the effects varied considerably from one class to another.

Key question
Did the workers benefit under the Third Reich?

Industrial workers

The working class was by far the largest social group in German society (see Table 13.1). The Nazi regime could not assume that the workers would be won over to the promised ideas of the *Volksgemeinschaft*. Under Weimar, many workers had belonged to independent trade unions and had generally voted for the Social Democrats and Communists.

At first, the Nazi regime wanted to establish its authority and closed down all the established trade unions (see page 233). As a result, workers lost the right of industrial bargaining. Consequently, management and the government controlled pay increases and were able to limit workers' freedom of movement.

Table 13.1: German society

	Working class	Middle classes			Peasants	Others
		White-collar workers	Self-employed	Government officials/ employees		
German society as a whole in 1933 (%)	46.3	12.4	9.6	4.8	20.7	6.2

Key date

Creation of German Labour Front: May 1933

In the place of the unions, from May 1933, the only available option to workers was to join the German Labour Front (DAF, *Deutsche Arbeitsfront*). Led by Robert Ley, DAF became the largest Nazi organisation in the Third Reich with a membership that increased from five million in 1933 to 22 million in 1939. It was not compulsory to join, but advisable to do so if you wanted to make the best of things. It became responsible for virtually all areas of work such as:

- Setting working hours and wages.
- Dealing harshly with any sign of disobedience, strikes or absenteeism.
- Running training schemes for apprenticeships.
- Setting stable rents for housing.
- Supervising working conditions through the DAF subsection called the Beauty of Labour (SdA, *Schönheit der Arbeit*). The SdA aimed to provide cleaning, meals, exercise, etc.
- Organising recreational facilities through the Strength through Joy (KdF, *Kraft durch Freude*). It provided very real opportunities to millions of workers: cultural visits, education, sports facilities and holiday travel. By 1939, it had over 7000 paid employees and 135,000 voluntary workers, organised in every factory and workshop employing more than 20 people. Official statistics showed that the number of people in KdF holidays had grown from 2.3 million in 1934 to 10.3 million in 1938.

A Nazi propaganda poster advertising the benefits of saving for 'Your own KdF car'. Workers enthusiastically paid millions of marks to the scheme but mass production of the Volkswagen, planned for 1939, was stopped until after the war.

Assessing the material effects of the Nazi regime on the workers is a highly complicated issue mainly because there are so many variables, such as age, occupation and geographical location. The obvious and most significant benefit for industrial workers was the creation of employment. For the many millions who had suffered from the distress of mass unemployment, the creation of jobs was accepted gratefully (see pages 276–81). Indeed, by the late 1930s Germany had achieved full employment and there was a growing shortage of workers.

Yet, to put that major benefit into context, it is important to bear in mind a number of key factors:

- Average workers' **real wages** only rose above 1929 levels in 1938. Also, workers were forced to pay extensive contributions for DAF and insurance/tax.

Real wages
The actual purchasing power of income taking into account inflation/deflation and also the effect of deductions, e.g. taxes.

Key term

Profile: Robert Ley 1890–1945

1890 – Born in the Rhineland, the son of a farmer
1914 – Graduated with a degree in chemistry
1914–17 – First World War pilot
1920–8 – Worked with the chemicals company IG Farben, but sacked for drunkenness
1924 – Joined the NSDAP and elected to the *Reichstag* in 1930
1933–45 – Leader of the German Labour Front
1939–45 – Lost influence to Todt and Speer
1945 – Committed suicide before trial by the Allies

Ley enjoyed a very significant power-base as the leader of DAF, which was the largest Nazi organisation. However, he failed to develop the institution to its political potential and simply exploited the position for his own self-advancement. He became an alcoholic and although he retained his position, he lost the support of other leading Nazis.

- The generalised picture disguises the fact that the biggest gains were clearly made by the workers associated with the boom in the rearmament industries, whereas those in consumer goods struggled to maintain their real incomes.
- Working hours increased over time. The average working week was officially increased from 43 hours in 1933 to 47 hours in 1939 – and as military demands grew, there was pressure on many workers to do more overtime.
- The fall in unemployment figures from the statistics owed much to the removal of women and Jews, and the introduction of male conscription of the army and labour service.

So, there is considerable evidence to suggest there was workers' discontent even before 1939. During the war, pressures increased further – especially from 1942 when bombing began to hit German industrial urban sectors. By 1944 the working week had grown to 60 hours.

Peasants and small farmers

Key question
Did the peasantry and small farmers benefit under the Third Reich?

The farming community had been attracted to the Nazis by the promise of financial aid, as it had suffered from a series of economic problems from the mid-1920s. Moreover, peasants felt increasingly that they were losing out to the growing urban society of industrial Germany. The Nazi ideology of 'Blood and Soil' promoted by Richard Darré (see profile on page 296) suggested real sympathy for the peasants. It portrayed them as racially the purest element of the *Volk*, the providers of Germany's food and the symbol of traditional German values.

Profile: Richard Darré 1895–1953

1895   – Born in Argentina, of German and Swedish parents

1914–18 – Served in the war and reached the rank of lieutenant

1920–5 – Studied at Halle and gained a doctorate in agriculture specialising in animal breeding

1928–30 – Published three books on Nazi views of race; the most significant was *The Peasantry as the Life-source of the Nordic Race*

1930   – Joined the Nazi Party

1933   – Appointed Reich Peasant Leader and Minister of Agriculture and Food

           – Responsible for introducing the Reich Entitled Law and the Reich Food Estate (see page 297)

1938   – Made leader of the Central Office for Race and Settlement (RuSHA)

1942   – Forced to resign from all his positions

1945   – Arrested and sentenced to seven years in prison in 1949, but died in 1953

Darré was more intellectual than many Nazi leaders. He was well travelled, fluent in four languages and eventually was awarded a doctoral degree for his studies. In 1930 he was drawn into the NSDAP and played an important role in the rise of the Nazis by creating an agrarian political organisation. He effectively exploited the rural unrest, winning electoral support in the countryside.

There were two elements to Darré's thinking:

- to restore the role and values of the countryside and to reverse the drive towards urbanisation by promoting the concept of 'Blood and Soil'
- to support the expansionist policy of *Lebensraum* and to create a German racial aristocracy based on selective breeding.

Initially, his agricultural reforms were well received by the Nazi regime and certainly helped to enable many farmers to recover in the mid-1930s. In particular, his ideas were supported by Himmler and they worked closely together in the RuSHA. However, Darré increasingly fell out with the leadership. His idealistic vision of a rural utopia was at odds with the economic demands of war production and in 1942 he was forced to resign by Hitler.

The Nazi regime certainly took initiatives on agriculture:

- Many farm debts and mortgages were written off and small farmers were given low interest rates and a range of tax allowances.
- The government maintained extensive tariffs to reduce imports.

- The Reich Entailed Farm Law of 1933 gave security of tenure to the occupiers of medium-sized farms between 7.5 and 125 hectares, and forbade the division of farms, in order to promote efficient agriculture.
- The Reich Food Estate, established in 1933, supervised every aspect of agricultural production and distribution, especially food prices and working wages (although its bureaucratic meddling became the focus of resentment, when, for example, it stipulated that each hen had to lay 65 eggs per year).

The economic realities meant that in practice the impact of Nazi agricultural policy was rather mixed. At first, all farmers benefited from an increase in prices between 1933 and 1936 and so farmers' incomes did improve markedly, although they only recovered to 1928 levels in 1938. However, it seems that by 1936–7 any benefits were giving way to growing peasant disillusionment. This was for several reasons:

- Agricultural production increased by 20 per cent from 1928 to 1938, but a significant drift of people to the towns continued – 3 per cent of the population. Wages were higher there, and agriculture just did not have the economic power to compete with other sectors of the economy.
- The positive aspects of the Reich Food Estate were accepted, but the regulations became increasingly resented.
- The Reich Entailed Farm Law also caused resentment and family discontent. In trying to solve the problem of excessive subdivision by passing on farms to just one child, farmers faced the very real dilemma of not being able to provide a future for their remaining children.

With the onset of the war in 1939 pressures on the peasantry developed in all sorts of ways. Men were increasingly conscripted to the military fronts, so increasing the shortage of agricultural labour. This resulted in the transportation to Germany of cheap forced labour of peasants from eastern Europe, e.g. Poles and Czechs. This also conflicted with Nazi thinking since the labourers were not even viewed as racially acceptable.

Key question
Did the landowners lose out?

Landowners

The landed classes had been initially suspicious of radical social change. They resented the political interference of the party, but above all they feared the Nazis would redistribute the large landed estates. However, they soon learned to live quite comfortably with the Nazi regime and in the years before 1939 their economic interests were not really threatened. Indeed, German victories in the early years of the war offered the chance of acquiring more cheap land. The real blow for the landowners actually came in 1945 when the occupation of eastern Germany by the USSR resulted in the nationalisation of land. The traditional social and economic supremacy of the German landowners was broken.

Mittelstand

Another social class that expected to benefit from the Nazi regime was the *Mittelstand*. Its problems were in many ways comparable to those of the peasantry. It had suffered from the decline in commerce in Germany since the First World War and it struggled to compete with the increasing power of big business and trade unions.

Key question
Did the *Mittelstand* benefit under the Third Reich?

Research has shown that in the elections 1930–3 the *Mittelstand* had voted for Nazism in greater proportion than the rest of German society and the Nazi regime was keen to take sympathetic measures to maintain that support:

- Money from the confiscation of Jewish businesses was used to offer low interest rate loans.
- The Law to Protect Retail Trade (1933) banned the opening of new department stores and taxed the existing ones, many of which were owned by Jews.
- Many new trading regulations were imposed to protect small craftsmen.

However, despite the Nazis' attempt to implement electoral promises made before 1933 and the economic recovery, the *Mittelstand* continued the decline that had started with Germany's industrialisation. The costs of small businesses meant that they could not compete with the lower costs of the large department stores. The problem was made worse because the Nazis needed big business to bring about rearmament.

The *Mittelstand* was getting older. In 1933, 20 per cent of the owners of small businesses were under 30 years old and 14 per cent over 60. By 1939 the corresponding figures were 10 per cent under 30 and 19 per cent over 60. In 1936–9 it is reckoned that the number of traditional skilled craftsmen declined by 10 per cent. The *Mittelstand* was being squeezed out.

Big business

The influence of big business is considered in more depth in Chapter 12 (pages 286–7), but it is clear that it generally benefited from the Nazis' economic programme. Despite an increasing range of government controls, the financial gains were impressive. The value of German industry steadily increased from the share price index and the improvement of salaries of management. Moreover, from 1938 the annexations and the conquests of war provided enormous opportunities for taking over foreign property, land and companies.

Key question
Did big business benefit?

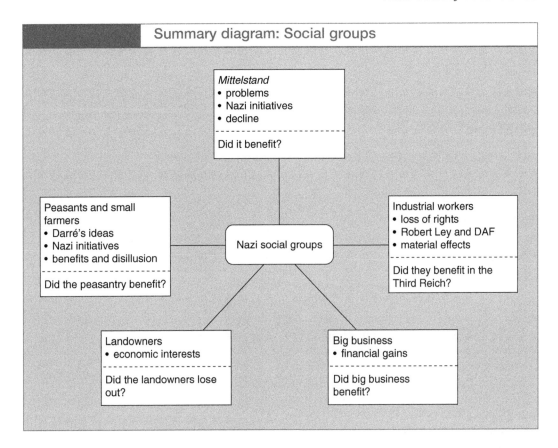

Summary diagram: Social groups

Mittelstand
• problems
• Nazi initiatives
• decline
- - - - - - - - - - - - - - - -
Did it benefit?

Peasants and small farmers
• Darré's ideas
• Nazi initiatives
• benefits and disillusion
- - - - - - - - - - - - - - - -
Did the peasantry benefit?

Nazi social groups

Industrial workers
• loss of rights
• Robert Ley and DAF
• material effects
- - - - - - - - - - - - - - - -
Did they benefit in the Third Reich?

Landowners
• economic interests
- - - - - - - - - - - - - - - -
Did the landowners lose out?

Big business
• financial gains
- - - - - - - - - - - - - - - -
Did big business benefit?

3 | Education and Youth

Key question
What were the aims of Nazi education?

In Nazi Germany, education became merely a tool for the consolidation of the Nazi system. Hitler expressed his views chillingly in 1933:

> When an opponent declares, 'I will not come over to your side', I calmly say, 'Your child belongs to us already … What are you? You will pass on. Your descendants, however, now stand in the new camp. In a short time they will know nothing else but this new community.'

Education in the Third Reich was therefore intended to **indoctrinate** its youth so completely in the principles and ethos of National Socialism that the long-term survival of the 'New Order' would never be brought into question. A National Socialist Teachers' League official wrote pompously in 1937:

Key term

Indoctrination
Inculcating and imposing a set of ideas.

> German youth must no longer – as in the Liberal era in the cause of so-called objectivity – be confronted with the choice of whether it wishes to grow up in a spirit of materialism or idealism, of racism or internationalism, of religion or godlessness, but it must be consciously shaped according to the principles which are recognised as correct and which have shown themselves to be correct: according to the principles of the ideology of National Socialism.

This was to be achieved not only through the traditional structure of the educational system, but also by the development of various Nazi youth movements.

Schools

The actual organisation of the state educational system was not fundamentally altered, although by a law of 1934 control was taken from the regional states and centralised under the Reich Ministry of Education, Culture and Science led by Reich Minister Bernhard Rust. The ministry was then able to adapt the existing system to suit Nazi purposes.

First, the teaching profession was 'reconditioned'. Politically unreliable individuals were removed and Jewish teachers were banned, and many women were encouraged to conform to Nazi values by returning to the home (see pages 310–11). Special training courses were arranged for those teachers who remained unconvinced by the new requirements. The National Socialist Teachers' League (NSLB, *Nationalsozialistische Lehrerbund*) was established and its influence and interference continued to grow. By 1937, it included 97 per cent of all teachers and two-thirds of the profession had been on special month-long courses on Nazi ideology and the changes to the curriculum.

Secondly, the curricula and syllabuses were adapted. To fit the Nazi Aryan ideal, much greater emphasis was placed on physical education. Fifteen per cent of school time was given over to it, and games teachers assumed an increased status and importance in the school hierarchy. On the academic front, Religious Studies was dropped to downgrade the importance of Christianity, whereas German, Biology and History became the focus of special attention:

- German language and literature were studied to create 'a consciousness of being German', and to inculcate a martial and nationalistic spirit. Among the list of suggested reading for 14-year-old pupils was *The Battle of Tannenberg*, which included the following extract: 'A Russian soldier tried to bar the infiltrator's way, but Otto's bayonet slid gratingly between the Russian's ribs, so that he collapsed groaning. There it lay before him, simple and distinguished, his dream's desire, the Iron Cross.'
- Biology became the means by which to deliver Nazi racial theory: ethnic classification, **population policy** and racial genetics were all integrated into the syllabus.
- History, not surprisingly, was also given a special place in the Nazi curriculum, so that the glories of German nationalism could be emphasised.

One final innovation was the creation of various types of élite schools. They were intended to prepare the best of Germany's youth for future political leadership, were modelled on the principles of the Hitler Youth, and focused on physical training, paramilitary activities and political education. The 21 *Napolas* (National Political Educational Institutions) and the 10 Adolf

Key question
How did German schools change under the Nazis?

Key date
Reich Ministry of Education created – control of education was taken away from *Länder*: 1934

Key term
Population policy
In 1933–45 the Nazi government aimed to increase the birth rate.

Hitler Schools were both for boys of secondary school age, and the three *Ordensburgen* for boys of college age.

Hitler Youth

Key question
How did the Hitler Youth try to indoctrinate Germany's young people?

The responsibility for developing a new outlook lay with the youth movements. There was already a long and well-established tradition of youth organisation in Germany before 1933, but at that time the Hitler Youth (HJ, *Hitler Jugend*) represented only one per cent of the total.

The term 'Hitler Youth' in fact embraced a range of youth groups under the control of its leader Baldur von Schirach and in the next six years the structure and membership of the HJ grew remarkably, although this was partly because parents were pressurised to enrol the children and by 1939 membership became compulsory. By then all other youth organisations had been abolished.

Table 13.2: Hitler Youth movements. The percentages indicate the percentage of total youth population aged 10–18 years who were members

Year	Number	Percentages
1932	200,000	1.5
1934	3,500,000	46.5
1936	5,400,000	62.8
1938	7,100,000	77.2

In all four groups shown in Table 13.3 there was a great stress on political indoctrination, emphasising the life and achievements of the *Führer*, German patriotism, athletics and camping. In addition, the sexes were moulded for their future roles in Nazi society. Boys engaged in endless physical and military-type activities, e.g. target shooting, and girls were prepared for their domestic and maternal tasks, e.g. cooking.

Table 13.3: Youth groups

Boys 10–14 years old	German Young People (DJ, *Deutsche Jungvolk*)
Boys 14–18 years old	Hitler Youth (HJ, *Hitler Jugend*)
Girls 10–14 years old	League of Young Girls (JM, *Jungmädel*)
Girls 14–18 years old	League of German Girls (BDM, *Bund Deutscher Mädel*)

Successes and failures

Key question
Did Nazi education succeed?

It is difficult to assess the success of any educational system. It depends on the criteria chosen and the 'evidence' is open to conflicting interpretations. Therefore, conclusions must be tentative.

Profile: Baldur von Schirach 1907–74

1907	– Born in Berlin, the son of an aristocratic German father and an American mother
1924	– Joined the NSDAP as a student of art history at Munich
1928	– Leader of Nazi German Students' League
1933–9	– Youth Leader of the German Reich
1939–40	– Joined the German army and won the Iron Cross
1940–5	– *Gauleiter* of Vienna
1945	– Arrested by the Allies and sentenced to 20 years' imprisonment at the Nuremberg trials in 1946
1967	– Publication of his book, *I Believed in Hitler*
1974	– Lived privately in West Germany until his death

Schirach's only real significant role was as 'Youth Leader of the German Reich', which gave him the responsibility to supervise all the youth organisations, 1933–9. He became obsessed with Hitler from the mid-1920s: he even wrote poetry to the *Führer*! He was not greatly respected by other leading Nazis, partly because of his effeminate nature. However, his loyalty and charm allowed him to remain influential with Hitler.

Teaching

The teaching profession certainly felt its status to be under threat, despite its initial sympathy for the regime. Thirty-two per cent were members of the party in 1936 – a figure markedly higher than the figure of 17 per cent of the Reich Civil Service as a whole. The anti-academic ethos and the crude indoctrination alienated many, while the party's backing of the HJ and its activities caused much resentment. Not surprisingly, standards in traditional academic subjects had fallen by the early years of the war. This was particularly the case in the various élite schools, where physical development predominated. By 1938 recruitment of teachers had declined and there were 8000 vacancies, and only 2500 were graduating from teacher training colleges. In higher education, the number of students had halved even before the war.

Youth conformity

The impact of the HJ seems to have been very mixed. In some respects the emphasis on teamwork and extracurricular activities was to be commended, especially when compared to the limited provision available in many European countries. So, the provision for sports, camping and music genuinely excited many youngsters, and for those from poorer backgrounds the HJ really offered opportunities. Most significantly, the HJ successfully conveyed to many youngsters an atmosphere of fun and a sense of belonging to the new Germany, as expressed by a young member of the Hitler Youth, Heinrich Metelmann:

'Youth serves the *Führer*. Every ten year old into the Hitler Youth.' The Nazi propaganda poster cleverly plays on the combined images of the young boy and Hitler sharing a common vision. It was produced in 1940, by which time war had started and membership was compulsory.

The structural system of that youth organisation was based on the military. Our group consisted of about 150–200 boys, subdivided into three troops – just like a company of soldiers. We met together, marched and played together in close comradeship until the age of 18 ... Every company had a *Heim* [home; often a barn or cellar] which we decorated in a nationalist/militarist style. Swastika flags, and other Nazi emblems had places of honour, as well as decorated pictures of our *Führer* ... But when we had our close togetherness there, we felt happy on our own. We were sure and proud that *we* were the future of Germany, come what may.

However, the HJ suffered from its over-rapid expansion and the leadership was inadequate. By the late 1930s it became more difficult to run the movement effectively and, as a result, the increasing Nazi emphasis on military drill and discipline was certainly resented by many adolescents; it was becoming institutionalised by the Nazi regime. Moreover, recent research suggests that sizeable pockets of the adolescent population had not been won over by 1939 and that alienation and dissent increased quite markedly. The regime even established a special youth section of the secret police and a youth concentration camp was set up at Neuwied.

A number of youth groups developed deliberately exhibiting codes of behaviour at odds with the expected social values of Nazism. 'Swing Youth' was one such craze among mainly middle-class youngsters who took up the music and imagery associated with the dance-bands of Britain and the USA. The ***Edelweiss Piraten*** was a general name given to a host of working-class youths who formed gangs, such as the 'Roving Dudes' and 'Navajos'. Their members had been alienated by the military emphasis and discipline of the Hitler Youth. They met up and organised their own hikes and camps which then came into conflict with the official ones. In several instances, 'Pirates' became involved in more active resistance, most famously at Cologne in 1944 when 12 of them were hanged publicly because of their attacks on military targets and the assassination of a Gestapo officer.

Edelweiss
A white alpine flower which served as a symbol of opposition.

Key term

Kittelbach Pirates from 1937. 'Pirates' was the label chosen by dissenting German youth. In what ways could these boys be seen as challenging Nazi ideals?

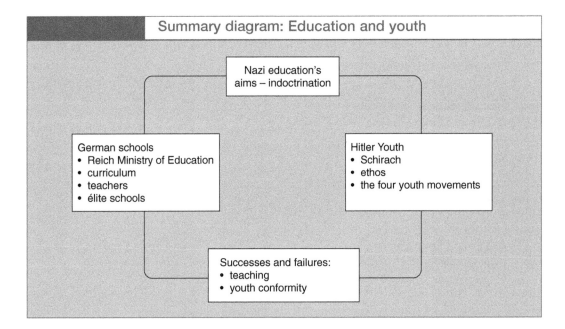

Summary diagram: Education and youth

Nazi education's aims – indoctrination

German schools
• Reich Ministry of Education
• curriculum
• teachers
• élite schools

Hitler Youth
• Schirach
• ethos
• the four youth movements

Successes and failures:
• teaching
• youth conformity

Key question
How did the Nazis regard religion?

4 | Religion

The rise of Nazism posed fundamental political and ethical problems for the Christian Churches, while Nazism could not ignore these well-established and powerful institutions.

In his rise to power Hitler avoided direct attacks on the Churches and number 24 of the party's 25-points programme spoke in favour of 'positive Christianity' which was closely linked to racial and national views (see page 177). However, there can be little doubt that Nazism was a fundamentally anti-Christian philosophy. Where Nazism glorified strength, violence and war, Christianity taught love, forgiveness and neighbourly respect. Moreover, Christianity was regarded as the product of an inferior race – Jesus was a Hebrew – and therefore, it could not be reconciled with Nazi *völkisch* thought. Some leading Nazis, such as Himmler and his deputy, Heydrich, openly revealed their contempt for Christianity. Hitler himself was more cautious, although what were probably his true feelings were revealed in a private conversation in 1933:

> Neither of the denominations – Catholic or Protestant, they are both the same – has any future left … That won't stop me stamping out Christianity in Germany root and branch. One is either a Christian or a German. You can't be both.

Teutonic paganism
The non-Christian beliefs of the Germans in ancient history (heathens).

Key term

The German Faith Movement

In place of Christianity, the Nazis aimed to cultivate a **teutonic paganism**, which became known as the German Faith Movement. Although a clear Nazi religious ideology was never fully outlined, the development of the German Faith Movement, promoted by

the Nazi thinker Alfred Rosenberg, revolved around four main
themes:

- the propagation of the 'Blood and Soil' ideology (see
page 292)
- the replacement of Christian ceremonies – marriage and
baptism – by pagan equivalents
- the wholesale rejection of Christian ethics – closely linked to
racial and nationalist views
- the **cult of** Hitler's **personality**.

However, the Nazi government knew that religion was a very
delicate issue and it initially adopted a cautious conciliatory
stance towards both the Churches to lull them into a false sense of
security while the Nazi dictatorship was being established.

Conciliation and conflict 1933–5

In his very first speech as Chancellor, Hitler paid tribute to the
Churches as being integral to the well-being of the nation.
Members of the SA were even encouraged to attend Protestant
Church services. This was done to give weight to the idea that the
Nazi state could accommodate Protestantism. The 'Day of
Potsdam' (see page 225) further gave the impression of a unity
between the Protestant Church and the state.

Likewise, the Catholic Church responded sympathetically to the
overtures of the Nazis. Catholic bishops, in particular, were
frightened of the possibility of a repeat of the so-called
Kulturkampf in the late nineteenth century (see page 6). So,
Catholic bishops were concerned to safeguard the position of the
Church under the Nazis and in July 1933 a **Concordat** was signed
between the Papacy and the regime (represented by Vice-
Chancellor Papen who was a Catholic). In the agreement it was
decided that:

- the Nazis would guarantee the Catholic Church religious
freedom
- the Nazis would not interfere with the Catholic Church's
property and legal rights
- the Nazis would accept the Catholic Church's control over its
own education
- in return, the Catholic Church would not interfere in politics
and would give diplomatic recognition to the Nazi government.

In the short term the Concordat seemed to be a significant
success. However, the courting of both of the Churches by the
Nazis was totally insincere and by the end of 1933 Nazi
interference in religious affairs was already causing resentment
and disillusionment in both Catholic and Protestant Churches.

The Nazi regime hoped that the Protestant Churches would
gradually be 'co-ordinated' through the influence of the group
known as the German Christians (*Deutsche Christen*). This group
hoped to reconcile their Protestant ideas with Nazi nationalist
and racial thinking by finding common ground. So, a new Church
constitution was formulated in July 1933 with the Nazi

Key terms

Cult of personality
Using the power
and charisma of a
political leader to
dominate the
nation.

Concordat
An agreement
between Church
and state.

Key question
Why did conciliation
lead to conflict?

Key dates

Concordat signed
with the Papacy:
July 1933

Creation of the
Confessional Church:
1934

Papal encyclical, *Mit
Brennender Sorge*,
issued: 1937

Profile: Pastor Martin Niemöller 1892–1984

1892	– Born in Lippstadt
1914–18	– U-boat commander, won the Iron Cross
1920–4	– Studied theology and ordained as a Protestant pastor
1934	– Co-founder of the Confessional Church
1937	– A critical sermon resulted in his arrest
1937–45	– Held in the camps of Sachsenhausen and Dachau
1946	– President of the Protestant Church in Hessen
1946–84	– A strong supporter of the World Peace Movement
1984	– Died in Wiesbaden, Germany

In the 1920s Niemöller was a nationalist, anti-communist and against the Weimar Republic – he even sympathised with Hitler in the rise of Nazism. However, during 1933 his doubts emerged because of Nazism's anti-Semitism and its attempt to control the Churches. Therefore, he played a crucial role in the formation of the Confessional Church and after a critical sermon he was imprisoned from 1937 to 1945.

sympathiser Ludwig Müller as the first Reich Bishop – an interesting application of the *Führerprinzip*.

However, such Nazi policies alienated many Protestant pastors, and there soon developed an opposition group, the Confessional Church (*Bekennende Kirche*), which upheld orthodox Protestantism and rejected Nazi distortions. Led by Pastor Niemöller, by 1934 the Confessional Church gained the support of about 7000 pastors out of 17,000. They claimed to represent the true Protestant Churches of Germany.

Churches and state

Key question
How did the relationship between the Churches and state change over time?

By 1935 it was clear that the Nazi leadership had achieved only limited success in controlling the Churches. It was torn between a policy of total suppression, which would alienate large numbers of Germans, and a policy of limited persecution, which would allow the Churches too much independence. In fact, although the ultimate objective was never in doubt, Nazi tactics degenerated into a kind of war of attrition against the Churches.

In order to destabilise the Churches, the Ministry of Church Affairs, led by Hanns Kerrl, was established. He adopted a policy of undermining both the Protestant and Catholic Churches by a series of anti-religious measures, including:

- closure of Church schools
- undermining of Catholic youth groups
- personal campaigns to discredit and harass the clergy, e.g. monasteries were accused of sexual and financial malpractices
- confiscation of Church funds
- campaign to remove crucifixes from schools
- arrest of more and more pastors and priests.

The Churches were undoubtedly weakened by this approach, but it also stimulated individual declarations of opposition from both Protestants and Catholics:

- Niemöller delivered a sermon in which he said that 'we must obey God rather than man'; he was interned in 1937 and was held in various concentration camps until the end of the war.
- The Pope, Pius XI, eventually vehemently attacked the Nazi system in his encyclical, or public letter, of 1937 entitled *With Burning Concern (Mit Brennender Sorge)*.

Clearly, the conflict between the Churches and the state was set to continue.

The outbreak of war initially brought about a more cautious policy, as the regime wished to avoid unnecessary tensions. However, following the military victories of 1939–40 the persecution intensified, as a result of pressure applied by anti-Christian enthusiasts, such as Bormann and Heydrich and the SS hierarchy. Monasteries were closed, Church property was attacked and Church activities were severely restricted. Even so, religion was such a politically sensitive issue that Hitler did not allow subordination of the Churches to give way to wholesale suppression within Germany.

Conclusions

The Nazis achieved only limited success in their religious policy. The German Faith Movement was a clearly a failure. Neo-paganism never achieved support on any large scale. The 1939 official census recorded only five per cent of the population as members, although it shows the direction that might have been taken, if the likes of Himmler had won the war.

Many individual Christians made brave stands against the Nazis. This made the dictatorship wary of launching a fundamental assault on religion, so German loyalty to Christianity survived in the long term despite Nazism. The historian J.R.C. Wright says: 'The Churches were severely handicapped but not destroyed. Hitler's programme needed time: he was himself destroyed before it had taken root.'

However, both the Catholic and Protestant Churches failed to provide effective opposition to Nazism. Neither was 'co-ordinated' so both enjoyed a measure of independence. Both could have provided the focus for active resistance. Instead, they preferred, as institutions, to adopt a pragmatic policy towards Nazism. They stood up for their own religious practices and traditions with shows of dissent, but generally denunciations of the regime were left to individuals.

The reasons for the Churches' reluctance to show opposition to the regime lay in their conservatism:

- They distrusted the politics of the left which seemed to threaten the existing order of society. The most extreme form of communism rejected the existence of religion itself.

Key questions
Did Nazi religious policy succeed in its aims? Did the Churches effectively oppose the Nazis?

- There was a nationalist sympathy for Nazism, especially after the problems of 1918–33. For many Church leaders it was too easy to believe that Hitler's 'national renewal' was simply a return to the glorious days before 1914. This was particularly true of the Lutheran Protestant Church, which had been the state Church in Prussia under Imperial Germany.
- Both Churches rightly feared the power of the Nazi state. They believed that any gestures of heroic resistance were more than likely to have bloody consequences. In such a situation, their emphasis on pastoral and spiritual comfort was perhaps the most practical and realistic policy for them.

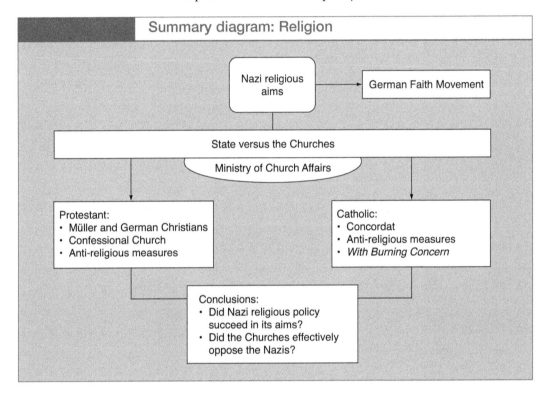

Summary diagram: Religion

Nazi religious aims → German Faith Movement

State versus the Churches

Ministry of Church Affairs

Protestant:
- Müller and German Christians
- Confessional Church
- Anti-religious measures

Catholic:
- Concordat
- Anti-religious measures
- *With Burning Concern*

Conclusions:
- Did Nazi religious policy succeed in its aims?
- Did the Churches effectively oppose the Nazis?

5 | Women and the Family

Key question
How and why was the role of women changing in society in the early twentieth century?

The first quarter of the twentieth century witnessed two important social changes in German family life:

- Germany's population growth had decelerated markedly, which is *not* to say that the actual population had declined. In 1900 there had been over two million live births per annum, whereas by 1933 the figure was below one million.
- Over the same period female employment expanded by at least a third, far outstripping the percentage increase in population.

Both of these trends had been partially brought about by long-term changes in social behaviour common to many industrialised countries. It was recognised that the use of contraception to limit family size would improve the standard of living and give better educated women the opportunity to have a vocation as well as children. However, Germany's recent past history exaggerated these developments. Economic mobilisation during the First World War had driven women into the factories, while the post-war difficulties caused by the inflation had encouraged them to stay on working out of economic necessity. In addition, the war had left a surplus of 1.8 million marriageable women, as well as many wives with invalided husbands. Finally, the changing balance of the economy in the 1920s had led to an increased demand for non-manual labour and the growth of mass-production techniques requiring more unskilled workers. These factors tended to favour the employment of women, who could be paid less than men.

The Nazi view towards women

The ideology of National Socialism was in stark contrast to the above social trends. Nazism fundamentally opposed social and economic female emancipation and had the following aims for women:

Key question
What was the ideal role of women in Nazi society?

- To have more children and to take responsibility for bringing them up.
- To care for the house and their husbands.
- To stop paid employment except for very specialist vocations such as midwifery.

In the view of the Nazis, nature had ordained that the two sexes should fulfil entirely different roles, and it was simply the task of the state to maintain this distinction. What this amounted to was that 'a woman's place was to be in the home'. Or, as the Nazi slogan presented it, they were to be devoted to the three German Ks: '*Kinder, Küche, Kirche*' ('children, kitchen and Church' – see the 'Ten commandments' for choosing a spouse, below). Such dogma was upheld by the party, even before 1933 – there was not a single female Nazi deputy in the *Reichstag*, and a party regulation of 1921 excluded women from all senior positions within its structure.

Nazi Ten Commandments for the choice of a spouse
1. Remember that you are German!
2. If you are genetically healthy, do not stay single.
3. Keep your body pure.
4. Keep your mind and spirit pure.
5. Marry only for love.
6. As a German, choose only a spouse of similar or related blood.
7. In choosing a spouse, ask about his forebears.
8. Health is essential to physical beauty.
9. Don't look for a playmate but for a companion in marriage.
10. You should want to have as many children as possible.

Nazi views on women tied in with their concern about the demographic trends. A growing population was viewed as a sign of national strength and status – a reflection of Germany's aspiration to the status of an international power. How could they demand nationalist expansionism in eastern Europe, if the number of Germans was in fact levelling out? It was therefore considered essential to increase the population substantially and, to this end, women were portrayed as primarily the mothers of the next generation – an image that suited Nazi anti-feminism.

Female employment

Initially, attempts to reduce the number of women in work seem to have been quite successful. Between 1933 and 1936 married women were in turn debarred from jobs in medicine, law and the higher ranks of the civil service. Moreover, the number of female teachers and university students was reduced considerably – only 10 per cent of university students could be female. Such laws had a profound effect on professional middle-class women, although their actual number was small.

Nazi incentives

In other sectors of the economy a mixture of party pressure and financial inducements was employed to cajole women out of the workplace and back into the home. From June 1933 interest-free loans of RM600 were made available to young women who withdrew from the labour market in order to get married. The effects of the Depression also worked in favour of Nazi objectives. They not only drastically reduced the number of female workers (although proportionately far less than male workers), but also enabled the government to justify its campaign for women to give up work for the benefit of unemployed men. On these grounds, **labour exchanges** and employers were advised to discriminate positively in favour of men. As a result of all this, the percentage of women in employment fell from 37 per cent to 31 per cent of the total from 1932 to 1937, although the policy was not entirely effective as the actual *number* of women employed in this period rose.

Nazi women's organisations

Women were quite specifically excluded from the Nazi machinery of government. The only employment opportunities available to them were within the various Nazi women's organisations, such as the National Socialist Womanhood (NSF, *National Sozialistische Frauenschaft*) and the German Women's Enterprise (DFW, *Deutsches Frauenwerk*), led by Gertrud Scholtz-Klink. Yet, the NSF and DFW were regarded by the party as mere tools for the propagation of the **anti-feminist** ideology by means of cultural, educational and social programmes. And so, when a campaign started in the NSF for enhanced opportunities for women within the party, its organisers were officially discredited.

Effects

However, by 1937 Nazi ideological convictions were already threatened by the pressures of economic necessity. The introduction of conscription and the rearmament boom from the mid-1930s soon led to an increasing shortage of labour, as the Nazi economy continued to grow. The anti-feminist ideology could only be upheld if economic growth was slowed down and that, in turn, would restrict the rearmament programme. Of course, Hitler was not prepared to sanction this. Consequently, market forces inevitably began to exploit this readily available pool of labour, and the relative decline in female employment was reversed. Between 1937 and 1939 it rose from 5.7 million to 7.1 million, and the percentage of women increased from 31 per cent to 33 per cent of the total workforce (see Table 13.4) At this point the government decided to end the marriage loan scheme (see below) for women who withdrew from the labour market.

Table 13.4: Women in regular manual and non-manual employment

	1932	1937	1939
Millions of women	4.8	5.7	7.1
Women as a percentage of the total	37	31	33

Note: the comparative figure for 1928 was 7.4 million.

The contradictions between theory and practice of female employment were exacerbated further with the onset of war. So, although the trend of female employment continued to increase, the Nazi regime did not fully exploit the valuable resource of women as munitions workers. Whereas British women were required to play a major role on the home front, German women remained underemployed right to the end of the war (see pages 348–9). This was due to:

- Germany's poor economic mobilisation
- the unconvincing appeal for women to do war work in arms factories
- women's farming responsibilities.

Marriage and family

The Nazi state was obsessed with a desire to increase Germany's population and a series of measures was promptly introduced:

- Marriage loans. The loan was worth just over half a year's earnings and a quarter of it was converted into a straight gift for each child that was born. (The scheme was introduced in June 1933, but progressively reduced from 1937.)
- Family allowances were improved dramatically, particularly for low-income families.
- Income tax was reduced in proportion to the number of children and those families with six or more did not pay any.
- Maternity benefits were improved.

Key question
What were the effects of Nazi population policy?

- The anti-abortion law introduced under the Weimar Republic was enforced much more strictly.
- Contraceptive advice and facilities were restricted.

Inevitably, these incentives and laws were backed up by an extensive propaganda campaign, which glorified motherhood and the large family. There were also rewards: the Honour Cross of the German Mother in bronze, silver and gold, awarded for four, six and eight children, respectively. Such glorification reached its climax in the coining of the Nazi slogan 'I have donated a child to the *Führer*' (as contemporary humorists soon pointed out, this was presumably because of Hitler's personal unwillingness or inability to father children of his own).

Table 13.5: Social trends in Nazi Germany 1933–9

	Marriages per 1000 inhabitants	Divorces per 10,000 existing marriages	Births per 1000 inhabitants
1933	9.7	29.7	14.7
1936	9.1	32.6	19.0
1939	11.1	38.3	20.3

The statistics in Table 13.5 show several trends:

- From 1933 the birth rate increased significantly, reaching a peak in 1939 (although thereafter it again slowly declined).
- The divorce rate continued to increase.
- The figure of marriages was fairly consistent (apart from the blip in 1939 – probably connected to the onset of the war).

The real problem for the historian is deciding whether Nazi population policy was actually *responsible* for the demographic trends. Interpreting population statistics is difficult because it involves so many different factors – social, economic and even psychological factors. Also, it is extremely hard to assess the *relative* significance of Nazi population policy over such a short period, when its background was the effects of the depression.

Lebensborn

Nazi population policy not only aimed to increase the number of children being born, but also tried to improve 'racial standards'. It led to the establishment of one of the most extraordinary features of Nazi social engineering, **Lebensborn**, set up by Himmler and the SS. Initially, the programme provided homes for unmarried mothers of the increasing number of illegitimate children who were seen as racially correct. Later, the institution also made the necessary arrangements for girls to be impregnated by members of the SS in organised brothels. It is reckoned that by the end of the regime about 11,000 children were born under these circumstances.

Key term

Lebensborn
Literally, the 'spring' or 'fountain of life'. Founded by Himmler and overseen by the SS to promote doctrines of racial purity.

Conclusion

Feminist historians have been highly critical of Nazi population and family policy that had reduced the status of women. One historian, Gisela Bock, in the 1980s viewed Nazi thinking on women as a kind of secondary racism in which women were the victims of a sexist–racist male regime that reduced women to the status of mere objects. Such an interpretation would, of course, have been denied by the Nazis who claimed to regard women as different rather than inferior. But some modern-day non-feminist historians have tried to explain the positive features of Nazi policy on women. Improved welfare services made life easier for women, especially in more isolated rural areas. Also, with husbands away during the war, women were protected from having to combine paid work with bringing up a family and running the household.

Yet, despite these different perspectives, Nazi policy objectives for women and the family could not be squared with the social realities of twentieth-century Germany. With the changing population trend and the increasing employment of women, Nazi views on women and the family were idealistic but impractical. Consequently, Nazi policy towards women and the family was contradictory and incoherent.

Key question
How successful was Nazi policy on women and family?

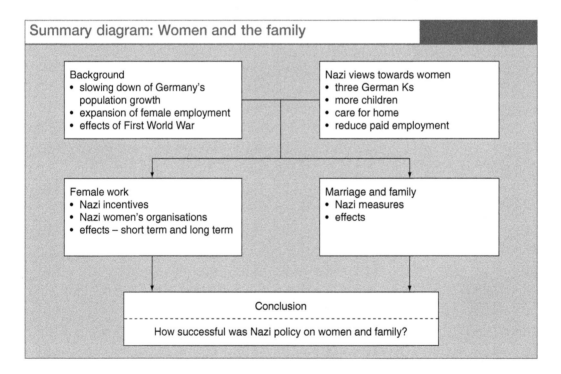

Summary diagram: Women and the family

Background
- slowing down of Germany's population growth
- expansion of female employment
- effects of First World War

Nazi views towards women
- three German Ks
- more children
- care for home
- reduce paid employment

Female work
- Nazi incentives
- Nazi women's organisations
- effects – short term and long term

Marriage and family
- Nazi measures
- effects

Conclusion
How successful was Nazi policy on women and family?

Key question
Who were the outsiders in the *Volksgemeinschaft*?

6 | Outsiders

Nazism claimed to create a *Volksgemeinschaft* in the Third Reich, although certain people were not allowed to be part of it and they were to be discriminated against and persecuted. Nazism was an all-embracing society, but only of those who conformed to their criteria, and there were certain groups who were definitely 'outsiders'.

Ideological opponents

This term could most obviously be applied to the socialists and communists, many of whom were sent to the early concentration camps in 1933 (see page 253). However, it increasingly became a term to cover anyone who did not politically accept the regime and, as the years went on, a broader range of political and ideological opponents was imprisoned or worse, e.g. Pastor Niemöller (see page 307).

The 'biologically inferior'

This covered all the races that, according to the Nazis, were 'inferior' or subhuman, such as Gypsies, Slavs and Jews (see below).

It also included the mentally and physically disabled. As early as July 1933 the Nazis proclaimed 'The Law for the Prevention of Hereditarily Diseased Offspring', which allowed for the compulsory sterilisation of those with hereditary conditions like schizophrenia, Huntington's chorea, hereditary blindness or deafness. In 12 years 350,000 people were sterilised under this law.

However, the policy went much further from 1939, when Hitler himself initiated the idea of using euthanasia for children with severe disabilities (such as Down's syndrome and cerebral palsy) by using the phrase 'mercy death'. No specific law permitted this, but patients were killed in asylums under the name of 'Operation T4'. About 70,000 were gassed in 1940–1 but, following public rumours and Catholic opposition, the operation was stopped (see page 351).

Key term

Asocials
The Nazis' desire to create a 'pure' 'national community' excluding the 'socially unfit'. The term 'asocial' covered any marginal group that deviated from the norms of society. It was applied in an elastic manner including Gypsies, vagabonds, prostitutes, alcoholics, homosexuals, criminals, 'idlers', even grumblers.

Asocials

The term was used very broadly to cover anyone whose behaviour was not viewed as acceptable. These social outcasts included alcoholics, prostitutes, criminals, tramps and the workshy: indeed any one else who did not, could not or would not perform their duties to the national community.

Those **asocials** who were 'orderly' but avoided work were rounded up and organised into a compulsory labour force; and those who were judged as 'disorderly' were imprisoned and sometimes sterilised or experimented on.

Homosexual men were also classed as asocials. They were seen as breaking the laws of nature and undermining traditional Nazi family values. In 1936 the Reich Central Office for the Combating of Homosexuality and Abortion was established. Between 10,000 and 15,000 homosexuals were imprisoned and those sent to camps were forced to wear pink triangles. Provided they were discreet, lesbians were not persecuted as badly as men, as they were not seen as a threat to society in the same way.

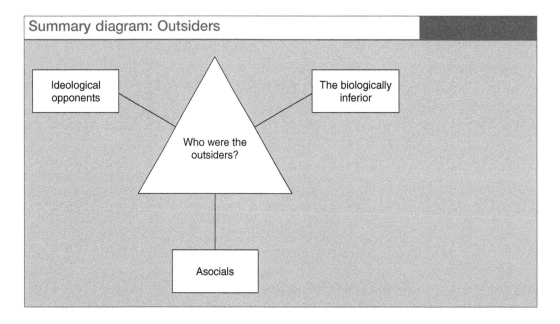

Summary diagram: Outsiders

7 | Nazi Anti-Semitism

The emergence of right-wing racist *völkisch* nationalism was clearly apparent before 1914 (see pages 14–15). Its attractions expanded in the aftermath of the First World War: the self-deception of the 'stab in the back' myth; the humiliation of the Versailles Treaty; and the political and economic weaknesses of the Weimar Republic. So, by the early 1920s, there were about 70 relatively small right-wing parties such as the Nazi Party.

In that environment Hitler was able to exploit hostility towards the Jews and turn it into a radical ideology of hatred. He was the product, not the creator, of a society that was permeated by such prejudices. Yet, it would be inaccurate to dismiss Hitler as just another anti-Semite. Hitler's hatred of Jews was obsessive and vindictive, and it shaped much of his political philosophy. Without his personal commitment to attack the Jews and without his charismatic skills as a political leader, it seems unlikely that anti-Semitism could have become such an integral part of the Nazi movement. He was able to mobilise and stir the support of the leading anti-Semitic Nazis.

It is all too easy to highlight the rhetoric of Nazi anti-Semitism as the reason for the success of the party. Certainly, 37.3 per cent of the population may have voted for Hitler the anti-Semite in July 1932, but the vast majority of Germans were motivated by unemployment, the collapse of agricultural prices and the fear of communism. Indeed, in a 1934 survey into the reasons why people joined the Nazis, over 60 per cent did not even mention anti-Semitism.

Therefore, the Nazi approach to anti-Semitism was **gradualist**. The early moves against Jews gave no suggestion of the end result. Indeed, for some Germans the discriminatory legislation was no more than Jews deserved. For the more liberal minded,

Key term

Gradualism
Changing by degrees; progressing slowly.

who found such action offensive, there was the practical problem of how to show opposition and to offer resistance. Once the apparatus of dictatorship was well established by the end of 1934, the futility of opposition was apparent to most people. Feelings of hopelessness were soon replaced by those of fear. To show sympathy for, or to protect Jews, was to risk one's own freedom or one's own life. It was an unenviable dilemma.

Legal discrimination

Key question
Did Nazi anti-Semitism change over time?

Key dates

First official boycott of Jewish shops and professions: 1 April 1933

Nuremberg Race Laws introduced: 15 September 1935

Many radical Nazis were keen to take immediate measures against Jewish people and their businesses, but the party's leadership was worried that it could get out of hand. And those concerns were confirmed when a one-day national boycott was organised for 1 April 1933. Jewish-owned shops, cafés and businesses were picketed by the SA, who stood outside urging people not to enter. However, the boycott was not universally accepted by the German people and it caused a lot of bad publicity abroad.

The Nazi leaders developed their anti-Semitism in a more subtle way. Once the Nazi regime had established the legal basis for its dictatorship (see pages 222–6), it was legally possible to initiate an anti-Jewish policy, most significantly by the creation of the Nuremberg Laws in September 1935. This clearly stood in contrast to the extensive civil rights that Jews had enjoyed in

Table 13.6: Major Nazi anti-Jewish laws 1933–9

Date		Law
1933	7 April	Law for the Restoration of the Professional Civil Service.
		Jews excluded from the government's civil service
	4 October	Law for the exclusion of Jewish journalists
1935	15 September	The Nuremberg Race Laws:
		Reich Citizenship Act. 'A citizen of the Reich is a subject who is only of German or kindred blood.'
		Jews lost their citizenship in Germany
		Law for the Protection of German Blood and German Honour. Marriages and extramarital relations between Jews and German citizens forbidden
1938	5 July	Decree prohibiting Jewish doctors practising medicine
	28 October	Decree to expel 17,000 Polish Jews resident in Germany
	15 November	Decree to exclude Jewish pupils from schools and universities
	3 December	Decree for the compulsory closure and sale of all Jewish businesses
1939	1 September	Decree for the introduction of curfew for Jews

Weimar Germany. The discrimination against Jewish people got worse as an ongoing range of laws was introduced (see Table 13.6). In this way all the rights of Jews were gradually removed even before the onset of the war.

Propaganda and indoctrination

Nazism also set out to cultivate the message of anti-Semitism; in effect to change people's attitudes so that they hated the Jews. Goebbels himself was a particularly committed anti-Semite and he used his skills as the Minister of Propaganda and Popular Enlightenment to indoctrinate the German people (see pages 260–2). All aspects of culture associated with the Jews were censored. Even more forceful was the full range of propaganda methods used to advance the anti-Semitic message, such as:

- posters and signs, e.g. 'Jews are not wanted here'
- newspapers, e.g. *Der Angriff*, which was founded by Goebbels; *Der Stürmer*, edited by the *Gauleiter* Julius Streicher, which was overtly anti-Semitic with a seedy range of articles devoted to pornography and violence
- cinema, e.g. *The Eternal Jew; Jud Süss*.

A particular aspect of anti-Semitic indoctrination was the emphasis placed on influencing German youth. The message was obviously put across by the Hitler Youth, but all schools also conformed to new revised textbooks and teaching materials, e.g. tasks and exam questions.

Terror and violence

In the early years of the regime, the SA, as the radical left wing of the Nazis, took advantage of their power at local level to use violence against Jews, e.g. damage to property, intimidation and physical attacks. However, after the Night of the Long Knives in June 1934 (see pages 237–9), anti-Semitic violence became more sporadic for two probable reasons. First, in 1936 there was a distinct decline in the anti-Semitic campaign because of the Berlin Olympics and the need to avoid international alienation. Secondly, conservative forces still had a restraining influence. For example, Schacht had continued to express worries about the implications of anti-Semitic action for the economy (although he resigned in 1937; see page 284).

The events of 1938 were on a different scale. First, the union with Austria in March 1938 resulted, in the following month, in thousands of attacks on the 200,000 Jews of Vienna. Secondly, on 9–10 November 1938 there was a sudden violent **pogrom** against the Jews, which became known as the 'Night of Crystal Glass' (*Kristallnacht*) because of all the smashed glass. *Kristallnacht* started in Berlin and spread throughout Germany with dramatic effects: the destruction of numerous Jewish homes and 100 deaths, attacks on 10,000 Jewish shops and businesses, the burning down of 200 synagogues and the deportation of 20,000 to concentration camps. The excuse for this had been the assassination of Ernst von Rath, a German diplomat in Paris, by

Key dates

Kristallnacht, anti-Jewish pogrom: 9–10 November 1938

Creation of the Reich Central Office for Jewish Emigration: 1939

Key term

Pogrom
An organised or encouraged massacre of innocent people. The term originated from the massacres of Jews in Russia.

Poster for the anti-Semitic film *The Eternal Jew*.

Herschel Grünspan, a Jew, on 7 November. Goebbels had hoped that the anti-Semitic actions might also win Hitler's favour, and compensate for Goebbels' disreputable affair with a Czech actress. Much of the anti-Semitic legislation (see also page 317) came in the months after the pogrom.

Forced emigration

From the start of the Nazi dictatorship some Jews had decided to leave Germany voluntarily. Many Jews with influence, high reputation or sufficient wealth could find the means to leave. The most popular destinations were Palestine, Britain and the USA, and among the most renowned *emigrés* were Albert Einstein, the scientist, and Kurt Weill, the composer.

However, from 1938 a new dimension to anti-Semitism developed – forced emigration. As a result of the events in Austria in 1938, the Central Office for Jewish Emigration was established in Vienna, overseen by Adolf Eichmann. Jewish property was confiscated to finance the emigration of poor Jews. Within six months Eichmann had forced the emigration of 45,000 and the scheme was seen as such a success that, in January 1939, Göring was prompted to create the Reich Central Office for Jewish Emigration run by Heydrich and Eichmann (see Table 13.7).

Table 13.7: The Jewish community in Germany 1933–45

	Jewish population	Emigrés *per annum*
1933	503,000	38,000
1939 (May)	234,000	78,000*
1945	20,000	N/A

* The cumulative figure of Jewish *emigrés* between 1933 and 1939 was 257,000.

It is therefore estimated that the Nazi persecution led to about half of the Jewish population leaving before the war. Technically, the Jews had voluntarily emigrated but they were forced to leave behind all their belongings. Given those circumstances, some assumed that this was just another phase in the history of European pogroms, and would pass. Others felt they were so rooted in Germany that they could not comprehend living elsewhere. Whatever the reason, the remainder decided to take their chances and stay in Germany, rather than lose their homes and all their possessions.

Conclusion

Despite the range of anti-Semitic measures of 1933–9, it is difficult to claim that the Nazis had pursued a planned overall policy to deal with the 'Jewish question'. In many respects the measures were at first haphazard. However, on one point it is very clear – the year 1938 marked an undoubted '**radicalisation**' of Nazi anti-Semitism. The laws, the violence connected with *Kristallnacht* and the forced emigration came together, suggesting that the regime had reached a pivotal year, a fact confirmed by the tone of the speech in the *Reichstag* by Hitler on 30 January 1939:

> If the international Jewish financiers in and outside Europe should succeed in plunging the nations once more into a world war, then the result will not be the Bolshevising [making communist] of the earth, and thus the victory of Jewry, but the annihilation of the Jewish race in Europe.

It is difficult to truly assess how popular the anti-Semitic policies of 1933–9 were with non-Jewish Germans. Certainly there was much anti-Semitism, and it is likely that the initial commercial and social discrimination was generally well received. But

Key question
Why was the year 1938 so significant?

Radicalisation
A policy of increasing severity.

Key term

attitudes to the aftermath of *Kristallnacht* are another matter. By
then, open opposition from non-Jewish Germans would have
been dangerous and there would have been serious consequences
for any dissenters.

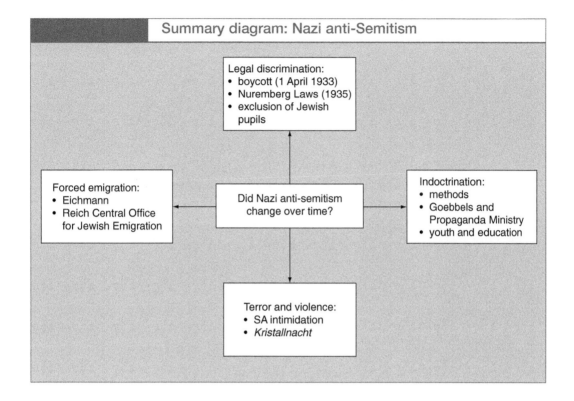

Summary diagram: Nazi anti-Semitism

Legal discrimination:
• boycott (1 April 1933)
• Nuremberg Laws (1935)
• exclusion of Jewish
  pupils

Forced emigration:
• Eichmann
• Reich Central Office
  for Jewish Emigration

Did Nazi anti-semitism
change over time?

Indoctrination:
• methods
• Goebbels and
  Propaganda Ministry
• youth and education

Terror and violence:
• SA intimidation
• *Kristallnacht*

8 | The Key Debate

How popular was the Nazi regime 1933–9?

Assessing the popularity of a regime is far from easy. It is hard
enough in a modern-day democracy, like Britain or Germany,
even when we have access to sophisticated methods of analysis.
Yet, trying to gauge the degree of consent and opposition to a
totalitarian dictatorship is even more difficult. There was not a
black and white distinction, as is shown by the spectrum in
Figure 13.1 on page 322. Moreover, shades of opinion were not
static – they changed over time. So can historians agree on this
one crucial question: how popular was the Nazi regime 1933–9?

The historical sources

Key question
Can historians assess
public opinion in Nazi
Germany?

Historians face serious problems trying to assess public opinion
on the popularity of regime. Significantly, Kershaw, in his book
The Hitler Myth: Image and Reality, states: 'We cannot quantify
Hitler's popularity at any given time during the Third Reich.'
The elections and plebiscites of the 1930s were rigged and the
media were effectively controlled. Nevertheless, two important

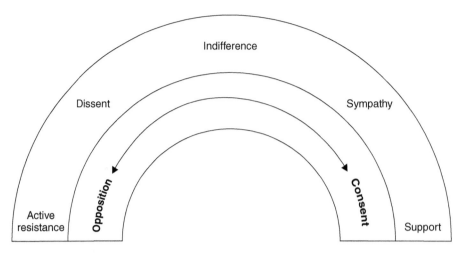

Figure 13.1: A suggested spectrum of public attitudes to the Nazi regime.

sources have been used to understand the nature of public opinion in Nazi Germany.

First, records of the *Gestapo* and SD. By the start of the war 3000 full-time officials co-ordinated information from a broad range of contacts across the whole country and produced analytical reports, such as this one:

> ... the illegal activity of the SPD is the same as that outlined in the newly published guidelines for the conspiratorial work of the KPD; the setting up of cells in factories, sports, clubs and other organisations. Since the former SPD carry on propaganda only by word of mouth, it is very difficult to get hold of proof of their illegal activities which would be used in court. (*Gestapo* report, 1937, of the Düsseldorf area)

Secondly, the records of SOPADE (the SPD in exile). Among the included monthly reports from the SPD's contacts travelling or working secretly underground, such as this one:

> It becomes increasingly evident that the majority of the people have two faces; one which they show to their good and reliable acquaintances; and the other for the authorities, the party officers, keen Nazis, for strangers. The private face shows the sharpest criticism of everything that is going on now; the official one beams with optimism and contentment. (SOPADE report 1937)

Such material is thought-provoking, yet it remains contentious and needs careful evaluation as the sources are highly subjective.

Support and sympathy

It is evident from Chapters 11–13 that many groups of people had good reasons to back the Nazi regime. It is important to highlight the following key factors:

Key question
Who supported the Nazis and why?

- The economic recovery, whether it was strong and genuine or weak and false, represented concrete gains for many German workers. The 'battle for work' substantially reduced the scar of mass unemployment from the human crisis of 1930–3. Although industrial workers may have resented the longer hours and the relatively low wages, they benefited from the restoration of full employment by 1939.
- The diplomatic successes of 1935–9 (which soon gave way to the military victories of 1939–41) were seen as real achievements in foreign policy. For a nation that had lost the First World War and endured the 'shame' of the Versailles Treaty, Hitler was seen as an effective leader in contrast to the failings of Weimar.
- The restoration of political and economic stability was well-received by many people, especially the middle classes, who were afraid of the threat of communism.
- Despite Nazi ideological objectives, many youngsters did enjoy the social and physical aspects of the Hitler Youth.
- The social benefits introduced through the Nazi welfare organisations, such as the KDF and SdA, had a broadly positive effect. Somehow the Nazi regime government did succeed with its practical changes in making the people feel that the government recognised their problems and anxieties.
- Traditional family values – at the expense of women's rights – were not so unpopular, particularly in the rural areas.

These factors contributed greatly, at the very least, to the German people's acceptance or, even, support of the regime (see Table 13.8).

Table 13.8: The results of public opinion polls taken in democratic West Germany, 1948–55

Question: Do you think National Socialism was a good idea only badly carried out? (October 1948)

Yes:	57%
No:	28%
I don't know:	15%

Question: Everything that was built up between 1933 and 1939 was destroyed by the war. Would you say that without the war Hitler would have been one of the greatest ever statesmen? (May 1955)

	Total	Male	Female
Yes, he would have been	48%	51%	45%
No, he would not have been	36%	38%	35%
I don't know	14%	9%	18%
Other answers	2%	2%	2%

Key question
Were the German people deluded by the regime?

Shaped consent

Nevertheless, popular consent was also deliberately 'shaped' by the Nazi regime. Nazi control of all means of communication effectively enabled them to have power over all propaganda and censorship. As shown on pages 262–4 there were limitations to this control, but in the years before the war the propaganda machine was successful in the sense that:

- It cultivated the Hitler myth of him as an effective leader – of almost messianic qualities which glorified him as a 'saviour'.
- It portrayed the Nazi regime and its *Volksgemeinschaft* model as a stabilising force which promised harmony and security after the civil strife and conflicts of the Weimar years.
- It played on frustrated German nationalism.

For many, it was perhaps easier to believe the propaganda than to question it. Historians can question the true impact of the propaganda or marvel at the gullibility of those who were taken in. But to have lived in a society where only one point of view was disseminated must have blunted anyone's powers of judgement. Many people could push to one side their doubts about the regime because of its perceived successes and their memories of Weimar failures.

Terror and surveillance

Also, the Third Reich developed a regime built on terror and intimidation and backed by surveillance. Of course, the terror was not quite as pervasive as was believed at the time (see pages 251–6); nevertheless the brutality must not be underestimated. Civil rights and freedoms were lost and the courts were increasingly made to deliver judgements and sentences which upheld the regime. Any 'outsiders' were sent to camps or held in prison. Therefore, 'an atmosphere of fear' was created where people were coerced into submission. In this way, not only the potential opposition but also the non-committed and the indifferent were made aware of the dangers. Those individuals who were prepared to question must have known that their actions were futile gestures which would end in personal sacrifice.

As the leading historian in this area, Hutteneberger, has written:

> Whatever the perceptible reserve and discontent of the workers, sections of the middle class, and the peasantry, the fact cannot be ignored that the leadership of the Third Reich largely succeeded in producing such a degree of conformity, indeed readiness to collaborate, that its plans, especially preparation for war, were not endangered from within.

Opposition: resistance and dissent

The Third Reich may have had Nazi totalitarian aspirations, yet it fell a long way short of winning the hearts and minds of the German population. Nevertheless, the real threat posed by opponents was fairly limited. Active resistance to undermine the Nazi state could only have come from the élites, and the disillusioned elements did not act together until the late 1930s. Nor did the conservative opposition enjoy a sufficiently strong and broad base of support at any time.

Key question
Who really were the opponents of Nazism?

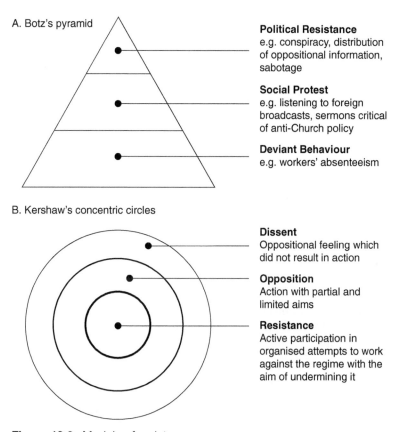

Figure 13.2: Models of resistance.

So in the years after the war historians tended to focus simply on those who actively resisted the regime. Marxist historians from East Germany concentrated almost exclusively on the role of the internal communist opposition and portrayed it as the means to Germany's liberation from fascism by the USSR. On the other hand, in West Germany, the historical writings of Hans Rothfels, *The German Opposition* (1948), and Gerhard Ritter, *The German Resistance* (1958), tended to highlight those famous individuals who valiantly fought for freedom and liberalism. Consequently, the focus of research was on the role of the traditional élites and conservatives.

However, a new generation of historians from the 1970s started to question the nature of the opposition by a completely new historical methodology. Mommsen adopted new research techniques to examine people's attitudes and beliefs at the grass-roots of society through oral history. This was initiated by the so-called Bavaria Project led by Huttenberger and then developed by leading English historians, Mason and Kershaw. The study of opposition to the Nazis has thus been broadened from the narrow area of active resistance to include anyone who did not conform to Nazi expectations.

Not surprisingly, such a methodology has its critics. Many see it as trying to play down active resistance and to exaggerate the importance of mere passive behaviour, which had little real effect on the regime. However, some historians, in an attempt to give clearer definition to the subtle differences of opposition, have proposed 'models' of resistance similar to the methods of social scientists. The models shown on page 325 are merely the suggestions of two historians who have tried to categorise opposition. None of them should be seen as providing all the answers to the problems raised. They are starting-points for discussion and analysis.

Much depends on the particular meanings applied to specific words. More significantly, there are dangers in the drawing of clear-cut boundary-lines; what emerges from all the research is that any individual's behaviour was rarely clear-cut. More often than not, most people exhibited a broad mixture of attitudes, variously shaped by religious, financial, moral or personal influences.

For example, according to Housden's levels of action, it was quite feasible for a Catholic priest to show opposition in the following ways:

• protest publicly over the Nazi euthanasia policy
• deliberately carry on traditional Catholic customs within the community.

Yet, the priest could at the same time:

• still be generally supportive of Nazi foreign/military policy
• sympathise with the more authoritarian nature of Nazi government.

It should also be borne in mind that attitudes were rarely static – circumstances changed over time. Indeed, some of the most important figures in the active resistance among the conservative élites had initially supported the Nazi regime (see page 234).

Conclusion

All the recent evidence suggests that the position of public opinion was a lot more 'fluid' than assumed previously. It may not be possible to give a straight and clear answer to the question of how many people opposed or supported the regime. Nevertheless, it is now possible to make a provisional assessment of the state of play. The range of dissent may have now been identified, but the underlying trend suggests that the regime enjoyed increasing popular support from its consolidation during the peace years – a position that was to be maintained until the winter of 1942–3. The regime enjoyed a trend of consensus that was not realistically threatened.

Some key books in the debate

M. Housden, *Resistance and Conformity in the Third Reich* (Routledge, 1997).

Ian Kershaw, *The Hitler Myth: Image and Reality in the Third Reich* (Oxford, 2001).

D. Peukert, *Inside Nazi Germany: Conformity, Opposition and Racism in Everyday Life* (Yale University Press, 1989).

Hans Rothfels, *The German Opposition* (1948).

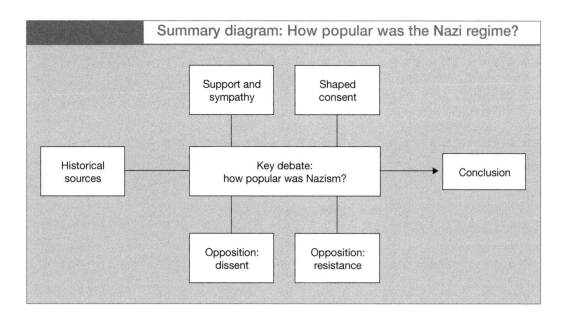

Summary diagram: How popular was the Nazi regime?

Study Guide: A2 Question

How far do you agree with the view that the Nazi regime was strong and successful throughout the period 1935–9? Explain your answer, using the evidence of Sources 1–3 and your own knowledge of the issues related to this controversy.

Source 1

From: W.S. Allen, The Nazi Seizure of Power, *published in 1968.*

The *Gestapo* report of December 1935 was even gloomier.

Protestants were secretly circulating anti-Nazi writing; the Catholic Church was systematically and ceaselessly trying to make its followers anti-Nazi. The lower classes were ripe for recruitment by the workers underground. People were still shopping in Jewish stores. Former Conservatives were disgusted with the party. Thus there were many elements dissatisfied with the Third Reich in 1935, for almost as many different reasons as there were identifiable groups. And that is one of the major reasons disaffection was not likely to produce any organised opposition or cohesive action against the NSDAP.

Source 2

From: Hans Mommsen, German Society and the Resistance Against Hitler, *published in 1999.*

During the second stage of its evolution, from 1935 to 1938, the resistance is marked by both the growth of conspiratorial forms of association (in particular among working-class resistance groups), and the consolidation of organisations in exile in Czechoslovakia, the Netherlands and France. Yet, even during this period, most resisters continued to deceive themselves by their belief that an anti-fascist mass movement would emerge to overthrow the Nazi regime. This kind of self-deception would find its reflection in illegal propaganda and information material. By the end of the period it had, however, become clear that the illegal groups which attempted to expand beyond a close circle of like-minded individuals were doomed to be crushed.

Source 3

From: Ian Kershaw, Hitler 1936–45, *published in 2000.*

To most observers, both internal and external, after four years in power the Hitler regime looked stable, strong and successful. Hitler's own position was untouchable. The image of the great statesman and national leader of genius, manufactured by propaganda, matched the sentiment and expectations of much of the population. The internal rebuilding of the country and the national triumphs in foreign policy, all attributed to his genius, had made him the most popular political leader of any nation in Europe. Most ordinary Germans – like most ordinary people anywhere most times – looked forward to peace and prosperity. Hitler appeared to have established the basis of these. He had restored authority to government. Law and order had been re-established. Few were concerned if civil liberties had been destroyed in the process. There was work again. The economy was booming. What a contrast this was to the mass unemployment and economic failure of Weimar democracy.

Of course, there was still much to do and many grievances remained. Not least, the conflict with the churches was the source of great bitterness.

Exam tips

In considering the nature of the Nazi regime, you are asked to consider two adjectives: strong and successful. You are asked to consider them 'throughout the period 1935–9'. You will need to use your cross-referencing skills again here to identify the issues the sources raise and then develop these issues from your own knowledge.

The quotation comes from Source 3, so begin there and identify points which you can put under the two headings: 'strong' and 'successful', each of which is subdivided with a yes and no column (yes this point suggests strength or no this point suggests weakness). Some points which indicate both strength and success can go under both headings, but if you separate it this way it will help you to see where the sources – and afterwards your own knowledge – help you to make distinctions. Now use Sources 1 and 2 to complete the picture from the sources. Note where there are links between them – for example on the issue of the Catholic Church (Sources 1 and 3).

Before you integrate your own knowledge into your plan, it will be helpful to read Chapters 11–13. Think about the nature and strength/weakness of opposition in Germany. The strength of a regime can be measured partly in terms of the strength or weakness of opposition to it. The regime also had its own sources of strength.

When deploying information of your own, always use the sources as a starting point to help you think about what own knowledge to use. See the points in Source 3 which show that 'Hitler's position was untouchable'. You can develop these from your own knowledge.

How will you measure 'successful'? It is not the same as 'strong'. Use the points in Source 3 as a starting point and add your own knowledge here, too. What will your conclusion be? Note that Source 3 indicates some limitations to success, as well as considerable successes. An argument along those lines could be developed if you wish to challenge the statement.

14 Germany at War 1939–45

POINTS TO CONSIDER

This chapter looks at the domestic impact of the war in Germany, rather than the conduct of military operations. Its effects will be considered within the broad context of racism, opposition, the direction of the economy and morale – issues that have already been raised in the previous three chapters. The following main themes will be explored:

- The military war
- The Nazi war economy
- Genocide
- Key debate: Why did the Holocaust happen and who was responsible?
- Civilian morale
- Resistance and repression
- Germany's military defeat

Key dates

1939	September 1	German invasion of Poland
	September 3	Britain and France declared war on Germany
	December	Hitler's war economy decrees
1941	June 22	'Operation Barbarossa' – German invasion of USSR
	August	Bishop Galen's sermon against euthanasia
	December 11	German declaration of war on USA
1942	January	Wannsee Conference – 'Final Solution' to exterminate the Jewish people
	February	Appointment of Albert Speer as Minister of Armaments
	November	German defeat at El Alamein
1942–3		White Rose student group; distribution of anti-Nazi leaflets
1943–4		Transportation of Jews from German-occupied Europe to death camps
1943	January	German surrender at Stalingrad

	February 18	Goebbels' speech rallied the people for a 'total war'
	July 24	Hamburg fire-storm
1944	June 6	Allied landings in Normandy, France
	July 20	Stauffenberg Bomb Plot failed to overthrow the regime
	August	Peak of German munitions production
	November	Execution of 12 Edelweiss Pirates in Cologne
1945	May 7–8	German surrender: occupation and division of Germany

1 | The Military War

Key question
Why was Germany so successful in 1939–41?

In *Mein Kampf* Hitler openly stated his ambitions for foreign policy. Indeed, some historians believe that Hitler had a clearly defined set of objectives, which amounted to a 'stage-by-stage plan':

• The destruction of the Treaty of Versailles and the restoration of Germany's pre-1914 boundaries.
• The union of all German-speaking peoples such as Austria, western Poland, the borders of Czechoslovakia (the Sudetenland) and provinces in Hungary and Romania.
• The creation of *Lebensraum* – the establishment of a Nazi racial empire by expanding into eastern Europe at the expense of the Slavic peoples, particularly in Poland and Russia.

In the years 1935–8 Germany rapidly made some key gains which changed the continental balance of power:

• The Treaty of Versailles was challenged by the creation of an airforce and by the introduction of a conscripted army of 555,000 (March 1935).
• The remilitarisation of the Rhineland (March 1936).
• The *Anschluss* ('union') with Austria (March 1938).
• The Munich Agreement which ceded the German-speaking Sudetenland to Germany (September 1938).

However, once Nazi Germany had militarily occupied the non-German lands of Czechoslovakia in March 1939, Britain and France found it difficult to tolerate further German expansionism and immediately guaranteed to uphold the independence of Poland. Thus, when the German armed forces attacked Poland on 1 September 1939 Britain and France were obliged to declare war.

Although Germany found itself committed to a major war in the autumn of 1939, which Hitler had not expected to wage until the mid-1940s, Germany was not militarily destined to fail from the start. The string of victories from September 1939 to November 1941 bears witness to the military power exerted by the Nazi war-machine and suggests that Germany did not have to go

Key dates

German invasion of Poland:
1 September 1939

Britain and France declared war on Germany:
3 September 1939

down the road to total collapse. However, by early 1943 Germany faced serious military reverses, but Germany's eventual defeat was not inevitable. It has to be explained, not merely assumed.

Initial victories

Without direct help from Britain or France, Poland was crushingly defeated by Germany's *Blitzkrieg* tactics within a few weeks. This gave the Germans access to valuable raw materials and labour as well as the aid received from the USSR under the terms of the **Nazi–Soviet Pact**. Hitler was, therefore, keen to maintain the military momentum and planned for an invasion of France to take place as early as November 1939. But the German attack was postponed several times, mainly because of the lukewarm attitude of senior army generals towards such an operation.

Phoney war

The German attack on the Western Front did not finally take place until May 1940, thus prolonging the Anglo-French '**phoney war**' for eight months. Hitler's thinking seems to have revolved around the idea of removing the threat posed by the Western democracies before turning east again. To that end Germany needed to 'destroy France' and to make Britain accept German aspirations on the continent. In this way it was hoped to force Britain, under the pressure of military circumstances, into a 'deal' with Germany.

The Low Countries and France

The German defeat of the Low Countries (Belgium and the Netherlands) and France within six weeks was a dramatic triumph for both the armed forces and Hitler. Diffident generals could hardly fail to be impressed by the *Führer*'s military and political handling of events. German popular opinion was relieved and triumphant. Hitler ruled not only in Berlin but also in Paris, Oslo, Vienna, Prague and Warsaw, while the Third Reich was bordered by the three 'friendly' powers of Spain, Italy and the USSR. It was assumed by many that the war was as good as over.

The Battle of Britain

If self-interest had prevailed, Britain would have settled with Germany. However, the new British Prime Minister, Churchill, refused even to consider negotiations. The implications of this stubbornness for Germany were clear-cut: Germany needed to secure air superiority in order to invade Britain and to disable its military and strategic potential. Thus, Germany's failure to win the **Battle of Britain** in the autumn of 1940 was significant. Yet, even more so was Hitler's personal decision to switch the military focus, and to start preparing for the invasion of the USSR even before Britain had been neutralised.

Operation Barbarossa

On 18 December 1940 Hitler issued Directive No. 21 for 'Operation Barbarossa', stating that 'The German armed forces must be prepared to crush Soviet Russia in a quick campaign

Nazi–Soviet Pact
A non-aggression pact of 1939 between the USSR and Germany that opened the way for the invasion of Poland.

Phoney war
Used to describe the war period from September 1939 to May 1940 because there was no real aggressive activity on the Western Front.

Battle of Britain
Name given to the air battle fought over the skies of southern England between the RAF and the Luftwaffe, July–October 1940.

Key dates

'Operation Barbarossa' – German invasion of USSR: 22 June 1941

German declaration of war on USA: 11 December 1941

even before the end of the war against England.' This decision can only be explained by Hitler's belief that *Blitzkrieg* tactics could also succeed in bringing a quick victory against the USSR, as they had against Poland, France and the Low Countries.

The German invasion of the USSR eventually took place on 22 June 1941. It was delayed by the need to invade Yugoslavia and Greece in order to secure Germany's southern flank. At first all went well. Vast tracts of Russian territory were occupied and thousands of prisoners were taken, so that by November 1941 German troops were only miles from Moscow and Leningrad.

Reasons for success

The German military advance was the high-point of the war and in the years 1939–41 it was phenomenally successful for the following reasons:

- France and Britain failed to take the initiative and Poland was left to fight alone.
- Germany's *Blitzkrieg* strategy of rapid advances outmanoeuvred all of its enemies in the first two years.
- The French defensive strategy was based on the Maginot Line and it proved to be powerless in the face of German *Blitzkrieg* tactics. As a result the French political and military leadership lost the will to resist.

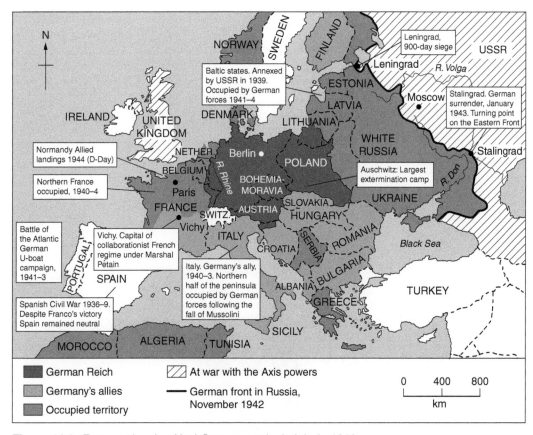

Figure 14.1: Europe, showing Nazi Germany at its height in 1942.

- Germany's expansion (from 1938) allowed it to exploit all the labour and resources of those countries for its own purposes.
- The USSR was taken by surprise by the German attack and was not really prepared.

However, despite Germany's successes, the military advance halted in December 1941. The Soviets had never lost the will to carry on fighting while Anglo-American aid and the snows of Russia combined to consolidate the Eastern Front. Hitler's gamble to break the USSR by launching a *Blitzkrieg* invasion had failed and Germany was now faced with the prospect of a long war on two fronts.

The 'turn of the tide'

December 1941 was significant in another sense too, for, in that month, the Japanese attack on the US naval base at **Pearl Harbor** 'globalised' the conflict. Although he was not obliged to do so, Hitler aligned Germany with Japan and declared war on the USA. This move was perhaps prompted by the USA's involvement in the **Battle of the Atlantic** even before Pearl Harbor. However, it did not fit easily with Germany's existing strategy and above all it turned the industrial capacity of the world's greatest power against it. It is tempting therefore to suggest that by the end of 1941 Hitler had lost the military and diplomatic grasp which had previously allowed him to shape international developments. Events were now very much running out of the *Führer*'s control.

Yet, although it appears that the events of December 1941 were the vital turning point for German fortunes in the war, this was certainly not apparent at the time. Throughout 1942 German forces pushed deep into the Caucasian oilfields with the objective of capturing Stalingrad, while the Afrika Korps drove the British back across North Africa into Egypt. It was the eventual failure of these two offensives that enabled contemporaries to see the winter of 1942–3 as the '**turn of the tide**': the British victory at El Alamein eventually led to the ejection of German forces from North Africa; and the encirclement and surrender of 300,000 troops at Stalingrad marked the beginning of the Soviet counter-offensive.

Defeat

From 1943 Germany's strategy was essentially defensive. Hitler was determined to protect 'Fortress Europe' from Allied invasion, but possibly his strategic and political thinking was losing touch with reality. Increasingly it became shaped by his belief in German invincibility and his own ideological prejudices about race and communism. For example, in spite of all the military difficulties, the creation of the new racial order continued – there was no postponement of the Final Solution. Hitler deluded himself into thinking that the alliance of the USSR and the Western Allies could not last and that this would then allow Germany to play off one against the other.

Key terms

Pearl Harbor
A US military base in the Pacific.

Battle of the Atlantic
The naval struggle between the Allied convoys and the German U-boats in the northern Atlantic.

Key question
When and why did the military balance turn against Germany?

Key dates

German defeat at El Alamein: November 1942

German surrender at Stalingrad: January 1943

Key term

Turn of the tide
The term used to describe the Allied military victories in the winter of 1942–3, when the British won at El Alamein in North Africa and when the Russians forced the surrender of 300,000 German troops at Stalingrad.

Key question
Why could Germany not resist the Allied advance?

Key dates

Allied landings in Normandy: 6 June 1944

German surrender: occupation and division of Germany: 7–8 May 1945

Key term

Unconditional surrender Roosevelt and Churchill's statement in 1943 that the Allies would not accept a negotiated peace.

However, Allied military co-ordination continued to work reasonably well. By the end of 1943 Anglo-American forces had linked up in Africa and had then established a hold on southern Italy, while Soviet forces had reconquered much of the Ukraine after the great tank victory at the battle of Kursk in July 1943. The war had also begun to have an impact on Germany itself. The massive bombing raids caused destruction and dislocation, although their exact strategic value has been questioned over the years. It was becoming clear that the war could not be won by Germany and that it faced total devastation unless the Allied demand for **unconditional surrender** was accepted.

Such realities prompted the attempted assassination of Hitler in July 1944 (see pages 335–6). Its failure meant that the war would have to be fought to the bitter end. Thus, strong German resistance forced the Western Allies to fight extremely hard in order to break out of the beach-head established in Normandy, France, in 1944, while in the east the Soviet advance progressed through eastern Europe in the face of desperate defensive measures. Yet, even then a blind optimism still prevailed in the minds of some Germans. It was not until 30 April 1945 that Hitler committed suicide when Soviet soldiers had advanced to within a mile of the Chancellery in Berlin. Only then was the German nation freed from the *Führer*'s command and Germany surrendered on 7–8 May.

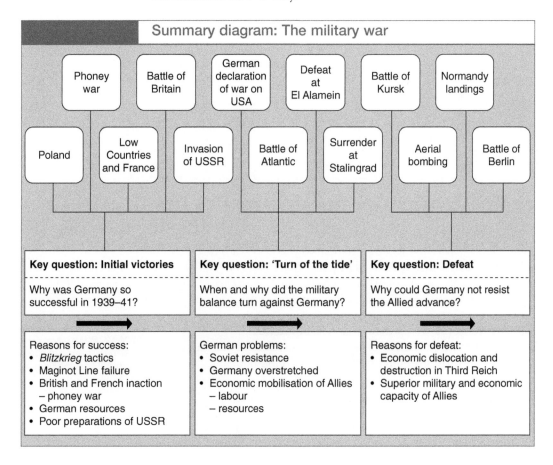

Summary diagram: The military war

| Phoney war | Battle of Britain | German declaration of war on USA | Defeat at El Alamein | Battle of Kursk | Normandy landings |

| Poland | Low Countries and France | Invasion of USSR | Battle of Atlantic | Surrender at Stalingrad | Aerial bombing | Battle of Berlin |

Key question: Initial victories

Why was Germany so successful in 1939–41?

Key question: 'Turn of the tide'

When and why did the military balance turn against Germany?

Key question: Defeat

Why could Germany not resist the Allied advance?

Reasons for success:
- *Blitzkrieg* tactics
- Maginot Line failure
- British and French inaction – phoney war
- German resources
- Poor preparations of USSR

German problems:
- Soviet resistance
- Germany overstretched
- Economic mobilisation of Allies – labour – resources

Reasons for defeat:
- Economic dislocation and destruction in Third Reich
- Superior military and economic capacity of Allies

2 | The Nazi War Economy

The string of military successes achieved by the German armed forces with their use of *Blitzkrieg* strategy up to December 1941 won Hitler and the regime valuable popular support. Moreover, it gave the impression of an economy that had not been over-strained by the demands of war. Such a view, however attractive, does not actually square with either Nazi intentions or the economic statistics.

The expansion of the Nazi economy

First, Hitler was determined to avoid the problems faced by Germany in the First World War and to fight the coming war with an economy thoroughly prepared for a major and perhaps extended conflict. To this end, a series of war economy decrees was issued by Hitler in December 1939 outlining vast programmes for every possible aspect of war production, e.g. submarines and aircraft. These plans suggest that the Nazis went well beyond the demands of *Blitzkrieg* and a limited war.

Secondly, in real and percentage terms, German military expenditure doubled between 1939 and 1941, as shown by Table 14.1. (However, the figures have important implications, as Britain trebled expenditure in the same categories.)

Key question
How did the German economy expand?

Key date
Hitler's war economy decrees: December 1939

Table 14.1: Military expenditure of Germany and Britain

Year	Germany (RM billions)			Britain (£ billions)		
	GNP	Military expenditure	Military expenditure as a % of GNP	GNP	Military expenditure	Military expenditure as a % of GNP
1937	93	11.7	13	4.6	0.3	7
1938	105	17.2	17	4.8	0.4	8
1939	130	30.0	23	5.0	1.1	22
1940	141	53.0	38	6.0	3.2	53
1941	152	71.0	47	6.8	4.1	60

Thirdly, food rationing in certain items was introduced from the very start of the war and the German labour force was rapidly mobilised for war so that, by the summer of 1941, 55 per cent of the workforce was involved in war-related projects – a figure which then only crept up to a high-point of 61 per cent by 1944. In this light it is hardly surprising that the first two years of war also witnessed a 20 per cent decline in civilian consumption.

The limitations of economic mobilisation

However, despite the intent of wholesale mobilisation the actual results, in terms of armaments production, remained disappointingly low. Admittedly, there was a marked increase in the number of submarines, but amazingly, Germany's airforce had only increased from 8290 aircraft in 1939 to 10,780 in 1941 while in Britain over the same period the number of aircraft had

Key question
To what extent did the Nazis fail to mobilise the economy during the war?

trebled to 20,100. Likewise, Hitler was astonished to learn when drawing up plans for the invasion of the USSR that the Germans' armoured strength totalled only 3500 tanks, which was just 800 more than for the invasion of the West.

It seems that despite the Nazi image of German order and purposefulness, the actual mobilisation of the German economy was marred by inefficiency and poor co-ordination. The pressures resulting from the premature outbreak of war created problems, since many of the major projects were not due to be ready until 1942–3. So, at first, there was undoubtedly confusion between the short-term needs and long-term plans of the Nazi leadership.

Nevertheless, this should not have been an impossible barrier if only a clear and authoritative central control had been established over the economy. Instead, a host of different agencies all continued to function in their own way and often in a fashion which put them at odds with each other. So, although there was a Ministry of Armaments, it existed alongside three other interested governmental ministries, those of Economics, Finance and Labour. In addition, there was political infighting between the leading Nazi figures – for example, the *Gauleiters* tried to control their local areas at the expense of the plans of the state and the party – and also considerable financial corruption.

There were a number of groups responsible for armaments: the Office of the Four-Year Plan, the SS bodies and the different branches of the armed forces, **Wehrmacht**, *Luftwaffe* and navy. The armed forces, in particular, were determined to have their way over the development of munitions with the very best specifications possible and as a result the drive for quality was pursued at the expense of quantity. The consequence of all this was that after two years of war, and with the armed forces advancing into the USSR, Germany's economic mobilisation for total war had not achieved the expected levels of armaments production.

Total war 1942–5

By the end of 1941, Germany was at war with Britain, the USSR and the USA and yet its armaments production remained inferior to that of Britain. Preparations for a new approach had begun in the autumn of 1941 and Hitler had issued a 'Rationalisation Decree' in December of that year which had intended to eliminate the waste of labour and materials.

However, it was the appointment of Albert Speer as Minister of Armaments in February 1942 that marked the real turning point. Speer had previously been the *Führer*'s personal architect and he enjoyed excellent relations with Hitler. He now used the *Führer*'s authority to cut through the mass of interests and to implement his programme of 'industrial self-responsibility' to provide mass production. The controls and constraints previously placed on business, in order to fit in with Nazi wishes, were relaxed. In their place a Central Planning Board was established in April 1942, which was in turn supported by a number of committees, each

Profile: Albert Speer 1905–81

1905	– Born in Mannheim
1924–8	– Trained as an architect at Karlsruhe and Munich
1931	– Joined the Nazi Party
1934	– Became Hitler's personal architect
1942	– Minister of Armaments
1946	– Sentenced to 20 years at the Nuremberg trials
1966	– Released from Spandau prison
1969	– Publication of his books, *Inside the Third Reich* and *Spandau: The Secret Diaries*
1981	– Died in London on a visit

Speer remains as an interesting, and significant, figure on several counts:

- He was a talented and able architect who was commissioned for the design of the German pavilion at the Paris Exhibition (1937) and the Reich Chancellery in Berlin. His close friendship with Hitler and their common interest in architecture allowed him to exert increasing political influence.
- He proved himself a skilful manager of the war economy, resulting in a fundamental increase in arms production, 1942–4.
- Despite his friendship with Hitler, he clashed with leading Nazis, particularly Himmler.
- He always claimed after the war that he opposed forced labour in the occupied countries, yet his opponents maintained that this policy had more to do with efficiency than morality, and even claimed that he was aware of the treatment of the Jews.

representing one vital sector of the economy. This gave the industrialists a considerable degree of freedom, while ensuring that Speer as the director of Central Planning was able to maintain overall control of the war economy. Speer also encouraged industrialists and engineers to join his ministerial team. At the same time, wherever possible, he excluded military personnel from the production process.

Speer was what would now be called a 'technocrat'. He simply co-ordinated and rationalised the process of war production and more effectively exploited the potential of Germany's resources and labour force. Speer was able to exert influence because of his friendship with Hitler and he used his personal skills to charm or blackmail other authorities. In this way, he took a whole range of other personal initiatives to improve production, such as:

- employing more women in the arms factories
- making effective use of concentration camp prisoners as workers
- preventing skilled workers being lost to military conscription.

Key date

Goebbels' speech rallied the people for a 'total war': 18 February 1943

The successes and limitations of Speer's economic rationalisation

In a famous speech in February 1943, after the German army surrender at Stalingrad, Goebbels invited the crowd to support 'total war'. However, the transformation of the Nazi economy really pre-dated Goebbels' propagandist appeal to 'total war' and was down to the work of Speer. As a result of Speer's first six months in power:

- ammunition production increased by 97 per cent
- tank production rose by 25 per cent
- total arms production increased by 59 per cent.

By the second half of 1944, when German war production peaked, it can be noted that there had been more than a three-fold increase since early 1942 (see Tables 14.2 and 14.3).

Table 14.2: Number of German, British, US and USSR tanks produced 1940–5

	Germany	Britain	USA	USSR
1940	1,600	1,400	300	2,800
1941	3,800	4,800	4,100	6,400
1942	6,300	8,600	25,000	24,700
1943	12,100	7,500	29,500	24,000
1944	19,000	4,600	17,600	29,000
1945	3,900	N/A	12,000	15,400

The ruins of Berlin in May 1945.

Table 14.3: Number of German, British, US and USSR aircraft produced 1940–5

	Germany	Britain	USA	USSR
1940	10,200	15,000	6,100	7,000
1941	11,000	20,100	19,400	12,500
1942	14,200	23,600	47,800	26,000
1943	25,200	26,200	85,900	37,000
1944	39,600	26,500	96,300	40,000
1945	N/A	12,100	46,000	35,000

Despite Speer's economic successes, Germany probably had the capacity to produce even more and could have achieved a level of output close to that of the USSR or the USA. He was not always able to counter the power of the party *Gauleiters* at a local level and the SS remained a law unto themselves, especially in the conquered lands. Indeed, although the occupied territories of the Third Reich were well and truly plundered, they were not exploited with real economic efficiency. Above all, though, from 1943 Speer could not reverse the detrimental effects of Anglo-American bombing.

After the war, 'blanket bombing' by the Allies was condemned by some on moral grounds and its effectiveness denied; indeed, critics pointed to Speer's production figures as proof that the strategy had failed to break the German war economy. However, it is probably more accurate to say that the effects of bombing prevented Germany from increasing its levels of arms production even further. The results of Allied bombing caused industrial destruction and breakdown in communications. Also, Germany was forced to divert available resources towards the construction of anti-aircraft installations and underground industrial sites. Because of this Germany was unable to achieve a total war economy. As it was, German arms production peaked in August 1944 at a level well below its full potential.

In the end, the Nazi economy had proved incapable of rising to the demands of total war and the cost of that failure was all too clearly to be seen in the ruins of 1945. (See also pages 357–60.)

> **Key date**
>
> Peak of German munitions production: August 1944

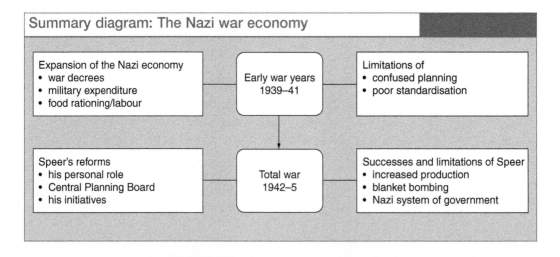

Summary diagram: The Nazi war economy

Expansion of the Nazi economy
- war decrees
- military expenditure
- food rationing/labour

Early war years 1939–41

Limitations of
- confused planning
- poor standardisation

Speer's reforms
- his personal role
- Central Planning Board
- his initiatives

Total war 1942–5

Successes and limitations of Speer
- increased production
- blanket bombing
- Nazi system of government

Key term

Ghetto
An ancient term used to describe the area lived in by the Jews in a city. In the years of Nazi occupation the Jews were separated from the rest of the community and forced to live in ghettos. The Jewish population was heavily concentrated and lived in appalling conditions.

Key question
How did Nazi anti-Semitism degenerate into genocide?

Key term

SS *Einsatzgruppen*
Means 'Action Units'. Four of the units were launched in eastern Europe after the invasion of Russia. They were responsible for rounding up local Jews and murdering them by mass shootings.

3 | Genocide

It is clear that the months before the war marked an undoubted radicalisation in Nazi anti-Semitism (see pages 318–20). However, at the time it was inconceivable to imagine that the Holocaust was possible. Who in 1939 could have predicted the scenario of the next six years? The suggestion that millions would be systematically exterminated would have defied belief. It is an event in modern European history which even now seems almost beyond rational comprehension, although it had a terrifying logic to it. For those who lived in occupied Europe it was easier and more comfortable to dismiss the rumours as gross and macabre exaggerations – the result of wartime gossip and Allied propaganda. Yet, the unbelievable did happen and it required not only the actions of a 'criminal' minority but also the passivity of the 'innocent' majority. In Germany the moral dimension has helped to make this historical debate a particularly impassioned one.

From emigration to extermination

Germany's victory over Poland in autumn 1939 (see page 332) meant that the Nazis inherited responsibility for an estimated three million Jewish people. Moreover, the beginning of a general European war made emigration of Jews to independent countries more difficult. However, plans to 'resettle' so many people placed such a great strain on food supplies and the transportation system that, in the short term, the Nazi leadership in Poland were compelled to create a number of Jewish **ghettos**, e.g. Warsaw, Krakow and Lublin.

The invasion of Russia in the summer 1941 marked a decisive development. From that time, it was seen as a racial war launched by the **SS *Einsatzgruppen*** which moved in behind the advancing armies. These four special 'Action Units' were responsible for rounding up local Jews and murdering them by mass shootings. During the winter of 1941–2 it is estimated that *Einsatzgruppen*

Table 14.4: The Nazi extermination of the Jews 1940–5

1940		First deportations of Jews from certain German provinces
1941	June	Action squads (*Einsatzgruppen*) of SS moved into the USSR behind the advancing armies to round up and kill Jews
1941	1 September	All Jews forced to wear the Yellow Star of David
1942	20 January	Wannsee Conference. Various government and party agencies agreed on the 'Final Solution' to the Jewish problem
	Spring	Extermination facilities set up at Auschwitz, Sobibor and Treblinka
1943	February	Destruction of Warsaw Ghetto
1943–4		Transportation of Jews from all over German-occupied Europe to death camps began
1945	27 January	Liberation of Auschwitz by Soviet troops

had killed 700,000 Jews in western Russia, but the bloody process clearly raised the practical implications for the Nazi leadership of finding a '**Final Solution**' to the Jewish question.

Nevertheless, there remains uncertainty and debate over when exactly it was decided to launch the genocide of the Jews (see pages 344–6). Options were probably being considered during autumn 1941, but it was only agreed as a result of the Wannsee Conference on 20 January 1942. There, in no more than a few hours, a meeting, chaired by Heydrich and organised by Eichmann, outlined the grim details of the plan to use gas to kill Europe's 11 million Jews.

In the course of 1942 a number of camps were developed into mass extermination centres in Poland, most notably Auschwitz, Sobibor and Treblinka. Most of the Polish Jews were cleared from their ghettos and then 'transported' by train in appalling conditions to their death in gas chambers. It is believed that, of the original three million Polish Jews, only 4000 survived the war. In 1943–4 Jews from all over Europe were deported to face a similar fate – so that by 1945 it is estimated that six million European Jews had been murdered.

Key term

Final Solution
A euphemism used by the Nazi leadership to describe the extermination of the Jews from 1941, although in the earlier years the term had been used before there was any real overall plan.

Key dates

Wannsee Conference. 'Final Solution' to exterminate the Jewish people: January 1942

Transportation of Jews from all over German-occupied Europe to death camps: 1943–4

Henru Pieck, *Behind Barbed Wire*. Painting drawn in Buchenwald concentration camp.

Profile: Reinhard Heydrich 1904–42

1904	– Born at Halle in Saxony, Germany
1922–8	– Joined the navy, but discharged (probably for a sexual offence against a woman)
1931	– Joined the NSDAP and the SS
1932	– Appointed leader of the newly created SD (the party's intelligence security service, see pages 252–3)
1934	– Worked closely with Himmler in the Night of Long Knives
1936	– Appointed Chief of Secret Police (but still under Himmler's authority)
1939	– Created Reich Central Office for Jewish Emigration
	– Appointed Head of RSHA (Reich Security Head Office
1941	– Reich Protector of Bohemia (Czech lands)
1942	– Chaired the Wannsee Conference meeting on 20 January to exterminate the Jews
	– Assassinated in May by the Czech resistance in Prague

Heydrich was undoubtedly talented – he was not only physically the image of the perfect Aryan, but also a good sportsman and a talented musician and linguist. Yet, his skills gave way to the dominating traits of selfishness, ambitious and brutality that earned him the title of 'butcher of Prague'. He advanced quickly within the SS, so at 32 he was appointed Chief of Secret Police. With his abilities he was responsible for:

- running the policing system of surveillance and repression
- implementing the Nazi racial policy
- chairing the notorious meeting at Wannsee Conference which agreed on the Final Solution.

Key question
Why were Gypsies persecuted?

Gypsies

In addition to Jews, Gypsies (Sinti and Roma) were also subject to racial persecution and became victims of Nazi genocide. Gypsies had been viewed as 'outsiders' throughout European history for several clear reasons:

- They were non-Christian and they had their own Romany customs and dialect.
- They were non-white – because they had originated from India in the late medieval period.
- Their 'traveller' lifestyle with no regular employment was resented.

So, even before the Nazi dictatorship and during Weimar's liberal years, there was official hostility towards Gypsies and, in 1929, 'The Central Office for the Fight against the Gypsies' was established.

By 1933 it is believed that the number of Gypsies in Germany was about 25,000 to 30,000 – and they, too, were beginning to suffer from the gradualist policy of Nazi discrimination:

- Gypsies were defined exactly like the Jews as 'infallibly of alien blood' according to the Nuremberg Laws of 1935.
- Himmler issued, in 1938, a directive titled 'The Struggle against the Gypsy Plague', which ordered the registration of Gypsies in racial terms.
- Straight after the outbreak of the war, Gypsies were deported from Germany to Poland – and their movements were severely controlled in working camps. Notoriously, in January 1940, the first case of mass murder through gassing was committed by the Nazis against Gypsy children at Buchenwald.

As with the Jews, the Gypsies during the war were the focus of ever-increasing repression and violence but there was no real, systematic Nazi policy of extermination until the end of 1942. In the first months of 1943 Germany's Gypsies were sent to Auschwitz camp and over 1943–4 a large proportion of Europe's Gypsy population from south-eastern Europe was exterminated: a figure between 225,000 and nearly 500,000.

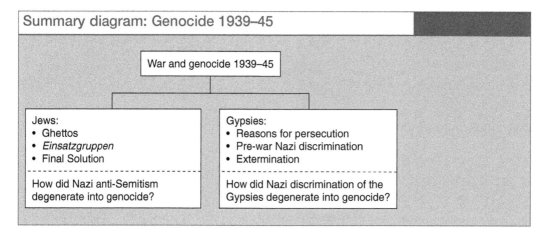

Summary diagram: Genocide 1939–45

4 | The Key Debate

The issue of the Holocaust remains one of the most fundamental controversies in history. The detached rational objectivity required of historical analysis is exceedingly difficult to achieve when the subject is so emotive, and in many respects so irrational. And yet, among all the historical and moral issues, there lies one crucial question:

Why did the Holocaust happen and who was responsible?

Intentionalists

For intentionalist historians, such as Fleming and Dawidowicz, Hitler remains the key. He is seen as having committed himself to the extermination of the Jews at an early stage in his political career. This was followed by a consistent gradualist policy which led logically from the persecution of 1933 to the gates of Auschwitz. In the simplest form they suggest that the Holocaust happened because Hitler willed it.

Goldhagen

Even more controversially, the American historian Daniel Goldhagen has recently suggested in his book *Hitler's Willing Executioners* that the Holocaust was 'intended' because so many ordinary Germans were prepared to participate in the Third Reich's darkest deed. This is explained according to Goldhagen by the fact that within German culture there had developed a violent variant of anti-Semitism which was set on eliminating the Jews. Such a view has resurrected the old argument of 'collective national guilt and shame', although in academic circles Goldhagen's ideas have not been generally well received. He has been condemned for:

- selecting his evidence to prove his thesis
- failing to recognise other overtly anti-Semitic cultures in pre-1933 Europe
- ignoring the role of many non-Germans in the murder of the Jews.

Structuralists

On the other hand, historians of the 'structuralist' school reject the idea of a long-term plan for mass extermination. Most notably, K. Schleunes has suggested that there was no direct path because there was a lack of clear objectives and because of the existence of rival policies. As a result, he describes the road to Auschwitz as a 'twisted one' and concludes, 'the Final Solution as it emerged in 1941 and 1942 was *not* the product of grand design'. Instead, the 'Final Solution', it is suggested, came to be implemented as a result of the chaotic nature of government within the regime. As a result, various institutions and individuals improvised a policy to deal with the military and human situation in eastern Europe by the end of 1941.

Therefore, according to the structuralist interpretation, the moral responsibility for the 'Final Solution' extends beyond Hitler's intentions to the apparatus of the regime. However, nearly all 'structuralist' historians emphasise that this in no way reduces the guilt of Hitler himself, who was in total agreement with such a policy. Mommsen, for example, concluded his analysis as follows:

> It cannot be proved, for instance, that Hitler himself gave the order for the Final Solution, though this does not mean that he did not approve the policy. That the solution was put into effect is by no means to be ascribed to Hitler alone, but to the complexity of the decision-making process in the Third Reich, which brought about a progressive and cumulative radicalisation.

However, structuralists have also distanced themselves from Goldhagen's view because they cannot accept the anti-German generalisations. The reality is, that for the majority of the young men in the action squads and in the camps, their actions were not motivated by any kind of zealous anti-Semitism, but by much more mundane factors. In his chilling description *One Day in Jozefow*, Christopher Browning has detailed how one unit carried out its grim task. What emerges is that the perpetrators were influenced by peer pressure, cowardice, careerism and alcohol – all exaggerated by a brutalising context which was entirely alien to their home environment.

Conclusion

This particular historical debate has proved to be a lively one and it looks set to run for a good while yet. The controversy has generated a very close scrutiny and analysis of all the available evidence, particularly in the past 20 years. So, although the exact details are not clear, it seems fair to conclude the following points about the 'Final Solution':

- It now seems that the initial arrangements for the implementation of the 'Final Solution' were haphazard and makeshift. Hitler and the Nazi leadership did not have any clear programme to deal with the Jewish question until 1941.
- No written order for the killing of the Jews from Hitler has been found, although in January 1944 Himmler publicly stated that Hitler had given him 'a *Führer* order' to give priority to 'the total solution of the Jewish question'. It should be remembered that Hitler's authority was such that it encouraged initiatives from below as long as they were seen to be in line with his overall ideological vision, and clearly Hitler had often spoken in violent and barbaric terms about the Jews from an early stage in his political career.
- Probably around autumn 1941 it was decided by the top Nazi leadership to launch an extermination policy and this was agreed at the Wannsee Conference in January 1942 by a broad range of representatives of Nazi organisations.

If these points are accepted, then it might be that the 'Final Solution' should be viewed as a pragmatic (practical) response to the confusion and chaos of war in 1941–2 rather than the culmination of long-term ideological intent.

Some key books in the debate

C. Browning, *Ordinary Men* (New York, 1992).

Michael Burleigh, *The Racial State: Germany 1933–45* (Cambridge, 1993).

L. Dawidowicz, *The War against the Jews* (Weidenfeld & Nicholson, 1975).

D. Goldhagen, *Hitler's Willing Executioners: Ordinary Germans and the Holocaust* (London, 1996).

K. Schleunes, *The Twisted Road to Auschwitz* (London, 1970).

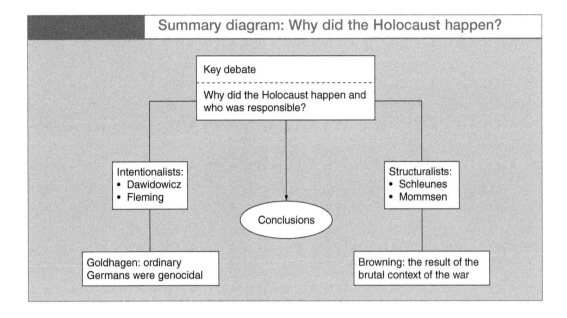

Summary diagram: Why did the Holocaust happen?

Key debate

Why did the Holocaust happen and who was responsible?

Intentionalists:
• Dawidowicz
• Fleming

Conclusions

Structuralists:
• Schleunes
• Mommsen

Goldhagen: ordinary Germans were genocidal

Browning: the result of the brutal context of the war

5 | Civilian Morale

Generally, the onset of the war underlined the totalitarian nature of the Nazi regime. The leadership no longer needed to show any regard for international opinion. However, within Germany the Nazis remained very aware of public opinion and the importance of keeping up the nation's morale.

The declaration of war in September 1939 was not met with the patriotic frenzy of August 1914. Rather the mass of people seemed to be resigned and apprehensive. However, the German strategy of *Blitzkrieg* was incredibly successful and the victories of 1939–40 gave the impression of military and economic strength. Most of the people's doubts were, therefore, put to one side. On Hitler's return journey from France back to Berlin he was met by ecstatic crowds, which were cleverly recorded in the newsreels.

Living and working conditions

Key question
How did the war affect people's living and working conditions?

The Nazi economy was not really ready for a major war in 1939 (see pages 288–90) and as a result, from the earliest days the Nazis had to introduce the rationing of food, clothes and basics like soap and toilet paper. Although the German population was adequately fed – even up until early 1944 its rations were about 10 per cent above the minimum calorific standard – the diet was very boring and restricted. By 1942 consumer goods began to decline and in the final 12 months of the war the situation worsened very dramatically with clear human consequences. For example:

• food rationing led to real shortages (and real hunger by 1945)
• clothes rationing was ended, but only because of the decline in clothes production
• boots and shoes were in short supply
• small luxuries, like magazines and sweets, were stopped.

'One battle, one will, one goal: victory at any cost!' Propaganda poster from May 1942. It conveys the image of ordinary men, women and children on the home front supporting German soldiers fighting on the military front.

Moreover, under the direction of Speer, the economy was geared even more to fighting a 'total war' (see pages 337–40). This meant that every part of German society was focused on the war effort and would have to make real human sacrifices:

- industry was organised more efficiently
- working hours were increased
- millions of foreign workers were encouraged to work (but under controls)
- non-essential businesses were closed.

Women

Most notably the war put great pressure on women; with so many men away during the war, women had to take on more responsibilities both in and out of the home. In fact, Speer even tried to mobilise the economy on a total war footing by suggesting the conscription of women workers. However, he encountered opposition from Hitler, who wished to retain the traditional roles of women in order to maintain civilian morale.

The Nazis were caught in the contradictions of their own ideology between the theory and practice of female employment. They were motivated by military expansionism which needed to

Key question
Why did the war put particular pressure on German women?

By 1943 Allied bombing of German cities had increased to the level that children in cities were being encouraged to go to the countryside for safety. The poster encourages parents to register their children aged 3–14 years for the programme, which was not compulsory.

Kommt mit in die Kinderlandverſchickung

Anmeldungen für die 3–10 jährigen erfolgen bei der NSV.
für die 10–14 jährigen in den Schulen

employ women effectively, so, in the final two years of the Nazi state, more and more women ended up at work. In the cities, long hours in arms factories made life very arduous, especially if women had to combine this with running a household and bringing up children. In the countryside, German women experienced considerable hardship meeting the continuous demands of running farms. The shortage of agricultural labour had created major problems from the 1930s (see pages 295–7), but once the young men were sent away for military service, it got worse. Yet, the government could not bring itself to renounce fully its anti-feminist stance. As an official in the NSF wrote, 'It has always been our chief article of faith that a woman's place is in the home – but since the whole of Germany is our home we must serve wherever we can best do so.'

Key question
What was the extent of Allied bombing on Germany?

Bombing

During the winter of 1942–3 it became impossible for Nazi propaganda and censorship to disguise the reality of the military defeats. Moreover, on the home front, the Anglo-American bombing began to hit the great urban centres of the Ruhr and Berlin day and night. Most famously, on the night of 24 July 1943 a massive raid on Hamburg created a fire-storm that killed 30,000 civilians and left an estimated one million homeless. And controversially, the bombing of Dresden on 13–15 February 1945 (12 weeks before the end of the war) saw 1300 heavy bombers drop over 3900 tons of high-explosive bombs and incendiary devices, destroying 13 square miles of the city.

Hamburg fire-storm: 24 July 1943

Execution of 12 Edelweiss Pirates in Cologne: November 1944

Key dates

By 1945 it is estimated that as a result of the air raids:

- 300,000 Germans were killed
- 800,000 were wounded
- 3.6 million homes were destroyed (20 per cent of the total housing).

Dissent

Key question
How did the war change German people's attitudes?

The effects of the Allied bombing on German civilians (as opposed to the effects on industry, see page 340) have been the subject of considerable discussion. Some have claimed that, despite the difficult circumstances faced by most Germans in the final two years of the war, there was no real sign of a decline of morale leading up to the collapse of the regime itself. Indeed, in the face of Allied mass bombing many people came together against the enemy. Rumpf therefore claims, 'Under the terrible blows of that terror from the skies the bonds grew closer and the spirit of solidarity stronger.'

However, especially from 1943 there was a growing mood of grumbling and complaint. Active resistance (see pages 353–6) was limited, but there was growing disaffection.

Youth

It seems that the appeal of the Hitler Youth became increasingly polarised between fanatics and the disaffected. It was made compulsory in 1939 with increased emphasis on military drill and discipline. Moreover, the standard of teachers and HJ leaders declined, as so many had to fight military service. Of course, the number of young Germans involved with the Pirates remained a small minority, yet interestingly, a youth leader wrote in 1942 that 'the formation of cliques, i.e. groupings of young people outside the Hitler youth … has particularly increased during the war, to such a degree that a serious risk of the political, moral and criminal breakdown of youth must be said to exist'. The Nazi response became increasingly harsh. Various gangs were rounded up by the *Gestapo* and had their heads shaved. In some cases, young people were sent to camps – and most notoriously 12 Edelweiss Pirates were publicly hanged in Cologne.

Churches

As Nazi persecution intensified from 1941 the Churches still posed no active threat to the strength of the regime. However, they did stand against the Nazis' ideology and their totalitarian aspirations. The evidence suggests that Church attendance increased during the war and many individual churchmen put

Profile: Dietrich Bonhoeffer 1906–45

1906	–	Born at Breslau
1923–31	–	Studied at Tübingen, Berlin, Rome and Barcelona
1931–3	–	Lecturer and student pastor at Berlin University
1933–5	–	Worked as a pastor on the outskirts of London
1935	–	Returned to Germany and joined the Confessional Church (see page 307)
1935–7	–	Ran a college to train pastors, but it was quickly closed down
1940–3	–	Banned from preaching and made contact with the active resistance movement
1943	–	Arrested by the *Gestapo* and held in various camps.
1945	–	Murdered in Flossenbürg concentration camp in April

From the very start Bonhoeffer was a consistent opponent of Nazism. However, by 1940, he had moved from religious dissent to political resistance. Over the next three years he:

Key term

Kreisau Circle Name given to the resistance group which met at the estates of Helmut von Moltke.

- helped Jews to emigrate
- was drawn into the **Kreisau Circle** and actively worked with the underground movement
- travelled secretly to Sweden to see an English bishop, Bell, in the hope that Britain would help the resistance.

An SS doctor wrote: 'in nearly 50 years as a doctor I never saw another man go to his death so possessed of the spirit of God'.

their own freedom and lives at risk in order to uphold their beliefs or to give pastoral assistance. It has been estimated that 40 per cent of the Catholic clergy and over 50 per cent of the Protestant pastors were harassed by the Nazis. Most famous were:

- Dietrich Bonhoeffer, whose opposition started as religious dissent but, from 1940, developed into political resistance which brought him into direct contact with elements of the conservative resistance.
- Bishop Galen of Münster, whose outspoken sermon attacking Nazi euthanasia policy in 1941 proved so powerful that the authorities recoiled from arresting him and actually stopped the programme.

Key date

Bishop Galen's sermon against euthanasia: August 1941

Indeed, a *Gauleiter* reported in June 1943: '... the war with all its sorrow and anguish has driven some families into the arms of the priests and the church ... in their weekly reports, the party regional organisations have repeatedly emphasised that the churches of both confessions – but especially the Catholic Church – are in today's fateful struggle one of the main pillars of negative influence upon public morale'.

Conclusion

Reports from the SD comment on civilian morale and public opinion and also tend to confirm that, from 1943, people became increasingly resigned to the coming disaster. By 1944, there had developed a major loss of confidence in the regime. Very interestingly, the source below highlights the deepening cynicism in the nation about the political and military situation after Stalingrad when there was broad criticism of the state and Hitler:

> A large section of the nation cannot imagine how the war will end and the telling of vulgar jokes against the state, even about the *Führer* himself, has increased considerably since Stalingrad. (An SD report, 1943)

Although it is true that active resistance to the war remained very limited (see pages 353–6), popular dissent in various forms developed, as Welch writes in his conclusion on *The Third Reich: Politics and Propaganda*:

> The debacle of Stalingrad undoubtedly affected the morale of the German people. It forced them to question Nazi war aims and led to a crisis of confidence in the regime amongst broad sections of the population.

Table 14.5: The three phases of the war in Germany

Main phases	Key military events	Developments in Germany
1939–41 The years of Nazi victories	Nazi control over Poland and northern and western Europe German invasion of USSR leading to control of most of western USSR	Introduction of food/clothes rationing Casualties limited
1941–3 The 'turn of the tide'	German declaration of war on USA following Japanese attack at Pearl Harbor German defeat at El Alamein German surrender at Stalingrad	'Final Solution' started to exterminate Jews Speer's reforms to mobilise the war economy More resistance developed, but isolated Creation of Kreisau Circle White Rose group of students at Munich
1943–5 'Total war' and defeat	Western Allies' invasion of France: D-Day USSR gained control of eastern Europe, including Berlin German surrender Western Allies' occupation of western Germany	Goebbels' speech rallied the people for a 'total war' Allied mass bombing of Germany, e.g. Hamburg fire-storm Manufacture of clothes ended and clothes rations suspended Stauffenberg's 'July plot' failed Auschwitz liberated by USSR Food only available on black market Dresden bombing: thousands killed in two nights by Allies Hitler's suicide in Berlin

Summary diagram: Civilian morale

6 | Resistance and Repression

'**Active resistance**' to the Nazi regime failed and the Third Reich only collapsed when Germany was defeated by the Allies. So those who organised activities aimed at subverting the regime – however gloriously and heroically portrayed – made enormous personal sacrifices without making any real impression on the Nazi stranglehold of power. The real question is: why did they fail?

Communists

Over half of KPD members were interned during the first year of Nazi rule and by 1935 the *Gestapo* had infiltrated the remains of the party leading to a series of mass trials. Nevertheless, the communist movement was never entirely broken and it went underground. Many small communist cells continued to be formed by Wilhelm Knöckel in many of the large German cities. The most famous of the communist cells was the so-called *Rote Kapelle* (Red Orchestra), a spy network which successfully permeated the government and military through the aristocratic sympathiser Schulz-Boysen. From 1938 to 1942 it transmitted vital information back to Moscow, but all the members were eventually caught and appallingly tortured.

However, the impact of communist activities should not be overstated and German communists failed because:

- They took their orders from Moscow and in the 1930s Stalin purged elements of the whole communist movement.
- They were fatally compromised by the period of co-operation with the USSR as a result of the Nazi–Soviet Pact, 1939–41.
- Even when the USSR and Germany did end up at war with each other in June 1941 the resistance groups remained very isolated.

Key question
Why was active communist resistance to the Nazi state so limited?

Key terms

Active resistance
Suggests opposition by words or action, which tries to undermine or even overthrow the state.

Rote Kapelle
Red Orchestra. The name given to the communist spy network which passed information to the USSR.

Active communist resistance to the Nazi state was limited and in the end it really became more geared towards self-preservation, so that it was ready for the day when Nazism would be defeated and the Soviet 'liberation' could take place.

Students: the White Rose group

The White Rose student resistance movement is probably the most famous of the youth groups because it went beyond mere dissent. It was led by brother and sister Hans and Sophie Scholl. *The White Rose* (the symbol of peace) was the name given to a series of leaflets printed in 1942–3 and distributed initially among the students of Munich University but in time to many towns in central Germany. The content of the leaflets was highly political and openly condemned the moral and spiritual values of the Nazi regime. One of the early leaflets was entitled 'Isn't every decent German today ashamed of his government?'

The group represented a brave gesture of defiance and self-sacrifice. However, from the start the group's security was weak and it was only a matter of time before the *Gestapo* closed in. In February 1943 the six leaders were arrested, tortured and swiftly executed. Sophie Scholl openly said to the court: 'What we wrote and said is in the minds of you all. You just don't say it aloud.'

Key question
Did the White Rose group achieve anything?

White Rose student group and the distribution of anti-Nazi leaflets: 1942–3

Key date

Conservative élites

It might seem surprising that the most influential active resistance emerged from the ranks of Germany's upper classes who dominated the civil service and, most particularly, the officer corps. After all, these were the very same conservative nationalists who had given sympathetic backing to Nazi authoritarianism (see pages 234 and 270–1). Yet, the army as an institution was not fully co-ordinated (until the summer 1944) and therefore it enjoyed a degree of freedom from Nazi control. Moreover, with its access to arms, the army had the real capacity to resist. For these reasons the development of the active resistance of the German élites formed around the army, although once again it was to fail in its primary objective.

Key question
Why did Germany's 'active resistance' fail to undermine the Third Reich?

Kreisau Circle

The opposition of the conservative élites emerged slowly and effective resistance began to re-emerge in the winter months of 1942–3 with the military disasters at El-Alamein and Stalingrad (see page 334). The so-called Kreisau Circle was a wide-ranging group of officers, aristocrats, academics and churchmen who met at the Kreisau estate of Helmut von Moltke. The conferences discussed ideas about plans for a new Germany after Hitler and, in August 1943, a programme was drawn up. The principles of the Kreisau Circle were politically conservative and strongly influenced by Christian values. Indeed, there were pacifist elements in the group who were opposed to a *coup* against Hitler.

Key date

Stauffenberg Bomb Plot failed to overthrow regime: 20 July 1944

Stauffenberg plot

Nevertheless, some individual members were supporters of what became the most far-reaching act of resistance to Hitler's Germany: the Bomb Plot of 20 July 1944. A number of the civilian resistance figures made contact with dissident army officers, such as Beck and Tresckow, in order to plan the assassination of Hitler and the creation of a provisional government. In the words of Tresckow just before the attempted assassination:

> The assassination must take place, whatever the cost. Even if it should fail, the attempt to seize power in Berlin must take place. The practical consequences are immaterial. The German resistance must prove to the world and to posterity that it dares to take the decisive step.

Eventually, the lead was taken by Colonel von Stauffenberg, who came to believe that the assassination of Hitler was the only way to end the Nazi regime. He placed a bomb in Hitler's briefing room at his headquarters in East Prussia on 20 July 1944. Unfortunately, for the conspirators, the briefcase containing the bomb was moved a few yards just a minute before it exploded.

Profile: Claus von Stauffenberg 1907–44

1907	– Born in Bavaria of an aristocratic military family
1926–30	– Joined the Bavarian Cavalry Regiment
1936–8	– Joined the War Academy and graduated first in his class
1939–43	– Fought in Poland, France, Russia and Africa
1942	– Witnessed atrocities in Russia. Started to associate with the Kreisau Circle along with Tresckow
1943	– Promoted to lieutenant-colonel
	– Badly injured in April when his staff car was strafed in Africa. Lost his eye, two left-hand fingers and his right forearm
1944	– After his recuperation he draw up the plan codenamed 'Operation Valkyrie' to kill Hitler. Several attempts aborted in the first half of the year. Detonated the bomb on 20 July at Hitler's headquarters in eastern Germany. Hitler was only injured. Stauffenberg arrested and shot late evening

Stauffenberg was a very able and committed soldier who initially admired Hitler. However, his strong Catholic moral outlook shaped his increasing doubts about the regime by 1941. He remained on the fringes of the Kreisau Circle in 1942–3, but he gave the resistance group a real purpose from early 1944. Stauffenberg personally took the initiative to carry out the assassination, but for his failure he paid the ultimate price – along with his brother.

A photograph taken of the room after Stauffenberg's bomb exploded. Despite the destruction Hitler was only slightly injured.

Hitler thus sustained only minor injuries. In the confused aftermath the generals in Berlin fatally hesitated, thus enabling a group of Hitler's loyal soldiers to arrest the conspirators and re-establish order. About 5000 supporters of the resistance were killed in the aftermath, including Stauffenberg, Beck, Tresckow, Rommel, Moltke and Goerdeler.

Conclusion

The conservative élites proved incapable of fundamentally weakening the Nazi regime and in that sense their active resistance failed. Among the reasons for this are:

- They only recognised the need to resist the regime after the crucial developments of 1934 and 1938, by which time it was too well established.
- The military oath tied the army to the Nazi regime and its leader.
- Hitler's diplomatic and military successes in 1938–42 undoubtedly blinded the élites. Even after the 'turn of the tide' and the growing knowledge of brutal actions, the majority of army generals did not work with the resistance.
- Planning and organisation of effective action was always fraught with difficulties. Their long-term political aims lacked clarity and practical plans were inhibited by the environment of suspicion and uncertainty in a police state.

In the end the bad luck and confusion of the Bomb Plot of 20 July reflected these difficulties.

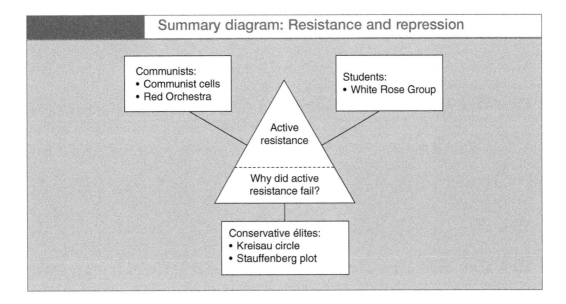

Summary diagram: Resistance and repression

7 | Germany's Military Defeat

Key question
Did Germany have to lose the war?

By May 1945 Germany lay in ruins. Nazi foreign policy had reached its destructive conclusion. Its ambitions had been extensive:

- To establish a 'greater Germany', which went well beyond Germany's 1914 frontiers.
- To destroy Bolshevik Russia.
- To create a new order based on the concept of Aryan racial supremacy.

The means to these ends had involved the acceptance of violence and bloodshed on a massive scale.

On a superficial level, Hitler's final failure in his ambitions could be explained by his strategic bungling. Hitler had always believed (along with most generals going back to Imperial Germany) that a war on two fronts had to be avoided. To this end he needed an alliance with Britain and/or France – or at least their neutrality – so that he could be free to launch an unrestrained attack in the east. Consequently, when Germany failed to secure either British neutrality or a British surrender in 1940–1, before attacking the USSR, the foundations for defeat were laid.

Germany had become engaged in a conflict for which it was not fully prepared. As has been seen on pages 288–90 and 336–8, at the start of the war Germany did not exploit fully the available resources and manpower. The alliance with Mussolini's Italy was also of little gain. Indeed, Italian military weakness in the Balkans and North Africa proved costly, since it diverted German forces away from the main European fronts. Yet, Hitler was driven on ideologically to launch an attack on the USSR with another *Blitzkrieg*.

The failure to defeat the USSR before the onset of winter in 1941, combined with the entry of the USA into the war, now tipped the balance. Britain was still free to act as a launchpad for a Western Front and also, in the meantime, could strike into the heart of Germany by means of aerial bombing. The USSR could maintain the Eastern Front by relying on its geography and sacrificing its huge manpower. As Stalin recognised, the Allied victory could be summarised in his words: 'Britain gave the time; America the money; and Russia the blood.'

Hitler had militarily misjudged the antagonists, and now all the resources and the industrial capacity of the world's two political giants were directed towards the military defeat of Germany. The following economic factors counted against Germany:

- The Four-Year Plan. In 1936 it was meant to make Germany 'fit for war within four years' but the German economy was not really ready for a long war in 1939. Its capacity was only strong enough to sustain a couple of short campaigns.
- Anglo-American bombing. German industry peaked in the production of weapons in summer 1944, yet the German armed forces could not fully benefit from this because of the detrimental effect of Allied air raids.
- From the start Germany was short of labour. Millions of workers were required to keep up the industrial and agricultural production, and the gaps were only partially filled by forced labourers and an increase in female employment.
- Germany was deeply in debt. The reserves in gold and foreign currencies were almost completely used up by 1939 and the Nazi state had run up a debt of roughly 42 billion *Reichsmarks*.
- The US economy was just too powerful. In 1944 the ratio of Germany's fuel supply compared to the supply of the Western Allies was 1:3. The USA sent massive support to the Allies, especially to the USSR which received 13,000 tanks and 15,000 planes.
- Soviet resources. The Soviet economy had undergone a ruthless industrialisation programme in the 1930s under Stalin and despite its limitations, Russia had vast resources of human manpower and raw materials, e.g. oil, coal and iron.

Such explanations might make historical analysis of Germany's defeat in the Second World War seem like a relatively straightforward exercise. However, before accepting such a simple view, it should be borne in mind that, even in 1942, Germany came very close indeed to capturing Stalingrad and to defeating Britain in Egypt. Such successes would have changed the course of the war and the final outcome might have been very different.

Germany in 1945

In the weeks before the capital fell to the Soviets a typical Berliner's joke began to circulate: 'Enjoy the war while you can! The peace is going to be terrible.'

It is no exaggeration to say that the German state had ceased to exist by May 1945. Hitler and Goebbels and a number of other Nazi leaders had committed suicide, while others had fled or been captured and arrested (see the profiles of the main

Key question
How serious was Germany's condition by 1945?

characters). Therefore, central government had broken down. Instead, Germany and Berlin had been divided by the Allies into four zones, each one with their own military commander giving orders and guidelines for the local economy and administration.

But, in the short term, the most telling problem facing Germany in that spring was the extent of the social and economic crisis.

Population displacement

At the end of the war it is estimated that one in two Germans were on the move:

- roughly 12 million German refugees fleeing from the east
- 10 million of the so-called 'displaced persons', who had done forced labour or had been prisoners in the various Nazi camps
- over 11 million German soldiers, who had been taken as prisoners of war: 7.7 million in camps in the west were soon released, whereas the 3.3 million in the USSR were kept in captivity until the 1950s, of whom one-third did not survive.

All these people posed a serious problem to the British and the Americans because of the lack of food.

Urban destruction

Major German cities, especially Cologne, Hamburg and Berlin, had been reduced to rubble because of Anglo-American bombing and Soviet artillery firing (see the photograph on page 339). Twenty per cent of housing had been completely destroyed, and a further 30 per cent badly damaged, which led many to accept sheltered accommodation or to escape to the countryside.

Food and fuel shortages

Food was the immediate problem, but it was soon to be exacerbated by the onset of winter at the end of 1945. The average recommended calorie consumption of 2000 calories sank to 950–1150 and, if it had not been for emergency relief from the Western Allies and care parcels from charities, starvation would have been far worse. This level of malnourishment led to illnesses such as typhus, diphtheria and whooping cough.

Economic dislocation

Surprisingly, the economy had not completely broken down, but it was very badly dislocated. Industrial capacity had obviously declined dramatically, but its destruction was exaggerated at the time. Moreover, the infrastructure of bridges and railways and the utilities, like gas and water, had broken down during the end of the war. Also, the state had massive debts, so Germany was once again facing the problem of a rising inflation causing a major black market in the supply of food and other goods.

The Third Reich had been destroyed in May 1945, but that left Germany in ruins. Violence, destruction and dislocation had brought it to **zero hour**.

Key term

Zero hour
Used in German society to describe Germany's overall collapse at the end of the Second World War.

Summary diagram: Germany's military defeat

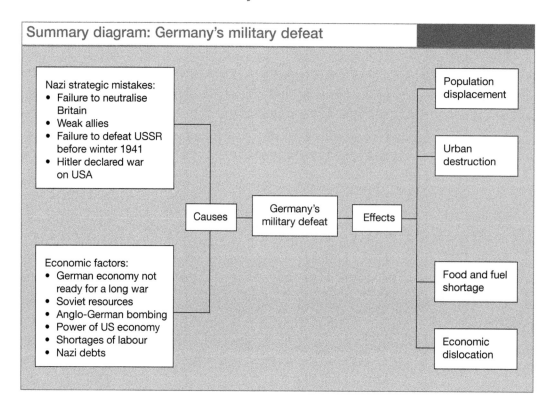

Nazi strategic mistakes:
- Failure to neutralise Britain
- Weak allies
- Failure to defeat USSR before winter 1941
- Hitler declared war on USA

Economic factors:
- German economy not ready for a long war
- Soviet resources
- Anglo-German bombing
- Power of US economy
- Shortages of labour
- Nazi debts

Causes → Germany's military defeat → Effects

- Population displacement
- Urban destruction
- Food and fuel shortage
- Economic dislocation

Study Guide: A2 Question

'The handling of the economy was poorly co-ordinated and this accounts for the weaknesses in German war production in the years 1939–45.' How far do you agree with this view?

Exam tips

The cross-references are intended to take you straight to the material that will help you to answer the question.

You are being asked to consider the accuracy of two judgements: whether the economy was poorly co-ordinated and whether this provides a complete explanation for the weaknesses in war production. You could, if you wish, challenge this view of war production by 1944, but you should still note that, relative to the Allies and relative to Germany's productive capacity, there are weaknesses to be accounted for.

To deal with the first part of the question consider the evidence of:

- the lack of clear central control and the existence of agencies with competing function in 1939–41 (pages 336–7)
- the polices of Speer from 1942: the extent to which they demonstrate both improved direction and improved performance of the economy (pages 337–8).

However, in spite of the dramatic improvements in economic performance under Speer, note the limitations to his successes which were still indicative of the limits of central control:

- the power of party *Gauleiters* at local level (page 340)
- the extent to which the SS remained a law unto themselves, especially in the conquered lands (pages 253–4 and 340).

Finally, consider other factors which account for weak economic performance, significantly the detrimental effect of Allied bombing.

In your conclusion you should make an explicit judgement in relation to both parts of the contention in the question.

Glossary

Active resistance   Suggests opposition by words or action, which tries to undermine or even overthrow the state.

Agrarian League   A *Junkers*-led organisation formed in 1893 with a third of a million members of farmers and landowners.

Alliance   An agreement where members promise to support the other(s), if one or more of them is attacked.

Anglo-French Agreement   A colonial agreement signed by France and Britain in 1904, which evolved into the *Entente Cordiale*.

Annexation   Taking over of another country against its will.

Anschluss   Usually translated as 'union'. In the years 1919–38, it referred to the paragraph in the Treaty of Versailles that outlawed any political union between Germany and Austria, although the population was wholly German.

Anti-capitalism   Rejects the economic system based upon private property and profit. Early Nazi ideas laid stress upon preventing the exploitation of workers and suggesting social reforms.

Anti-feminist   Opposing female advancement.

Anti-German determinist   Believes that the collapse of Weimar democracy and the rise of Nazi dictatorship were bound to happen because of Germany's long-term history and the national character of its people.

Anti-Marxism   Opposition to the ideology of Karl Marx.

Anti-modernism   Strand of opinion which rejects, objects to, or is highly critical of changes to society and culture brought about by technological advancement.

Anti-Semitism   The hatred of Jews.

Arbitration treaty   An agreement to accept the decision by a third party to settle a conflict.

Armistice   An agreement to cease fire before drawing up a peace settlement.

Arms race   A competition between two or more powers for military supremacy. Each power competes to produce larger numbers of weapons, greater armies or superior technology.

Article 48   Gave the Weimar president the power in an emergency to rule by decree and to override the constitutional rights of the people.

Aryan   Technically it refers to the family of Indo-European languages. Yet, racists in the nineteenth century defined it as the non-Jewish people of northern Europe.

Asocials   The Nazis' desire to create a 'pure' 'national community' excluding the 'socially unfit'. The term 'asocial' covered any marginal group that deviated from the norms of society. It was applied in an elastic manner including Gypsies, vagabonds, prostitutes, alcoholics, homosexuals, criminals, 'idlers', even grumblers.

Associationism   Having a strong identity or affiliation with a particular group.

Authoritarianism   A broad term meaning government by strong non-democratic leadership.

Autonomy   The right of self-government.

Avant garde   A general term suggesting new ideas and styles in art.

Balance of trade The difference in value between exports and imports. If the value of the imports is above that of the exports, the balance of the payments has a deficit that is often referred to as being in the red.

Balanced budget A financial programme in which a government does not spend more than it raises in revenue.

Battle of Britain Name given to the air battle fought over the skies of southern England between the RAF and the Luftwaffe, July–October 1940.

Battle of the Atlantic The naval struggle between the Allied convoys and the German U-boats in the northern Atlantic.

Belgian neutrality Britain had guaranteed Belgian neutrality by the 1839 Treaty of London. Notoriously, Bethmann referred to it in 1914 as 'a scrap of paper', a comment which contributed to the harshness of the Treaty of Versailles, as it was taken to mean that Germany did not respect treaties.

Bilateral trade treaty A trade agreement between two countries or parties.

Black market The underground economy where goods are sold at unregulated prices.

'Blank cheque' The name given to the telegram sent by Wilhelm II and Bethmann telling Austria that Germany would support whatever action was necessary to deal with Serbia.

Blitzkrieg Literally 'lightning war'. It was the name of the military strategy developed to avoid static war. It was based on the use of dive-bombers, paratroopers and motorised infantry.

Bolsheviks Followers of Bolshevism – Russian communism.

Bourgeoisie The upper and middle classes who owned the capital and the means of production (factories and mines).

Brinkmanship The strategy of pushing one's opponent to the limit in a dangerous situation with the aim of forcing them to concede.

Buffer state The general idea of separating two rival countries by leaving a space between them. Clemenceau believed that the long-established Franco-German military aggression could be brought to an end by establishing an independent Rhineland state (though this was not implemented because Wilson saw it as against the principle of self-determination).

Bundesrat The Federal Council 1871–1918. It comprised 58 members nominated by the assemblies of the 25 states.

Burgfriede A (political) truce.

Cartel An arrangement between businesses to control the level of production and prices. This in effect creates a joint monopoly.

Central Powers The name for Germany and its allies: Austria-Hungary, Turkey and Bulgaria.

Coalition A government made up of members from several parties.

Concordat An agreement between Church and state.

Conscription The length of time of compulsory service for men in the army.

Constitution The principles and rules that govern a state.

Constitutional monarchy Where the monarch has limited power within the lines of a constitution.

Convoy system Organised naval protection of the merchant navy. From 1917 the British Admiralty introduced a system for the Royal Navy to counter the threat of submarines to merchant ships.

Cult of personality Using the power and charisma of a political leader to dominate the nation.

Dardanelles campaign Took place at the Gallipoli peninsula of Turkey in 1915.

British (and Empire) and French troops aimed to capture Constantinople and secure a sea route to Russia. The attempt failed, with heavy casualties on both sides.

Demilitarisation   The removal of military personnel, weaponry or forts. The Rhineland demilitarised zone was outlined by the Treaty of Versailles.

Diktat   A dictated peace. The Germans felt that the Treaty of Versailles was imposed without negotiation.

Diplomacy   The art and practice of negotiating between states with regard to issues of peace-making, trade, war and economics.

Divine right of kings   The belief that kings are God's representatives and have the authority to rule their subjects.

Dualism   A government system in which two forces co-exist, e.g. the Nazi Party and the German state (and the Communist Party and the Soviet state).

Edelweiss   A white alpine flower which served as a symbol of opposition.

Ersatzkaiser   Means 'substitute emperor'. After Marshal Hindenburg was elected president, he provided the *ersatzkaiser* figure required by the respectable right wing – he was a conservative, a nationalist and a military hero.

Exports   Goods sold to foreign countries.

Expressionism   An art form which suggests that the artist transforms reality to express a personal outlook.

Fatherland Party   *Vaterlandspartei.* A conservative right-wing party which supported the government's pursuit of the war and annexations.

Federal structure   Where power and responsibilities are shared between central and regional governments, for example, the USA.

Federalism   A government in which several states divide responsibilities between central and regional authority.

Final Solution   A euphemism used by the Nazi leadership to describe the extermination of the Jews from 1941, although in the earlier years the term had been used before there was any real overall plan.

'First past the post'   An electoral system that simply requires the winner to gain one vote more than the second placed candidate. It is also referred to as the plurality system and does not require 50 per cent plus one votes. In a national election it tends to give the most successful party disproportionately more seats than its total vote merits.

Franco-Russian Alliance   A military alliance signed between Russia and France in 1894.

Freikorps   Means 'free corps' who acted as paramilitaries. They were right-wing, nationalist soldiers who were only too willing to use force to suppress communist activity.

Führerprinzip   'The leadership principle'. Hitler upheld the idea of a one-party state, built on an all-powerful leader.

Gauleiter   Means 'leader of a regional area'. The Nazi Party was organised into 35 regions from 1926.

Geostrategy   Political and military planning constrained by geographical factors.

German October   The revolutionary uprising in Germany in 1923 is often referred to as the German October, but it is a confusing term. Mass protests started before this, in the summer of 1923, though the uprising did not actually come to a head until October 1923 (which was also emotionally associated with the Bolshevik Revolution in Russia in October 1917).

Gestapo   Secret State Police – *Geheime Staats Polizei.*

Ghetto   An ancient term used to describe the area lived in by the Jews in a city. In the years of Nazi occupation the Jews were separated from the rest of the community and forced to live in ghettos. The Jewish population was heavily concentrated and lived in appalling conditions.

Gleichschaltung 'Bringing into line' or 'co-ordination'.

GNP Gross national product: the total value of all goods and services in a nation's economy (including income derived from assets abroad).

Gradualism Changing by degrees; progressing slowly.

Gradualism or reformism The ideas of evolutionary socialism grew out of the writings in the late 1890s of Eduard Bernstein, who argued that capitalism was not in economic demise and he refuted Marx's predictions. He therefore believed that socialism would be achieved through capitalism – as workers gradually won rights, their cause for grievance would be diminished.

Great Depression The severe economic crisis of 1929–33 that was marked by mass unemployment, falling prices and a lack of spending.

Great Power A nation or state that has the ability to exert its influence on a global scale through its economic, military and diplomatic strengths. In 1900 the five major continental Great Powers were Britain, France, Germany, Russia and Austria-Hungary.

Guns or butter A phrase used to highlight the controversial economic choice between rearmament and consumer goods.

Hakatisten The German Society for the Eastern Marches was known as the *Hakatisten*, named after its founders Hansemann, Kennemann and Tidemann. It campaigned for a repressive anti-Polish policy.

Hard currency A currency that the market considers to be strong because its value does not depreciate. In the 1920s the hardest currency was the US dollar.

High treason The crime of betraying one's country, especially by attempting to overthrow the leader or government.

Holy Roman Empire Formed in the ninth century, but by 1800 had become a loose empire of separate states.

Horst Wessel A young Nazi stormtrooper killed in a fight with communists in 1930. The song he wrote became a Nazi marching song and later virtually became an alternative national anthem.

'Hottentot election' The name given to the *Reichstag* election of 1907, when the government's nationalist patriotic campaign played on the colonial war against the rebels in German South West Africa.

Hyper-inflation Prices spiralled out of control because the government increased the amount of money being printed. As a result, it displaced the whole economy.

Imperialism Rule by an Emperor. It has come to mean one country taking political and economic control of another territory.

Imports Goods purchased from foreign countries.

Indirect/direct taxes Direct taxes are on income. Indirect ones are customs duties and taxes on goods and services.

Indoctrination Inculcating and imposing a set of ideas.

Inheritance tax The tax on the estate, or total value of the money and property, of a person who has died. Also known as estate tax and death duty.

Intentionalists Interpret history by emphasising the role (intentions) of people who shape history.

Jameson Raid In 1895–6 Leander Jameson, a British colonial administrator, led a force of 500 into the Transvaal in the hope of overthrowing the Boer government. It was a complete failure.

Japanese Alliance An alliance signed by Japan and Britain in 1902 but limited to the Pacific region.

Junkers The conservative landowning aristocracy, especially those from eastern Germany.

Kaiser Emperor. The regime of 1871–1918 is known as the *Kaiserreich*, translated as Imperial Germany or the Second Empire.

Kaiserreich Translated as Imperial Germany or the Second Empire.

Kanzler The Chancellor.

KRA *Kriegsrohstoffabteilung*: War Raw Materials Department.

Kreisau Circle Name given to the resistance group which met at the estates of Helmut von Moltke.

Kripo Criminal police responsible for the maintenance of general law and order.

Kulturkampf A struggle for culture or civilisation. Bismarck's anti-Catholic policy of the 1870s.

Labour exchanges Local offices created by the state for finding employment. Many industrialised countries had labour exchanges to counter mass unemployment.

Labour market Comprises the supply of labour (those looking for work) and the demand for labour from employers. These two forces within the labour market determine wage rates.

Landtag Within the federal structure each state had its own assembly.

League of Nations The international body initiated by President Wilson to encourage disarmament and to prevent war.

Lebensborn Literally, the 'spring' or 'fountain of life'. Founded by Himmler and overseen by the SS to promote doctrines of racial purity.

Lebensraum Living space.

Mandates The name given by the Allies to the system created in the peace settlement for the supervision of all the colonies of Germany (and Turkey) by the League of Nations.

March converts Those who joined the NSDAP immediately after the consolidation of power in January–March 1933.

Marxism The ideology of Karl Marx, who believed that the working classes will overthrow the ruling classes by revolution.

Marxist historians A school of historians who believe that history has been deeply shaped by economic circumstances. They are influenced by the ideology of the philosopher Karl Marx.

Mass suggestion A psychological term suggesting that large groups of people can be unified simply by the atmosphere of the occasion. Hitler and Goebbels used their speeches and large rallies to particularly good effect.

Mediterranean Agreements A series of agreements signed by Britain, Austria and Italy to maintain the status quo in the eastern Mediterranean, which was clearly directed against Russia.

Mein Kampf 'My struggle'. The book written by Hitler in 1924, which expresses his political ideas.

Mittelstand Can be translated as 'the middle class', but in German society it tends to represent the lower middle classes, e.g. shopkeepers, craft workers and clerks. Traditionally independent and self-reliant, but it increasingly felt squeezed out between the power and influence of big business and industrial labour.

Mutual guarantee agreement An agreement between states on a particular issue, but not an alliance.

Nacht und Nebel (**Night and Fog**) Name given to a decree by Hitler in December 1941 to seize any person thought to be dangerous. They should vanish into *Nacht und Nebel*.

National Opposition   A title given to various political forces that united to campaign against Weimar. It included the DNVP, the Nazis, the Pan-German League and the Stahlhelm – an organisation of ex-soldiers. The 'National Opposition' opposed reparation payments.

Nationalism   The belief in – and support for – a national identity.

Nazi–Soviet Pact   A non-aggression pact of 1939 between the USSR and Germany that opened the way for the invasion of Poland.

New functionalism   A form of art that developed in post-war Germany which tried to express reality with a more objective view of the world.

New objectivity   Artists in favour of the 'new objectivity' broke away from the traditional romantic nostalgia of the nineteenth century.

New Order   A phrase given by the Nazis to the economic, political and racial integration of Europe under the Third Reich.

Night of the Long Knives   A crucial turning point when Hitler arranged for the SS to purge the SA leadership and murder about 200 victims, including Ernst Röhm, Gregor Strasser and Kurt von Schleicher.

November criminals   Those who signed the November Armistice and a term of abuse to vilify all those who supported the democratic republic.

Ottoman Empire   The Ottoman Empire, or Turkish Empire, lasted from 1299 to 1922. The sultanate was dissolved in 1922 and the state of Turkey became a republic.

Pan-German League   *Alldeutscher Verband*. A right-wing nationalist movement formed in 1893. It supported expansionism and many of its supporters were anti-democratic, anti-socialist and anti-Semitic.

Paramilitary units   Informal non-legal military squads.

Passive resistance   Refusal to work with occupying forces.

Pearl Harbor   A US military base in the Pacific.

Phoney war   Used to describe the war period from September 1939 to May 1940 because there was no real aggressive activity on the Western Front.

Plebiscite   A vote by the people on one specific issue – like a referendum.

Pogrom   An organised or encouraged massacre of innocent people. The term originated from the massacres of Jews in Russia.

Polarisation   The division of society into distinctly opposite views (the comparison is to the north and south poles).

Polycracy   A government system with an increasing range of competing power blocs.

Population policy   In 1933–45 the Nazi government aimed to increase the birth rate.

Proletariat   The industrial working class who, in Marxist theory, would ultimately take power in the state.

Proportional representation   A system that allocates parliamentary seats in proportion to the total number of votes.

Radicalisation   A policy of increasing severity.

Rapallo Treaty   This was not an alliance, but a treaty of friendship between Germany and Russia.

Reactionary   Opposing change and supporting a return to traditional ways.

Real wages   The actual purchasing power of income taking into account inflation/deflation and also the effect of deductions, e.g. taxes.

Recession   Period of economic slowdown, usually accompanied by rising unemployment.

Rechtsstaat   A state under a rule of laws.

Red Threat A 'Red' was a loose term used to describe anyone sympathetic to the left. It originated from the Bolshevik use of the red flag in Russia.

Reichstag The Imperial Parliament elected by all male voters aged over 25.

Reinsurance Treaty An agreement signed in 1887 between Russia and Germany accepting that that if either were at war, the other would remain neutral, unless France or Austria were the object of attack.

Reparations Payments of money (and gold) and the transfer of property and equipment from the defeated to the victor after war.

Revisionist In general terms it is the aim to modify or change something. In this context, it refers specifically to a historian who changes a well-established interpretation.

Revolution from below The radical elements in the party, e.g. the SA, that wanted to direct the Nazi revolution from a more local level rather than from the leadership in Berlin.

Revolutionary socialism The belief of socialists in the need for revolution to bring about fundamental social change.

Revolutionary stewards *Obleute*. Left-wing activists who organised strikes and demonstrations against the war. They did much to create the workers' councils (soviets) in 1918–19.

Ribbentrop Bureau Name given to the office created by Joachim von Ribbentrop, who ran his own personal 'bureau' to oversee foreign affairs.

Risk fleet theory As Germany was unable to challenge the Royal Navy directly in terms of size, the expansion of the German fleet was based on what Tirpitz described as the 'risk fleet theory'. The aim of this was to build a fleet based in the North Sea of sufficient size to pose a serious threat to British strategy.

Rote Kapelle Red Orchestra. The name given to the communist spy network which passed information to the USSR.

RSHA Reich Security Office, which amalgamated all police and security organisations.

Russo-Japanese War The war fought between Russia and Japan in 1904–5 over the clash of ambitions in Asia.

SA *Sturm Abteilung* became known in English as the Stormtroopers. They were also referred to as the Brownshirts after the colour of the uniform. They supported the radical socialist aspects of Nazism.

Sammlungspolitik A 'policy of concentration' to integrate the range of conservative forces.

Schlieffen Plan Germany's military strategy in 1914. Its purpose was to avoid a two-front war by winning victory on the Western Front before dealing with the threat from Russia on the Eastern Front. It aimed to defeat France within six weeks by a massive German offensive in northern France and Belgium in order to seize Paris quickly.

SD Security service.

Second revolution Refers to the aims of the SA, led by Ernst Röhm, which wanted social and economic reforms and the creation of a 'people's army' – merging the German army and the SA. The aims of 'a second revolution' were more attractive to 'left-wing socialist Nazis' or 'radical Nazis', who did not sympathise with the German conservative forces.

Self-determination The right of people of the same nation to decide their own form of government. In effect, it is the principle of each nation ruling itself. Wilson believed that the application of self-determination was integral to the peace settlement and it would lead to long-term peace.

Siegfriede A victory peace, which would establish Germany's supremacy in Europe.

Social Darwinism   A philosophy that portrayed the world as a 'struggle' between people, races and nations. It was deeply influenced by the theory of evolution based on natural selection.

Social Democratic Party   The SPD was the main working-class party in Germany.

Social imperialism   A phrase suggesting that a government played on imperialism to preserve the domestic social peace.

Socialist republic   A system of government without a monarchy that aims to introduce social changes for collective benefit.

Soviet   A Russian word meaning an elected council. Soviets developed during the Russian Revolution in 1917. In Germany many councils were set up in 1918, which had the support of the more radical and revolutionary left-wing working class.

Soviet republic   A system of government without a monarchy that aims to introduce a communist state organised by the workers' councils and opposed to private ownership.

Spartacus League   A small group which believed that Germany should follow the same path as communist Russia. The fundamental aim of the Spartacists was to create a soviet republic based on the rule of the proletariat through workers' and soldiers' councils.

Sphere of influence   An area or region over which a state has significant cultural, economic, military or political influence.

Splendid isolation   In the nineteenth century Britain had been the strongest power because of its navy and empire, therefore it had no need to sign alliances with others. (However, although Britain was still isolated in 1900, it faced increasing pressures from France, Germany and Russia and the isolation appeared less attractive.)

SS   *Schutz Staffel* (protection squad); became known as the Blackshirts, named after the uniform.

SS Einsatzgruppen   Means 'Action Units'. Four of the units were launched in eastern Europe after the invasion of Russia. They were responsible for rounding up local Jews and murdering them by mass shootings.

'Stab in the back' myth   The distorted view that the army had not really lost the First World War and that unpatriotic groups, such as socialists and Jews, had undermined the war effort. The myth severely weakened the Weimar democracy from the start.

Stalemate   A deadlock in war where neither side makes progress.

State within a state   A situation where the authority and government of the state are threatened by a rival power base.

Structuralists   Interpret history by analysing the role of social and economic forces and structures. Therefore, they tend to place less emphasis on the role of the individual.

Supreme Army Command   The highest level of command in the German army.

Tariffs   Taxes levied by an importing nation on foreign goods coming in, and paid by the importers.

Teutonic paganism   The non-Christian beliefs of the Germans in ancient history (heathens).

Third Reich   Third Empire: the Nazi dictatorship 1933–45. It was seen as the successor to the Holy Roman Empire and Imperial Germany 1871–1918.

Three Emperors' Alliance   An informal alliance between Austria-Hungary, Germany and Russia, announced officially in 1872 and renewed in 1881.

Toleration   Acceptance of alternative political, religious and cultural views.

Total war A war that spared neither the military nor the civilian population, forcing Germany to use the power of the state as a means of mobilising its economic potential.

Totalitarian A system of government in which all power is centralised and does not allow any rival authorities.

Triple Alliance The military alliance of Germany, Austria and Italy was formed in 1882 out of the Austro-German Dual Alliance of 1879.

Triple Entente The name given to the alignment of the powers Russia, France and Britain, which evolved between 1894 and 1907. Only France and Russia were actually in alliance.

Turn of the tide The term used to describe the Allied military victories in the winter of 1942–3, when the British won at El Alamein in North Africa and when the Russians forced the surrender of 300,000 German troops at Stalingrad.

Unconditional surrender Roosevelt and Churchill's statement in 1943 that the Allies would not accept a negotiated peace.

Unilateral disarmament The disarmament of one party. Wilson pushed for general (universal) disarmament after the war, but France and Britain were more suspicious. As a result only Germany had to disarm.

Unrestricted submarine warfare Germany's policy in the First World War to attack all military and civilian shipping in order to sink supplies going to Britain.

Vernunftrepublikaner 'A rational republican' – used in the 1920s to define those people who really wanted Germany to have a constitutional monarchy but who, out of necessity, came to support the democratic Weimar Republic.

Volk Often translated as 'people', although it tends to suggest a nation with the same ethnic and cultural identities and with a collective sense of belonging.

Völkisch Nationalist views associated with racism (especially anti-Semitism).

Volksgemeinschaft 'A people's community'. Nazism stressed the development of a harmonious, socially unified and racially pure community.

Vote of no confidence A motion put before a parliament by the opposition in the hope of defeating or weakening the government. In Britain, the passing of a vote of no confidence would lead to a general election.

***Waffen* SS** The armed SS: the number of *Waffen* SS armed divisions grew during the war from three to 35.

War bonds In order to raise money for the war, Imperial Germany encouraged people to invest into government funds in the belief they were helping to finance the war and their savings were secure.

War guilt The term originated from the Treaty of Versailles 1919, which forced Germany to accept blame for causing the war. Later, it became the focus of great historical discussion.

War of attrition A long, drawn-out war aimed at wearing down the enemy.

Wehrmacht The German army.

Weimar Republic Took its name from the first meeting of the National Constituent Assembly at Weimar. The Assembly had moved there because there were still many disturbances in Berlin. Weimar was chosen because it was a town with a great historical and cultural tradition.

Weltpolitik 'World policy'; the imperial government's strategy from 1897 to expand Germany's military and political influence.

White-collar workers Workers not involved in manual labour.

White Terror The 'Whites' were seen as the opponents (in contrast to the Reds). The 'White Terror' refers to the suppression of the soviet republic in Bavaria in March 1919.

Wilhelmine A term for the period of German history, 1890–1918. It refers to the rule of Wilhelm II, in contrast to the Bismarckian era, 1871–90.

Zero hour Used in German society to describe Germany's overall collapse at the end of the Second World War.

Zollverein The customs union of German states. It created a free trade area by removing internal customs, but upholding customs on imports from foreign trade partners.

Index